REBUILDING JEWISH LIFE IN GERMANY

REBUILDING JEWISH LIFE IN GERMANY

EDITED BY JAY HOWARD GELLER
AND MICHAEL MENG

RUTGERS UNIVERSITY PRESS
NEW BRUNSWICK, CAMDEN, AND NEWARK,
NEW JERSEY, AND LONDON

Library of Congress Cataloging-in-Publication Data
Names: Geller, Jay Howard, editor. | Meng, Michael, editor.
Title: Rebuilding Jewish life in Germany / edited by Jay Howard Geller and Michael Meng.
Description: New Brunswick, New Jersey: Rutgers University Press, [2020] | Includes bibliographical references and index.
Identifiers: LCCN 2019017599 | ISBN 9781978800724 (cloth) | ISBN 9781978800717 (pbk.)
Subjects: LCSH: Jews—Germany—History—1945–1990. | Jews—Germany—History—1990– | Jews—Germany—Intellectual life. | Germany—Ethnic relations.
Classification: LCC DS134.26 .R43 2020 | DDC 305.892/4043—dc23
LC record available at https://lccn.loc.gov/2019017599
A British Cataloging-in-Publication record for this book is available from the British Library.

♾ The paper used in this publication meets the requirements of the American National Standard for Information Sciences—Permanence of Paper for Printed Library Materials, ANSI Z39.48-1992.
www.rutgersuniversitypress.org
Manufactured in the United States of America

CONTENTS

REBUILDING JEWISH LIFE IN GERMANY

INTRODUCTION

Jay Howard Geller and Michael Meng

On the morning of 26 March 2012, Germans woke up to the news that the city of Frankfurt had elected Peter Feldmann of the Social Democratic Party as mayor in a run-off election. This development was particularly noteworthy because he was the city's first center-left mayor in seventeen years and had won only second place in the initial election. However, there was added significance because Feldmann was Jewish—only the second Jew elected as mayor of a major German city since 1945 and the first in Frankfurt since 1933, when Nazi agitation had compelled Ludwig Landmann to resign his office. It is extremely unlikely, however, that Feldmann's Jewish heritage affected the election in any significant way.[1] In 2018, he won reelection with over 70 percent of the vote.

For foreign Jewish observers, Feldmann's victory was a sign of how far Germany had come and how at home Jews felt in a unified Germany.[2] A few months after Feldmann began his second term of office, the *New York Times* ran a profile of a popular, openly Jewish gangsta rap star in Germany who went by the stage name Sun Diego.[3] At the other end of the cultural spectrum, Daniel Barenboim was serving as the general music director of the Berlin State Opera and the Staatskapelle Berlin. During the early 2000s, Germany's leading highbrow weekly news magazine, *Die Zeit*, was under the editorship of Josef Joffe, a German-Jewish journalist. Though the official Jewish community of Germany remains relatively small—approximately ninety-eight thousand Jews among a general population of eighty-two million—individual Jews have notable roles in German public life, and it is possible to live a Jewish religious and cultural life in Berlin and other major metropolises.[4]

That is not to say that Jewish life has been normalized in Germany in the sense that it is identical to the everyday lives of non-Jewish, nonimmigrant citizens or residents of Germany. Indeed, police still guard Jewish schools, synagogues, and other institutions, and visitors must be searched before entry. Anti-Israel demonstrations can easily descend into anti-Semitism and use slogans reminiscent of Nazi rhetoric.[5] In early April 2018, the German federal government tacitly acknowledged the increasingly hostile atmosphere for Jews in Germany among segments of the country's population and decided to appoint a commissioner on anti-Semitism, a position technically known as the Commissioner for Jewish Life in Germany and for the Fight against Anti-Semitism. Only days after Feldmann's election, an Israeli was attacked in broad daylight in Berlin's trendy and generally affluent Prenzlauer Berg district for wearing a kippa.[6] In contrast to the situation with Jewish community elites, many ordinary Jews who had hoped to make a life in Germany no longer wish to remain in the country.[7] Nonetheless, the situation has changed significantly compared to the first decades after 1945.

Through much of the history of the Bonn Republic (the old West Germany), the Jewish community was small, often insular, and focused on its institutions. Initially, culturally German Jews in particular—as opposed to Eastern European Jews in Germany—coalesced around the Central Council of Jews in Germany (Zentralrat der Juden in Deutschland), statewide Jewish associations, and the newspaper *Allgemeine Wochenzeitung der Juden in Deutschland.* Most Jews worked in commerce, but for a variety of reasons, German banks would not advance start-up capital to Jews, so Jewish loan societies fulfilled that function, placing them somewhere between financial institutions and charitable funds and reinforcing the community's inward-looking nature. Additionally, most Jews in Germany after 1948 had a pronounced Zionist orientation, possibly to compensate for daring to settle (or resettle) in the "land of the perpetrators."

The demographics of the community were also in flux in the country's initial decades. Right after 1949, there were roughly equal numbers of German Jews and Eastern European Jews; however, the German Jews were largely older and were frequently married to non-Jews. Nonetheless, in many cities, German Jews controlled the levers of Jewish communal power. By the late 1960s, the Jewish community in Germany consisted overwhelmingly of Eastern European Jews and their children. Concomitantly, prewar German Liberal Judaism did not regain a significant foothold in Germany, and Orthodox Judaism following an Eastern European model predominated for those who chose to affiliate with a synagogue.

During the first decades after the war, Jewish communal leaders such as Hendrik George van Dam and Karl Marx promoted Jewish interests, often quietly through official channels or even back channels, relying on personal connections and humble appeals for support. While several German universities did offer courses on Jewish topics, the academic study of Judaism remained dominated by Christian scholars. Only a handful of Jews taught Jewish history or Jewish studies at German universities before the 1980s, with the postwar Free University of Berlin the main focal point, as opposed to one of Germany's tradition-rich medieval universities. In literature, most Jewish authors writing in the German language cast their views backward rather than illuminating contemporary German-Jewish society.

Some individual Jews engaged in the public sphere, though the most visible among them had lived in Germany before the war (as opposed to Jews who had previously resided in various areas of Eastern Europe). Hans Rosenthal had a highly successful career as a radio and television quiz show host and president of the Tennis Borussia Berlin soccer club, but he was also a high-ranking official in the Berlin Jewish community. Alfred Ries was president of the Werder Bremen soccer club. A very small number of West German Jews entered politics, mainly on behalf of the Social Democratic Party, including Bundestag members Jakob Altmaier, Peter Blachstein, and Jeanette Wolff; federal constitutional court member and Schleswig-Holstein justice minister Rudolf Katz, who did not affiliate with the official Jewish community; and North Rhine–Westphalia justice minister Josef Neuberger, who held Jewish communal offices. In 1965, Herbert Weichmann became the mayor of Hamburg—he was the first Jewish mayor of any German city since the Holocaust and the only one during the era of the Bonn Republic. While Weichmann was a successful and popular leader, he ascended to the mayoralty purely by accident. A local politician in the second tier, he came to office initially as interim mayor when the previous office holder resigned over a marriage scandal. Weichmann, the accidental mayor, served for six years. At one point, there were discussions about him running for president of the Federal Republic of Germany, but he declined to pursue the high office, feeling that Germans would not have accepted a Jewish president in 1969.[8]

By the 1970s, change was under way in West Germany. A social democratic–liberal coalition under Chancellor Willy Brandt governed the country. The left-wing student movement was highly visible and vocal. Even within the Jewish community, pressure for change was growing. Members of the generation born and raised in Germany felt more integrated into non-Jewish society than their parents and frequently held different views about mixed marriages than the older generation. They also sought greater democracy within the Jewish community, a more nuanced view of Israel, and a more critical relationship with West German political elites. It was clear that although the Jewish community had not appreciably grown in size (hovering around thirty-two thousand), it had become more comfortable with its place in Germany. A college for Jewish studies was established in Heidelberg in 1979 and a national Jewish archive was set up in the same city in 1987. Jewish topics became the subject of study at more German universities, and in 1982, a large Jewish bookstore opened in Munich. Members of the Jewish community in Frankfurt, which arguably had the most diverse Jewish life in West Germany, felt comfortable literally demonstrating to make their demands known and to stop anti-Semitism. In 1985, they took over a theater stage to prevent a performance of Rainer Werner Fassbinder's play *Garbage, the City, and Death*, which had anti-Semitic overtones. Two years later, demonstrators successfully protested the removal of the archaeological remains of Frankfurt's famous ghetto for the construction of a municipal public works building. These acts signaled both a desire for public recognition as Jews and an acknowledgment that Jews saw West German society as their home, which they wished to shape in both the present and the future.

In the German Democratic Republic (GDR), the organized Jewish community was small to begin with and shrank further under the impact of Communist anti-Semitism in the early 1950s. Nonetheless, a Jewish presence persisted in East Germany, though for many years the community had only a nonordained rabbi and, after his death in 1965, no rabbi at all until the 1980s. Additionally, anti-Zionism became a part of official East German political discourse, and the Jewish community remained under Stasi surveillance (like most groups in East German society), though it also had some support for its religious needs. At the same time, a handful of individuals from Jewish backgrounds who were not involved in the official Jewish community played an outsized role in the cultural, intellectual, and even political life of East Germany. Novelists Anna Seghers, Stefan Heym, Arnold Zweig, and Jurek Becker were among the most prominent writers of Jewish descent in either Germany between 1949 and 1990. Alexander Abusch, Hermann Axen, and Albert Norden had long and successful careers in the East German Communist Party, while Leo Zuckermann had to flee to West Berlin as a wave of virulent anti-Semitism swept the Soviet bloc from 1951 to 1953.

The events of 1989 and 1990, which bought German reunification, fundamentally changed Jewish life in Germany. A wave of Soviet, and then post-Soviet, Jews to Germany exponentially increased the size of the community, bringing tremendous challenges and opportunities. On one hand, Jewish communal organs struggled to integrate and care for the newcomers. Additionally, most of the immigrants viewed their Jewishness as a "national" or cultural identity—not a religious one—in contradistinction to longtime community members. On the other hand, the rapid growth of the community was accompanied by a reexploration of Jewish culture and a blossoming of Jewish life within Germany. In recent years, diverse Jewish institutions, Jewish cultural festivals, and even Jewish-oriented restaurants and shops have been more conspicuous than at any time since 1945. Moreover, a wave of Jewish Israelis has added to the cultural mix. With Israelis and Russian Jews present and active in German cultural and social life, notions of "What is Jewish?" and "Who is a Jew?" have grown more complicated. A different sensibility regarding Jews pervades the German public, and Jewish sensitivities are no longer so easily overlooked or ignored by political and cultural leaders. The government's negative reaction to a regional court decision in 2012 that threatened to end the legal circumcision of young boys indicates an understanding of the situation of Jews in Germany. At the same time, Jews in Germany have noticed a marked increase in manifestations of everyday anti-Semitism in schools, on the soccer pitch, and on the street, though debate rages over who is most responsible for this upsurge: the German Far Right, German Far Left, or Muslim immigrants to Germany.[9] What seems to be increasingly evident, however, is that significant numbers of German citizens—like their counterparts in other countries in Western and Eastern Europe—seem to be moving in a nationalistic direction that might weaken German commitments to acceptance of and solidarity with religious-cultural minorities such as Jews, among other minority groups living in contemporary Germany.[10]

Scholarship on Jews in Postwar Germany

With this basic history as its focus, this volume offers new perspectives on the history of Jews in West, East, and reunited Germany. To situate the volume's scholarly intervention, it might be useful to survey the scholarship that has been written hitherto on the history of Jews in postwar Germany. While there is a growing literature in German on the history of Jews in Germany after 1945, there is comparatively less written on this topic in English,[11] with the notable exception of the significant literature that now exists on the immediate postwar years in general and on the history of Jewish displaced persons (DPs) in particular.[12] Shortly after the collapse of Hitler's empire, occupied Germany became, ironically, a relatively safe refuge for some 250,000 Jews fleeing from a violent outburst of anti-Semitism in Eastern Europe, above all in Poland.[13] Most of the Jews who fled to Germany had little interest in staying there and soon migrated, typically to the United States or Israel (after its founding in 1948). Despite the brevity of their stay in postwar Germany, Jewish DPs established a vibrant social, political, religious, and cultural life, which has garnered considerable attention from scholars.

In contrast, the Jews who decided to stay in or return to Germany have received considerably less attention from scholars until only very recently. For many years, historians largely ignored the reestablishment of Jewish life in Germany and its broader significance for postwar German history, with only a handful of studies on the subject appearing from 1945 to 1989.[14] Yet the situation changed significantly after the collapse of Communism and German reunification in 1989–1990. In the ensuing years, a number of scholars published broad surveys or edited volumes on Jewish life in Germany—particularly West Germany—since 1945, though few of them were fundamentally archival studies.[15] By the 2000s, a wave of dissertations, monographs, surveys, and edited volumes based on intense research reexamined the topic in greater detail, often at the communal level.[16] Similarly, the small Jewish community in East Germany and Jewish-German relations in the GDR have received increased attention since the mid- to late 1990s.[17] Only in 2018, however, did there appear in English a truly comprehensive and chronologically ordered history of Jews in Germany since 1945—an English-language edition of a multiauthor volume, edited by Michael Brenner and first published in German in 2012. Relying on previously inaccessible Jewish community records and surveying topics such as demographics, institutions, religion, culture, and relations with non-Jewish Germans, it depicts the changing nature of Jewish life in Germany from the perspectives both of regular community members and of high politics, elites, and institutions over the course of many decades.[18]

Scholarship on Jews in the GDR, based on the very rich archival material that the Communist regime left in its wake, has been heavily focused on the regime's (at times hostile) policy toward the Jewish community, with several important exceptions.[19] Scholars such as Mario Keßler and Karin Hartewig have explored the history of Jewish Communists who returned to East Germany with the fervent belief that Germany could rebuild itself after Nazism only through the establishment of a Communist regime.[20] By contrast, historians such as Jay Howard Geller have demonstrated that the East German Jewish community, while heavily restricted by the regime's policies, was nevertheless able to secure some support from the state for its religious and cultural institutions; the same could be said about Jews—and non-Jews—in the GDR who were able to carve out some space to remember and reflect on the Holocaust, as Michael Meng has shown in his work on Jewish sites in postwar Germany.[21]

The scholarship on West Germany has been animated broadly by three central issues, often in comparison to East Germany. First, historians in particular have been keen to describe the actual process of rebuilding Jewish life in post-Holocaust Germany by documenting the reconstruction of Jewish organizations, institutions, and communities.[22] Second, historians, literary scholars, and others have been interested in examining the relationship between Jews and Germans after the Holocaust with regards to such issues as the memory of the Holocaust, the return of Jewish property, and the outbreak of anti-Semitism after 1945.[23] And third, the question of identity—namely, how Jews in Germany think of themselves as "Jews" living in the "land of the perpetrators"—has received considerable attention from cultural historians, anthropologists, and literary scholars.[24]

The latter two themes have dominated the scholarship that has recently emerged on the contemporary period, as the size of the Jewish community in reunited Germany grew substantially thanks to the immigration of Russian Jews after the collapse of the Soviet Union. Indeed, scholars continue to be intrigued by questions of memory and identity.[25] Nevertheless, these questions are inflected in the new historical context of reunified Germany, a context shaped not only by a larger, more diversified Jewish population but also by an increasingly diverse German society. Currently, Germany has some ten million foreigners living within its borders, and almost nineteen million people come from a so-called migration background (*Personen mit Migrationshintergrund*). As Germany's demographics have changed, the country seems more than ever to be pulled between the countervailing trends of cosmopolitanism and nationalism. In such a changing situation, questions about identity and memory have become more complicated.

The Intervention of This Volume

It has been three decades since German reunification and approximately two decades since scholars engaged newly opened archives to illuminate Jewish life and relations between Jewish and non-Jewish populations in the two Germanys. Since then, many of the original investigators have reappraised their initial assessments, and new scholars have expanded the breadth of the literature. At the same time, the first decades of the so-called Berlin Republic now fall under the rubric of contemporary history. This volume profits from these changes while also embracing work in the fields of literature studies, film studies, and sociology.

Since the Jewish community in West Germany was small and often insular, its institutions and leading personalities were particularly important. Jay Howard Geller opens this volume with an examination of the origins and early struggles of the Central Council of Jews in Germany (Zentralrat der Juden in Deutschland), the principal representative of Jewry in West Germany. It was by no means certain that significant numbers of Jews would remain in Germany or that they would unify for representative purposes. Indeed, they only did so in reaction to the real possibility of (non-Jewish) German government officials or (non-German) Jewish groups setting the agenda for their community and making decisions on their behalf. Even so, the Central Council struggled for financial stability and respect in its early years and looked to non-Jewish German politicians for support. Building on the themes and chronology presented in Jay Howard Geller's essay, Andrea Sinn's examination of the West German Jewish community's leadership—specifically that of prominent Jewish newspaper publisher Karl Marx and Central Council general secretary Hendrik G. van Dam—focuses on these leaders' roles in justifying the continued presence of Jews in the "land of the perpetrators," including serving as watchdogs of Germany's nascent democracy and as advocates for reparations. However, Marx and van Dam differed on the role that the Jewish community in Germany should play vis-à-vis the West German federal government. While the journalist advocated for an intermediary position between German officials and foreign Jewish groups, the community administrator wanted to focus on the community's own needs. Additionally, van Dam struggled to maintain cooperation between the Central Council's members and foreign Jewish organizations that neglected or denigrated the needs of the Jewish community in postwar Germany.

Indeed, the presence of Jews in Germany after the Holocaust could be seen as a challenge to the State of Israel, founded in 1948, in part as a home for displaced Jews. As shown by Jason Lustig, the German-born rabbi and archivist Bernhard Brilling's quest to establish a comprehensive Jewish archive in West Germany as the successor of the prewar General Archive of German Jews (Gesamtarchiv der deutschen Juden) conflicted with the aspirations of the Central Archives for the History of the Jewish People, located in Jerusalem, to be a single, monumental archive for the Jewish people—including the Diaspora—in the Jewish state. Consequently, the West German state, interested in fostering its relationship with Israel, lent Brilling little support, and Communist East Germany and Poland would not transfer their archival holdings. Both the modest archive that Brilling did establish in Germany and the Central Archives for the History of the Jewish People in Jerusalem reflected the realities of (German-) Jewish life after the Holocaust and visions for the future of the Jews anchored in their experience of the past. Similarly, German-Jewish refugees in the United States, Great Britain, and Israel established branches of the Leo Baeck Institute for the study of historic German-speaking Jewry. Though not a part of their effort, the Institute for the History of the German Jews (Institut für die Geschichte der deutschen Juden) served as an analog to the Leo Baeck Institutes, but as Miriam Rürup shows, the institute's leaders struggled to achieve acceptance both from non-Jewish German archivists and historians, who challenged their objectivity, and from fellow former-German Jews, who questioned their right to preserve and interpret German-Jewish history. Meanwhile, Israel laid claim to the Hamburg Jewish community's archives, which had survived the Nazi years intact. Rejecting this negation of the Diaspora and involuntary "ingathering of the exiles" (or of their material heritage), Hamburg Jews saw the preservation of their archives in situ as a way to establish a claim of continuity and legitimization for their postwar community. Only after several decades did the Institute for the History of the German Jews receive the recognition and respect demanded by its work, and the presence of an extensive Jewish archive in Hamburg was seen as facilitating research on the broader history of Hamburg in addition to specifically Jewish history.

Looking at Jewish life and institutions in Frankfurt, Tobias Freimüller illuminates the tensions that internally divided the city's Jewish community from the late 1940s to the 1980s. While the leadership of the postwar Jewish community was in the hands of "German" Jews, who claimed legal and symbolic continuity with the prewar community, most Jewish community members were former DPs from Eastern Europe who had no roots in Frankfurt and could not relate to the city's storied Jewish past. They were soon joined by immigrants or remigrants from Israel. Without a common past, support for Israel and Zionism served as a source of shared identity. Later, the generation of Frankfurt Jews born after the war tried to find a place between the conservative Jewish establishment and the city's vibrant leftist activist scene.

The GDR, colloquially known as East Germany, presented a different set of challenges for Jews and Judaism. Moreover, East Germany's appeal to Jews was very different from that of West Germany. Many individuals of Jewish heritage made a conscious choice to settle in East Germany for ideological reasons or for the opportunity to build a better, more humane Germany after the Holocaust. However, the reality of life under German Communism—including eruptions of anti-Semitism, persistent anti-Zionism, and insensitivity to the needs of Jewish victims of the Nazis—was often at variance with their vision for Germany's future. Considering the weakness of institutional Jewish life in East Germany, small size of the community, and disproportionate prominence of some leftist Jewish intellectuals in the GDR, focusing on certain individuals illuminates both the promise and the disillusionment associated with the Jewish experience in the "Workers' and Farmers' State."

Among those Jews who initially saw great promise in East Germany was Helmut Eschwege, a noted historian. For a time, he was willing to assist the Communist regime, including working as a Stasi informant, though he did depart from the GDR's anti-Zionist stance, as Alexander Walter shows in his contribution to this book. As an individual attempting to negotiate between his support for the regime and his Jewish heritage, Eschwege stands as a significant example of the challenges of sustaining some semblance of Jewish life in the Communist East. A much more vocal critic of the regime was Stefan Heym. In a capacious chapter that spans everything from Heym's friendship with Robert Havemann and Wolf Biermann, to the political implications of those friendships, to his critical relationship with the Socialist Unity Party of Germany (SED) dictatorship, Cathy Gelbin provides a rich analysis of Heym as a committed socialist who nevertheless challenged the regime so as to improve it. In doing so, her chapter offers a more nuanced portrait of Jewish contributions to East German life and culture.

One of the most well-known individuals of Jewish heritage to return to East Germany was Ernst Bloch. As Michael Meng discusses in his chapter, Bloch initially became attracted to East Germany as a possible place to build a new kind of society that promised to offer an expansive notion of human freedom. Meng attempts to untangle precisely what "freedom" means for Bloch especially as it pertains to death, so as to demonstrate the richness of Bloch's "eschatological" Marxism in the postwar era. Katja Garloff explores the central tension between displacement and settlement in postwar German-Jewish history and culture by turning to the literary work of Barbara Honigmann, who lived in East Germany before embarking on a successful career as a German-language writer in Strasbourg, France. Specifically, Garloff explores the theme of displacement through Honigmann's reflections on the return of her parents to post-Holocaust Germany, while she examines the theme of settlement—uneasy, to be sure—through Honigmann's narration of visits to Jewish cemeteries as spatial embodiments of the German-Jewish past. After examining these two themes, Garloff concludes that "place-making" enables displaced subjects to find a new sense of home in the Diaspora.

Despite the small size of the active Jewish community in East Germany, there is a relatively large and vibrant scholarly literature on the topic, which Constantin Goschler reviews and categorizes. Indeed, perspectives on the history of Jews in East Germany have undergone a number of interpretive turns in the last thirty years. The initial wave of research, relying on then newly opened archives, stood in the shadow of the Cold War and stressed the instrumentalization of Jews and Jewish-related issues by the East German state and Communist Party. Later, scholars began to consider Jewish life in East Germany, reflecting on questions of Jewish identity and Holocaust memory. In his chapter, Goschler looks forward and proposes widening the circle of individuals covered by Jewish biography in the GDR; transcending the traditional parameters of 1945, 1949, and 1990 in considering "East German" Jewish history; adopting a transnational approach to the topic; considering waves of community construction; and interrogating notions of Jewish identities, which may compete or overlap with each other.

Following German reunification and the collapse of the Soviet bloc, the Jewish community experienced a massive transformation occasioned by the influx of Jews and people of Jewish descent from the former Soviet Union. Joseph Cronin sheds light on the ways that Jewish leaders in Germany and non-Jewish German politicians understood this phenomenon. Indeed, their disparate views and needs led to uncertainty and controversy regarding the regulation of Jewish immigration and care for immigrants. While the Soviet government used patrilineal descent to assign Jewish "nationality" to Soviet citizens, Jewish religious communities have historically used matrilineal descent to determine belonging. As a result of this discrepancy, thousands of former Soviets were admitted to Germany as Jews but were not eligible for membership in the official Jewish community, and structural obstacles prevented their formal conversion to Judaism. After years of misunderstandings between German government officials and the Jewish community as well as of ill feeling between Russian Jews (who saw their identity as cultural) and Jewish community leaders in Germany (who maintained the primacy of religion), the Central Council of Jews in Germany convinced German state governments to permit indirect use of the Jewish religious (or "halakhic") definition of Jewishness to determine eligibility for post-Soviet Jewish immigration to Germany.

The two final essays in this volume, by Jill S. Smith and Irit Dekel, turn to the contemporary situation. Through an analysis of Dominik Graf's crime drama *Im Angesicht des Verbrechens* (*Face to Face with the Crime*), Smith explores the complex, multilayered history of Jewish migration to Germany within the broader context of debates about multiculturalism and difference in reunified Germany. On one hand, she interprets the crime drama as an expression of German anxieties about ethnocultural differences and concomitant hopes that assimilation will prevail, while, on the other hand, she views the series as suggesting the possibility of embracing cultural differences in a manner that transforms German culture into something new. In short, Smith touches on the profound tension between assimilation and pluralism in German society and culture today.

In the final essay of the volume, Irit Dekel picks up on this theme as well. Examining the reactions of the German and Hebrew press to Israeli migration to Berlin, she shows the complexities of this striking post-1989 development. In particular, Dekel contrasts the ways in which Germans view the migration of Jews to Berlin as evidence of their country's putative transformation into a "cosmopolitan" nation to the ways in which the migrants themselves view it as both liberating and constraining in regards to their own nationalistic-ethnic affiliations. By detailing this contrast, Dekel emphasizes the central role that national identity continues to play in discussions and experiences of migration.

If taken as a whole, the essays in this volume not only make a contribution to the now sizeable literature on Jews in postwar Germany but also enrich our understanding of German politics, society, and culture after Nazism—and particularly of themes such as nationalism, memory, migration, freedom, and difference in the postwar era.

NOTES

1. Canan Topçu, "Herr Feldmann von der SPD," *Jüdische Allgemeine*, 8 March 2012.

2. For example, Ofer Aderet, "Germany Elects First Jewish Mayor of Frankfurt since Holocaust," *Haaretz* online, 26 March 2012, https://www.haaretz.com/jewish/1.5208510; Benjamin Weinthal, "Frankfurt Elects 1st Jewish Mayor since Holocaust," *Jerusalem Post*, 29 March 2012; Abigail [no last name], "Jew Elected Mayor of Frankfurt, Germany—Why This Isn't News," *Heeb Magazine* online, 5 April 2012, http://heebmagazine.com/jew-elected-mayor-of-frankfurt-germany-why-this-isnt-news/35059.

3. "Jewish Rapper Carves Niche in Germany's Booming Hip-Hop Scene," *New York Times*, 12 May 2018.

4. The core Jewish population of Germany in 2017 was 98,594, based on community registration. It was estimated that 116,500 Jews lived in Germany in 2017, including several thousand not registered with the community. The "enlarged Jewish population," which includes non-Jewish individuals who live in Jewish households, was approximately 225,000. Sergio DellaPergola, "World Jewish Population, 2017," *American Jewish Year Book* (2017): 339–340.

5. Jörn Hasselmann, "Araber wollten Israeli attackieren," *Der Tagesspiegel*, 21 July 2014.

6. Hannes Heine, "'Ich wollte mir das nicht gefallen lassen'. Der Israeli Adam Armush wurde von drei Arabisch sprechenden jungen Männern angegriffen, weil er eine Kippa trug," *Der Tagesspiegel*, 19 April 2018.

7. Ann-Kristin Tlusty, "'Ich möchte Deutschland mittelfristig verlassen,'" *Die Zeit* online, 19 May 2018, https://www.zeit.de/gesellschaft/2018-05/antisemitismus-erfahrungen-protokolle-zeit-online-community.

8. Uwe Bahnsen, *Die Weichmanns in Hamburg. Ein Glücksfall für Deutschland* (Hamburg: Hans Christians, 2001), 355–357; "Jewish Mayor Says He Refused Bonn Presidency," *New York Times*, 25 April 1969 (late city edition). Twenty-four years later, another prominent German Jew, Ignatz Bubis, came to a similar conclusion. Stephen Kinzer, "Germany Considers Jew as President," *New York Times*, 27 March 1993 (late edition).

9. Matthias Bartsch et al., "Das große Unbehagen," *Der Spiegel*, 10 September 2012, 30–32; Griff Witte and Luisa Beck, "After Refugee Influx, Germany Confronts Imported Anti-Semitism," *Washington Post*, 29 April 2018.

10. Rita Chin, *The Crisis of Multiculturalism in Europe: A History* (Princeton, N.J.: Princeton University Press, 2017), 254–260; Rita Chin et al., *After the Nazi Racial State: Difference and Democracy in Germany and Europe* (Ann Arbor: University of Michigan Press, 2009).

11. Among German-language books that survey the history of Jews in Germany after 1945, see Erica Burgauer, *Zwischen Erinnerung und Verdrängung. Juden in Deutschland nach 1945* (Reinbeck: Rowohlt, 1993); Susanne Schönborn, ed., *Zwischen Erinnerung und Neubeginn. Zur deutsch-jüdischen Geschichte nach 1945* (Munich: Meidenbauer, 2006); Anthony Kauders, *Unmögliche Heimat: Eine deutsch-jüdische Geschichte der Bundesrepublik* (Munich: Deutsche Verlags-Anstalt, 2007); and Michael Brenner, ed., *Geschichte der Juden in Deutschland von 1945 bis zur Gegenwart: Politik, Kultur und Gesellschaft* (Munich: C. H. Beck, 2012).

12. Angelika Konigseder and Juliane Wetzel, *Waiting for Hope: Jewish Displaced Persons in Post–World War II Germany*, trans. John A. Broadwin (Evanston, Ill.: Northwestern University Press, 2001); Hagit Lavsky, *New Beginnings: Holocaust Survivors in Bergen-Belsen and the British Zone in Germany, 1945–1950* (Detroit, Mich.: Wayne State University Press, 2002); Zeev W. Mankowitz, *Life between Memory and Hope: The Survivors of the Holocaust in Occupied Germany* (Cambridge: Cambridge University Press, 2002); Atina Grossmann, *Jews, Germans, and Allies: Close Encounters in Occupied Germany* (Princeton, N.J.: Princeton University Press, 2007); Margarete Myers Feinstein, *Holocaust Survivors in Postwar Germany, 1945–1957* (Cambridge: Cambridge University Press, 2010); Avinoam J. Patt and Michael Berkowitz, eds., *"We Are Here": New Approaches to Jewish Displaced Persons in Postwar Germany* (Detroit, Mich.: Wayne State University Press, 2010).

13. On the outbreak of anti-Semitism in Poland, see David Engel, "Patterns of Anti-Jewish Violence in Poland, 1944–1946," *Yad Vashem Studies* 26 (1998): 43–85; Anna Cichopek, *Pogrom Żydów w Krakowie* (Warsaw: Żydowski Instytut Historyczny, 2000); Krystyna Kersten, *Polacy, Żydzi, komunizm. Anatomia półprawd 1939–1968* (Warsaw: Niezależna Oficyna Wydaw, 1992); Bożena Szaynok, *Pogrom Żydów w Kielcach 4 lipca 1946* (Warsaw: Bellona, 1992); Natalia Aleksiun, *Dokąd dalej? Ruch syjonistyczny w Polsce, 1944–1950* (Warsaw: Trio, 2002); August Grabski, Maciej Pisarski, and Albert Stankowski, *Studia z dziejów i kultury Żydów w Polsce po 1945 roku* (Warsaw: Trio, 1997); Jan Gross, *Fear: Antisemitism in Poland after Auschwitz* (New York: Random House, 2006); Bożena Szaynok, *Ludność żydowska na Dolnym Śląsku 1945–1950* (Wrocław: Wydawn. Uniwersytetu Wrocławskiego, 2000).

14. Harry Maor, "Über den Wiederaufbau der Jüdischen Gemeinden in Deutschland seit 1945" (PhD thesis, Universität Mainz, 1961); Doris Kuschner, "Die Jüdische Minderheit in der Bundesrepublik Deutschland. Eine Analyse" (PhD thesis, Universität Köln, 1977); Anson Rabinbach and Jack Zipes, eds., *Germans and Jews since the Holocaust: The Changing Situation in West Germany* (New York: Holmes & Meier, 1986); Micha Brumlik et al., eds., *Jüdisches Leben in Deutschland seit 1945* (Frankfurt: Jüdischer Verlag bei Athenäum, 1986); Robin Ostow, *Jews in Contemporary East Germany: The Children of Moses in the Land of Marx* (Houndmills, U.K.: Macmillan, 1989).

15. Burgauer, *Zwischen Erinnerung und Verdrängung*; Michael Cohn, *The Jews in Germany, 1945–1993: The Building of a Minority* (Westport, Conn.: Praeger, 1994); Uri Kaufmann, *Jewish Life in Germany Today*, trans. Susan Schwarz (Bonn: Inter Nationes, 1994); Günther Ginzel, ed., *Der Anfang nach dem Ende: Jüdisches Leben in Deutschland bis heute* (Düsseldorf: Droste, 1996); Y. Michal Bodemann, ed., *Jews, Germans, Memory: Reconstructions of Jewish Life in Germany* (Ann Arbor: University of Michigan Press, 1996).

16. Lynn Rapaport, *Jews in Germany after the Holocaust: Memory, Identity, and Jewish-German Relations* (New York: Cambridge University Press, 1997); Jael Geis, *Übrig Sein—Leben "danach." Juden deutscher Herkunft in der britischen und amerikanischen Zone Deutschlands 1945–1949* (Berlin: Philo, 2000); Anke Quast, *Nach der Befreiung. Jüdische Gemeinden in Niedersachsen seit 1945* (Göttingen: Wallstein, 2001); Ruth Gay, *Safe among the Germans: Liberated Jews after World War II* (New Haven, Conn.: Yale University Press, 2002); Donate Strathmann, *Auswandern oder Hierbleiben? Jüdisches Leben in Deutschland und Nordrhein 1945–1960* (Essen: Klartext, 2003); Anthony Kauders, *Democratization and the Jews: Munich, 1945–1965* (Lincoln: University of Nebraska Press, 2004); Jürgen Zieher, *Im Schatten von Antisemitismus und Wiedergutmachung. Kommunen und jüdische Gemeinden*

in Dortmund, Düsseldorf und Köln 1945–1960 (Berlin: Metropol, 2004); Jay Howard Geller, *Jews in Post-Holocaust Germany* (New York: Cambridge University Press, 2005); Schönborn, *Erinnerung*; Kauders, *Unmögliche Heimat*; Alon Tauber, *Zwischen Kontinuität und Neuanfang. Die Entstehung der jüdischen Nachkriegsgemeinde in Frankfurt am Main 1945–1949* (Wiesbaden: Kommission für die Geschichte der Juden in Hessen, 2008).

17. See Peter Monteath, "The German Democratic Republic and the Jews," *German History* 22, no. 3 (2004): 448–468.

18. Michael Brenner, ed., *A History of Jews in Germany since 1945: Politics, Culture, and Society*, trans. Kenneth Kronenberg (Bloomington: Indiana University Press, 2018). Contributors include Brenner, Dan Diner, Constantin Goschler, Norbert Frei, Lena Gorelik, Atina Grossmann, Anthony Kauders, Tamar Lewinsky, and Yfaat Weiss.

19. See Lothar Mertens, *Davidstern unter Hammer und Zirkel: Die Jüdischen Gemeinden in der SBZ/DDR und ihre Behandlungen durch Partei und Staat, 1945–1990* (Hildesheim: Olms, 1997); Jutta Illichmann, *Die DDR und die Juden: Die deutschlandpolitische Instrumentalisierung von Juden und Judentum durch die Partei- und Staatsführung der SBZ/DDR von 1945 bis 1990* (Frankfurt am Main: Peter Lang, 1997); Ulrike Offenberg, *"Seid vorsichtig gegen die Machthaber": Die Jüdischen Gemeinden in der SBZ und der DDR, 1945–1990* (Berlin: Aufbau, 1998).

20. Mario Keßler, *Die SED und die Juden—zwischen Repression und Toleranz* (Berlin: Akademie, 1995); Karin Hartewig, *Zurückgekehrt. Die Geschichte der jüdischen Kommunisten in der DDR* (Cologne: Böhlau, 2000).

21. Geller, *Jews in Post-Holocaust Germany*; Jay Howard Geller, "Representing Jewry in East Germany, 1945–1953: The Jewish Community between Advocacy and Accommodation," *Leo Baeck Institute Year Book* 47 (2002): 195–214.

22. See, for example, Geller, *Jews in Post-Holocaust Germany*; Quast, *Nach der Befreiung*; Strathmann, *Auswandern oder Hierbleiben*; Zieher, *Im Schatten von Antisemitismus*; Andrea Sinn, *Jüdische Politik und Presse in der frühen Bundesrepublik* (Göttingen: Vandenhoeck & Ruprecht, 2014).

23. Frank Stern, *Im Anfang war Auschwitz: Antisemitismus und Philosemitismus im deutschen Nachkrieg* (Gerlingen: Bleicher, 1991); Constantin Goschler, *Wiedergutmachung: Westdeutschland und die Verfolgten des Nationalsozialismus (1945–1954)* (Munich: Oldenbourg, 1992); Jeffrey Herf, *Divided Memory: The Nazi Past in the Two Germanys* (Cambridge, Mass.: Harvard University Press, 1997); Werner Bergmann and Rainer Erb, *Anti-Semitism in Germany: The Post-Nazi Epoch since 1945*, trans. Belinda Cooper and Allison Brown (New Brunswick, N.J.: Transaction, 1997); Constantin Goschler, *Schuld und Schulden: Die Politik der Wiedergutmachung für NS-Verfolgte seit 1945* (Göttingen: Wallstein, 2005); Norbert Frei, José Brunner, and Constantin Goschler, eds., *Praxis der Wiedergutmachung: Geschichte, Erfahrung und Wirkung in Deutschland und Israel* (Göttingen: Wallstein, 2009); Michael Meng, *Shattered Spaces Encountering Jewish Ruins in Postwar Germany and Poland* (Cambridge, Mass.: Harvard University Press, 2011).

24. John Borneman and Jeffrey M. Peck, *Sojourners: The Return of German Jews and the Question of Identity* (Lincoln: University of Nebraska Press, 1995); Bodemann, *Jews, Germans, Memory*; Leslie Morris and Jack Zipes, eds., *Unlikely History: The Changing German-Jewish Symbiosis, 1945–2000* (New York: Palgrave, 2002); Y. Michal Bodemann, *A Jewish Family in Germany Today: An Intimate Portrait* (Durham, N.C.: Duke University Press, 2005); Andrea Sinn, *"Und ich lebe wieder an der Isar": Exil und Rückkehr des Münchner Juden Hans Lamm* (Munich: Oldenbourg, 2008).

25. Jeffrey M. Peck, *Being Jewish in the New Germany* (New Brunswick, N.J.: Rutgers University Press, 2007).

CHAPTER 1

THE POLITICS OF JEWISH REPRESENTATION IN EARLY WEST GERMANY

Jay Howard Geller

Since 1950, the Central Council of Jews in Germany (Zentralrat der Juden in Deutschland) has been the principal representative body for the organized Jewish communities in Germany and their chief mediator with the German federal government. Despite the relatively small size of its constituency—just under one hundred thousand individuals in 105 Jewish communities in 2017[1]—the Central Council has a notable role in German public affairs. Non-Jewish German politicians consider the opinions of the Central Council's leadership when making decisions regarding Jewish affairs, including memorialization of the Holocaust and the regulation of rituals such as circumcision and kosher slaughter of animals.[2]

Considering the Central Council's political prominence and central role in organized Jewish life in Germany, it is important to illuminate its origins and early years. Close examination demonstrates that despite its importance, this group's establishment was a reaction to external circumstances and not the result of factors deriving entirely from the Jews then living in Germany. Moreover, in its early years, the organization had a relatively marginal role in the West German government's relations with the Jews, broadly speaking, and was even dependent on the (non-Jewish) government for its survival.

During the years of Allied occupation before the establishment of the Federal Republic of Germany, there was not a single unified Jewish community in Germany. At best, one can speak of two distinct groups separated by cultural, religious, and political differences.[3] The larger of the two communities consisted of Eastern European Jews, who had mainly come to Germany after their liberation from the concentration camps. While it may seem paradoxical that non-German Jews who had been liberated from Nazi German camps would come to Germany (and specifically Western Germany) of their own volition, this is precisely what happened. Faced with the persistence of anti-Semitism in Eastern Europe and the rise of discriminatory Communist regimes, tens of thousands of Jewish survivors of the Holocaust and Jews who had spent the war in the Soviet Union made the decision not to return permanently to their hometowns but rather to flee to the relative safety of the Western Allies' occupation zones in Germany. While some did settle in German cities, the vast majority congregated in refugee camps under the auspices of the Allied armies, the United Nations Relief and Rehabilitation Administration (UNRRA) and, later, the International Refugee Organization (IRO).

These Jews, known as displaced persons (DPs), had a different pre-Holocaust cultural, religious, and political experience from Western European Jews. Their native milieu was Yiddish-speaking (or bilingual, with Yiddish and a European national language). While many of them had lost their Jewish faith in the camps or had secularized before the Holocaust, Orthodox Judaism was practically the only variety of Jewish religion practiced by DPs. Additionally, prewar politics among Eastern European Jews were intensely Jewish, with competition between Labor Zionists, Bundists, Revisionist Zionists, and other specifically Jewish political parties that were unpopular or unknown in Western Europe.

In addition to the Jewish refugees from Eastern Europe, who numbered as many as two hundred thousand, there were also remnants of pre-Holocaust German Jewry. After liberation on 8 May 1945, many German Jews who had survived the camps returned to their hometowns or congregated in large cities. Other Jews, who had survived in hiding or through their marriages to non-Jewish spouses, emerged from the shadows. Some German Jews returned to Germany from their exile abroad. These Jews were culturally German. Their politics were German liberal or social democratic, and their religious practice was overwhelmingly Liberal Judaism, a variety of Jewish rite largely unknown outside of Central Europe. As they recommenced their personal and professional lives in German cities, they reestablished synagogues and Jewish communal institutions. In their efforts, they looked chiefly to German governments on the local level and even state level for assistance. For collective political representation, they organized themselves into state associations (*Landesverbände*) and zonal "interest representations" (*Interessenvertretungen*). In total, the German Jews did not number more than twenty thousand and were likely far fewer.

With nothing to return to in Eastern Europe, most Jewish DPs wished to leave Europe permanently. A large number of them, possibly the majority, desired to settle in Palestine in the hope that it would soon be home to a Jewish state. However, the British, who still controlled Palestine under the terms of a League of Nations mandate and who faced a disintegrating situation between Palestine's

Jewish and Arab populations, did not wish to permit Jewish immigration to the territory. Additionally, immigration to the United States was either not possible or not desired. For the most part, the Jewish DPs found themselves stuck in DP camps. There, they built up microsocieties that both drew upon the culture of prewar Jewish Eastern Europe, which was no longer extant, and the culture of Zionist Palestine, which they regarded as their future home. The camps had schools for children and occupational retraining programs for adults, religious institutions, a flourishing press, and entertainment venues. They received assistance from American and international Jewish welfare agencies, as well as the U.S. Army and UNRRA and IRO. Some DPs lived in camps but worked in German cities. Nonetheless, they did not see themselves setting down permanent roots on German soil and intended to leave when they could. Meanwhile, many DPs, most notably in the American zone of occupation, slipped out of the camps and Germany and traveled to Mediterranean ports to hazard the illegal journey to Palestine.

Politically, the Jewish DPs organized themselves on a camp-by-camp basis and later into organizations, known as Central Committees, for all DPs in a given zone of occupation. Generally speaking, they had very few ties to the German Jews, who were much fewer in number, culturally and religiously very different, and who intended to remain permanently in Germany. And this is how the situation concerning the two Jewish communities remained until 1948.

At the same time, Jews living in Germany had to reckon with a boycott by their foreign coreligionists. During the summer of 1948, the World Jewish Congress (WJC), meeting in Montreux, Switzerland, proclaimed "the determination of the Jewish people never again to settle on the bloodstained soil of Germany."[4] A. Leon Kubowitzki, general secretary of the WJC from 1945 to 1948, called for the dissolution of the Jewish communities in postwar Germany, whose existence, in his view, somehow mitigated German guilt for the Holocaust.[5] DP leader Pessach Piekatsch also spoke against Jews remaining in in Germany: "We feel no responsibility toward those DPs who choose to remain. By helping the Gemeinden [Jewish communities established by German Jews] to achieve permanence we encourage DPs to remain too."[6] Looking back on that time four decades later, DP leader Norbert Wollheim, who had been born in Germany, saw things similarly: "I didn't destroy Germany. I have no duty to build it up again. I can't. For me, Germany is one big cemetery."[7]

Another sign of how foreign Jewish groups viewed the future of Jewish life in Germany was the dispensation of property owned by German Jews killed in the Holocaust whose heirs either could not be found or did not make a claim. Control of this ownerless Jewish property was not assigned to the actual, existing Jewish communities in postwar Germany but rather to the Jewish Trust Corporation (JTC) and the Jewish Restitution Successor Organization (JRSO), as per the terms of an agreement between the Western Allies and these foreign

Jewish groups. The JTC and JRSO directly or indirectly promoted the dissolution of organized Jewish life in Germany and intended to use proceeds from the sale of properties to support Jewish life elsewhere. Naturally, the impoverished communities of German Jews protested this decision, which both undermined their own financial well-being and tacitly signaled disapproval of their remaining in Germany.[8]

In the course of 1948, the situation on the ground in Germany changed dramatically. With the establishment of Israel as an independent state, Jewish DPs were free to leave the Western Allies' occupation zones and immigrate to the new Jewish state. Concomitantly, the stream of Jewish refugees to Western Germany ceased. As a result, the number of Eastern European Jewish DPs in diminished from 150,000 to 66,000, and the numbers continued to shrink further. Israel intended to accommodate all the DPs by the end of 1949. Under these circumstances, the American occupation authorities began to consolidate and close DP camps. To many outside observers, this seemed to mark the end of a Jewish presence in Germany, but in fact, this would not be the case.

Thousands of German Jews and Eastern European Jewish DPs remained in Germany despite the wishes of the Israeli government and Jewish relief organizations. Soon, the U.S. Office of Military Government (OMGUS), the American occupation authority, accepted the new reality. The OMGUS adviser for Jewish affairs, Harry Greenstein, met military governor Lucius Clay and summarized his views: "It is his conviction that it is possible for Jews to build a future for themselves and their families in Germany and felt it would be a tragic mistake on the part of the Jews to make Germany 'Judenrein.'"[9]

More consequential for all sides was the establishment of the Federal Republic of Germany in May 1949. As representatives of the people of Western Germany worked to create a federal government, it was clear that the Americans were going to relinquish responsibility for many aspects of governance and relations between the state and civil society, including the supervision of Jewish affairs. Under these circumstances, American occupation authority leaders were of the opinion that it was important for all the Jews in Germany—Eastern European DPs and German Jews—to unite, and Harry Greenstein endeavored to bring the DP communities and the German-Jewish groups together. U.S. high commissioner John J. McCloy favored a central organization for all the Jews in Germany.[10]

Greenstein organized a series of conferences on the future of Jewish life in Germany. At the most important of the conferences, in Heidelberg on 31 July 1949, Greenstein spoke bluntly about the reality of the situation: "This conference has been planned on the premise that there are at the present time[,] and there will continue to be, Jewish communities in Germany." While recognizing the controversial debate on this issue, he proclaimed that it was time to merge the DP and German-Jewish communities. Moreover, he wanted conference participants to "agree on the desirability of setting up an over-all Jewish organization which will make it possible for us to plan together for all of the Jews in Germany."[11]

McCloy also supported the reestablishment of Jewish life in Germany, though his remarks on the matter evince a certain naïveté and even condescension. He attacked the notion that a country as large and important as Germany would not have a substantial Jewish community, and he even went so far as to say that it was odd that the Jews could not live in Germany as in other countries. He ascribed the high degree of residual anti-Semitism in Germany to the effect of repeated, intense propaganda under the Nazis and expected that it would be some time before the atmosphere changed. However, in his opinion, the Jews in Germany needed to contribute to the change in German attitude. They had to comport themselves with honesty and courage. Moreover, he called the development of the Jewish community in Germany as an indicator of "Germany's progress toward the light." The entire world would be watching. Oddly, though, he seemed to place the onus on the Jews: "The success of those that remain will to a large extent depend on the extent to which that community becomes less a community in itself and merges with the general community."[12]

One of the greatest obstacles to forming a unitary organization for all Jews in Germany was the division between Jewish DPs and German Jews, exacerbated by the large size of the DP population. However, now that almost all DPs willing to emigrate had actually left the country, the two groups could plan for a shared future. On the suggestion of German-Jewish leader and Bavarian politician Philipp Auerbach, delegates at the Heidelberg conference formed a committee with the goal of founding an umbrella organization for all existing Jewish groups in Germany. DP leaders Pessach Piekatsch and Josef Rosensaft endorsed the idea, but the latter absurdly stated, "The primary objective of the proposed organization should be to enlighten those who intend to remain here, that there is no place for them in Germany."[13] In any event, they intended to meet again on 4 September 1949 to discuss proposals for the new body.[14]

Despite the plans for unity, tensions between DPs and German Jews did not disappear, and diverging visions prevailed. Leaders of the German Jews complained that the DPs' Central Committee tried to determine the form of the future organization. Not to put too fine a point on it, the German Jews' regional representatives informed the Jewish community of Frankfurt that "by preempting possible decisions, the Central Committee has shown that it will be very difficult to work with it."[15] A speedy unification did not occur. Major Abraham Hyman, Harry Greenstein's successor as Jewish affairs adviser to McCloy, tried to explain the failure: "In the first place, the community is impoverished from the standpoint of leadership." He added that many Jews could not decide whether to stay or emigrate, "with the most articulate elements pulling in diametrically opposite directions."[16]

Not only were the Americans disappointed by the delay, but German politicians who supported reconciliation with the Jews were also frustrated. The inability of the Jews to speak with a single voice hindered German efforts to open a German-Jewish dialogue. Without a Jewish interlocutor, discussion began concerning the appointment of an official Jewish adviser within the West German government.[17] The controversy over this proposal lasted nearly a year. Although most Jewish leaders in Germany eventually spoke out in opposition, it initially found support among some prominent Jews in Germany. Karl Marx, publisher of the *Allgemeine Wochenzeitung der Juden in Deutschland*, wrote to federal president Theodor Heuss, "It seems to me that clarification of all these questions will only be possible if the federal government would decide to consult a Jewish advisor, at least for the first few years."[18] Government officials worked on the details of the proposed office, and according to the state secretary of the interior in the Federal Chancellery, "For domestic and foreign policy reasons, it seems desirable to the Federal Chancellor [Konrad Adenauer] to set up a Department of Jewish Affairs in the Ministry of the Interior." The proposed department within the Interior Ministry not only would handle cultural matters but also would "have the task of ensuring that Jewish interests are sufficiently taken into account in legislation and administration." Adenauer wanted Ernst G. Löwenthal to assume the office.[19] Löwenthal, who had been born in Cologne and fled to Britain during the Nazi era, was in Wiesbaden on the staff of the Jewish Cultural Reconstruction, the cultural branch of the JRSO.

The idea of a Jewish department within the West German government quickly encountered opposition from German-Jewish organizations. The Jewish community of Frankfurt and the Interest Representation of Jewish Communities in the American Zone came out against the plan. At a meeting of the Interest Representation in December 1949, delegates demanded that the federal government "discuss the questions that concern the Jews in Germany with their democratically elected representations," namely, the Interest Representation.[20] In March 1950, Philipp Auerbach wrote to the Federal Chancellery to express his opposition to the plan. He demanded that the federal government consult only with the democratically elected representatives of the Jewish communities and threatened that any Jew who took the office would be excluded from the Interest Representation.[21] However, all this opposition did not resolve the problem: Jews in Germany still did not speak with a single voice, and the West German government still did not have a partner for German-Jewish dialogue. Even Auerbach had to admit to federal interior minister Gustav Heinemann that "it has not been possible to date to merge all the Jewish organizations in the Federal Republic into one democratic organization. We have united only 90% of all Jewish fellow citizens in the Coordinating Council of Jewish Organizations in the US Zone." In fact, several important Jewish communities were outside the American zone, including in Hamburg and Cologne, and many leading Jews lived in Northern Germany, including Karl Marx and Norbert Wollheim.[22]

Meanwhile, Karl Marx worked behind the scenes for the implementation of the proposal, and he advised the federal government on how best to promote it. He suggested renaming the proposed office: "At the same time, I am taking the liberty of asking you to check whether it is not possible for the department, which is to be established, to be called the Reparations Department. In the view of most Jewish circles domestically and abroad, such a designation may be particularly desirable because a Jewish Department existed under the former German government."[23]

According to Luitpold Werz of the Federal President's Office, Marx told Heuss that the biggest problem with the office was its appellation.[24] While the idea of (non-Jewish) German government officials appointing an official representative for the Jews was inherently offensive, Marx had hit upon an additional point of insult: the office's name. It is remarkable that German politicians and civil servants failed to see the similarity between the name of their proposed office, the Department for Jewish Affairs (Referat für Jüdische Angelegenheiten), and the name of the office run by Adolf Eichmann during the Holocaust, the Jewish Department (Judenreferat).

Considering the mixed signals—opposition by Auerbach and support from Marx—federal chancellor Konrad Adenauer sought clarification of the situation. Since Munich-based Auerbach was the most important German-Jewish leader in the American zone, Adenauer asked, "What about the opinion of the Jews in the British and French zones?"[25] During a visit to Berlin in April 1950, Adenauer met with local Jewish community chairman Heinz Galinski and Siegmund Weltlinger, who had been the Berlin city government's adviser for Jewish affairs. He asked the two Berlin Jews for their opinions regarding the proposal for a federal Jewish department, and they supported the idea. Weltlinger recalled, "I urgently recommended the establishment of a Jewish Department in the Federal Republic, despite or rather precisely because of the protest of certain Jewish circles, which fundamentally reject cooperation with German authorities and are fanatically under the spell of a hate psychosis." Turning to Galinski's view, Weltlinger wrote, "Mr. Galinski also supported these remarks, advocated for a department, and recommended Dr. Löwenthal, who is personally known to him." Adenauer responded very positively to this opinion.[26]

The situation had reached an impasse. The leadership of the West German federal government and state apparatus wanted a partner for German-Jewish dialogue and needed someone to provide counsel on sensitive matters concerning the Jews—thus the seeming need for a department, or official adviser, for Jewish Affairs. However, many Jewish leaders in Germany strongly opposed the creation of such a post, while other Jewish leaders endorsed the proposal. At the same time, the Jews living in Germany proved unable to form their own unitary organization, which could have represented them in public life and acted as an intermediary to the government. The situation was untenable in the long term.

In the end, the critical catalyst for Jewish organizational unity came from the World Jewish Congress (WJC), despite its infamous resolution from 1948. WJC president Nahum Goldmann—who was raised and educated in pre-Nazi Germany—supported unitary representation for the Jews in Germany, but he did not have time to take charge of matters personally. Yet without WJC leadership, it seemed that nothing was going to happen "because Jewish leaders in Germany were too busy stabbing each other in the back," in the estimation of an American Jewish Committee representative in Paris. With the situation continually adrift, Gerhard Jacoby, WJC envoy in Germany, and A. L. Easterman, WJC political director in London, took the initiative. At their invitation, Jewish delegates from throughout Germany met on 8 July 1950 for initial talks. Despite making progress, they could not conclude all plans for an umbrella organization and arranged to have a second meeting on 19 July. Heinz Galinski of Berlin insisted that Jews from East Germany be included. Meanwhile, a delegate from the Jewish Agency insisted that there were no more Zionists in Germany and called German Jews' ties to world Jewry into question, an accusation that angered northern German-Jewish leader Norbert Wollheim. Nonetheless, Gerhard Jacoby ended the meeting with the observation that the WJC was pleased that the Jews in Germany would found a united organization.[27]

On 19 July 1950, Jewish leaders from throughout Germany met in Frankfurt to establish an umbrella organization for all Jews living in Germany. Almost from the beginning, the meeting was mired in conflict. Although most of the federal states and large cities of West Germany were represented, Heinz Galinski from Berlin regretted "that no representative of the German Democratic Republic was invited. This absolutely should have happened. Also in the directorate, which is to be founded, the Jews from the G.D.R. [must] have a seat."[28] Some delegates wanted Galinski to function as the delegate for Berlin and East Germany, which he rejected: "Berlin and the East Zone are two different things. He represents both parts of Berlin, but not the G.D.R. outside of Berlin. If the latter is not represented, the Berlin community will not be able to cooperate." But the delegate from Hessen opposed participation by the Jewish community in East Germany and its representation in Bonn, the West German capital. Another source of conflict was the new organization's areas of competency. The powerful heads of statewide Jewish representative bodies feared a diminution of their power. Norbert Wollheim from Northern Germany wanted Jewish state associations to retain all responsibility for regional matters.[29]

A four-person directorate and fifteen-person council would lead the new organization. For the directorate, Philipp Auerbach of Bavaria nominated himself; Heinz Galinski, head of the Berlin Jewish community; Norbert Wollheim, a leader of the DPs in the British zone; and Pessach Piekatsch, a leader of the DPs in the American zone. Beneath the directorate would be a council with three seats for the Jewish communities in the American zone, three seats for the Jewish communities in the British zone, one seat for the French zone, three seats for Berlin, one seat for the Soviet zone (East Germany), three seats for the central committee of Jewish DPs in the American zone, and one seat for the central committee of Jewish DPs in the British zone. The founders unanimously named the new group the Central Council of Jews in Germany, with its base of operations in Frankfurt. Josef Klibansky and Hendrik George van Dam, both lawyers, were to draft the organization's statutes.[30]

The two men could hardly have been more different. Klibansky was a bold advocate for Jewish interests, but his leadership of the Jewish Bank for Industry and Commerce caused many Jews to accuse him of unethical, if not illegal, business practices, such as dubious bookkeeping, violation of currency regulations, and financial relations with blackmarketeers. (As a result of his aggressive and controversial behavior during the trial of Philipp Auerbach two years later, in 1952, he was found in contempt of court and drew unwelcome attention to the Jewish community in West Germany.) In contrast, Hendrik van Dam was accustomed to working within the system. His Dutch-born father had been an antiques and art dealer with a royal warrant of appointment from Wilhelm II, and his maternal grandfather had served as a city councilman in Bremen. After studying at various German universities, Hendrik van Dam earned a doctorate in law at the University of Basel, in Switzerland, in 1934. He spent most of the 1930s in the Netherlands and the war years primarily in Britain. After the war, he helped reestablish the legal administration in Oldenburg and worked for the Jewish Relief Unit in the British zone of occupation. Yet despite their differences, it fell to these two men to lay the groundwork for the most important Jewish institution in Germany.

Foreign reaction to the formation of the Central Council was mixed. According to a representative of the American Jewish Committee (AJC), Germany's outstanding Jewish leaders formed the directorate, while the council consisted of "second-rank 'machers.'" He described Heinz Galinski of Berlin as "plodding" but "honest and diligent, no great intellectual." East German representative Julius Meyer was called "a little-educated business promoter who has done good work for Jewish causes in East Berlin and in the East Zone." However, he was considered to be very close to the Soviets. Hendrik George van Dam was very positively assessed: "His integrity is beyond question."[31]

The second meeting of the Central Council took place on 20 August 1950 in Munich and dealt with organizational matters as well as the critical question of how to let the government and the wider public know about the Central Council. Delegates debated issuing a press release versus making private contacts to certain individuals.[32] Hendrik George van Dam was asked to serve as secretary-general of the group, and he commenced work on 15 October. Eventually, he moved the

Central Council's secretariat to Hamburg, where he lived, and the British occupation authorities arranged for van Dam to receive office space.[33] Gradually, administrator van Dam and Düsseldorf-based publisher Karl Marx became the mouthpieces for the group and the two most notable behind-the-scenes activists for the Jews in West Germany.[34] Van Dam's appointment was particularly consequential, and he provided stability and continuity of leadership since the Central Council had no lay leader as president. Moreover, the two most prominent German-Jewish leaders in Western Germany soon exited the scene: Wollheim emigrating in 1951, and Auerbach committing suicide in 1952 after being convicted of fraud and misappropriation of funds.

It was not long after its formation that the Central Council had to address the issue that had instigated its establishment—namely, Federal Chancellor Adenauer's wish to found a Department for Jewish Affairs. On 10 September, the federal interior minister asked the Central Council for its opinion on appointing Rabbi Aron Ohrenstein to the post. The majority of Central Council members were opposed to the proposal, as they worried that the officeholder would have no real power to make important decisions but would be held accountable if things went badly. Several Central Council members characterized the position as that of a whipping boy (*Prügelknabe*). However, the delegate from the Jewish Agency said that federal interior minister Gustav Heinemann had told him that the lack of such an office hindered any progress on the reparations question. Ultimately, the delegates wrote to the Interior Ministry that they did not wish for any official to receive this appointment.[35] This opposition from the Central Council should be no surprise, since the existence of such a position might have lessened the influence or authority of the Central Council.

In fact, the new organization had to struggle for attention and recognition from the Allies, German authorities, and foreign Jewish groups alike. To alter its standing with the Allies, Central Council directorate members, accompanied by WJC representative Gerhard Jacoby and JDC representative Sam Haber, met with American high commissioner John J. McCloy on 29 November 1950.[36] Foreign Jewish groups took note of the Central Council's activities, and an observer from the AJC worried that the Central Council would be too close to the WJC and would "arrogate to itself the authority on all important matters affecting the Jews in Germany."[37] The Israeli consul in Munich, Eliahu Livneh, supported the group and told its leaders "that Israel does not forget its children, wherever they live."[38] However, when it came to negotiating with the West German government regarding Holocaust reparations, Israel and the Conference on Jewish Material Claims against Germany (the "Claims Conference") took the lead. The Central Council did not have a seat at the table, though it did have a vote on ratifying the reparations settlement and benefited from it.[39] The Jewish Restitution Successor Organization, which the Allies had designated as the heir to ownerless Jewish property in Germany, worried that the Central Council would lead direct negotiations with the West German federal government regarding restitution. Such a move would have rendered the New York–based restitution organization irrelevant.[40] In fact, in January 1951, the Central Council resolved to establish the Central Welfare Office for the Jews in Germany (Zentralwohlfahrtsstelle der Juden in Deutschland) to strengthen its own case and to aid poor Jews, yet the Central Welfare Office too struggled for recognition.[41]

Soon, the Central Council looked to German politicians for attention. On 31 May 1951, Hendrik George van Dam wrote to federal president Theodor Heuss to request that he help improve relations between Jews and the West German government. The Central Council believed that it was time to change the state of affairs and asked Heuss to make the government and, particularly, federal chancellor Konrad Adenauer aware of this desire.[42] The letter was not just a plea for help in improving the climate for Jews; it was also a means to seek recognition, and Heuss's staff forwarded the letter to the Interior Ministry. Soon a civil servant replied to the Office of the Federal President. He cited numerous instances of cooperation between the government and the Central Council and added that ever since the Interior Ministry's recognition of the Central Council, "it [the Central Council] is treated as the rightful representative of the Jews and the Jewish religious communities in the area of Federal Republic. I would be grateful if this were brought to the attention of the Federal President."[43]

Nonetheless, a delegation from the Central Council did not meet with a representative of the West German state until March 1952.[44] Only on 21 March 1952 did Heuss receive envoys from the Central Council, and on 1 April, a similar delegation met with Adenauer.[45] However, the government's efforts to establish a meaningful relationship with Jews focused principally on foreign Jews. By the time the Central Council representatives finally met with Adenauer, West Germany, Israel, and the multinational Claims Conference were already engaged in negotiations over Holocaust reparations. Consequently, the Central Council played almost no role in that endeavor. Only after the conclusion of an agreement could the Central Council establish its relationship with the federal government on a new basis.

Considering the importance of its relations with the government and financial stresses on the organization, a topic of ongoing debate within the organization was where the Central Council should have its base of operations. Hendrik van Dam had moved the group's office to Hamburg soon after becoming secretary-general, but that decision did not find universal approval. For some, and particularly for foreign Jewish envoys to the Central Council, Munich was the natural place for the organization to reside. At the time, it had the largest Jewish population in West Germany, the most Jewish offices, and an Israeli consulate. However, the Munich option was problematic. First of all, most Jews in and near Munich were Eastern European DPs (or former DPs) who intended to emigrate from Germany. Moreover, Munich was far from Bonn, the seat of power in West Germany. Another problem was that Philipp Auerbach, who had utterly dominated Jewish political life in Munich, was under arrest for fraud and other crimes involving reparations funds. As a result, having Germany's leading Jewish representative organization in Munich became unthinkable.

To others, it seemed natural that the group should have its headquarters in Bonn, the federal capital, but there were distinct disadvantages to that option as well. Not only would it have given the impression that the Central Council existed solely for externally directed political activity, but it would have also alienated Jews in East Germany, who were officially members of the group.[46] In the end, the Central Council leaders selected Düsseldorf, in the Rhineland region of West Germany.[47] In many ways, it was a natural choice. It was already home to several German-Jewish professional and social organizations. Karl Marx's newspaper was based there. And it was close, but not *too* close, to Bonn (approximately seventy-five kilometers, or one hour's drive). Ultimately, the decision to move the offices to Düsseldorf signaled a balance between independence and intensification of the relationship with the federal government.[48]

Not only did the Central Council wish to achieve full recognition, but it also needed to ensure its very existence. In January 1953, van Dam wrote to federal interior minister Robert Lehr about the significance of the Central Council: "Hereby is a unitary representation vis-à-vis the federal government, as well as foreign Jewish organizations, guaranteed." But the Central Council's existence did not seem certain to van Dam. He continued, "It is therefore our view that the central representation of the Jewish communities should be granted a federal subsidy that enables it to carry out its duties independently. All actions of the Central Council today can only take place in an atmosphere of provisionality and uncertainty, which serves neither the independence nor the vigor of a statutory body."[49] In fact, within a few months, the Central Council began to receive a subvention from the West German government.[50] Such payments were critical for the Central Council's viability. But the federal government's ongoing relationship with the JRSO, foreign Jewish reparations authorities, and Israeli diplomats caused continuing concern for the organization. Van Dam and his colleagues in the Central Council felt it necessary over and over to lobby for full recognition. On 3 November, they wrote to several government ministries, "For the exercise of the rights and interests of the Jewish community in Germany with the federal authorities, only the Central Council of Jews in Germany is authorized to represent the Jewish communities of the Federal Republic. Representation by foreign organizations or spokespersons will not be recognized by the Central Council in the future. Decisions that affect the interests of the Jewish community in Germany are binding on the Central Council only if it was involved in the negotiations or has commented on them in a timely manner."[51] Although their position was probably not truly threatened, particularly after the conclusion of the Luxembourg Agreement for reparations, it would be years before the small Jewish community in the Federal Republic of Germany was considered a full member of the broader international Jewish community.[52] Meanwhile, the Central Council pursued a two-track strategy with representatives of the West German state and government: the cultivation of ties to national political leaders, whose approbation brought the group respect and a public profile, and an ongoing relationship with ministerial officials and civil servants, who could help with mundane (but necessary) issues such as funding.[53]

The establishment of a single, united representation for all Jews living in Germany was not easy. After liberation, the Jewish community was divided between Eastern European DPs and German Jews, with the former group considerably larger than the latter. However, the establishment of Israel in 1948 ultimately resolved the imbalance. With the ability to immigrate to the Jewish state, the number of Eastern European Jews in Germany diminished significantly by 1950.

Meanwhile, there was a greater need for unity than ever. For several years, the American military occupation government had rendered assistance to the Jews, particularly through the offices of the adviser for Jewish affairs, but in 1949 that option was also coming to an end, as a German civilian federal government began to take over many areas of competency from the Allies. The Americans recommended that all Jews living in Germany unite for representative purposes, while at the same time, the new West German federal government was interested in Jewish matters. The Jews presented no interlocutor to government offices and were unable to speak with a single voice on important issues. The federal government's attempt to set up a Department for Jewish Affairs within the Federal Interior Ministry failed as a result of Jewish opposition, but it did, however, serve as a stimulus for the establishment of a single representative institution. With help from the WJC, Jewish groups from throughout Germany founded the Central Council of Jews in Germany. Beginning in 1950–1951, German politicians had a partner for German-Jewish dialogue, and the Jewish communities in Germany had a single organization to speak in their name.

Despite these steps, the Central Council struggled for recognition and respect. Jewish groups abroad competed with it to represent Jewish interests in Germany or to represent the Jews vis-à-vis the West German federal government. Only in 1952, after West Germany, Israel, and the Claims Conference began negotiations for Holocaust reparations, were delegates from the Central Council received by the federal president and the federal chancellor. And only after the conclusion of the Luxembourg Agreement for reparations did the Central Council receive a subsidy from the German federal government that ensured its existence and signified solid recognition from the state. Nearly seven decades later, the organization is prominent in German public life, but neither its establishment nor its status came easily.

ABBREVIATIONS

BArch. Bundesarchiv Koblenz
CJH. Center for Jewish History
LAB. Landesarchiv Berlin
USHMM. United States Holocaust Memorial Museum
ZA. Zentralarchiv zur Erforschung der Geschichte der Juden in Deutschland

NOTES

1. Sergio DellaPergola, "World Jewish Population, 2017," *American Jewish Year Book* (2017): 339–340; "Jüdische Gegenwart in Deutschland," Bundeszentrale für politische Bildung, 6 October 2016, http://www.bpb.de/geschichte/zeitgeschichte/deutschlandarchiv/234438/juedische-gegenwart-in-deutschland-die-migration-russischsprachiger-juden-seit-1989.

2. "Federal Republic of Germany," *American Jewish Year Book* 97 (1997): 337; Karen E. Till, *The New Berlin: Memory, Politics, Place* (Minneapolis: University of Minnesota Press, 2005), 173; Zentralrat der Juden in Deutschland, "Zentralrat steht unmissverständlich zum Denkmal für die ermordeten Juden Europas," 14 February 2004, http://www.zentralratdjuden.de/de/article/223.zentralrat-steht-unmissverständlich-zum-denkmal-für-die-ermordeten-juden-europas.html; Zentralrat der Juden in Deutschland, "Gegen das Schächt-Verbot," 25 July 2008, http://www.zentralratdjuden.de/de/article/1839.gegen-das-schächt-verbot.html; Mariam Lau, "Etwas ist zerbrochen," *Die Zeit*, 13 September 2012.

3. See Michael Brenner, *After the Holocaust: Rebuilding Jewish Lives in Postwar Germany*, trans. Barbara Harshav (Princeton, N.J.: Princeton University Press, 1997), 7–77; Jay Howard Geller, *Jews in Post-Holocaust Germany, 1945–1953* (New York: Cambridge University Press, 2005), 17–52.

4. World Jewish Congress, "Germany," *Resolutions Adopted by the Second Plenary Assembly of the World Jewish Congress, Montreux, Switzerland, June 27th–July 6th, 1948* (London: Odhams Press, [1948]), 7.

5. "Wir und Deutschland," undated, BArch, B 122, 2083; Protokoll der Sitzung der vorläufigen Direktoriums des Zentralrates, 29 November 1950, ZA, B.1/7, 221.7.

6. "Report of Conference Held in the Office of the Adviser on Jewish Affairs," 13–14 March 1949, Center for Jewish History / YIVO, RG 294.1, 76.

7. Interview with Norbert Wollheim, part 2, 17 May 1991, United States Holocaust Memorial Museum, RG 50.030*0267, tape 3.

8. The JRSO and many Jewish communities in Germany agreed that the communities would receive properties they needed for their work, while others would go to the JRSO, but in many cases, the communities and the JRSO fought it out in West German courts. Michael Meng, *Shattered Spaces: Encountering Jewish Ruins in Postwar Germany and Poland* (Cambridge, Mass.: Harvard University Press, 2011), 33–38.

9. Report by Harry Greenstein, 22 March 1949, Center for Jewish History / YIVO, RG 347.7.1, 33.

10. Hendrik George van Dam, "Die Juden in Deutschland nach 1945," in *Judentum. Schicksal, Wesen und Gegenwart*, vol. 2, ed. Franz Böhm and Walter Dirks (Wiesbaden: Franz Steiner, 1965), 901.

11. "Introductory Remarks by Harry Greenstein, Adviser on Jewish Affairs," *Conference on "The Future of the Jews in Germany,"* Office of Adviser on Jewish Affairs (Heidelberg: Office of Adviser on Jewish Affairs, [1949]), 5.

12. "Remarks by John J. McCloy, High Commissioner US Zone, Germany," in *Conference on "The Future of the Jews in Germany,"* 20–22, quotes on 22.

13. "Formation of a Dachkommitee," in *Conference on "The Future of the Jews in Germany,"* 32–33, quote on 32.

14. "Report of the Commission Appointed to Formulate Tentative Plans for the Establishment of the Dachkommitee," in *Conference on "The Future of the Jews in Germany,"* 57.

15. Interessenvertretung to Jewish Community Frankfurt am Main, 19 August 1949 and 28 August 1949, ZA, B.1/13, A.409, quote from 28 August 1949.

16. "Final Report of Major Abraham S. Hyman," 30 January 1950, Center for Jewish History / YIVO, RG 347.7.1, 33.

17. Karl Marx to Konrad Adenauer, 20 September 1949, BArch, B 136, 5862.

18. Karl Marx to Theodor Heuss, 15 September 1949, BArch, B 122, 2086.

19. State Secretary of the Interior in the Federal Chancellery to Minister of the Interior Gustav Heinemann and Minister of Finance Fritz Schäffer, 28 November 1949, BArch, B 136, 5862.

20. Interessenvertretung der Jüdischen Gemeinden und Kultusvereinigungen der amerikanischen Zone to Konrad Adenauer, 16 December 1949, BArch, B 136, 5862; "Protokoll über die Sitzung des Vorstandes der Jüdischen Gemeinde in Frankfurt am Main," 7 December 1949, ZA, B.1/13, A.4.

21. Philipp Auerbach to Federal Chancellery, 6 March 1950, BArch, B 136, 5862.

22. Philipp Auerbach to Gustav Heinemann, 24 March 1950, BArch, B 136, 5862.

23. Karl Marx to Herbert Blankenhorn, 24 December 1949, BArch, B 136, 5862.

24. Luitpold Werz, "Aufzeichnung," 23 February 1950, BArch, B 122, 2083.

25. Konrad Adenauer's commentary on letter from Philipp Auerbach to Federal Chancellery, 6 March 1950, BArch, B 136, 5862.

26. "Aktennotiz! Betr. Besuch Adenauer," 19 April 1950, LAB, B Rep. 2, 4866.

27. "WJC Woos German Jewry," 24 July 1950, Center for Jewish History / YIVO, RG 347.7.1, 35; "Eine Gesamtorganisation in Deutschland vor der Gründung," *Allgemeine Wochenzeitung der Juden in Deutschland*, 14 July 1950, 5.

28. "Protokoll der am 19. Juli 1950 14 Uhr in Frankfurt a. M. Hebelstr. 17 stattgehabten Sitzung zum Zwecke der Konstituierung einer Gesamtvertretung der Juden in Deutschland," 19 July 1950, ZA, B.1/7, 221.1.

29. "Protokoll der am 19. Juli 1950 14 Uhr in Frankfurt a. M. Hebelstr. 17 stattgehabten Sitzung zum Zwecke der Konstituierung einer Gesamtvertretung der Juden in Deutschland," 19 July 1950, ZA, B.1/7, 221.1.

30. "Protokoll der am 19. Juli 1950 14 Uhr in Frankfurt a. M. Hebelstr. 17 stattgehabten Sitzung zum Zwecke der Konstituierung einer Gesamtvertretung der Juden in Deutschland," 19 July 1950, ZA, B.1/7, 221.1.

31. "A 'Roof Organization' Is Born," 23 July 1950, Center for Jewish History / YIVO, RG 347.7.1, 35.

32. "Protokoll des Zentralrates der Juden in Deutschland," 20 August 1950, ZA, B.1/7, 221.2.

33. H. G. van Dam, *10 Jahre Zentralrat der Juden in Deutschland. Jahresbericht 1960* (Düsseldorf: Zentralrat der Juden in Deutschland, 1960), 5–6.

34. Andrea Sinn, *Jüdische Politik und Presse in der frühen Bundesrepublik* (Göttingen: Vandenhoeck & Ruprecht, 2014); Y. Michal Bodemann, "'How Can One Stand to Live There as a Jew . . .': Paradoxes of Jewish Existence in Germany," in *Jews, Germans, Memory: Reconstructions of Jewish Life in Germany*, ed. Y. Michal Bodemann (Ann Arbor: University of Michigan Press, 1996), 30–32; Michael Brenner, "East European and German Jews in Postwar Germany, 1945–1950," in *Jews, Germans, Memory*, ed. Bodemann, 59.

35. "Protokoll der Sitzung des Direktoriums des Zentralrates," 15–16 October 1950, ZA, B.1/7, 221.5.

36. "McCloy beriet mit Zentralrat," *Allgemeine Wochenzeitung der Juden in Deutschland*, 8 December 1950, 5; "Besprechung von Mitgliedern des vorläufigen Direktoriums mit Mr. J. McCloy," 29 November 1950, ZA, B.1/7, 221.6.

37. "Shall Jews Remain in Germany? An Observer's Report from Inside Germany," November 1950, Center for Jewish History / YIVO, RG 347.7.1, 33.

38. "Summarisches Protokoll der Sitzung des Zentralrates," 7 January 1951, ZA, B.1/7, 221.9.

39. "Protokoll über die Sitzung des Zentralrates der Juden in Deutschland," 20 July 1952, ZA, B.1/7, 221.21; "Protokoll," 14 September 1952, ZA, B.1/7, 221.27; van Dam, "Die Juden in Deutschland nach 1945," in *Judentum*, 906; Nana Sagi, *German Reparations: A History of the Negotiations*, trans. Dafna Alon (Jerusalem: Magnes, 1986); Ronald W. Zweig, *German Reparations and the Jewish World: A History of the Claims Conference*, 2nd ed. (London: Routledge, 2013), 144.

40. Ruth Schreiber, "The New Jewish Communities in Germany after World War II and the Successor Organizations in the Western Zones," *Journal of Israeli History* 18, nos. 2–3 (Autumn 1997): 177.

41. Norbert Wollheim to Hendrik George van Dam, 21 January 1951, Hendrik George van Dam to Interior Minister, 25 February 1951, Interior Ministry to Central Council, 29 March 1951, ZA, B.1/7, 157; "Zentralwohlfahrtsstelle der Juden in Deutschland (in Gründung)," 19–20 August 1951, B.1/11, 15 (Zugang 96/10).

42. Hendrik George van Dam to Theodor Heuss, 31 May 1951, BArch, B 106, 36.

43. Federal Interior Ministry to Federal President's Office, 29 July 1951, BArch, B 106, 36.

44. Prior to that time, some individual German-Jewish leaders, including Norbert Wollheim, had met state and government officials. See "Gespräch zwischen Bundespräsident Theodor Heuss und Norbert Wollheim am 19. Januar 1950 in Kiel—Niederschrift," 19 January 1950, *Zwischen Moral und Realpolitik. Deutsch-israelische Beziehungen, 1945–1965. Eine Dokumentensammlung*, ed. Yeshayahu A. Jelinek (Gerlingen: Bleicher, 1997), 135–138; "Brief von Norbert Wollheim an Shalom Adler-Rudel mit Bericht über das Treffen mit Bundespräsident Theodor Heuss," 4 April 1950, *Zwischen Moral und Realpolitik*, 145.

45. "Aufzeichnung," 21 March 1952, BArch, B 122, 2080; Leopold Golschmidt, "Empfang bei Professor Heuss," *Allgemeine Wochenzeitung der Juden in Deutschland*, 28 March 1952, 5; "Bericht über die Bespechung des Direktoriums des Zentralrates der Juden in Deutschland und dessen Generalsekretär mit dem Bundeskanzler Dr. Adenauer," ZA, B.1/5, 213.

46. "Protokoll des Zentralrates der Juden in Deutschland," 29–30 April 1951, ZA, B.1/7, 221.13.

47. "Beschlussprotokoll der Sitzung des Direktoriums," 4 May 1952, ZA, B.1/7, 221.19.

48. Sinn, *Jüdische Politik*, 189.

49. "Memorandum," BArch, B 106, 21407, 5 January 1953.

50. Norbert Schäfer to Carl Gussone, 2 October 1953, BArch, B 106, 21407; Norbert Schäfer and Carl Katz to Gussone, 28 October 1953, BArch, B 106, 21407; "Tätigkeitsberichte des Generalsekretärs," 10 December 1953, ZA, B.1/7, 120.

51. Carl Katz and Hendrik George van Dam to Ministerialrat Dr. Fiegel of the Ministry of the Interior, Katz and van Dam to Abraham Frowein of the Foreign Office, and Katz and van Dam to Walter Roemer of the Ministry of Justice, 2–3 November 1953, ZA, B.1/7, 101.

52. Lilli Marx, "Renewal of the German-Jewish Press," in *After the Holocaust: Rebuilding Jewish Lives in Postwar Germany*, trans. Barbara Harshav (Princeton, N.J.: Princeton University Press, 1997), 127; Michael Cohn, *The Jews in Germany, 1945–1993: The Building of a Minority* (Westport: Praeger, 1994), 93.

53. Sinn, *Jüdische Politik*, 305–306.

CHAPTER 2

WE HAVE THE RIGHT TO EXIST HERE

JEWISH POLITICS AND THE CHALLENGES OF *WIEDERGUTMACHUNG* IN POST-HOLOCAUST GERMANY

Andrea A. Sinn

According to a census taken in 1950, the Jewish population in the Federal Republic of Germany and West Berlin had fallen to 21,974 from roughly 250,000 during the immediate postwar years, mainly due to the emigration of the vast majority of Jewish Holocaust survivors from Eastern Europe.[1] For a variety of reasons, these individuals had fled or been driven or deported from their countries of origin during or as a result of the war, and they were therefore categorized pursuant to the United Nations' definition as displaced persons (DPs). A large number of these non-German Jews had refused or been unable to return to their home countries after the end of the Second World War and hence lived for variable lengths of time in the Allied zones of occupation, where they waited for the permissions necessary to leave for a new homeland.[2] Despite this disproportionally large decrease of population, in 1954, seventy Jewish communities, arranged into thirteen state associations (*Landesverbände*), existed in the Federal Republic of Germany and West Berlin.[3] In retrospect, it is tempting to interpret this presence as a sign of the gradual consolidation of the Jewish community in this area. At the time, however, many Jews in Germany saw themselves in contradictory terms: they often justified their continued presence in the "land of the perpetrators" with their sense of responsibility for the democratic development of West Germany, while at the same time viewing the country as only a temporary place of residence.[4] To some extent, this way of thinking mirrored the stance that influential Jews, such as former German rabbi Dr. Leo Baeck and American rabbi

Abraham Klausner, and international Jewish organizations, like the World Jewish Congress (WJC), had taken against the continuation of Jewish life in Germany immediately after the end of the Second World War. They regarded the large Jewish presence in the Allied zones of occupation as no more than temporary and insisted that the reestablishment of Jewish life in Germany should not be encouraged considering the strongly negative view of Jews held by the majority of Germans.[5] In light of the various forms of isolation and stigmatization that Jews in Germany experienced during the postwar years, there was a need for the emerging spokesmen of the newly established Jewish communities and state associations as well as for the nationwide representation of Jews through the Central Council of Jews in Germany (Zentralrat der Juden in Deutschland). The Central Council was founded in 1950 to step up efforts to consolidate the community and help it stand its ground when confronting the competing and conflicting German, Jewish, and international conceptions of Jewish life in Germany voiced at the time.[6]

Utilizing a wide range of primary-source materials located in various German private, city, and state archives, this essay documents the unique challenges that Jews in Germany confronted when seeking to secure and advance Jewish life there during the early 1950s. Moreover, this article asserts that at a time when many Jews felt guilty and judged their own or others' decisions to remain in Germany after the Shoah as unacceptable, a number of high-ranking Jewish functionaries defended the right of Jewish communities to exist in the newly founded West German state. Ultimately, as will be shown, it was their fierce commitment and political positioning that guided the community and resulted in securing its financial and practical support from international Jewish organizations in 1953, despite strong differences of opinion. This was a crucial first step that, together with subsidies subsequently granted by the German state, formed the necessary existential basis for the revival of Jewish life in the Federal Republic of Germany.

The intense political discussions of the question of material and moral compensation for victims of Nazi persecution and the Holocaust serve as an especially revealing example of the conflicting views and the difficult process of rapprochement between various actors within and outside of Germany after 1945. Even though the issue of restitution was referenced by the first general secretary of the Central Council, lawyer Dr. Hendrik G. van Dam,[7] as "the crucial factor which led to the founding of the Central Council"[8] (a positively connoted interpretation frequently cited in modern scholarship), restitution demonstrates better than anything else how complex, conflictive, and competitive the nature of Jewish politics proved following the end of the Second World War. As a matter of fact, as early as 1946, the question of restitution had been a key theme in the German-Jewish community newspaper today known as *Jüdische Allgemeine*.[9] At that time, it was the first priority of the newspaper's chief editor, journalist Karl Marx,[10] to denounce the failures of both Allied occupiers and German officials on this matter. It is thus hardly surprising that three years later, it was he who published West German chancellor Konrad Adenauer's first statement on the question of restitution for Jewish survivors, in November 1949. In an interview with Marx (which was to serve as the basis of a news story), Adenauer had not only promised the Jews in Germany security but also announced the newly established government's commitment to a broad compensation indemnification for every Jew that had been harmed during the years of the Nazi regime.[11] It was, however, the chancellor's government policy statement on 27 September 1951[12] that marked the starting point for official negotiations among German, Jewish, and Israeli parties, which concluded in September 1952 with the signing of the Luxembourg Agreement, the Federal Republic of Germany's first major international restitution treaty.[13]

To this day, three key aspects of the Holocaust restitution negotiations between Jews and Germans have attracted considerable attention in scholarly literature: *Wiedergutmachung*, a German term encompassing all actions intended to compensate the losses suffered by people who were persecuted for racial, religious, or political reasons under National Socialist rule; the fact that being confronted with the question of German reparations to Jews at the end of the 1940s brought the representatives of the existing DP and German-Jewish committees throughout the country together at a decisive meeting in Frankfurt am Main, where on 19 July 1950 they merged and established a consolidated representative political body (the Central Council of Jews in Germany); and the lengthy negotiations between German, Jewish, and Israeli representatives that eventually resulted in the conclusion of a reparation agreement between the Federal Republic of Germany and the State of Israel.[14] The heated discussions between different Jewish groups in Germany concerning their positioning and their tense relations with international Jewish organizations are also integral, but substantially less attention has been paid to these all-too-often overlooked parts of the negotiations for restitution and compensation payments.[15]

Consequently, this essay sets out to offer an in-depth analysis of Jewish politics and the challenges of *Wiedergutmachung* faced by Jews in post-Holocaust Germany, with a focus on the position that two of the most prominent representatives of the Jewish community in Germany—Karl Marx and Hendrik G. van Dam—adopted both on this question in general and toward (restitution claims of) Jewish organizations outside of Germany in particular. In analyzing this crucial chapter of Germany's post-Holocaust history from a Jewish perspective, this essay invites readers to consider the negotiations about restitution collectively as a significant indicator of the recognition and later acceptance of the Jewish minority in Germany. This approach will allow for new insights not only into the process of negotiating a future for Jews in the Federal Republic but also regarding the changing position of Germany's Jewish minority in the international community.

A Challenging Task: Jews in Germany on the Question of Restitution after 1945

Before even beginning to consider approaching third parties with regard to restitution claims, Jews in Germany had to gain clarity of their own values and goals so that their spokespeople could convincingly articulate their thoughts, interests, demands, and needs. Did they see themselves in the role of observers? Did they expect to actively contribute to the debate on future compensation legislation? Or did they want to pursue the objective of becoming mediators in the forthcoming restitution negotiations between the West German government and representatives of both the State of Israel and international Jewish organizations?

When considering the position of Karl Marx, who by the end of the 1940s had secured the powerful position of chief editor of the *Jüdische Allgemeine*, his interests are obvious and quickly summarized. Through his journalistic work, Marx went out of his way to call attention to failures regarding restitution payments and legislation on the parts of the Allied and German authorities. In addition, he hoped to initiate a broad public debate aimed at improving the situation for Jewish Holocaust survivors. Simultaneously, however, he worked hard to position himself as a mediator between Germans and Jews—that is to say, between the German federal government and the Jewish community in Germany as well as between the German and Israeli governments.

Marx's desire to present himself as the leading representative of all Jews in Germany led to frequent clashes between the editor and representatives of the newly founded Jewish communities and state associations, who condemned his well-meant yet uncoordinated set of actions. An example of such practices occurred in late 1949, when Marx—without consultation or prior notice—held a meeting with Kurt Schumacher, the leader of both the German Social Democratic Party and its principal spokesman on the Jewish question during the early postwar years. As soon as this became known, Norbert Wollheim, a German Jew and Auschwitz survivor who organized Jewish life in the British occupation zone, criticized Marx for (intentionally) creating a situation in which the editor would be perceived as official representative of *all* Jewish communities.[16] In response to this incident, Wollheim saw no alternative to introducing a resolution, endorsed by the Central Committee of Liberated Jews in the British Zone, that publicly condemned any type of independent campaign.[17] After this and other incidents, Marx promised to be more considerate and aimed to search for common ground and a common level of communication. However, difficulties persisted even after the Central Council was established in July 1950 and claimed to represent the interests of all Jews living in Germany.[18]

Despite the continuing tensions between the national Jewish umbrella organization, primarily represented by van Dam, and the self-appointed spokesman, Karl Marx, the Central Council reaffirmed its commitment to working together with the *Jüdische Allgemeine* on issues such as restitution, not however without having created a set of new rules deemed necessary for the safeguarding of its interests and for the success of the actions undertaken.[19] The number and intensity of these altercations raise the question of how these disputes about matters of competence affected the behavior of Germany's Jewish postwar representation with regard to the question of restitution. Few other methods could be more suited to study these two representatives' position than a close analysis of the incessant stream of newspaper and journal articles both men published over the course of two decades predominantly (though not exclusively) in the *Jüdische Allgemeine*.

At the beginning of 1950, both Marx and van Dam were actively involved in calling for restitution, reparation, and compensation payments for victims of Nazi persecution.[20] As a lawyer and expert on restoration and restitution, van Dam made use of his legal knowledge and sent out a myriad of statements and resolutions adopted by the directorate of the Central Council of Jews in Germany. These publications are particularly insightful as they provide a greater understanding of how van Dam categorized and conceptualized the issue. As part of his analysis of the legal basis for reparation claims on the part of the State of Israel, he explained, for example, that in his opinion, "*Wiedergutmachung*, before it poses a complicated legal problem, . . . presents a moral and political one. This applies as much to the German as to the Jewish nation."[21] He also pressed German and Israeli authorities alike for the immediate opening of negotiations without intermediation in the hopes that an agreement between Israel and the Federal Republic of Germany might bring an end to the German-Jewish communities' state of international isolation.[22]

Marx shared van Dam's view as regards the need to expedite the restitution process. Yet by no means did he focus on that issue alone. It was his stated goal not only to make his newspaper available as a platform for detailed analysis and critical articles concerning this topic but also to stress the multidimensional nature of the subject matter and promote a differentiated approach to reporting.[23] The longer the discussions continued, the more evident it became that Marx considered it the "special task" of the Jews in Germany "to ensure that what had been started would be completed."[24] Moreover, Marx claimed that the Jews in Germany "through repeated warnings and admonitions made a not insignificant contribution . . . to creating a sound basis . . . for future negotiations between Jews and Germans." Following Adenauer's 1951 government statement, Marx went even further and declared—in accordance with his private interests—that taking on the role of "intermediary between the Germans, who are committed to the declaration of their government, and the Jews all over the world, but above all, however, in Israel," was the future task of the Jewish community in Germany.[25] This interpretation stood in stark contrast to the position adopted by van Dam, who more and more frequently defended the Central Council's right to sole representation of the Jewish community in Germany and refused to act as an intercessor for the German Federal government.[26] Instead, van Dam made an effort, as historian Anthony Kauders has characterized it, to "conduct a Jewish discourse about Jews in Germany, without simply saying what Jews living outside of Germany wanted to hear."[27]

In other words, while Marx's topical coverage reiterated the intermediary role Jews in Germany (had) played and praised every step taken by the West German government with a view to addressing the question of restitution for its positive impact, van Dam's articles became more and more focused on defending the interest and claims of the Jews in Germany. A closer look at the German-Jewish functionaries' relationship with international Jewish organizations can help put van Dam's strong intervention on behalf of the Jewish minority in the newly established West German state into perspective and will make it possible to relate the attitudes Marx and van Dam adopted on the given topic to the official policy approach chosen by the spokespeople of Germany's Jewish minority.

Partners or Competitors? Jews in Germany and International Jewish Organizations in the Context of the Early Restitution Negotiations

Once Allied troops had liberated the European continent and informed the world of the horrors of Nazism and the enormity of the Holocaust, the question of whether it was at all possible or desirable to restore Jewish life in post-Holocaust Germany was fiercely debated. As mentioned earlier, one of the most powerful statements against the continuation of Jewish life in "the land of the perpetrators" was issued by the Second Assembly of the WJC that took place in Montreux, Switzerland, from 27 June to 6 July 1948.[28] Referring to the general consensus to refrain from settling in Spain after the expulsion of the Jews in 1492, this international federation of Jewish communities and organizations condemned the idea of a Jewish return to Germany and declared unequivocally "the determination of the Jewish people never again to settle on the bloodstained soil of Germany."[29]

The WJC reinforced this attitude with another declaration issued shortly after the establishment of the Central Council, which stated that "the representatives [of Jews] in Germany will not be allowed to send a voting delegation to the forthcoming World Congress."[30] In addition, German-Jewish officials were excluded from active participation in any of the meetings leading up to the signing of the Luxembourg Agreement. One major reason for this was that, according to the Jewish majority's view, it was not the task of Jews in Germany to voice German-Jewish interests. In fact, many Jews outside Germany were of the opinion that, in accordance with the plan to terminate Jewish life in Germany, only properties essential for the communities' religious and cultural activities should be (provisionally) conserved. They contended that the rest of the communal Jewish property in Germany should benefit those Jews who did survive and resettled elsewhere, as well as the Jewish communities worldwide, who were responsible for their integration. Consequently, those in favor of this argument did not acknowledge the newly founded Jewish communities in Germany, but considered the so-called successor organizations—the Jewish Restitution Successor Organization (JRSO) in the U.S. zone of Germany, the Jewish Trust Corporation for Germany (JTC) in the British zone, and the Branche Française de la Jewish Trust Corporation in the French zone—to be the legitimate legal representation of all German-Jewish claims.[31] These organizations, which merged in 1951 into the Conference of Jewish Material Claims against Germany (Claims Conference), had been established during the late 1940s to prosecute the restitution claims of the "heirless assets" of German Jewry, including property owned by Jewish communities before 1933, as well as the holdings of German Jews who had perished in the Holocaust.[32]

With regard to the matter of restitution negotiations, the international Jewish organizations' position and resulting legal understanding caused a crucial conflict of interest with the Jewish communities in West Germany. Even though they constituted only a small fraction of the once vital centers of German-Jewish life, their members fought to be recognized as the legal successors of the destroyed German-Jewish communities in order to assert restitution claims of synagogues, cemeteries, hospitals, old-age homes, and so on.[33] This important facet of the restitution negotiations shows that the fight for recognition that was carried out between the international Jewish organizations and the Jews in Germany had not only a moral but also a crucial financial dimension that featured prominently on the agenda of the process of rapprochement.

Reaching a unified position on any decision regarding the question of restitution proved to be particularly difficult during the year that preceded the signing of the Luxemburg Agreement in September 1952. According to van Dam's annual report discussing the events over the course of the first half of 1951, "The categorical condemnation of the continued presence of Jews in Germany by Jews abroad, and especially by Jews in Israel, had been subject to many consultations and protestations" by the spokespeople of the Jewish community in Germany.[34] However, a year later, his description of the relationship between the Jewish communities in Germany and international Jewish organizations, which he expressed in an interview, pointed already to a more positive trend in the climate of opinion. Aiming to make sense of the change of the overall condition, van Dam's retrospective assessment of the difficult process of restitution negotiations is of particular interest. In April 1953, he explained, "Today, following a period of understandable restraint, close contacts are maintained with World Jewry. After all, Joint and Jewish Relief Unit already worked in Germany shortly after the end of the war. . . . The Central Council views the Jews in Germany as a central element of world Jewry and acts accordingly in all matters that affect Jews in the world. It should be noted that, in this respect, all bodies representing the Jews in Germany carefully avoided filing restitution claims on their behalf. This voluntary restraint should be put to their credit."[35]

Admittedly, this "voluntary restraint" that van Dam stressed in this conversation did not come naturally but was the result of many exhausting discussions among the elected representatives of the Jews living in Germany at the time.

A close reading of contemporary sources, such as letters and minutes of meetings, reveals that a few weeks after a conference on the question of restitution held in Munich on 28 January of 1951 did not produce any results,[36] the directorate of the Central Council had a particularly intense debate on the subject in general, and the Central Council's relationship to the international Jewish organizations in particular.[37] Although there was widespread consensus among the participants that good relations existed with a few relevant individuals, including the European director of the WJC, Noah Barou,[38] worries steadily grew among a number of German-Jewish representatives who feared that going forward this might not be sufficient considering the changing political landscape in Germany. The fact that the western Allies gradually handed control over regional and state affairs to German authorities raised the question whether the Jews in Germany could afford to renounce their own priorities in favor of those of Jews living outside of the country or if it was time to approach the federal government directly to protect their own interests. While Auschwitz survivor Heinz Galinski, who was the leader of the Jewish community in West Berlin and later chairman of the Central Council, insisted on "practicing realpolitik," which for him meant to "finally tread the path to the [West German] government and explain our position very clearly,"[39] Marx and van Dam most urgently advised against "demanding something as German Jews . . . that pertained to World Jewry." At the same time, the Central Council general secretary reminded the members of the organization's directorate that a number of questions existed "that the foreign Jews are not interested in [and that] there the Central Council would have to take necessary measures." To this end it was decided that the Central Council should establish contacts with the West German federal government, but that any discussion should be limited to addressing inner-German problems. The German-Jewish representatives were particularly careful at the time of the vote not to compete or to openly take a stand against the outstanding claims of the international Jewish organizations since they were still expecting to receive an invitation to the next global restitution summit to be organized by the Jewish Agency in Paris.[40]

There was considerable disappointment among the representatives of Germany's Jews when they did not receive an invitation either to the Paris meeting in the spring of 1951 or to the even larger New York conference in October of that same year.[41] The latter was attended by twenty-three different American and international Jewish organizations and led to the establishment of the

Conference on Jewish Material Claims against Germany (Claims Conference), an organization that was to play a leading role in the restitution negotiations between Jewish organizations and the State of Israel on the one hand and the West German federal government on the other hand.[42] The fact that the organization's board of directors included two representatives of each founding member but did not involve any representatives of the small Jewish community in post-Holocaust Germany caused enormous concern on the part of the German-Jewish representation regarding the continued existence of a Jewish community in Germany and the assertion of their restitution claims before both courts and institutional authorities.[43]

Karl Marx took these developments at the beginning of 1951 as an occasion to refine the Central Council's tasks in contrast to those of the international Jewish organizations. He protested "repeatedly and vehemently against [their] attempts to isolate the Jews in Germany" and made it abundantly clear that "preserving and protecting all interests vis-à-vis the [West German] federal government (first and foremost concerning the question of moral and material compensation)" belonged to the exclusive responsibility of the Central Council.[44]

The depicted policy decisions of the international Jewish organizations' leadership also provide a convincing explanation of why van Dam vehemently demanded the right of the Jews in Germany to participate fully in the ongoing negotiations for compensation in early October 1951. Statements and letters composed at the time demonstrate that the general secretary agreed in principle with journalist Karl Marx and other members of the Central Council's directorate that "the foreign organizations should refrain from discriminating against the Jews in Germany (as was the case when excluding the Jewish community in Germany from the conferences, first in Paris and then also in New York)." Interestingly, however, in a letter to the members of the Central Council's directorate and the organization's council, state associations, as well as the Jewish communities in Berlin, Bremen, Hamburg and Cologne, dated 15 November 1951, van Dam carefully explained and justified why he was convinced that a close partnership with the international Jewish organizations was of vital importance, despite their lack of willingness to cooperate with the German-Jewish community:

> Due to their small size, their social differentiation, and age distribution, the Jews *in Germany* cannot play the role they once had. Its relevance essentially consists in providing *a connection to world Jewry* and in embodying, to some extent, the "good will," the good reputation of a former era of German Jewry. Of course, it should not go unrecognized that the existence of a Jewish community in Germany, however small, serves as a sort of alibi for the German democracy, one of the reasons for the controversy surrounding German Jewry's right to exist. Yet, this is also the cause for the interest in this Jewish group, which is disproportionate to its numerical and cultural significance. Hence, the Jews in

> Germany and its representation cannot be overlooked, but this attention also gives rise to the risk that they might inaccurately estimate reality. The reason for the interest on the part of non-Jewish bodies is temporary, with the exception of one decisive factor: the relation to world Jewry. Only this sort of connection can provide us—given the weak state of the religious foundation of Judaism in Germany—the strength for self-preservation.[45]

Based on the above considerations, van Dam concluded "that—from a Jewish perspective—the only feasible option is to decide for a close cooperation with the Jews abroad." Moreover, he urged "the Jews living in Germany, who put in a lot of the groundwork for the reinstatement of the rule of law since 1945, also in the interest of the Jews living abroad, to be pragmatic and remain calm. . . . The fact that the international Jewish organizations are mistaken cannot be the reason for Germany's Jews to aggravate the situation by our own misconduct. On the contrary, it can only have a positive impact for the Jewish communities if they act in the spirit of cooperation and coordination, thus demonstrating their understanding for and handling of the situation." Last but not least, he recommended—for strategic considerations—"that the Central Council should consider becoming a member of the WJC while simultaneously calling for an adequate representation of the Jews in Germany in all bodies of the organization."

In connection with the contemporary developments, this detailed statement provides valuable information on van Dam's policy decision-making process. Unlike some of the members of the Central Council's directorate, van Dam opposed any form of isolated action. Instead, he called for the development of an autonomous opinion among Germany's Jews and aimed to play an active role in politics through the accession of the Central Council to the WJC and the aforementioned conventions.[46]

Van Dam was able to convince the members of the Central Council's directorate to follow his recommendation not to contact the West German federal government immediately. Yet and despite the support of the president of the WJC, Nahum Goldman, who advocated for trustful cooperation with the Central Council among the various members of his organization,[47] relations between the Jews in Germany and the representatives of the Claims Conference did not improve quickly. In late March 1952, for example, van Dam complained in a letter to Dr. Eliahu Livneh, the consul of Israel in Germany, that the Claims Conference still refused to share information or collaborate with the Central Council, despite agreements to the contrary.[48] Ultimately, this attitude prompted van Dam to publicly call on the foreign Jewish organizations "to grant Jews in and from Germany a fair say. . . . The Jews in and from Germany are very well capable of voicing their interest themselves, without being patronized. The political paternalism is not only an abuse, but also too expensive in the long run."[49]

It seems that the harsher tone of this statement reflected, in essence, the deteriorating mood among Germany's Jews. In the eyes of the members of the Central Council's directorate, in particular those from Munich and Stuttgart, neither concerns nor requests of the Central Council had been sufficiently taken into account by the representatives of the international Jewish organizations when negotiating for restitution payments. Consequently, these members spoke in favor of ending the collaborative arrangement with the Claims Conference.[50] Even in this difficult situation, van Dam succeeded once again in convincing the skeptics among the representatives to continue the Central Council's cooperation with international Jewish organizations. Nevertheless, the difficulties and tensions that were already discernible at the outset of the year continued in the future.[51] Nonetheless, the Central Council was repeatedly pressured to refrain from approaching the West German government to prevent any (unnecessary) duplication of action. Two ultimatums in the summer of 1952 clearly exemplify the severity of the ongoing conflict. First, Moses Leavitt, representative of the American Jewish Joint Distribution Committee (the Joint) and chairman of the Claims Conference, threatened to permanently exclude the Central Council from becoming a member of the Claims Conference if the Jews in Germany bypassed international Jewish organizations and directly talked to the West German federal government about the allocation of resources.[52] Then almost simultaneously, representatives of the Joint announced that they would immediately end support for the Jews in Germany if the Central Council stopped cooperation with the Claims Conference.[53]

In order not to jeopardize the ongoing negotiations between the West German government and the State of Israel and to avert a long-term social and financial isolation of the Jewish community in Germany, the Central Council continued its cooperation with the Claims Conference beyond August 1952. This decision was also significantly influenced by the fact that the German government had, at this point, successfully established contact with Jewish organizations outside of Germany and was about to sign a major reparations agreement. In other words, contrary to the immediate postwar years, the West German government was no longer dependent on the Jews in Germany to establish and build these connections. Against this background, a breakdown of relations with the international Jewish organizations seemed rather inappropriate and potentially detrimental.[54]

It was not until after the signing of the Luxemburg Agreement on 10 September 1952 that the Central Council's relations with international Jewish organizations entered a new phase. Since West Germany committed to pay three billion marks to Israel and 450 million marks to the Claims Conference, it became possible and necessary for the disparate Jewish partners to discuss the allocation of the newly available restitution funds. Nonetheless, this process was rather slow and difficult. While the Central Council was finally recognized as a member of the Claims Conference in October 1952,[55] months passed before the Claims

Conference was able to make effective decisions on how the resources could be used.[56] In the end, it was not until early May 1953 that a first agreement between representatives of the Claims Conference and the Central Council was reached, allowing the Jews in Germany to apply for an annual subsidy to cover all aspects of the work of the Central Welfare Office for Jews in Germany (Zentralwohlfahrtsstelle der Juden in Deutschland e.V., ZWST), founded in 1951.[57] However, despite the principal agreement of the Claims Conference to take the needs of the postwar Jewish communities in Germany into consideration and to support their national institutions, the president of the WJC, Nahum Goldmann, soon stated a widely acknowledged opinion: "The Jewish communities and the Central Council respectively can by no means rely on the [Claims] Conference alone, but will have to devote attention to the financial resources available in Germany, namely the successor organizations, as well as the federal and state [*Länder*] finances."[58] This was precisely what the Central Council focused upon during the next couple of years as financial support from both of these parties proved necessary to secure the work of the Central Council and the German-Jewish welfare organization in the long term.[59]

Conclusion

After Hitler's war against the Jews, it did not seem likely that any of the Jewish survivors would choose to settle permanently in post-Holocaust Germany. In fact, the vast majority of Jewish survivors perceived their existence in the Allied zones of occupation as nothing more than a miserable stopover on their way to a new homeland, still to be defined. Yet a small number of Jews started to engage in the process of restoring Jewish communal structures in Germany. Numbering roughly twenty thousand members during the 1950s and 1960s, approximately half of whom were former Jewish DPs, the Jewish communities in Germany continued to grow thereafter and now have nearly one hundred thousand officially registered members.[60]

A close analysis of the return of Jews and Jewish institutions to post-Holocaust Germany illustrates that the project of rebuilding Jewish life was appreciated by German politicians for political reasons. However, the continued anti-Jewish, if not outright anti-Semitic, environment in "the land of the perpetrators" led the majority of world Jewry to reject the idea of a Jewish presence in Germany. In short, during the early postwar years, instability, uncertainty, and isolation characterized the situation of Jews in Germany, undermining attempts to rebuild Jewish life in Germany.

A detailed examination of contemporary inner-Jewish debates on restitution matters suggests that the newly emerging Jewish leadership in Germany had difficulties uniting and found itself torn between the aspiration to represent the interests of the Jewish community in Germany vis-à-vis third parties and an appreciation for the need to respect international Jewish organizations' demand to serve this function. Yet against all odds and despite the German-Jewish community's initial isolation, the high profile representatives of Germany's Jewish minority developed a self-supporting strategy to counteract the stigmatization and furthermore underlined and defended their claim "We have a right to exist here."[61]

Even though individuals like Karl Marx or Heinz Galinski repeatedly argued for taking isolated action, the Central Council, committed to representing the interests of all Jews living in Germany, agreed with its general secretary that the task of rebuilding the Jewish life in the Federal Republic of Germany could not be tackled with their own means alone. The establishment of dialogue concerning the question of restitution between the West German government on the one hand and the State of Israel and international Jewish organizations on the other hand merely served to confirm the Central Council's decision to follow van Dam's line of reasoning and work toward finding a way to establish an effective cooperation between the Jews in Germany and international Jewish organizations. Ultimately, international Jewish institutions' acknowledgment of a Jewish presence in Germany in the 1950s, which the Jewish communities in Germany had eagerly sought for several years, was of vital importance as it provided essential financial and practical support that laid the foundation for Jewish structures that continue to exist today. Beyond that, the settlement of the dispute also provided the basis for continuously improving inner-Jewish relations. Following the example of the Claims Conference, the WJC and the World Zionist Organization also approved the accession of a German-Jewish representation to their organizations in the late 1950s—a development often interpreted as both a noticeable sign of a successful policy implementation and another important step toward securing a Jewish presence in Germany in the long run.

NOTES

This article is based on and continues my study of *Wiedergutmachungspolitik* first published in *Jüdische Politik und Presse in der frühen Bundesrepublik* (Göttingen: Vandenhoeck & Ruprecht, 2014). For the purpose of this article, all German quotes have been translated into English by the author.

1. The population census was carried out on 13 September 1950. Letter from the German Federal Statistical Office (Statistisches Bundesamtes) to Hans Lamm, 5 October 1955, *Zentralarchiv zur Erforschung der Geschichte der Juden in Deutschland*, Heidelberg (ZA), B.1/7 (Zentralrat), 152.

2. For more information concerning the experiences of Jewish DPs in postwar Germany, see Atina Grossmann and Tamar Lewinsky, "Erster Teil: 1945–1949 Zwischenstation," in *Geschichte der Juden in Deutschland von 1945 bis zur Gegenwart: Politik, Kultur und Gesellschaft*, ed. Michael Brenner (Munich: C. H. Beck, 2012), 67–152; and Angelika Königseder and Juliane Wetzel, *Waiting for Hope: Jewish Displaced Persons in Post–World War II Germany* (Evanston, Ill.: Northwestern University Press, 2001).

3. The statistical census from 1954 listed seventy Jewish communities in West Germany that had 20,429 members. ZA, B.1/7.152, "Juden in Deutschland Ergebnisse einer bevölkerungsstatistischen Erhebung (Frühjahr 1954)," ZA, B.1/7 152. For earlier postwar statistical

information, see, for example, Harry Maòr, "Über den Wiederaufbau der jüdischen Gemeinden in Deutschland seit 1945" (PhD diss., Mainz University, 1961 [1949]), 19, table 2.

4. In 2012, historian Anthony Kauders pointed out that there are several possible reasons for this nonpresence, among them "the impossibility of Germany as *Heimat* after the Shoah; the large number of Displaced Persons from Eastern Europe in the Western zones of occupation and Federal Republic; or Israel as the new Jewish homeland in the Zionist narrative after 1948." In addition, he argued that owing to a sense of guilt for living in the "land of the perpetrators," Jews in Germany "suspended any notion of *Heimat* as an emotional homeland and at the same time tried to make sense of how Germany might become their place in an abstract, de-essentialized way." Anthony Kauders, "The Emotional Geography of a Lost Space: Germany as an Object of Jewish Attachment after 1945," in *'Heimat': At the Intersection of Memory and Space*, ed. Friederike Eigler and Jens Kugel (Berlin: DeGruyter, 2012), 193–207, here 193f.

5. For a convincing interpretation of the situation for Jews in post-Holocaust Germany, see Dan Diner, "Im Zeichen des Banns," in *Geschichte der Juden*, ed. Michael Brenner (Munich: C. H. Beck, 2012), 15–66. See also Tamara Anthony, *Ins Land der Väter oder der Täter? Israel und die Juden in Deutschland nach der Schoah* (Berlin: Metropol, 2004), 27–74, 119–130; and Anthony Kauders, *Unmögliche Heimat: Eine deutsch-jüdische Geschichte der Bundesrepublik* (Munich: Deutsche Verlags-Anstalt, 2007).

6. See the contribution by Jay Howard Geller in this volume.

7. For biographical details on Dr. Hendrik G. van Dam (1906–1973), who served as the first Central Council's general secretary from 1950 until 1973, see Andrea Sinn, *Jüdische Politik und Presse in der frühen Bundesrepublik* (Göttingen: Vandenhoeck & Ruprecht, 2014), 84–115.

8. Hendrik G. van Dam, "Die Juden in Deutschland nach 1945," in *Judentum: Schicksal, Wesen und Gegenwart*, ed. Franz Böhm and Walter Dirks, vol. 2 (Wiesbaden: F. Steiner, 1965), 888–916, here 900.

9. Initially restricted to four pages (and later, eight), this periodical at first resembled a bulletin before developing into a fully grown newspaper. Over the course of its existence, the newspaper repeatedly changed its name. Founded in April 1946 as *Jüdisches Gemeindeblatt für die Nord-Rheinprovinz und Westfalen*, the newspaper was renamed *Allgemeine Wochenzeitung der Juden in Deutschland (AWJD)* in 1949. From 1973 to 2002, it was published under the name *Allgemeine Jüdische Wochenzeitung*. Since 2002, the newspaper has been called the *Jüdische Allgemeine*, which is—for reasons of simplification—the name referenced throughout this article. For details, see Sinn, *Jüdische Politik*, 117–161.

10. For biographical details on Karl Marx (1897–1966), who edited the *Jüdische Allgemeine* from 1946 until 1966, see Sinn, *Jüdische Politik*, 56–84.

11. Karl Marx, "Bekenntnis zur Verpflichtung," *AWJD*, 25 November 1949. See also Marx, "Juden in Deutschland," in *Brücken schlagen: Aufsätze und Reden aus den Jahren 1946 bis 1962 von Karl Marx*, ed. Hans Lamm and Hermann Lewy (Düsseldorf: self-published, 1962), 88–97, here 90.

12. *Verhandlungen des Bundestags*, 1. WP Sten. Berichte (stenographic record), Deutscher Bundestag, 165. Sitzung, Bonn, 27 September 1951, 6697f., accessed 29 September 2019, http://dipbt.bundestag.de/doc/btp/01/01165.pdf; Wolfgang Benz, "Das Luxemburger Abkommen 1952: Moral, Pragmatismus und politische Vernunft," *Tribüne* 46, no. 183 (2007): 110–118, here 113.

13. On 10 September 1952, representatives of the Conference of Jewish Material Claims against Germany ("Claims Conference"), Israel, and West Germany signed the Luxembourg Agreement for reparations. For more details, see Benz, "Das Luxemburger Abkommen 1952"; and Jay Howard Geller, *Jews in Post-Holocaust Germany, 1945–1953* (Cambridge: Cambridge University Press, 2005), 221–226.

14. For a general introduction to the multifaceted and disputed process of individual and/or collective facets of *Wiedergutmachung* (to make good again) in the Federal Republic of Germany, see, for example, Hans Günter Hockerts, "Wiedergutmachung in Deutschland:

Eine historische Bilanz 1945–2000," *Vierteljahrshefte für Zeitgeschichte* 49 (2001): 167–214. Concerning legislation, individual experiences, and limitations of *Wiedergutmachung*, see also, for example, Constantin Goschler, *Schuld und Schulden: Die Politik der Wiedergutmachung für NS-Verfolgte seit 1945*, 2nd ed. (Göttingen: Wallstein, 2013); Norbert Frei, José Brunner, and Constantin Goschler, eds., *Die Praxis der Wiedergutmachung: Geschichte, Erfahrung, und Wirkung in Deutschland und Israel* (Göttingen: Wallstein, 2009); and Jürgen Lillteicher, *Raub, Recht und Restitution: Die Rückerstattung jüdischen Eigentums in der frühen Bundesrepublik* (Göttingen: Wallstein, 2007). Concerning the conditions surrounding the Central Council's establishment, see Y. Michal Bodemann, "Staat und Ethnizität: Der Aufbau der jüdischen Gemeinden im Kalten Krieg" in *Jüdisches Leben in Deutschland seit 1945*, ed. Micha Brumlik et al. (Frankfurt: Jüd. Verlag bei Athenäum, 1988), 49–69; Geller, *Jews*; and Sinn, *Jüdische Politik*. For a detailed analysis of the early relations between the Federal Republic of Germany and the State of Israel, see Yeshayahu Jelinek, *Deutschland und Israel, 1945–1965: Ein neurotisches Verhältnis* (Berlin: DeGruyter, 2004); and Lorena De Vita, "Overlapping Rivalries: The Two Germanys, Israel, and the Cold War," *Cold War History* 17, 4 (2017): 351–366.

15. Jay Howard Geller's *Jews in Post-Holocaust Germany* remains one of the very few studies that address the different distribution of roles within the Jewish community in West Germany and in West Berlin, see esp. "The Jewish Community and the West German Government before Reparations" and "West Germany and Reparations to Israel and World Jewry," in Geller, *Jews*, 185–256.

16. To gain insight into the dispute between Marx and Wollheim, see, for example, Norbert Wollheim to the Chawerim J. Dreifuss, M. Goldschmidt, H. Goldstein, S. Heimberger, C. Katz, N. Prager, and H. Salomon, letter, 2 October 1949, Staatsarchiv Hamburg (StAHH), 522-2 Jüdische Gemeinde Hamburg (collection), Akt 522-2, file 2005-1.

17. StAHH, 522-2 Jüdische Gemeinde Hamburg, Akt 522-2 (2005-1), Norbert Wollheim to the Chawerim J. Dreifuss, M. Goldschmidt, H. Goldstein, S. Heimberger, C. Katz, N. Prager, and H. Salomon, 2 October 1949.

18. ZA, B.1/7.221.1, "Protokoll der am 19. Juli 1950 in Frankfurt a.M. stattgefundenen Sitzung zum Zwecke der Konstituierung einer Gesamtvertretung der Juden in Deutschland." See also Michael Brenner and Norbert Frei, "Zweiter Teil: 1950–1967—Konsolidierung," in Brenner, *Geschichte der Juden*, 153–293, here 153–163; Geller, *Jews*, 70–89; Andrea Sinn, "'Ungewöhnliche Schwierigkeiten und Situationen: Über die Anfänge einer organisierten jüdischen Nachkriegsgemeinschaft in Deutschland," in *Transit US-Zone: Überlebende des Holocaust im Bayern der Nachkriegszeit*, ed. Sybille Steinbacher (Göttingen: Wallstein, 2013), 166–183.

19. ZA, B.1/7.221.4, "Protokoll der Sitzung des Zentralrats," 6 September 1950.

20. Van Dam, "Die Juden," 900.

21. ZA, B.1/7.126, H. G. van Dam, "Das Problem der Reparationen und Wiedergutmachung für Israel," 1 July 1950.

22. ZA, B.1/7.126, H. G. van Dam, "Das Problem der Reparationen und Wiedergutmachung für Israel," 1 July 1950. See also H. G. van Dam, "Verrinnende Zeit," *AWJD*, 9 November 1951; H. Torren, "Jüdischer Optimismus," *AWJD*, 28 December 1951.

23. The complexity of the topic and the editor's approach are expressed in articles such as AjW, "Restitution und Erziehung: Der Jüdische Weltkongreß zur Deutschlandfrage," *AWJD*, 22 September 1950; and H. G. van Dam, "Rückerstattungsrechtliche Verbindlichkeiten des Deutschen Reiches," *AWJD*, 6 July 1951.

24. Karl Marx, "Jom Kippur—Tag der Versöhnung—Tag der Besinnung," *AWJD*, 5 October 1951.

25. Karl Marx, "Jom Kippur." Concerning the reception and acceptance of these efforts, see Brenner and Frei, "Zweiter Teil," 216f.

26. H. G. van Dam, "Unteilbarkeit des Rechts," *AWJD*, 12 October 1951.

27. Kauders, *Unmögliche Heimat*, 127. Van Dam expressed this position, for example, in G. Neuland, "Tolerierung der Unzulänglichkeit?," *AWJD*, 22 September 1950.

28. For the history of the WJC, see Zohar Segev, *The World Jewish Congress during the Holocaust: Between Activism and Restraint* (Berlin: DeGruyter, 2014); Shlomo Shafir, "Der Jüdische Weltkongress und sein Verhältnis zu Nachkriegsdeutschland (1945–1967)," *Menora. Jahrbuch für deutsch-jüdische Geschichte* 3 (1992): 210–237.

29. World Jewish Congress, "Germany," in *Resolutions Adopted by the Second Plenary Assembly of the World Jewish Congress, Montreuax, Switzerland, June 27th–July 6th, 1948* (London: [1948]), 7.

30. "Erste Tagung des Jüdischen Weltkongresses in Deutschland—Eine Gesamtorganisation in Deutschland vor der Gründung," *AWJD*, 14 July 1950.

31. No Jewish successor organization was created in the Soviet zone of occupation. For a discussion of the Jewish property policy and the role of Jewish successor organizations in postwar Germany, see Hans Günter Hockerts, "Anwälte der Verfolgten: Die United Restitution Successor Organization," in *Wiedergutmachung in der BRD*, ed. Constantin Goschler and Ludolf Herbst (Munich: Oldenbourg, 1989), 249–271; and Charles I. Kapralik, *Reclaiming the Nazi Loot: The History of the Jewish Trust Corporation for Germany* (London: Jewish Trust Corporation, 1962).

32. For detailed information about the Claims Conference, see Dean Silvers, "The Future of International Law as Seen through the Jewish Material Claims Conference against Germany," *Jewish Social Studies* XLII, 3–4 (1980): 215–228; and Ronald W. Zweig, *German Reparations and the Jewish World: A History of the Claims Conference*, 2nd ed. (London: Cass, 2001).

33. For more details, see Ayaka Takei, "The Jewish People as the Heir: The Jewish Successor Organizations (JRSO, JTC, French Branch) and the Postwar Jewish Communities in Germany" (PhD diss., Waseda University, 2004); and Andrea Sinn, "Restoring and Reconstructing Jewish Communities: Munich for Jews after World War II," *Studies in Contemporary Jewry* 30 (2018): 78–99.

34. ZA, B.1/7.246, "Bericht des Generalsekretärs für die Periode Januar-August 1951."

35. Archive of the *Jüdische Allgemeine*, Berlin (Archiv JA), Central Council Collection (ZR) 1950–1960, "Deutschland-Tagebuch 1953: Interview mit Dr. H. G. van Dam," 28 April 1953.

36. Archiv JA, ZR 1950–1960, "Protokoll der Sitzung des vorläufigen Direktoriums des Zentralrats," 6 January 1951; ZA, B.1/7.246, "Bericht des Generalsekretärs für die Periode Januar-August 1951."

37. Unless otherwise stated, the following quotes are taken from ZA, B.1/7.221.13, "Protokoll der Direktoriumssitzung des Zentralrats," 29/30 April 1951.

38. See ZA, B.1/7.854, Norbert Wollheim to H. G. van Dam, 7 November 1951; ZA, B.1/7.121, H. G. van Dam to the members of the Central Council's directorate and council, state associations, as well as the Jewish communities in Berlin, Bremen, Hamburg and Cologne, 15 November 1951; ZA, B.1/7.221.18, "Summarischer Bericht über die Sitzung des Zentralrats," 18/19 November 1951.

39. Concerning Heinz Galinski's positioning, see "Mahnruf zum gegenseitigen Verstehen," *AWJD*, 12 January 1951.

40. ZA, B.1/7. 221.13, "Protokoll der Direktoriumssitzung des Zentralrats," 29/30 April 1951.

41. See, for example, ZA, B.1/7.857, "Protokoll der Besprechung des Direktoriums," 7 October 1951. Concerning the early beginnings and intentions of the WJC, see Leon Kubowitzki, ed., *Unity in Dispersion: A History of the World Jewish Congress*, 2nd rev. ed. (New York: WJC, 1948), 228–232; Nana Sagi, *German Reparations: A History of the Negotiations* (New York: St. Martin's Press, 1986), 16–27; and Shafir, "Der Jüdische Weltkongress," 212.

42. Nahum Goldmann, *Staatsmann ohne Staat: Autobiographie* (Cologne: Kiepenheuer & Witsch, 1970), 314.

43. ZA, B.1/7.121, H. G. van Dam to the members of the Central Council's directorate and council, state associations, as well as the Jewish communities in Berlin, Bremen, Hamburg and Cologne, 15 November 1951; . . . x [Karl Marx], "Der Verlauf der Zentralratstagung:

Wiedergutmachungsfragen im Vordergrund—Sorge um die Existenz der jüdischen Gemeinden in Deutschland," *AWJD*, 5 September 1952.

44. Karl Marx, "Jüdische Arbeit in Deutschland: Konstellation und Aufgaben der jüdischen Organisationen," *AWJD*, 26 October 1951.

45. This and the following quotes are taken from ZA, B.1/7.121, H. G. van Dam to the members of the Central Council's directorate and council, state associations, as well as the Jewish communities in Berlin, Bremen, Hamburg and Cologne, 15 November 1951.

46. See van Dam, "Eine gemeinschaftliche Aufgabe: Zur Tagung des 'Council of Jews from Germany' und des 'Zentralrats der Juden in Deutschland,'" *AWJD*, 6 June 1952.

47. ZA, B.1/7.221.18, "Protokoll der Tagung des Zentralrats," 18/19 November 1951.

48. ZA, B.1/7.126, H. G. van Dam to Eliahu Livneh, 28 March 1952.

49. Van Dam, "Eine gemeinschaftliche Aufgabe: Zur Tagung des 'Council of Jews from Germany' und des 'Zentralrats der Juden in Deutschland,'" *AWJD*, 6 June 1952. See also ZA, B.1/7.221.21, "Beschluss des Direktoriums des Zentralrats auf der Zentralratssitzung," 20 July 1952.

50. ZA, B.1/7.221.21, "Protokoll über die Sitzung des Zentralrats," 20 July 1952. See also ZA, B.1/7.857, H. G. van Dam to the members of the Central Council's directorate, 6 October 1952.

51. Demands and threats that were exchanged between the different actors while seeking a mutual acceptable compromises can be traced in ZA, B.1/7.120, H. G. van Dam to the executive board and members of the Conference on Jewish Material Claims Against Germany; ZA, B.1/7.221.21, "Beschluss des Direktoriums des Zentralrats auf der Zentralratssitzung," 20 July 1952; ZA, B.1/7.121, H. G. van Dam to the members of the Central Council's directorate and the working group of Jewish lawyers in the Federal Republic of Germany, 3 August 1952; and ZA, B.1/7.221.25, "Protokoll der Zentralratstagung," 31 August 1952.

52. ZA, B.1/7.121, H. G. van Dam to the members of the Central Council's directorate and the working group of Jewish lawyers in the Federal Republic of Germany, 3 August 1952.

53. ZA, B.1/7.120, H. G. van Dam to the members of the Central Council's directorate, 3 August 1952; and ZA, B.1/7.221.22, "Protokoll der Sitzung des Direktoriums des Zentralrats," 10 August 1952.

54. ZA, B.1/7.221.25, "Protokoll der Zentralratstagung," 31 August 1952.

55. ZA, B.1/7.857, H. G. van Dam to the members of the Central Council's directorate, Report Nr. 2, 9 October 1952.

56. ZA, B.1/7.857, Nahum Goldmann to H. G. van Dam, 3 October 1952.

57. ZA, B.1/7.221.36, "Beschlussprotokoll der erweiterten Direktoriumssitzung des Zentralrats"; ZA, B.1/7.221.37, "Protokoll der Sitzung des erweiterten Direktoriums des Zentralrats," 3 May 1953; ZA, B.1/7.120, Heinz Galinski to H. G. van Dam, 13 May 1953. The establishment of the ZWST is discussed in Georg Heuberger, ed., *Zedaka: Jüdische Sozialarbeit im Wandel der Zeit. 75 Jahre Zentralwohlfahrtsstelle der Juden in Deutschland, 1917–1992* (Frankfurt: ZWST and Jewish Museum Frankfurt, 1992).

58. ZA, B.1/7.857, H. G. van Dam to the members of the Central Council's directorate, 6 October 1952.

59. ZA, B.1/7.221.38, "Beschlussprotokoll der Direktoriumssitzung," 28 June 1953. One major subsidy came since late 1953 from Germany's Federal Ministry of the Interior that agreed to promote the cultural efforts of the Central Council: 1953 25,000 DM; 1954 45,000 DM; 1955 40,000 DM; 1956 40,000 DM; 1957 45,000 DM; 1958 45,000 DM; 1959 45,000 DM; 1960 33,750 DM; 1961 45,000 DM; 1962 60,000 DM; 1963 60,000 DM; 1964 60,000 DM; 1965 60,000 DM; 1966 90,000 DM; 1967 100,000 DM; 1968 100,000 DM; 1969 120,000 DM; 1970 100,000 DM; 1971 140,000 DM; 1972 165,000 DM; 1973 180,500 DM. For correspondence discussing the reasons for the increase of the subsidies (e.g., cuts of the financial support paid by the Claims Conference, general inflation, higher personnel cost, expenses for the

Jüdischer Pressedienst), see Bundesarchiv Deutschland (BArch), B106 (Bundesministerium des Innern), 35457.

60. Zentralrat der Juden in Deutschland, accessed 29 September 2019, https://www.zentralratderjuden.de/der-zentralrat/aufgaben/.

61. The Jewish communities' right to exist in Germany is referenced, for example, in ZA, B.1/7.857, "Protokoll der Zentralratstagung," 31 August/1 September 1952.

CHAPTER 3

BERNHARD BRILLING AND THE RECONSTRUCTION OF JEWISH ARCHIVES IN POSTWAR GERMANY

Jason Lustig

In 1955, Bernhard Brilling set sail from Tel Aviv for Germany. A German-born rabbi and archivist, Brilling had seen his life and career cut short by the rise of Nazism. He had worked at the Jewish communal archive in Breslau from 1927, when he was still a rabbinical student at the Jüdisch-Theologisches Seminar (Jewish Theological Seminary) in the city, through his 1933 ordination, continuing up until his incarceration at Buchenwald after Kristallnacht and subsequent flight to Palestine in 1939.[1] Now Brilling was returning to Germany on assignment from the Jewish Historical General Archives (ʾArkhiyon kelali le-toldot yisraʾel, or JHGA) in Jerusalem, which aimed to gather the archives of European Jewry looted during the Holocaust under the banner of the "ingathering of the exiles (*ḳibbuts galuyot*) of the past."[2] He was one figure among many searching for as-yet-unrecovered historical records that had been looted by the Nazis and were now scattered throughout state archives around Europe. The Jerusalem archivists for whom Brilling worked dreamt of creating a central repository for the study of the Jews by gathering these materials—whether in the original, as was preferred, or by cataloging and microfilming. It was an ambition given voice in 1969, when the Jerusalem archive took the name of the Central Archives for the History of the Jewish People (ʾArkhiyon merkazi le-toldot ha-ʿam ha-yehudi), an idea of a "national archive" of the Jewish people with Jerusalem at its center.[3] But for Brilling, return to Germany presented the possibility to fulfill dreams to rebuild his life and attain professional opportunities he felt he had been cruelly denied and to create a new archive of German Jewry—in Germany.

Brilling had found adjustment to life in Palestine difficult, and without an archival position, it seems his prewar experience went unrewarded. As he worded it in a 1955 letter to Saul Kagan at the Conference of Jewish Material Claims Against Germany, he was "one of the surviving German Jewish historians and archivists who were deprived by the Nazis of the fruits of their scientific research work," work to which he desperately hoped to return.[4] With limited possibilities for advancement in Tel Aviv, Brilling ultimately resettled in Germany. There, he tried with limited success to create a new central archive of German Jewry under the auspices of the Zentralrat der Juden in Deutschland (Central Council of Jews in Germany) and with, he and his colleagues hoped, the financial support of the federal government. By gathering archival materials scattered by the Nazis' regime of looting and plunder, or in carrying forth the continuing mission to document Jewish history, he hoped to reconstitute in some measure the Gesamtarchiv der deutschen Juden (General Archive of the German Jews), established in Berlin in 1905, which had gathered files from hundreds of German-Jewish communities, as well as his own Breslau archive, which had come to serve as a regional archive of the Jews in Silesia.[5] And the government support, if they had garnered it, would have marked the stark difference between the Nazis' efforts to confiscate and control Jewish archives during and following Kristallnacht and the possibility of a German state friendly to continued Jewish settlement.

Brilling ultimately failed to create such an archive. The German-Jewish communities offered limited support and were generally unwilling to openly compete with the Israelis, who successfully restricted Brilling's project to a collection of microfilms. Still, Brilling's dreams of archival reconstruction highlight the multiple meanings, challenges, and limits of rebuilding Jewish life and lives after the Holocaust. For Brilling, creating a new Gesamtarchiv der deutschen Juden would have been a practical means of the reconstruction of his personal and professional life, it would have allowed for the reconstruction of scattered archival collections, and it would have served as a powerful symbol of the reconstruction of Jewish life in Germany. As such, Brilling's archival aspirations were profoundly personal, manifesting his own dreams of personal rehabilitation and professional revitalization, in contrast to the Israelis' efforts, which—despite the fact that they were undertaken by a privately managed research institution—were closely aligned with national aspirations to mark the State of Israel as a "Jewish" state through the gathering of historical records and artifacts. Instead, for Brilling, reconstructing archives stood in for the possibilities of one individual's struggle for survival and reconstruction. His inability to achieve these goals in his lifetime demonstrates the limits of the immediate postwar years, when so many Jewish leaders around the world (including some in Germany) believed that the chapter of Jewish life and culture in that bloodstained land had more or less come to its conclusion. By contrast, the increasing vitality of German Jewry in the 1980s and 1990s was reflected in the creation of institutions such as the Zentralarchiv zur Erforschung der Geschichte der Juden in Deutschland (Central Archive for the Research of the History of the Jews in Germany) in Heidelberg in 1987, which gathered the files of postwar German-Jewish life, and the Centrum Judaicum in Berlin in 1995, which came to possess a portion of the prewar Jewish Gesamtarchiv files that had long remained in East German state archives.

Archives present a useful lens to consider postwar reconstruction because the work of gathering historical records was and remains not just about giving order to the past but also about shaping the future. Especially after the Second World War, archives held symbolic and practical importance. In the mid-1950s, at the same moment the Israeli archives received German-Jewish communal records, the West German government took possession of files the western Allies had confiscated after the war from the Politisches Archiv des Auswärtiges Amt (Political Archive of the Foreign Office).[6] For both, receiving archives symbolized political sovereignty and ties to the past. For the Germans, taking back their administrative files symbolized the Federal Republic's diplomatic rehabilitation. For the Israelis, the Jewish community archives of the Diaspora held cultural significance. The so-called ingathering of the exiles of the past to Jerusalem seemed to mark the transfer of Jewish life in Europe from the mere past to history and to legitimize the State of Israel's claim that it constituted its successor.[7] Such archival transfers present a curious combination of a return to a status quo, inasmuch as returning archives reflected West Germany's renewed sovereignty and reentry into the family of nation-states, alongside new directions. Indeed, the whole process was reminiscent of the long tradition of postwar settlements including the transfer of records to successor states—in this case, with western Germany marked as the West's accepted successor to the series of historic German states and governments and Israel staking a claim that it was a successor to European Jewry.[8]

The Israeli archivists' efforts to gain archives also reflected the possibilities, and challenges, of institutional successorship. The Israelis did not imagine the Jewish Historical General Archives as a reconstituted Gesamtarchiv. Indeed, their aspiration was to include the records of Jews all over the world, and not just Germany, even if that was an early area of interest. But the Berlin archive still carried gravitas. When the Gesamtarchiv der deutschen Juden was established in 1905 under the auspices of the Deutsch-Israelitische Gemeindebund (Union of German Jewish Communities) and the German branch of the B'nai B'rith fraternal order, it was the first centralized and professionally managed archive of Jewish history, and it became the premier Jewish historical archive.[9] By the outbreak of the Second World War, the Gesamtarchiv held the files of hundreds of German-Jewish communities. It also inspired Jews around the world to create archives on its model. In 1920, Eugen Täubler, the Gesamtarchiv's founding director, spoke of a network of nationally organized central archives for each country of Jewish settlement, and over the years, Jews in Austria, the United States, and even Palestine looked to the Gesamtarchiv as a model.[10] Even the name of the Jerusalem-based Jewish Historical General Archives was consciously chosen to echo the Berlin archive. Further, the archivists in Jerusalem were nearly all of German origin, with Georg Herlitz of the Central Zionist Archives (and one of the leaders of the JHGA) a onetime assistant director of the Berlin archive. When the JHGA gained many of the Gesamtarchiv's files in 1950, it seemed to mark it as a successor to the Berlin archive. It was for this reason that in the inaugural issue of the *Leo Baeck Institute Year Book* in 1956, Daniel Cohen, himself a German Jew and at that time assistant director of the JHGA—he would become its leader the following year—described the work of the Jerusalem archivists as a kind of successor to the General Archive of the German Jews. As he explained, "By taking care of the German archives, publishing the sources relating to the history of the Jews in Germany, and by enlisting young historians of German origin, . . . [we] endeavour to carry on the tradition of the Gesamtarchiv in the changed circumstances."[11]

However, Brilling's efforts and even his emigration to Germany show how the Jerusalem archivists' narrative of the "ingathering of the exiles" of archives (and people) was neither monolithic nor without resistance.[12] Eugen Täubler, who fled Germany in 1941 and resettled with his wife, Selma Stern, in Cincinnati, wrote after the war that Jacob Jacobson, Täubler's successor as director of the General Archive from 1921 until his own deportation to Theresienstadt in 1943, should be tasked with reestablishing the Gesamtarchiv in England, where he settled after the war.[13] And Brilling's dreams of reconstructing archives in Germany presented a more direct challenge to the Israelis. In a curious coincidence, the *Leo Baeck Institute Year Book* published an essay by Brilling immediately following Cohen. Together, Cohen's "Jewish Records from Germany in the Jewish Historical General Archives in Jerusalem" and Brilling's "Jewish Records in German Archives" were clearly intended to highlight where scholars could find various historical materials. However, the pairing underscores the differences in outlook between Cohen and Brilling, who ostensibly was working for the Jerusalem archive. For in Brilling's report on his search for archives, he concluded not with the idea of bringing them to Jerusalem but instead by calling on the West German government to reproduce these files as microfilms and make them available to scholars.[14]

Indeed, though Brilling's work was supported by the Jerusalem archive, he proved to have a divergent idea about what archival reconstruction might look like. He dreamt of a new central Jewish archive in Germany itself as a direct successor to the Gesamtarchiv (in opposition to the JHGA's claim to take up that archive's mission and mantle), and thereby to create for himself a post where he could conduct his own research. For Brilling, such an archive might provide him a scholarly career that had been snatched away; it was also, he argued, a means to contribute to the "cultural reestablishment of German Jewry."[15] On the eve of the twentieth anniversary of the Kristallnacht pogrom that had preceded both his flight to Palestine as well as the Gestapo's confiscation of Jewish archives across Germany, Brilling spoke of his planned archive as a reaffirmation of the rootedness of German-Jewish life in its historical environment.[16] Similarly, Hans Hertz, the longtime antagonist to Israeli efforts to extract the Jewish archives of Hamburg, expressed his support for Brilling's effort as a kind of "re-rooting of our Jewish fellowmen in Germany," whereas Cohen claimed once that leaving archives in Germany would provide a "birth-certificate," lending these communities historical legitimacy.[17] Brilling's dream was thereby a direct repudiation of the Jerusalem archive's efforts. As he argued in 1960, the principle of removing Jewish archives was perhaps the proper path when Jews were fleeing the Nazi regime, but he insisted that now "a new solution must be found." Arguing that the historic files only made sense within the context of German history, Brilling called for the "repatriation" of archives taken to Jerusalem.[18] In the end, the debate over where a central archive of Jewish history should be, and the historical records of German Jewry specifically, was both a question of to whom they belonged (as in the debates over restitution) as well as a profoundly personal question between different émigré archivists like Cohen, Brilling, and others who had fled Germany for Palestine in the 1930s. On the whole, one might say that Jews' efforts to gather and reconstitute archives after the Holocaust mirrored the challenge of diaspora—both the dispersion of documents throughout the pathways of history and especially in the rupturing experience of the Holocaust and also the scattering of individuals in a German-Jewish diaspora, with the German Jews in Israel/Palestine, the United Kingdom, and the United States—not to mention those survivors who remained in Germany and those who, like Brilling, returned to Germany—all struggling over the contested legacy of German Jewry.

Brilling's postwar ambitions for archival reconstruction began with his time as a rabbinical student in Breslau. Brilling was born in 1906 in Tremessen (Trzemeszno), a small town outside Posen, and at the age of twenty he enrolled in rabbinical studies at the Jüdisch-Theologisches Seminar (Jewish Theological Seminary) in Breslau, where he was ordained in 1933. In 1927, shortly after entering the seminary, Brilling began work as an assistant at the archive of the Breslau Jewish community. The archive had been formed in 1924 by the rabbi Aron Heppner, once an active and early supporter of the Gesamtarchiv. Prior to the First World War, Heppner, who then lived in Koschmin (Koźmin), had been one of the Berlin archive's most effective collectors, gathering historical materials from Jewish communities throughout Posen and Silesia, and he was even considered as the General Archive's leader in 1920.[19] That year, though, Heppner relocated to Breslau, where he would head the community archive. As early as 1914, the Jewish community had sought to organize its files, and a decade later it established the Gemeindearchiv (community archive) in August 1924, at the same moment as its communal newsletter (*Gemeindeblatt*)—apparently in an effort to form the institutions befitting one of the larger Jewish communities in Germany.[20] This archive initially contained, as the name implied, the administrative files of the Breslau Jewish community. Soon, though, it grew into what Brilling would later call the "Jewish Provincial-Archive of Silesia," holding files from over twenty local communities.[21]

Brilling's experience at the Breslau archive clearly left a strong impression on the twenty-one-year-old rabbinical student. In December 1927, he jotted some notes on "the importance of a Jewish communal archive." As he wrote, "An archive is no superfluous luxury . . . but rather an absolute necessity."[22] Such earnestness reflected the beginnings of a strong passion for archives, a driving factor in Brilling's career as rabbi, historian, and archivist from then until his death in 1987. In these years, Brilling busied himself with historical work and genealogy at the expense of pursuing a rabbinical pulpit. He worked as a teacher and published pieces on local history and bibliography, with an emphasis on economic history and Jewish professions, especially goldsmithing, and was a corresponding member of Arthur Czellitzer's Berlin-based Gesellschaft für jüdische Familienforschung (Society for Jewish Genealogy).[23] He also worked closely with Jacob Jacobson, the leader of the Gesamtarchiv in Berlin, and spent time in Hamburg working to organize the Jewish community's files in the aim of developing a local archive.[24] All this was brought to an end with Kristallnacht, when the Breslau archive, like most other Jewish community archives, was confiscated by the Gestapo, which had issued instructions to take care that, in the planned sacking of synagogues, historical records be preserved.[25] Brilling and Heppner were incarcerated at Buchenwald, and Heppner, then over seventy years of age, died shortly thereafter. When Brilling returned to Breslau, Gestapo leader Fritz Arlt returned the keys to the archive, and he continued his work, now as the director of the archive. However, Arlt advised Brilling to emigrate, and Brilling fled to Palestine, prematurely ending his efforts to pursue his doctoral studies.[26]

In Palestine, Brilling struggled to rebuild his life. He helped establish the Society for Jewish Genealogy in Tel Aviv, a direct successor to Czellitzer's genealogical society, and he sought work as an archivist but found little professional success.[27] He found work in the municipality of Tel Aviv, but the city did not have an official archive or archivist. In part, Brilling's inability to find suitable work reflected the reality of his status as a refugee. A number of scholars have written about the so-called Fifth Aliyah as a wave of immigration to Palestine characterized by an influx of German Jews and their financial and intellectual capital, as a crucial moment in the development of the Yishuv or Jewish settlement in Palestine.[28] However, the reality of refugee life was one of heavy burdens. Georg Herlitz, Täubler's former assistant at the General Archive and since 1919 the leader of the Zionistische Zentralarchiv (Zionist Central Archives) in Berlin, fled to Palestine in October 1933 at the behest of the Zionist Organization, bringing his archives with him, but found that the Palestine Office lacked the funds to reopen the archive until 1935.[29] Alex Bein, another German-Jewish archivist who made his way to Palestine in 1933, faced similar challenges but proved an important foil to Brilling.[30] Bein—who would in 1956 become Israel's first state archivist—had worked from 1927 to 1933 at the Prussian Reichsarchiv, a military archive based in Potsdam.[31] Upon arriving in Palestine, Bein also had difficulty securing archival work, only finding a position at Herlitz's newly reestablished Central Zionist Archives in 1935. Brilling had started working at the Breslau communal archive the very same year Bein began at the Reichsarchiv, but it seems that Bein's years there provided a professional imprimatur in a way that Brilling never could muster. Despite his years of work in Breslau, Brilling never had any official archival training until he took part in a seminar run by Bein and Herlitz in 1952.[32] Still, Brilling saw himself first and foremost as an archivist, heading correspondence with a self-typed letterhead proclaiming himself the "former archivist of the Breslau synagogue-community" despite the fact that he only held the position for a few weeks following Heppner's passing.[33] As he entered the postwar years, he continued to work to rebuild his life, holding three hopes: that he might locate his Breslau archive, find work as an archivist, and eventually create a new archive for postwar Germany.

When Brilling came to Germany in 1955, he was tasked with preparing reports for the Jewish Historical General Archives on the contents of state archives around Germany elsewhere, including Amsterdam, which would allow them to catalog and microfilm material and in some instances secure records through restitution.[34] At the same time, though, he began to make plans for a life in Germany. In 1942, he had written that many Jewish refugees in Palestine—including himself, seemingly—would likely return to their countries of origin after the war.[35] It seems, then, that he believed Palestine would be for him but a brief sojourn; in 1951, Brilling—still unhappy with his lot in Tel Aviv—inquired if the Central Council of Jews in Germany required an archivist.[36] And so, when he returned to Germany in 1955 to Germany to search out archives on behalf of Meisl's Jewish Historical General Archives, he began to search for support for his dream for a new archive in Germany. In January 1956, Brilling turned to Hendrik George van Dam, general secretary of the Central Council, with a detailed proposal for establishing "an archive for the history of the Jews in Germany as a demand of reparations."[37] Explaining that the key archives before the war were the Berlin Gesamtarchiv and his own Breslau communal archive, he declared that the "reestablishment" of an archive of German Jewry, as a direct successor to the work of the Berlin Gesamtarchiv and his Breslau archive, could "represent an attempt to put right [*gut zu machen*] the crimes of the Nazis against the spirit." It also might provide a way forward for those—like himself—whose work in Jewish historical scholarship had been cut off by the rise of Nazism and the Second World War. He proposed that all state, municipal, and even estate (*ständisch*) archives be combed "file by file" for material relating to the Jews, which could be duplicated both for a German archive as well as for the Jerusalem archives, providing additional security for the materials.[38]

With this plan, Brilling found eager ears. A year after the Central Council of Jews in Germany was established in 1950, its historical commission was tasked with "securing the historically significant sources and monuments"[39] In 1953, Harry Goldstein of the Verband der Jüdischen Gemeinden Nordwestdeutschlands (Association of Jewish Communities in Northwest Germany), based in Hamburg, called for archives and libraries to be gathered to that city.[40] When pressed by Charles Kapralik, the leader of the Jewish Trust Corporation (JTC) in Britain, Goldstein insisted that they did not oppose sending materials to Jerusalem but merely wanted to examine the material and see what was necessary for "administrative" purposes; he claimed it would be easier to do this in one place than scattered across the British zone.[41] Nevertheless, a number of German Jews held onto hope that they might be able to keep some of the materials. Carl Katz of Bremen declared in May 1954 that whatever hope they still had to keep historical materials required having an appropriate archivist.[42] In the fall of 1955, just a few months before Brilling issued his memorandum on an archive, Hans Lamm, chair of the Central Council's cultural arm, had spoken similarly of creating a "Central Archive of the Jews in Germany."[43] All the while, the German Jews looked to a new archival cache to be the basis of their archive. It had been long known that the archives of the Jewish community of Königsberg had been brought westward during the war and were stored at the State Archive in Göttingen, but their fate was in question. Charles Kapralik of the Jewish Trust Corporation initially believed that the files, having originated in what was now Russian-occupied territory, must be returned there, but this proposal met with strong resistance.[44] By the time Brilling traveled to Germany in 1955, the files were still there. The following spring, van Dam and Lamm both hoped these files might be the kernel of their archive and Brilling would be the one to manage them.[45] And so, when van Dam circulated Brilling's notes on the state of Jewish archives in Germany to community leaders, he found that community leaders supportive, noting that Brilling's suggestions had reminded them of the fact that there did not exist a central archive or library for Jews in Germany, which they hoped to correct.[46]

Van Dam and the Central Council decided to pursue the plan. He reached out to Paul Hübinger of the Ministry of the Interior with a request to create a special "archive division for the history of Jews in Germany" under the Federal Archive (Bundesarchiv), which would collect microfilms and other materials, with a state appropriation of 30,000 deutsche marks (about 7,200 dollars at the time, or 69,000 dollars in 2019 terms) and a state appointment of an archivist—presumably Brilling—to manage the project.[47] Meanwhile, in March 1956, Brilling returned to Tel Aviv but remained unsatisfied with his lot there. He believed that he deserved a position (and salary) more befitting his perceived status as one of a select group of former Jewish archivists, but his uncompleted doctorate and lack of archival training left him at a disadvantage. And so he held two seemingly dissonant hopes: to be promoted in Tel Aviv and to establish an archive in Germany. At the same time, van Dam repeatedly inquired with Hübinger and waited for a response from the German government. But a full year later, in February 1957, van Dam had not yet even secured a meeting with the appropriate bureaucrats.[48]

Consequently, Brilling became increasingly impatient, concerned that the initiative would dissolve.[49] The result of such uncertainty was that Brilling maintained contingencies in both Israel and Germany; the question was what would come together first. On 14 March 1957, Brilling wrote to Alex Bein, now Israel's state archivist, with his proposal for a new German-Jewish archive, and asked if Bein might support him in his hopes of advancement in Tel Aviv. Brilling also held out hope that he might be appointed director of the Jewish Historical General Archives when Josef Meisl retired later that year, a position that he felt was his right, since he was, alongside the Gesamtarchiv's Jacob Jacobson, "the sole real veteran Jewish communal archivist"—a view following from his opinion that his Breslau archive and the Gesamtarchiv had been the only true prewar Jewish archives.[50] However, unbeknownst to Brilling, Meisl had already declared privately that Brilling was unsuitable.[51] And so Bein wrote Brilling that he would lend his support, but he also applied pressure. He insisted that Brilling's proposed archive could not be a successor to the Gesamtarchiv, a role already fulfilled, he claimed, by the Jerusalem archives. Bein pressed Brilling to explain to his colleagues in Germany that he proposed not to create an "archive" but rather wanted to collect photocopies, and certainly not originals.[52] Here, Bein echoed a general approach of privileging archives in Israel with originals. In 1954, Bein had expressed his view to the Hamburg mayor Kurt Sieveking that "filming is in no way equivalent to the source."[53] Similarly, Bein had been writing to Jewish leaders in Germany that when it came to the Königsberg files, the originals must go to Jerusalem and any new archive in Germany must be dedicated only to files originating in the postwar era.[54] What is more, "if one wants to establish a central Jewish archive in Germany," Bein insisted to Lamm, "it will require only photocopies and microfilms . . . [and] original material of recent date which is necessary for current work and the purposes of restitution."[55] On the whole, Bein expressed confusion about the possibility of a Jewish archivist appointed by the Ministry of the Interior, mostly seeing it as counterproductive.[56]

Ultimately, Brilling caved to Bein's pressure. Perhaps he felt he needed Bein's recommendation for any career advancement if he were to remain in Tel Aviv. Brilling insisted that his proposal was quite clear, but he conceded that he could write to van Dam "in the interest of high scientific goals in which we, as archivists, are all interested."[57] That same day, Brilling drafted a letter to van Dam explaining that his proposed archive would in no way serve as a competitor with the Jewish Historical General Archives in Jerusalem, which, he wrote, "should be greatly credited with securing the rescue of the files of Jewish communities." Instead, Brilling said, his effort should be seen as part of a "combined effort with [the JHGA] and other Jewish archives in the interest of science [*Wissenschaft*] and the general goal of studying the history of the German Jews." However, after writing the letter, it seems that Brilling sat on it, presumably mulling it over, for over two weeks before placing it in the post.[58]

In the summer of 1957, Brilling again returned to Germany, this time to finish his doctorate under Karl Heinrich Rengstorf, the New Testament scholar in Münster. A year later, he completed his thesis on "Die Juden und die Stadt Breslau im 16. und 17. Jahrhundert." He hoped that, perhaps, with his doctorate in hand he might be appointed Tel Aviv's municipal archivist. It seems, though, that his future in Israel was nonexistent; he just didn't know it yet. Bein did write a recommendation on Brilling's behalf, but he remained something of a *persona non grata* among the Jerusalem archivists and was particularly disliked by Daniel Cohen, who received Meisl's job that year. Reflecting on the question of the Königsberg and Brilling's potential hiring to manage a "Central Archive of the German Jews," Daniel Cohen was irate: "The whole matter is a scandal," he wrote.[59] Shortly thereafter, when the matter of the Königsberg stalled, Cohen again complained that it was "probably another . . . monkey-business with Brilling."[60]

All this time, Brilling remained in Germany to continue his research and push for the creation of his archive. In 1958, he again detailed an archival plan, arguing that such an archive could "carry forward the memory of the history of the German Jews" and the "tradition" of the Berlin and Breslau archives. Concluding, he suggested that in such a manner, these archives could be "continued."[61] And so, van Dam secured the support of the Ministry of Interior to support the creation of a position for an archivist for the Central Council, and they moved forward with plans to form the archive in Hamburg, to open in April 1959.[62] However, to Brilling's chagrin, the Central Council decided to appoint him only on a temporary basis; they recognized that creating an archive would require "considerable means and work" but only had enough funds to fund the position for a single year.[63] Brilling was furious. Jotting down some notes, he complained, "I am an archivist without an archive!"[64] Along the same lines, Hans Hertz in Hamburg and Brilling's teacher Karl Heinrich Rengstorf wrote to the Central Council and insisted that the project be better supported. As Hertz and Rengstorf put it, the effort was necessary as a "new General Archive of the German Jews for our time."[65] Nevertheless, shortly thereafter Hertz and Rengstorf decided that the best path forward was to bring Brilling back to Münster where he could pursue his archival work under Rengstorf.[66]

Brilling's effort failed for a number of reasons. By the time that Brilling began this effort in earnest in the second half of the 1950s, most of the most lucrative caches of looted archival materials—particularly a large portion of the former Gesamtarchiv files—had already been extracted from Germany to the Jerusalem archives. Moreover, the political situation made it difficult. The West German state clearly preferred dealing with Israel both for reasons of publicity and the development of a positive relationship with the young Jewish state and also because West German officials, while hoping to foster Jewish life in Germany, did not truly expect a Jewish community to flourish there.[67] Further, it would prove impossible to secure archives in eastern Germany, such as portions of the Gesamtarchiv that were in the German Democratic Republic's Zentralarchiv (central archive) in Potsdam, and Poland, where Brilling's Breslau files had made their way to Warsaw's Jewish Historical Institute (Żydowski Instytut Historyczny).[68] Limited to microfilms of existing materials, the Jewish communities in Germany had limited resources to pursue collecting records already preserved in state archives.

And so Brilling, this "archivist without an archive," settled in Münster. There, he worked with Rengstorf at the Institutum Judaicum Delitzschianum, a center for Jewish studies—originally founded to promote missionary work among Jews—named for the nineteenth-century scholar Franz Delitzsch and reestablished in Münster by Rengstorf in 1948. As the head of the "Division for the History of the Jews in Germany" (Abteilung für die Geschichte der Juden in Deutschland), Brilling gathered microfilms and other historical materials. And he still dreamed of "an extensive new Gesamtarchiv of the German Jews," as Rengstorf put it in 1960.[69] Indeed, the next year, when Brilling expressed his hope to gather materials relating to Berlin and eastern Germany, he claimed that the result might be that the "Jewish archives of Germany"—by which in context he clearly meant the tradition of the Gesamtarchiv and his Breslau archive, which he had just discussed—"could be recreated."[70]

When Brilling and Rengstorf spoke of an aspiration to make a new Gesamtarchiv, their goal was to recreate or reconstruct archives, which had been scattered during the Second World War—and even afterward. In 1960, Brilling explained the major goal of his archive to be the "repatriation" of the files of Jewish communities that had been removed from Germany to Israel.[71] Reaching out to the Association of Jewish Communities in Northwest Germany, Brilling explained that it was quite difficult for Jewish and non-Jewish scholars in Germany to use the materials that had been sent to Jerusalem, and he asked for funds to microfilm them.[72] It seemed they were not particularly forthcoming with the funds. But he aimed to microfilm portions of his former Breslau archives, which after the war found their way to Jewish Historical Institute in Warsaw, and tried—but failed—to secure the portions of the former Gesamtarchiv that were held in Potsdam.[73] Similarly, writing in 1961, Brilling declared his aim was to "recreate" the archives that had existed before the war.[74] He slowly accumulated material—by 1973 could boast of one hundred thousand pages of material in microfilm—but these achievements were modest by the standard he set, of recreating the archives that had existed before the war.[75] And so Brilling's language of creating a "new" Gesamtarchiv and reconstructing archives spoke to the challenge of rebuilding Jewish life in Germany after the Holocaust. For if he used the language of recreating the Gesamtarchiv, the reality was that any new archive would be profoundly distinct from that which came before. Indeed, Brilling's effort presents a key case of the dreams of postwar reconstruction and their practical limitations, especially in the immediate postwar years when so many felt that Jewish life in Germany was at its end. For Brilling, the possibility of creating another Gesamtarchiv might represent the possibility of continued Jewish existence in Germany and also present a claim that Germany could be the home to a hegemonic cultural center of German Jewry rather than its diaspora.

Brilling's story is one of someone who wanted to rebuild his life and to reconstruct his archives, and in both instances he was mostly unsuccessful. Plagued by professional failures, he was ultimately unable to find a position in Israel, returning to Germany, and there his efforts to create a new archive were mostly ineffective. But his effort represents a divergent approach to archival reconstruction from the work of Israeli archivists who gathered files to the Jewish Historical General Archives in Jerusalem. And it also demonstrates the limits of such reconstruction in terms of both the specific details of the postwar years, when the Israelis insisted that Jewish life in Germany was at its end and exerted great pressure to limit it, as well as the general possibility to "reconstruct" prewar archives. Brilling's efforts exemplify the then unrealized potentials for cross-currents and headwinds of efforts to rebuild Jewish life in its full variety, and they also gesture at the basic limitations of the idea of reconstruction. One must ask to what extent it would have even been possible for Brilling to "reconstruct" the prewar archives. Both Brilling and the Israelis sought to reconstitute and reconstruct these archives, or at least their archival materials, but in the end the effort to reconstruct something utterly destroyed was futile—instead they all, to varying degrees of success and failure, ended up constructing something radically new that reflected the new realities of Jewish life after the Holocaust.

It is for this reason useful to consider how Brilling's dream of a new central archive "as a demand for cultural reparations," which he first outlined in his 1956 memorandum, would come into being about a generation later. In April 1985, Helmut Kohl—speaking to commemorate the fortieth anniversary of the liberation of Bergen-Belsen—proposed the creation of an "Archive for Research on the History of the Jews in Germany."[76] Just before Brilling's death in 1987, such an archive opened: the Zentralarchiv zur Erforschung der Geschichte der Juden in Deutschland (Central Archive for the Research of the History of the Jews in Germany) at the Hochschule für Jüdische Studien in Heidelberg under the direction of Eberhard Gönner. For Peter Honigmann, who directed the Heidelberg archive from 1991 to 2016, the connection was clear, and he indicated the archive as a successor to Brilling's efforts as well as the Gesamtarchiv.[77] And at just this same time, as the Zentralarchiv was established in Heidelberg, Jews in East Germany were working toward what would become the Centrum Judaicum at the New Synagogue (Neue Synagoge) in Berlin. When it opened in 1991, it would house the files of the former Gesamtarchiv that had been in East Germany's Zentralarchiv since the late 1950s.[78] In this light, the question of creating archives for German Jews was never about the past—it was always a question of the present and future vitality of Jewish existence in Germany. If in the 1950s many felt this was an impossibility, by the 1990s it was manifested through the formation of such historical archives, giving shape to the present and the possibilities of reconstructing Jewish life in Germany by ordering the past.

NOTES

1. On Brilling, see Helmut Richtering, "Bernhard Brilling zum Gedenken," *Gedenkschrift für Bernhard Brilling*, ed. Peter Freimark and Helmut Richtering (Hamburg: Hans Christians, 1988), 9–13; see also Robert Jütte, *Die Emigration der deutschsprachigen "Wissenschaft des Judentums": Die Auswanderung Jüdischer Historiker nach Palästina, 1933–1945* (Stuttgart: Franz Steiner, 1992), 23, 99–100.

2. Jason Lustig, "Who Are to Be the Successors of European Jewry? The Restitution of Jewish Communal and Cultural Property," *Journal of Contemporary History* 52, no. 3 (2017): 519–545. Also Alex Bein, "*Din ve-ḥeshbon me-nesi'ati le-'eiropah be-shlikhut ha-'arkhiyon ha-tsiyoni ha-merkazi*," 19 December 1949, Central Zionist Archives (CZA), Jerusalem, L33/1439; Bein, "Kibbuts Galujoth auch für jüdische Archive," *Allgemeine Wochenzeitung der Juden in Deutschland*, 20 October 1950 and 27 October 1950.

3. On the name change, see "Yesod ḥevrah ha-'arkhiyon ha-merkazi le-toldot ha-'am ha-yehudi," 13 March 1969, Central Archives for the History of the Jewish People (CAHJP), Jerusalem, P28/6/42; "The Central Archives for the History of the Jewish People," *Tsiyon* 34, no. 2 (1969): 265–270; Daniel Cohen, "The Gathering of Jewish Records to Israel," 5 August 1969, American Jewish Archives (AJA), Cincinnati, MS-687 18/20, 11.

4. Bernhard Brilling to Saul Kagan, 11 October 1955, Jüdisches Museum Frankfurt (JMF), SB1680.

5. See, among others, Lynn H. Nicholas, *The Rape of Europa* (New York: Random House, 1994); Jonathan Petropoulos, *Art as Politics in the Third Reich* (Chapel Hill: University of North Carolina Press, 1996); Michael J. Kurtz, *America and the Return of Nazi Contraband: The Recovery of Europe's Cultural Treasures* (Cambridge, Mass.: Harvard University Press, 2006), esp. 1–43; Alan E. Steinweis, *Studying the Jew: Scholarly Antisemitism in Nazi Germany* (Cambridge, Mass.: Harvard University Press, 2006); Dirk Rupnow, *Täter, Gedächtnis, Opfer: Das "Jüdische Zentralmuseum" in Prag 1942–1945* (Vienna: Picus, 2000).

6. On this, see Astrid M. Eckert, *The Struggle for the Files: The Western Allies and the Return of German Archives after the Second World War* (Cambridge: Cambridge University Press, 2004).

7. See Lustig, "Who Are to Be the Successors?"

8. See Ernst Posner, "Effects of Changes of Sovereignty on Archives," in Ernst Posner, *Archives and the Public Interest: Selected Essays*, ed. Ken Munden (Chicago: Society of American Archivists, 2006), 168–181.

9. On the General Archive, see Lustig, "'A Time to Gather': A History of Jewish Archives in the Twentieth Century" (PhD diss., University of California–Los Angeles, 2017), 95–157; Barbara Welker, "Das Gesamtarchiv der deutschen Juden. Zentralisierungsbemühungen in

einem föderalen Staat," in *Jüdisches Archivwesen*, ed. Frank M. Bischoff and Peter Honigmann (Marburg: Archivschule Marburg, 2007), 39–74.

10. "Archiv der österreichisch-jüdischen Kultus-Gemeinden," 1905, CAHJP, A/W 1706; "Zikhron devarim mi-yeshivah muḳdeshet le-ba'ayot he-hisṭoriyah ha-'ivrit," 27 April 1937, CAHJP, IHS/17d; Isidore S. Meyer, "The American Jewish Historical Society," *Journal of Jewish Bibliography* 4, nos. 1–2 (January–April 1943): 6, 21; Eugen Täubler, "Das Forschungs-Institut für die Wissenschaft des Judentums: Organisation und Arbeitsplan," in *Aufsätze zur Problematik jüdischer Geschichtsschreibung*, ed. Eugen Täubler and Selma Stern-Täubler (Tübingen: J. C. B. Mohr, 1977), 39.

11. Daniel Cohen, "Jewish Records from Germany in the Jewish Historical General Archives in Jerusalem," *Leo Baeck Institute Year Book* 1 (1956): 331–345.

12. On Jewish emigration from the State of Israel in the 1950s, see Ori Yehudai, "Forth from Zion: Jewish Emigration from Palestine and Israel, 1945–1960" (PhD diss., University of Chicago, 2013).

13. Eugen Täubler to Jewish Theological Seminary, 2 June 1948, Universitätsbibliothek Basel, NL 76 E1 #353.

14. Bernhard Brilling, "Jewish Records in German Archives," *Leo Baeck Institute Yearbook* 1 (1956): 346–359.

15. Bernhard Brilling, "Aufgaben des Archivs des Zentralrats," n.d., JMF, SB0440.

16. Bernhard Brilling, "Die Aufgaben eines Archivs für die Geschichte der Juden in Deutschland: Zum 20. Jahrestag der Vernichtung der jüdischen Archive in Deutschland im November 1938," 1958, JMF, SB1676; SB1672.

17. Hans Hertz to Hendrik George van Dam, 25 March 1959, JMF, SB0440; Daniel Cohen to Mark Uveeler, 16 August 1955, CZA, L33/1270.

18. Bernhard Brilling, "Das Prinzip der Rettung jüdischer Gemeindearchivalien aus Deutschland," 1960, JMF, SB1676.

19. See Otto Marcus, "Rabbiner Dr. Aron Heppner, Anlässlich seines 100. Geburtstages," July 1965, JMF, SB1610; cf. CAHJP, M5/12, which has extensive correspondence between Heppner and the Gesamtarchiv; see also "Bewerbungen um die Stellung eines Archivars," 1920, CAHJP, M5/19.

20. See "Zum Geleit!" *Breslauer Jüdisches Gemeindeblatt*, 8 August 1924, which notes the importance of a paper as something that other large communities had; cf. "Sitzung der Bibliothekskommission," Breslau, 10 May 1914, National Library of Israel (NLI), ARC Ms. Var. 308/01/188.

21. See, for instance, Bernhard Brilling, "Das jüdische Archivwesen in Deutschland," *Der Archivar* 13 (1960): 271–290; also Brilling, "Das Archiv der Synagogengemeinde Breslau," *Breslauer Jüdisches Gemeindeblatt*, January 1933, 1; Brilling, "Zum 10 jährigen Bestehen des Breslauer jüdischen Gemeindearchivs," August 1934, JMF, SB1607.

22. Bernhard Brilling, handwritten note, 1 December 1927, JMF, SB1607.

23. A detailed list of Brilling's publications is found in "Bibliographie Bernhard Brilling, 1928–1968," *Theokratia: Jahrbuch des Institutum Judaicum Delitzschianum* 1 (1970): 195–223; 3 (1979): 263–270. See especially Brilling, "Die jüdischen Familien von Zülz O.-S. 1725," *Jüdische Familien-Forschung* 4, no. 3 (September 1928); Brilling, "Die familiengeschichtlichen Quellen des Archivs der Breslauer Synagogengemeinde," *Jüdische Familien-Forschung* 10 (1934); and various correspondence between Czellitzer and Brilling, JMF, SB0683.

24. Bernhard Brilling to his parents, 18 April 1928, JMF, SB1677; Jacob Jacobson, "Tätigkeitsbericht," November 1929, Centrum Judaicum, 1, 75 C Ge 2; Brilling, "Vita," 4 July 1938, JMF, SB0644.

25. Reinhard Heydrich, "Massnahmen gegen Juden in der heutigen Nacht," 10 November 1938, in *Reichskristallnacht: Der Judenpogrom vom 7. bis November 1938—Urheber, Täter, Hintergründe: mit ausgewählten Dokumenten*, ed. Wolf-Arno Kropat (Wiesbaden: Kommission für die Geschichte der Juden in Hessen, 1997), 214–216. Also see Ernst Zipfel to

Generaldirektor der Staatsarchiv, 28 November 1938, Bundesarchiv Lichterfelde, R1506/7, and the attached "Verordnung zur Sicherheit des Schrift- und Archivguts der Juden in Deutschland," Geheimes Staatsarchiv an alle Staatsarchive, 4 January 1940, Geheimes Staatsarchiv—Preußisches Kulturbesitz, Berlin–Dahlem, I. HA Rep. 178/1153.

26. Bernhard Brilling, "Das jüdische Archivwesen in Deutschland," *Der Archivar* 10 (1960); Brilling to Fritz Grabowski, 10 February 1960, JMF, SB0550.

27. Invitation, *Verein für jüdische Familienforschung*, 4 March 1941, JMF, SB0682.

28. See, for instance, Miriam Getter, "Ha-'aliyah mi-germaniyah be-shanim 1933–1939: Ḳelitah ḥevratit-kalkalit mul ḳelitah ḥevratit-tarbutit," *Cathedra* 12 (1979): 125–147; Jütte, *Die Emigration der deutschsprachigen, Wissenschaft des Judentums nach Palästina*; Hagit Lavsky, "German Jewish Interwar Migration in a Comparative Perspective: Mandatory Palestine, the United States, and Great Britain," in *Ethnicity and Beyond: Theories and Dilemmas of Jewish Group Demarcation*, ed. Eli Lederhendler (Oxford: Oxford University Press, 2011), 115–144.

29. See Georg Herlitz, *Mein Weg nach Jerusalem: Erinnerungen eines Zionistischen Beamter* (Jerusalem: Rubin Mass, 1964), 161.

30. See Bein, *Hier kannst du nicht jeden grüßen* (New York: Georg Olms Verlag, 1996), 253–266.

31. On the Reichsarchiv, see Walter Vogel, *Der Kampf um das Geistige Erbe. Zur Geschichte der Reichsarchividee und des Reichsarchivs als "geistiger Tempel deutscher Einheit"* (Bonn: Bernard & Graefe, 1994); Matthias Hermann, "Das Reichsarchiv (1919–1945). Eine archivalische Institution im Spannungsfeld der deutschen Politik" (PhD diss., Humboldt-Universität, Berlin, 1993, 2 vols.).

32. Brilling, "Ḳitsur toldot ḥayay!," 13 March 1955, JMF, SB1671; cf. "Ḳurs le-hakhsharat 'arkhiona'im mada'iim," 13 October 1952, CZA A198/13, which details the course of the training program.

33. See, for instance, Bernhard Brilling to E. G. Löwenthal, 12 September 1951, JMF, SB0661; Bernhard Brilling, "Die Juden-Akten des Stadtarchivs Göttingen," January 1956, CAHJP R3/56.

34. A number of the finding aids in the CAHJP still include Bernhard Brilling's reports. See, for instance, Brilling, "Die Juden-Akten des Stadtarchivs Göttingen," January 1956, CAHJP R3/56; Brilling, "Verzeichnis der Israelitsichen Kirchenbücher aus Mecklenburg," January 1956, CAHJP, R3/51; Brilling, "Bemerkungen zu dem Verzeichnis der Juden-AKten aus dem Archiv des Etatsministeriums Königsberg/Ostpreussen," January 1956, CAHJP, R3/49.

35. Bernhard Brilling to Director of the Department of Education, Jerusalem, 16 January 1942, JMF, SB0641, 1.

36. Bernhard Brilling to E. G. Löwenthal, 12 September 1951, JMF, SB0661, 2.

37. Bernhard Brilling, "Ein Archiv für die Geschichte der Juden in Deutschland, als eine Forderung der Wiedergutmachung," 24 January 1956 JMF, SB1676.

38. Brilling, "Ein Archiv für die Geschichte der Juden."

39. "Beschlußprotokoll der Tagung des Rates," 20 August 1951, Zentralarchiv zur Erforschung der Geschichte der Juden in Deutschland (ZA), B. 1/7 Nr. 221.15.

40. Goldstein to JTC, 6 July 1953, CAHJP, JTC/Lon/575.

41. Verband der Jüdischen Gemeinden Nordwestdeutschlands to Charles Kapralik, 23 March 1954, CAHJP, JTC/Lon/576a.

42. Carl Katz (Israelitische Gemeinde Bremen) to Central Council, 10 May 1954, ZA, B. 1/7 241.

43. Hans Lamm, "Programmvorschalge für das Kulturdezenat des Zentralrats der Juden in Deutschland," September 1955, ZA, B. 1/7 Nr. 221.59.

44. Hannah Arendt to Gershom Scholem, 20 October 1952, NLI, ARC 4°1599/02 23.6.

45. Dr. Forstreuter to Bernhard Brilling, 29 February 1956, Israel State Archives (ISA), HZ-19-303; Hans Lamm to Alex Bein, 28 February 1957, ISA, G-14-12648; van Dam to Berthold Simonsohn, 5 March 1957, CZA, L33/1268.

46. Hendrik George van Dam to "Direktoriumsmitglieder und Stellvertreter, an alle Landesverbände und die Gemeinden Berlin, Bremen, Hamburg, und Köln," 8 March 1956, ZA, B. 1/7 241; Alfons Jonas to Central Council, 9 March 1956, ZA, B. 1/7 241.

47. Hendrik George van Dam to Paul Hübinger, 10 February 1956, ZA, B. 1/7 241; Hendrik George van Dam to Fritz Manasse, 15 March 1956, ZA B. 1/7 241. For currency conversion, see R. C. Bidwell, *Currency Conversion Tables: A Hundred Years of Change* (London: Rex Collings, 1970), 22–24; and "CPI Inflation Calculator," U.S. Department of Labor, accessed 20 September 2019, https://data.bls.gov/cgi-bin/cpicalc.pl.

48. Hendrik George van Dam to Paul Hübinger, 11 May 1956, ZA, B. 1/7 241; Hendrik George van Dam to Brilling, 25 February 1957, JMF, SB1680.

49. Bernhard Brilling to Hendrik George van Dam, 17 May 1956, JMF, SB1680; Bernhard Brilling to Hendrik George van Dam, 19 November 1956, JMF, SB1680; Bernhard Brilling to Hendrik George van Dam, 22 February 1957, JMF, SB1680.

50. Bernhard Brilling to Alex Bein, 14 March 1957, CZA, L33/1268.

51. Josef Meisl to Siegfried Ascher, 12 September 1956, CAHJP, P35/34.

52. Alex Bein to Bernhard Brilling, 21 March 1957, JMF, SB1680.

53. Alex Bein, "Du"ḥ ʿal śiḥati ʿim ro'sh ha-ʿir hamburg," 16 June 1954, CAHJP, P28/6/37.

54. Alex Bein to Hans Lamm, 11 March 1957, ISA, G-14-12648; Alex Bein to Heinz Galinski, 11 March 1957, CZA, L33/1268.

55. Alex Bein to Hans Lamm, 11 April 1957, CZA, L33/1268.

56. See Alex Bein to Hans Lamm, 11 March 1957, ISA, G-14-12648.

57. Brilling to Alex Bein, 27 Mar. 1957, JMF SB1680.

58. Bernhard Brilling to Hendrik George van Dam, 27 March 1957, JMF, SB1680, also dated 14 April 1956, CZA, L33/1268.

59. Daniel Cohen to Issachar Ben-Yaacov, 25 April 1957, CZA, L33/1268.

60. Daniel Cohen to Bertl Trude, 26 June 1957, CZA, L33/1268.

61. Bernhard Brilling, "Die Aufgabe eines Archiv für die Geschichte der Juden in Deutschland: Zum 20. Jahrestag der Vernichtung der jüdischen Archive in Deutschland im November 1938," 1958, JMF, SB1676; SB1672.

62. Hendrik George van Dam to Zweig, 30 June 1958, ZA, B. 1/7 241; Bernhard Brilling to Hendrik George van Dam, 1 December 1958, JMF, SB0440; Hans Hertz to Hendrik George van Dam, 26 February 1959, JMF, SB0440.

63. Hans Lamm to Hans Hertz, 5 May 1959, ZA, B. 1/7 241; "Tätigkeitsbericht des Direktoriums," June 1959, ZA, B. 1/7 246.

64. Bernhard Brilling to Hans Hertz, 7 May 1959, JMF, SB0440.

65. Hans Hertz, Karl Heinrich Rengstorf, and Bernhard Brilling to Central Council, 5/6 June 1959, JMF, SB0440.

66. Karl Heinrich Rengstorf to Hans Hertz, Staatsarchiv Hamburg (StAHH), 133-1 III 215-1/4/2, Bd. IV.

67. See, for instance, Heinz von Trützschler to Abraham Frowein, August 1954, "Entwurf," Politisches Archiv–Auswärtiges Amt, Berlin, B10 1670.

68. Bernhard Brilling to Bundesarchiv, 8 July 1960, JMF SB1608. Also see Bernhard Brilling, "Archiwum Gminy Zydowskiej we Wroclawiu," *Biuletyn Zydowskiego instytutu Historycznego przy C.K. Zydow w Polsce*, November 1950, 15–17, which details the fate of the Breslau archive. It should be noted that the files are also held digitally by the U.S. Holocaust Memorial Museum in Washington, D.C., and that the "Branniana" section (of materials originating from Markus Brann), which Brilling claimed was mostly missing, can be found there.

69. Bernhard Brilling, "Aktennotiz: Besprechung mit Prof. R. am 3.7.1959," 3 July 1959, JMF, SB0540; Karl Heinrich Rengstorf to the State Secretary of the Federal Chancellery, 6 July 1960, JMF, SB0544.

70. Bernhard Brilling to Association of Jewish Communities in Northwest Germany, 25 April 1960, JMF, SB0533d.

71. Bernhard Brilling, "Das Prinzip der Rettung jüdischer Gemeindearchivalien aus Deutschland," 1960, JMF, SB1676.

72. Bernhard Brilling to Association of Jewish Communities in Northwest Germany, 25 April 1960, JMF, SB0533d.

73. Bernhard Brilling to Bundesarchiv, 8 July 1960, JMF, SB1608.

74. Bernhard Brilling to the Labor and Social Affairs Minister of the State of North Rhine–Westphalia, 23 January 1961, JMF, SB1608.

75. "Ein Institut von hohem Rang: Existenz des Institutum Judaicum ist gesichert," 30 May 1973, JMF, SB0495.

76. Helmut Kohl, "Ansprache in Bergen-Belsen zum 40. Jahrestag der Befreiung der Gefangenen aus den Konzentrationslagern," 21 April 1985, accessed 26 December 2017, http://helmut-kohl.kas.de/index.php?menu_sel=17&menu_sel2=&menu_sel3=&menu_sel4=&msg=1344. Also published as Helmut Kohl, "Die Geheimnis der Erlösung heißt Erinnerung. Ansprache in Bergen-Belsen zum 40. Jahrestag der Befreiung der Gefangenen aus den Konzentrationslagern, gehalten am 21. April 1985 in Bergen Belsen," in *Die unentrinnbare Gegenwart der Geschichte* (Bonn: Presse- und Informationsamt der Bundesregierung, 1988), 3–18.

77. Peter Honigmann, "Geschichte des jüdischen Archivwesens in Deutschland," *Archivar* 55, no. 3 (2002): 223–230; Peter Honigmann, "Das Heidelberger Zentralarchiv zur Erforschung der Geschichte der Juden in Deutschland," *Menorah* 12 (2001): 345–370.

78. Barbara Welker, "Das Archiv der Stiftung, Neue Synagoge Berlin–Centrum Judaicum," *Menorah* 12 (2001): 325–344.

CHAPTER 4

WHOSE HERITAGE?

EARLY POSTWAR GERMAN-JEWISH HISTORY AS REMIGRANTS' HISTORY—THE CASE OF HAMBURG

Miriam Rürup

In December 2007, the weekly German newspaper *Die Zeit* published a report on German Jews who had fled Nazi Germany for safety in the United States. Carol Kahn Strauss, the daughter of émigrés from Dortmund and the executive director of the Leo Baeck Institute in New York—one of the world's leading centers for the study of German Jewry—used the occasion to promote a "revolutionary idea." She proposed to relocate "the heart of the institute," its renowned archive, from New York to Berlin. She argued,

> Those emigrants, who have supported us for fifty years, even financially, are now passing away. We think that what we collect and document here, mostly in German, is part of German history and should be in Germany. . . . This history is becoming increasingly less relevant in New York. In Germany it is increasingly important. There, those materials will not degenerate, as far as one can say something about the future.[1]

Not everyone shared Strauss's perspective. Marion Kaplan, a professor at New York University and the daughter of German-Jewish refugees, reacted angrily. In an open letter to Ismar Schorsch, president of the Leo Baeck Institute (LBI), she wrote,

> The notion that the archives would "degenerate" in New York is dubious. Why should this be the case? . . . While it is true that the German-Jewish refugee generation is thinning out and that the children of these refugees have blended into the American Jewish community, the conclusion does not follow that the LBI will be unable to find financial support in exactly that American Jewish community. . . . Finally, with regard to those thousands of refugees

> and survivors who donated their memoirs, letters, diaries, and other precious papers to the LBI, most did so because—and confident that—their documents would be safe in America. I doubt they would have done so had they known that the materials with which they escaped from Germany would eventually end up back in Germany. They entrusted a Jewish institution in the United States with their treasured documents, not a Jewish institution in Germany. Their intentions alone should make the LBI pause before sending the archives to Germany.[2]

The larger, symbolic conflict illuminated by these two statements dates back to the early years of postwar German history and remains relevant today—namely, who are the heirs to the heritage of German Jewry, and for whom have the documents and records of former German Jews been preserved?

This conflict over material remnants gained its true importance from the symbolic issues at stake. While Strauss and Kaplan focused on an institution in New York in 2007–2008, a similar debate took place in Hamburg as early as the immediate postwar years and culminated in the establishment of the Institute for the History of the German Jews (Institut für die Geschichte der deutschen Juden) in 1966. The origins, early years, and precise character of the institute elucidate the fundamental struggle over who is in charge of German-Jewish history and whether there was meant to be a German-Jewish historiography within postwar Germany at all. The actors involved in this dispute over memory and heritage were non-Jewish and Jewish Germans, former German Jews, remigrants to Germany, German-born Israelis, and of course Zionists seeking to endow the new Israeli state with a Jewish-national legacy and heritage.

The conflict in Hamburg began, in fact, in Jerusalem, as the Jewish Historical General Archives (today, the Central Archives for the History of the Jewish People) attempted to collect all traces of Jewish heritage in postwar Europe and bring them to Israel. These early attempts focused not merely on archival documents but also on other objects of Jewish cultural heritage, such as books and libraries,[3] ritual objects, and profane material remnants seized by the Nazis.[4] This essay will focus on the story of the archival remnants of Hamburg's historic Jewish community. In Hamburg, one of the biggest archives of Jewish life in Germany survived the war unharmed, documenting four hundred years of Jewish life in Germany. City officials as well as representatives of the Jewish community of Hamburg were reluctant to give "their" material away, regarding it as part of their Hamburg (Jewish) heritage. In the end, some of the originals remained in Hamburg and some were brought to Jerusalem, while the respective missing portions were microfilmed so that the complete collection was accessible in both countries. Moreover, Hamburg committed itself to funding a research institute that would henceforth work with those files and on that heritage.

The years leading to the opening of the institute—the first scholarly center for German-Jewish history in postwar Germany—were conflict-ridden and indicate the difficult context in which early postwar German-Jewish history developed. The broader context has to be seen as part of German *Vergangenheitsbewältigung* (coming to terms with the past), when German-Jewish emigrants observed the diffident reconstruction of Jewish life in postwar Germany from afar. German-Jewish historians such as Heinz Mosche Graupe, the institute's founding director, and Joseph Wulf, who intended to work for the Hamburg institute, demanded to be respected as scholars in the field of contemporary German history in general and had to fight for recognition as legitimate German historians by convincing not only their (non-Jewish) German colleagues but also their fellow former German Jews.

The German-Jewish emigrants who founded branches of the Leo Baeck Institute in their countries of refuge—Britain, the United States, and Israel—expressly declared that they did not intend to establish a branch of the Leo Baeck Institute in Germany.[5] However, when the Institute for the History of the German Jews was founded in Hamburg, it was expected to take over the "practical role of a German Leo Baeck Institute."[6] Those expectations were expressed by the German side in order to further legitimize the establishment of such an institute.

Rebuilding Jewish Life in Germany

Both remigrants as well as those who had either survived in Germany in hiding or come to Germany as displaced persons (DPs) and decided to stay were part of a new beginning of Jewish life in Germany. This revival of Jewish life in the country of the perpetrators drew part of its legitimization from the existing heritage and remnants of Jewish life on the ground, such as the Hamburg Jewish community archives. And yet this development was a disputed topic among Jews and Zionists alike. From the Zionist (and later Israeli) perspective, Diaspora Judaism was seen as something that was meant to be overcome. Furthermore, rebuilding Jewish life in the country of the perpetrators was regarded nearly as an act of treason to the Jewish people.[7] From the angle of the Allied occupiers, remigration of political and Jewish emigrants was regarded as a way to enhance the rebuilding of a democratic post-Nazi society. From that perspective, Jews were seen as transmitters of democratic values and thus needed for the emerging European "West." A third group, exiled Jews, looked upon Germany with skepticism and were hesitant to return permanently to their former homeland, which had turned into a country of perpetrators. And even when they did return, they often kept the foreign passports they had received during their years of living abroad.[8] The fact that those remigrants remained skeptical and hesitant toward postwar Germany was nourished by a climate that they must have experienced as hostile.

Having been expatriated and stripped of their German citizenship by the National Socialists, they were no longer regarded as full members of German society. Everyday reality demonstrated to the remigrants that they were not necessarily welcome.[9] While non-Jewish Germans emphasized their own suffering and pointed to the bombed-out cities, the remigrants were regarded as well-fed returnees, who had survived in comparably safe surroundings and were now presumably only coming back to raise questions of German guilt, supposedly full of hatred—if not even bearing ideas of revenge.[10] Furthermore, Jewish and non-Jewish emigrants waited in vain for a clear call to return to Germany.[11] Most Jewish remigrants to Germany were very hesitant about returning to "accursed soil," and most of those who did return did not initially intend to resettle in Germany.[12] Additionally, there were many emigrants who did not think about returning and who declared those feelings publicly.[13]

The conflict over returning to Germany was intertwined with a discussion of rebuilding Jewish life and thus reestablishing Jewish culture in Germany. Aspects of the reconstruction included Jews who chose to remain in Germany after having witnessed the end of the war in Germany or who had come to the Allied zones as DPs and material remnants such as the Jewish community archives that served as the foundation for the Hamburg institute. Focusing on the emerging field of German-Jewish historiography in postwar Germany, we will see how closely linked both aspects were in those early discussions. The specific Hamburg case enables us to address the overall questions of who is in charge of the Jewish legacy—namely, the heritage of Jewish existence in Germany. Part of this original Hamburg debate centered on the following questions: Where should this heritage be kept, where should Jewish life be rebuilt after the war, and whose heritage is it? The perception of a Jewish community archive as part of *German*-Jewish heritage would call for leaving it in its country of origin—that is, Germany. This can be seen as a decentralized take on Jewish heritage, recognizing and accepting the ongoing existence of Diasporic Jewish life. By contrast, a centralized perspective would claim the remnants as part of a mainly *Jewish* heritage, which is owned by the Jewish people and should ultimately be removed from postwar Germany and brought to Israel.[14] Both cases raise questions, such as: Who would work with this material, who are the ones rightfully claiming the legitimacy to write German-Jewish history, and where would this occur? Thus we will now have a look at both the emerging field of German-Jewish history and the struggle over the archival remnants.

Jewish Historians and German-Jewish History

After the end of the Second World War, there was hardly any interest in studying German-Jewish history in Germany. One possible reason was the reluctance in Germany to deal at all with the recent past at all. Furthermore, it seemed impossible and inappropriate to focus on Jewish history while omitting the years of Nazi persecution. To put it differently, dealing with German-Jewish history would have also meant tackling the question of how Germans became perpetrators who excluded, expelled, and ultimately exterminated their fellow German (Jewish) citizens. Those who worked on German-Jewish history in those early postwar years did so as emigrants and published not in German journals but rather mainly in the *Leo Baeck Institute Year Book* after the establishment of the Leo Baeck Institute in 1955, whose primary audience was not Germans—either Jewish or non-Jewish—but rather the community of survivors and fellow emigrants in Israel, the United States, and the United Kingdom.[15] Thus there was no German or German-Jewish voice for German-Jewish history within Germany in the first decade after the war ended.

In the immediate postwar years, no university professor in West Germany taught Jewish history, and the very few professors who taught Jewish studies (not Jewish *history*) were employed within faculties of Christian theology or were (mostly Jewish) remigrants. One of the very early remigrants to Germany was Adolf Leschnitzer, who taught German-Jewish history at the Free University in Berlin beginning in 1952 and even then only a single course in the summer term. He kept his American citizenship and maintained his primary residence in the United States.[16] Nonetheless, the Free University practically became a hotbed of German-Jewish emigrants returning to study and teach Jewish studies in Germany, including Franz Neumann, Ernst Fraenkel, Ossip K. Flechtheim, and Jacob Taubes, to name a few. This was partially due to the fact that this postwar institution was not tainted with a Nazi past and could be seen as an academic answer to the call for a renewal of German society. Those early scholarly remigrants became educators of a whole new generation of (non-Jewish) German historians, including Arno Herzig, Stefi Jersch-Wenzel, Monika Richarz, and Reinhard Rürup, who went on to produce seminal works in the field of German-Jewish history. Those historians were born in the mid- to late 1930s and had received their university educations in postwar Germany. Especially in the 1960s, they formed the first group of young, non-Jewish historians dealing with Jewish history. Hence the generational change brought about a shift in German-Jewish historiography or, to be more precise, in the way that the history of German Jewry was addressed within general German history. The founders of this German-Jewish historiography were quite different from those who had tried to establish a *Wissenschaft des Judentums* (scholarly study of Judaism) before the National Socialist regime. Before 1933, it was exclusively Jewish historians dealing with Jewish history. Now it was non-Jewish historians working through a German lens. As a consequence, early on, Jewish history became part of German historiography. Many of those postwar historians of Jewish history chose as a starting point for their research the question and failure of emancipation, including Arno Herzig,[17] Reinhard Rürup, and even earlier, Eva G. Reichmann, who published *Hostages of Civilization: A Study of the Social Causes of Anti-Semitism in Germany* in 1945 (republished in German in 1951 as *Die Flucht in den Hass. Die Ursachen der deutschen Judenkatastrophe*). What made her work and that of these other early historians special was the view of the emancipation of German Jews as a test case for the overall social emancipation that took place in the nineteenth century.[18]

Jewish historians, by contrast, encountered great reservations—if not aggression—from their non-Jewish colleagues when they ventured into the field of German history, especially when focusing on the recent National Socialist past. Having suffered from German and Nazi history, they were considered incapable of having an "objective" perspective on German history.[19] This reproach can be seen in the 1949 Josef von Báky film *Der Ruf* (*The Last Illusion*), starring Fritz Kortner as an emigrant who returns to Germany to take up a professorship at the University of Göttingen. This common accusation must have deeply hurt director von Báky as well as Jewish actor Kortner, who fled Germany in the 1930s.

In fact, the institutionalization of Jewish history took place outside of academia; or rather, those Jewish historians who studied and did scholarly work in Germany in the early postwar years remained outside the ivory tower. One such example is Hans Lamm, a Jewish historian born in Munich. He had immigrated to the United States and soon after the end of the war returned to Germany as an interpreter during the Nuremberg trials. His dissertation, the first concise history of German Jewry from 1933 onward, was submitted in 1951 but remained unpublished.[20] He founded the Ner Tamid Verlag, the earliest postwar press to specialize in both scholarly and pedagogical works with a clear Jewish focus. In 1960, he published and edited a volume on behalf of the Association of German Student Unions (Verband Deutscher Studentenschaften) entitled *Erziehungswesen und Judentum. Die Darstellung des Judentums in der Lehrerbildung und im Schulunterricht*, which dealt with how to teach Jewish history and culture in German schools.[21] In general, German scholars have regarded the early placement of German-Jewish historical research outside the university system not only as an anti-Jewish reflex[22] but also possibly as part of a Jewish self-isolation and a lack of audience, as Reinhard Rürup has noted. Before the war, Jewish historians such as Leopold Zunz, Heinrich Graetz, and Moritz Steinschneider wrote for a predominantly Jewish audience—an audience that was tragically missing after the Second World War.[23]

Whose Sources? Struggle over the Archives

It is in this setting that a major conflict between Israel and Germany—or, to be more precise, between Jerusalem and Hamburg—led to the founding of the first research institute on Jewish history in Germany. The core of this conflict was the question, Whose heritage is it to claim? The introductory example of Carol Kahn Strauss's suggestion to "return" the documents of the German-Jewish émigrés to their country of origin shows how contentious the question of where historical archives are located can be. Archives not only serve as means for historians to do research but also are often seen as an essential foundation of a common heritage, which needs to be administered and owned by the group who claims its legacy. The history of the Institute for the History of the German Jews, located in Hamburg—the first postwar center for research on Jewish history in Germany—has its roots in this negotiation process. In the 1950s, the city of Hamburg was on the verge of legal struggles over archival material covering four hundred years of German-Jewish history in the Hamburg State Archive.[24] However, these would be struggles over more than simply archival files. Ultimately, they pointed to questions over quite a different kind of *return*—namely, whether the Jews may return to Germany or whether their "archival remnants" should rather "return" to their people, now living in Israel.

While most other Jewish archives in German cities were confiscated or destroyed during the Nazi years, the impressive archives of the former Jewish community of Hamburg were saved from confiscation in 1938 by means of being transferred into storage at the Hamburg State Archive (Staatsarchiv Hamburg). The material of Hamburg's Jewish community was passed to the city literally under the eyes of the Gestapo; when the Gestapo confiscated the Jewish community building at Rothenbaumchaussee 38 after Kristallnacht, in November 1938, the documents were brought to the Hamburg State Archive. The material was transferred as a "Depositum" and remained property of the Jewish community—a community, however, that was expelled and destroyed by Nazi persecution.

After the war, the Jewish Historical General Archives in Israel (later renamed the Central Archives for the History of the Jewish People) announced its claim to all Jewish heritage, including community materials. Israeli archivists collected the remnants of Jewish community files throughout Germany and attempted to do so in Hamburg.[25] After years of legal quarrels, Hamburg and Jerusalem reached an agreement in 1959. Hamburg agreed to establish (and fund) a research institute that would be committed exclusively to research on German-Jewish history. This struggle must be seen within the larger framework of a new Jewish existence in Germany, a Zionist state in Israel that was reluctant to accept Jewish life in post-Shoah Germany, and German state actors and German civil society trying to come to terms with the past.

The main arguments in favor of transferring the material to Israel were as follows: (1) a nation-state needed a national archive, (2) all Jewish material should be concentrated in order to make it more accessible for researchers, (3) the material should serve as a worthy memorial of a culturally rich yet obsolete Jewish past in the Diaspora, and lastly (4) it would save the material from future destruction in a presumably continuingly hostile society. The attempts to move and preserve the materials could build on earlier efforts undertaken by the Zionist movement. Already at the very beginning of Nazi persecution, Zionist scholars, including Ben-Zion Dinur, Yitzhak Baer, and Georg Herlitz, tried to save documents and bring them to Palestine, and Herlitz founded the Zionist Archives, which moved from Berlin to Jerusalem in 1933.[26]

Initial conversations about establishing a research institute for Jewish history in Hamburg date back to the 1950s. In 1953, Fritz Fischer, a scholar of German contemporary history who did not specialize in Jewish history, formed the Working Group for the History of the Jews in Hamburg (Arbeitsgemeinschaft für die Geschichte der Juden in Hamburg). An additional idea from this era was to establish a central Jewish community archive in Hamburg. Indeed, Rabbi Bernhard Brilling, who had worked as a Jewish communal archivist in Breslau before the war, returned to Germany from Israel in 1957 and fostered this project. While he organized a small department of German-Jewish history within the University of Münster, the project of an independent institute was realized only three decades later and not in Hamburg. Instead, the Central Archive for the Research on the History of the Jews in Germany (Zentralarchiv zur Erforschung der Geschichte der Juden in Deutschland) was established in Heidelberg and opened in 1987. In Hamburg, meanwhile, a lawsuit was imminent.

In 1953 the Jewish Trust Corporation for Germany (JTC) applied for "restitution" of the Jewish community archive to the Jewish people—that is, to Israel. At first, the Hamburg Jewish community supported this claim. By 1957, however, the community was firmly established; its members intended to stay permanently in Germany, and its leaders changed their opinion and wanted to keep the materials in Hamburg. City officials of Hamburg refused to hand over those materials. In this dispute, the Israeli side was represented by Alex Bein, director of the Central Zionist Archives in Israel, and Daniel J. Cohen, director of the Central Archives for the History of the Jewish People until 1986. Bein was a German-born and -trained historian who previously had served as an archivist at the Reichsarchiv in Potsdam. Cohen also had roots in Germany and came from Hamburg. Thus even the negotiators on the Israeli side had German backgrounds.[27]

Additionally, the struggle was not merely between "Israelis" and "Germans," since some Jews were in favor of keeping Jewish heritage as German-Jewish heritage and in Germany. Among them were Jacob Jacobson, director of the Central Archives of German Jews in Berlin before the war, who had helped systematically organize the material in Hamburg; Hans W. Hertz,[28] who had played an active part in moving, and thus saving, the Hamburg archives in the first place; Eric Warburg, a remigrant to Germany; and Max Plaut, the sole survivor of the prewar board of Hamburg's Jewish community.[29] They argued that since they had been invited back to Hamburg by none other than the mayor, Max Brauer, himself a remigrant, they also needed and wanted their heritage close by and in the country they considered home. For them, handing over the material to Israel was seen as completing the Nazi attempt to destroy all Jewish traces within Germany.

Hamburg was not the only location where German Jews insisted on keeping their historic archives. The Bavarian Jewish Community, with the support of the Central Council of Jews in Germany (Zentralrat der Juden in Deutschland), insisted on keeping its prewar collection of Jewish material. For these Bavarian Jews, the collection was proof of the long Jewish heritage in Germany. Moreover, they regarded it not only as German-Jewish heritage but also as German heritage in general.[30]

Another group of protagonists was far more critical of this approach and wanted to transfer the material to Israel as part of the heritage of the Jewish people. As A. Landsberg wrote, "The history of Jews in Hamburg and more generally: the history of German Jews overall is terminated and over. There are no grounds whatsoever for a veritable (and lively!) new beginning."[31] In this group's opinion, which echoed the overall Israeli view, the Diaspora was to be overcome and all heritage there dissolved and "returned" to Israel. The Zionist idea of "ingathering of the exiles" hence quite literally included the gathering of Jewish material and archival remnants to Israel.[32] The struggle over archival material was basically a conflict about the centrality of Israel and the continuing existence of a diaspora, especially a German-Jewish diaspora.

In 1959, finally, a Solomonic solution was found: the archive would be split into two parts, with each side keeping the originals of some materials and receiving microfilm or paper copies of others.[33] The material was divided along rather vague lines. Hamburg would keep the materials that would help reconstruct the history of the city of Hamburg and its special relation to its Jewish citizens (i.e., the "external" history), while the materials sent to Israel had a focus on the religious aspects of the Jewish community (i.e., the "internal" history).[34] The city of Hamburg established and funded the Institute for the History of the German Jews to conduct historical research with the Hamburg Jewish community's files. Professor Dietrich Gerhardt of the University of Hamburg supported the project, and the banker Eric M. Warburg, who had also returned to Germany from his exile in the United States in 1956, gave financial assistance. Joseph Wulf, a historian of National Socialism with a Jewish-Polish background, was invited to work at the institute and accepted the offer, though he ended up not taking the position.[35] It required yet another few years until Mosche Graupe was appointed as director on 19 November 1964, and the institute officially opened on 4 May 1966.

Whose History? Non-Jewish German Historians of Contemporary German History

A second arena of conflict was the question of who was eligible to tell the story of Jewish life in Germany. Initially, the founders of the Institute for the History of the German Jews had chosen Karl Heinrich Rengstorf as the first director. A professor of Protestant theology and director of the Institutum Judaicum

Delitzschianum at the University of Münster,[36] Rengstorf was involved in sketching out the idea of such a research institute early on. After attempting to establish a Jewish archive in Münster, he joined forces with the Hamburg initiators and supported the establishment of an institute in Hamburg.[37] Shortly before taking over the position as founding director, however, Jewish voices protested his appointment. Not only was Rengstorf not Jewish, but he was also one of the founders of the Lutheran-Protestant Mission among Israel (Evangelisch-Lutherischer Zentralverein für Mission unter Israel), an association in favor of converting the Jews. Although he defended his take on his "mission to the Jews" as one that took place in a Christian-Jewish dialogue, to the Jews who raised criticisms about his appointment, this was not acceptable—especially not in postwar Germany. Erich Lüth, spokesman of the Hamburg Senate and involved in the first steps of postwar Jewish-Christian dialogue in Hamburg in a truly reconciliatory context, understood the reservation. In a note to city officials, he explained the problem with this choice: "It is disturbing for the Jewish public to see their own documents not being administered and interpreted by a neutral scholar, but by kind of a militant missionary."[38] In the end, support for Rengstorf faded away, and he withdrew his appointment in February 1964 before the institute even opened.

Finding a replacement proved challenging. It now was obvious that the next choice had to be someone not only with an untainted biography but also capable of the required scholarly work. The Hamburg Senate appointed Heinz Mosche Graupe as the first director of the newly founded institute. Born in Berlin in 1906, he had immigrated to Palestine in 1933. As an academic scholar, however, he had a difficult time finding a suitable position and worked as a teacher and, after 1948, for the municipality of Haifa. In Germany he had studied philosophy, history, and Judaic studies, with his main focus on the history of Jewish thought. Even before his immigration to Palestine, he had studied in the Yishuv at the Hebrew University of Jerusalem and afterward completed a rabbinic degree in Berlin at the Higher Institute for the Scholarly Study of Judaism (Hochschule für die Wissenschaft des Judentums). Both of his parents perished in the Holocaust, yet he decided to follow the "call" to Hamburg when he was invited to become the first director of the Institute for the History of the German Jews. He came back to work and live in Germany in 1964.

Although the first research institute of its kind focusing on German-Jewish history, the institute did not become the first choice as a German partner for Jewish émigré scholars,[39] possibly as a result of the conflict over the appointment of the institute's first director. Another development in the field of German and Jewish historiography seemed to be more inviting. In 1959–1960, another institute was founded in Hamburg: the Research Center for the Study of National Socialism (Forschungsstelle zur Erforschung des Nationalsozialismus), today called the Research Center for Contemporary History in Hamburg

(Forschungsstelle für Zeitgeschichte in Hamburg). Werner Jochmann, the director of the institute, had been a postdoctoral assistant for the eminent historian Fritz Fischer[40] before turning his back on medieval history in order to pursue more contemporary research questions, especially about the failure of the Weimar Republic and its political successor, National Socialism.

Both German and Jewish historians, still struggling to find the right angle to deal with the recent past, characterized the emerging postwar field of "contemporary German history." Mostly, German postwar historiography did not address the question of the Nazi period, and if so, it did not analyze the Holocaust and persecution of the Jews. Rather, it dealt with the question of how and why the democratic system of the Weimar Republic failed. Furthermore, German academic historians considered themselves as writing about National Socialism from a neutral or "objective" standpoint, while they considered Jewish historians as biased and writing a victim-focused history, ignoring the "systemic" aspects of Nazi history and not getting to the real core of the history of National Socialism.[41] This divide could still be seen in the "*Historikerstreit*" of the 1980s and the famous exchange of correspondence between Martin Broszat and Saul Friedländer in 1987.[42]

Werner Jochmann, the first director of this institute of contemporary history, was born in 1921. The Nazi past definitely formed his perspective of the role of contemporary history. Jochmann had been a member of the Hitler Youth, worked for the Labor Service, and served in the German army during World War II. He was very active not only as a historian but also within the Protestant Church in the context of enhancing Jewish-Christian dialogue as a religious project. And just as was the professional approach of Heinz Mosche Graupe, he also insisted on making the results of his scholarly research accessible to a broader public, which led to cooperation with the State Agency for Civic Education (Landeszentrale für politische Bildung).[43] This state-funded institution, which still exists, offers adult education and provides schools with background material for their history and political science instruction to foster a well-educated civil society based on the ideas of tolerance and democracy.

In his research, Jochmann combined a strong interest in Jewish history with the history of National Socialism. This two-track approach also had its origins in early criticism that Jochmann received from a Jewish colleague, Shaul Esh, from the Institute for Contemporary Jewry in Israel, who was also born in Hamburg. Esh pointed out to Jochmann that his collection of documents about the history of Nazism lacked Jewish sources and did not refer to any of the works of Jewish scholars. This criticism led to a long conversation—first in letters, then in mutual visits—between Jochmann and Esh and indeed strengthened Hamburg's ties with Israel and Jewish academics as well as with the LBI in London.

The Research Center for the Study of National Socialism quickly turned into *the* place to go for many German-Jewish historians who had emigrated from

Germany and lived abroad yet who also wanted to have a scholarly address in Germany.[44] Quite interestingly, the professional links between the LBI and the research center were far closer than the links between the LBI and the Institute for the History of the German Jews. Thus in 1974, when the LBI put together the very first panel on German-Jewish history ever to be organized at a German *Historikertag*, the LBI did not approach Peter Freimark (then the director of the Institute for the History of the German Jews) but rather Werner Jochmann as its partner in Germany. Of course, such academic relations always have a personal reason as well.[45] However, reasons for this might just as well lie somewhere else, beyond mere personal affinity. It clearly was easier and more viable for emigrated Jewish historians of German-Jewish history to work with non-Jewish Germans than to acknowledge and accept that there were Jewish remigrants to Germany who were establishing a new Jewish existence there. It seems that in the case of the LBI and the Research Center for the Study of National Socialism, we see an echo of what Dan Diner has called the Jewish "ban" on Germany.

What History?

Lots of prominent guests, including leading members of the University and local politicians, such as former mayors Max Brauer and Kurt Sieveking, attended the opening ceremony of the newly founded Institute for the History of the German Jews and made welcoming remarks. They named three main motives for the establishment of such an institute: (1) to correct the "maliciously distorted image of the Jew";[46] (2) to prove the immense importance of Jews within Hamburg and Jewish contributions specifically to the city of Hamburg, as if not to let intellectual annihilation follow the city's physical destruction; and (3) to work closely with the sources and documents of the Hamburg Jewish community.

It was an institution funded by German money and researching the history of a religious minority within German history, but taking on the perspective of the Jews—*not* that of non-Jewish politics about Jews. It was clearly a rarity in many ways, and for many years it was the only such research institution in Germany. The scholarly profile of the institute addressed an academic audience and had a clear educational function. Especially under the institute's second director, close ties were established with the State Agency for Civic Education.[47] Thus very early on, the institute chose a two-track understanding of Jewish historiography in Germany: traditionally academic historical basic research together with the transfer of its findings to the decidedly non-Jewish German public.

Prominent Jewish contemporaries such as Norbert Wollheim publicly declared the role of historiography as the core discipline to address the question of "why" and "how" National Socialism could have happened, regarding history as the "teacher of mankind."[48] German Jews explicitly stated their right to reclaim their part within general German history. Their own history as Jews in Germany had to be considered as part of German history, and thus they perceived themselves as German historians just like other historians. As Wollheim stated, "After all, our history was taken away from us Jews in Germany on 9 November 1938. The same history, which was already shaped by our ancestors some sixteen hundred years ago in the old town of Cologne."[49] His claim must also be seen as an answer to the field of National Socialist historiography, in which, for example, the renowned journal *Historische Zeitschrift* had introduced a special section on the "Jewish question," giving room to studies by the Propaganda Ministry's special Institute for the Study of the Jewish Question, established in 1934.[50]

The main research focus of the Hamburg institute's first director, Heinz Mosche Graupe, was the history of ideas. The first volume of the institute's publication series was entitled *Die Entstehung des Modernen Judentums: Geistesgeschichte der Deutschen Juden, 1650–1942*.[51] The book not only proved to be popular and widely read but was also translated into Hebrew and English. When Graupe retired in 1972, he continued to live in Hamburg and later moved to Frankfurt. Only in 1988 did he decide to move to the United States, where he lived with his son in Chicago. Graupe was not only a remigrant who was willing to settle in Germany as a victim of Nazi persecution, but he was also eager to enter into a conversation with the broader German public about their very own Jewish heritage as part of German humanistic culture and heritage. Thus it is no accident that his first (and main) publication was written for a broad audience. Whether this "conversation" was one-sided or not is difficult to judge. What is interesting to see is that Jewish remigrants, such as Graupe, did not necessarily return as the victim seeking revenge—a fear that continued beneath the surface in German academia and beyond. Their approach rather was the question of how to address and reconcile the both rich and tragic legacy of German-Jewish life in their work as historians of German-Jewish history. They were looking for an explanation for the failure of a seemingly golden age of successful emancipation. That this one-sided love affair came to such a bitter end demanded clarification. By putting it in a larger perspective, they inherently reached out to a broader public beyond academia, as can be seen in the cases of Hans Lamm and Heinz Mosche Graupe.

Conclusion

In 1984, Hans W. Hertz, one of the activists who had moved the Jewish community's records to the Hamburg State Archive (where they had remained safe during the war) and who had facilitated the foundation of the Institute for the History of the German Jews, received an honorary doctorate degree from the University of Hamburg. Part of the rationale of the committee that approved his award was to honor his involvement in "saving" Hamburg's Jewish heritage.[52] In this decade, historiographical developments such as the history workshop movement[53] and the new social history brought about an openness that made it possible to address the "Jewish question" and claimed that "subjectivity" was a legitimate perspective. Moreover, scholarship on Jewish history, drawing on Jewish sources originating in Germany and archived in Germany, was not a disputed topic anymore. As the honoring of Hertz with an honorary degree shows, it had become part of a newfound pride in a city's Jewish heritage.

At the beginning I asked, "Whose heritage?" The struggle surrounding the archival material in Hamburg—as was the case in many German cities—can be seen as a test of how Jewish historians tried to rebuild their lives in Germany after the Second World War and on how many different levels they needed to resolve conflicts in order to gain respect and legitimacy for their efforts.

The antagonists who claimed that Jewish history in Germany was over and argued for a transfer of Jewish community files to Israel put forward four main arguments for doing so: (1) a nation-state needed a national archive, (2) all Jewish material should be concentrated in order to make it more accessible for researchers, (3) it would serve as a worthy memorial, and (4) the material should be saved from supposed future destruction. From this perspective, the priority of Jewish history was *not* to focus on its entanglement with German history, but rather the emphasis was put on the need to unite Jewish heritage in the newly founded Jewish state.

Those Jews who wanted to write history *within* Germany and as part of a *joint* German-Jewish history did so in order to reclaim their heritage. Not only were fellow Jews outside of Germany reluctant to accept Jewish scholarship on German soil, but "German" historians did not consider Jewish historians as being able to do research within the field of recent German history, alleging a lack of objectivity. Jewish historiography, in a way, had to wait until the earliest of the cultural turns, the history workshop movement, transformed subjectivity into an asset. The contemporary history institute that accepted not only Jewish scholars but also a Jewish angle within its approach toward history was the Research Center for Contemporary History (Forschungsstelle für Zeitgeschichte) in Hamburg.[54] There was one common aspect of postwar "German contemporary history" and "Jewish contemporary history": both addressed the question, How could it happen? The answer to this question, however, was sought in different historical eras. For the "Germans," it was the failure of the Weimar Republic; for the "Jews," it was the flaws and ultimately the failure of German emancipation.

Researching and writing history is a question of sovereignty and community/nation-building. Thus the struggle over "whose heritage?" became a central issue in early postwar scholarship by German-Jewish historians writing about the recent past. For them, writing German-Jewish history, even when focusing on the most recent and painful era, was part of reclaiming their heritage and, with it, sovereignty over their own history.

NOTES

1. Wolfgang Büscher, "Die Stimmen von New York," *Die Zeit* online, 27 December 2007, accessed 31 May 2018, http://www.zeit.de/2008/01/Emigranten/seite-12. I am very grateful to the editors of this book for helping shape my argument along the way. Special thanks to Jay Geller for all his additional editorial help with this text. I am much obliged to Björn Siegel and Georg Wamhof for commenting on previous versions.

2. Prof. Marion Kaplan to Rabbi Ismar Schorsch, 25 April 2008; sent as a copy to Miriam Rürup by Marion Kaplan, 2 November 2014.

3. For the case of the library of the Jewish community of Hamburg, see Alice Jankowski, "Die Jüdische Bibliothek und Lesehalle in Hamburg. Eine Gebrauchsbibliothek als Spiegelbild jüdischen Lebens, Kultur und Geschichte der Hansestadt." (master's thesis, Humboldt Universität zu Berlin, Institut für Bibliothekswissenschaft, 2003), and Alice Jankowski, "'Bibliothek, Buch, Leser.' Zur Geschichte der Hamburger jüdischen Gemeindebibliothek," *Theresienstädter Studien und Dokumente* 12 (2005): 179–212.

4. See for this broader story Elisabeth Gallas, *"Das Leichenhaus der Bücher." Kulturrestitution und jüdisches Geschichtsdenken nach 1945* (Göttingen: Vandenhoeck & Ruprecht, 2016), esp. 34, 241f., and 140–148; and Elisabeth Gallas, "Documenting Cultural Destruction: The Research Project of the Commission on European Jewish Cultural Reconstruction, 1944–1948," in *Als der Holocaust noch keinen Namen hatte. Zur frühen Aufarbeitung des NS-Massenmordes an Jüdinnen und Juden / Before the Holocaust Had Its Name: Early Confrontations of the Nazi Mass Murder of the Jews*, ed. Regina Fritz, Éva Kovács, and Béla Rásky (Vienna: New Academic, 2016), 45–61.

5. See Peter Freimark, "Vom Hamburger Umgang mit der Geschichte einer Minderheit. Vorgeschichte und Gründung des Instituts für die Geschichte der deutschen Juden," *Zeitschrift des Vereins für Hamburgische Geschichte* 74/75 (1989): 97–108, here 104f.

6. "Damit könnte das hamburgische Institut in die praktische . . . Rolle eines deutschen Leo Baeck-Instituts hineinwachsen," in *Vermerk über die Gründung eines Instituts für die Geschichte der Juden in Deutschland*, 26 November 1962, Archive of the Institute for the History of the German Jews (henceforth, IGdJ Archive), file 02-001ff., folder 02-002, p. 3.

7. See for this also Gallas, *"Das Leichenhaus der Bücher,"* 150f. Dan Diner framed this as the Jewish "ban on Germany" (*Bann über Deutschland*). See Dan Diner, *Rituelle Distanz. Israels deutsche Frage* (Munich: Deutsche Verlags-Anstalt, 2015).

8. See for individual examples Jessica Gienow-Hecht, "Zuckerbrot und Peitsche. Die Rolle von Remigranten in der Medienpolitik der USA und der US-Zone," in *Remigranten und Remigration in den Medien der Nachkriegszeit*, ed. Axel Schildt and Claus-Dieter Krohn (Hamburg: Hans Christians, 2002), 23–49, here 30f.

9. Tobias Winstel, "'Healed Biographies'? Jewish Remigration and Indemnification for National Socialist Injustice," *Leo Baeck Institute Year Book* 49 (2004): 137–152.

10. See for this issue also Fritz Kortner's autobiography, *Aller Tage Abend. Eine Autobiographie* (Munich: Droemer Knaur, 1959), 560f.

11. See various articles in Helmut G. Asper, ed., *Wenn wir von Gestern reden, sprechen wir über Heute und Morgen. Festschrift für Marta Mierendorff zum 80. Geburtstag* (Berlin: Edition Sigma, 1991); and Schildt and Krohn, eds., *Remigranten und Remigration*. For the special case of the discussion about a "call for remigration" to Hamburg, see Ursula Büttner, "Schwierige Rückwanderung nach Hamburg. Wie Briten und Deutsche den jüdischen Flüchtlingen im Wege standen," in *"Auch in Deutschland waren wir nicht wirklich zu Hause." Jüdische Remigration nach 1945*, ed. Irmela von der Lühe, Axel Schildt, Stefanie Schüler-Springorum (Göttingen: Wallstein, 2008), 40–68, here 52.

12. Winstel, "'Healed Biographies'?," 139.

13. See, for example, Peter Mertz, *Und das wurde nicht ihr Staat. Erfahrungen emigrierter Schriftsteller mit Westdeutschland* (Munich: C. H. Beck, 1985), and Hermann Kesten, *Ich lebe nicht in der Bundesrepublik* (Munich: List, 1964).

14. For archival remnants being collected by Israeli institutions, see Inka Arroyo, "Raison d'être der Central Archives for the History of the Jewish People als virtuelles 'Staatsarchiv' der Diaspora," in *Jüdisches Archivwesen. Beiträge zum Kolloquium aus Anlass des 100. Jahrestags der Gründung des Gesamtarchivs der Deutschen Juden; zugleich 10. Archivwissenschaftliches Kolloquium der Archivschule Marburg, 13.–15. September 2005*, ed. Frank M. Bischoff and Peter Honigmann (Marburg: Archivschule, 2007), 75–96. For committees collecting Jewish traces in postwar Europe, see Elisabeth Gallas, "*Leichenhaus der Bücher*," 97ff. and 188ff.

15. See Michael Brenner, "Vergessene Historiker. Ein Kapitel deutsch-jüdischer Geschichtsschreibung der fünfziger und sechziger Jahre," in *"Auch in Deutschland waren wir nicht wirklich zu Hause." Jüdische Remigration nach 1945*, ed. Irmela von der Lühe, Axel Schildt, Stefanie Schüler-Springorum (Göttingen: Wallstein, 2008), 207–223, here 209.

16. See Monika Richarz, "Zwischen Berlin und New York. Adolf Leschnitzer—der erste Professor für jüdische Geschichte in der Bundesrepublik," in *Deutsche, Juden, Völkermord. Der Holocaust als Geschichte und Gegenwart*, ed. Jürgen Matthäus and Klaus-Michael Mallmann (Darmstadt: wbg Academic, 2006), 73–86.

17. Arno Herzig, *Judentum und Emanzipation in Westfalen* (Münster: Aschendorff, 1973).

18. See Arno Herzig, "Deutsch-jüdische Geschichte. Methodischer und inhaltlicher Wandel seit den 1960er Jahren," *Transversal* 14 (2013): 9–13. See also Eleonore Sterling, *Er ist wie du. Antisemitismus in Deutschland 1815–1950* (Munich: Chr. Kaiser, 1956), and Paul Massing, *Rehearsal for Destruction: A Study of Political Anti-Semitism in Imperial Germany* (New York: Harper, 1949) (German translation 1959); Eva G. Reichmann, *Hostages of Civilisation: the Social Sources of National Socialist Anti-Semitism* (London: Gollancz, 1950). On Eva Reichmann, see Kirsten Heinsohn, "Diaspora as Possibility and Task—The Plea of a German-Jewish Woman," in *Diaspora Identities: Exile, Nationalism and Cosmopolitanism in Past and Present*, ed. Kirsten Heinsohn and Susanne Lachenicht (Frankfurt: Campus, 2009), 130–147; and Kirsten Heinsohn, "'Also, ich bin eine Deutsche nicht mehr, eine Engländerin werde ich nie sein.' Erfahrungen und Deutungen einer emigrierten Wissenschaftlerin. Beitrag zum Themenschwerpunkt 'Europäische Geschichte–Geschlechtergeschichte,'" *Themenportal Europäische Geschichte* (2009), www.europa.clio-online.de/essay/id/fdae-1494.

19. However, Jews expressed a similar view—namely, that Germans, as former perpetrators, naturally could not judge history objectively. Norbert Wollheim, *Zum 9. November 1948. Rede an die Jüdische Gemeinde Hamburg auf der Gedenkstunde zum zehnten Jahrestag des Beginns der Pogrome in Deutschland*, ed. Central Committee of Liberated Jews in the British Zone (Bergen-Belsen: Unzer Sztyme, 1948), 7.

20. Hans Lamm, "Über die innere und äussere Entwicklung des deutschen Judentums im Dritten Reich" (PhD diss., Universität Erlangen, 1951).

21. Verband Deutscher Studentenschaften, Ekkehart Krippendorff, and Dieter Bielenstein, eds., *Erziehungswesen und Judentum. Die Darstellung des Judentums in der Lehrerbildung und im Schulunterricht* (Munich: Ner-Tamid-Verlag, 1960). On the case of Lamm, see Andrea Sinn, *"Und ich lebe wieder an der Isar." Exil und Rückkehr des Münchner Juden Hans Lamm* (Munich: Oldenbourg, 2008), and Brenner, "Vergessene Historiker," 215.

22. Klaus Kempter, *Joseph Wulf. Ein Historikerschicksal in Deutschland* (Göttingen: Vandenhoeck & Ruprecht, 2013), and Nicolas Berg, *Der Holocaust und die westdeutschen Historiker. Erforschung und Erinnerung* (Göttingen: Wallstein, 2003).

23. Reinhard Rürup, "An Appraisal of German-Jewish Historiography," *Leo Baeck Institute Year Book* 25 (1990): xviii–xix.

24. For the character and richness of the material, see, for example, Ina Lorenz, "Editorische Bermerkungen," *Die Juden in Hamburg zur Zeit der Weimarer Republik. Eine Dokumentation*, vol. 1 (Hamburg: Hans Christians, 1987), v–vii, and Jürgen Sielemann, "Hamburger

Gemeindeakten im Staatsarchiv Hamburg," in *Jüdisches Archivwesen. Beiträge zum Kolloquium aus Anlass des 100. Jahrestags der Gründung des Gesamtarchivs der Deutschen Juden; zugleich 10. Archivwissenschaftliches Kolloquium der Archivschule Marburg, 13.–15. September 2005*, ed. Frank M. Bischoff and Peter Honigmann (Marburg: Archivschule, 2007), 97–110.

25. Denise Rein, "Die Bestände der ehemaligen jüdischen Gemeinden Deutschlands in den Central Archives for the History of the Jewish People in Jerusalem. Ein Überblick über das Schicksal der verschiedenen Gemeindearchive," *Der Archivar* 55, no. 4 (2002): 318–327. For the case of Hamburg, see Björn Siegel, "Verworrene Wege. Die Gründungsphase des IGdJ," in *50 Jahre, 50 Quellen. Festschrift zum Jubiläum des Instituts für die Geschichte der deutschen Juden*, ed. Institut für die Geschichte der deutschen Juden (Hamburg: Institut für die Geschichte der deutschen Juden, 2016), 26–53, esp. 29, and Arroyo, "Raison d'être," in *Jüdisches Archivwesen*, 82ff.

26. Arroyo, "Raison d'être," in *Jüdisches Archivwesen*, 77ff.; Robert Jütte, "Der Beitrag deutsch-jüdischer Einwanderer zum Aufbau eines Archivwesens in Israel," *Der Archivar* 43, no. 3 (1990): 396–414, here 396ff.

27. For this, see Siegel, "Verworrene Wege," in *50 Jahre, 50 Quellen*, 30–34. This echoes an observation by Dan Diner in his book on the Luxembourg Accords in 1951: Whereas every party spoke English or Hebrew during official negotiations, when off the record, they quickly reverted to their common German. Dan Diner, *Rituelle Distanz*.

28. In the meantime, the role of Hertz as the "savior" of the Hamburg archive is being critically reassessed. Currently, Jonas Stier is working on an MA thesis about Hertz's role in the conflict surrounding Hamburg's Jewish heritage ("Hans W. Hertz und die fotografische Dokumentation jüdischer Friedhöfe. Akteure, Motive und Netzwerke in Hamburg, 1937–1960"). See also Jürgen Sielemann, "Skrupellose Denunziation. Die personenkundliche Arbeit des Staatsarchivs Hamburg im 'Dritten Reich,'" *Der Archivar* 70, no. 3 (2017): 385–390; and Gunnar B. Zimmermann, "Hertz, Hans W.," in *Hamburgische Biografie*, ed. Franklin Kopitzsch and Dirk Brietzke, vol. 6 (Göttingen: Wallstein, 2012), 125–127. For Hertz's position, see also his memorandum on the founding of the Arbeitsgemeinschaft für die Geschichte der Juden in Hamburg, 15 August 1953, IGdJ Archive, file 02-001ff., folder 02-002.

29. For the German-Jewish supporters of keeping the material in Germany, see Sielemann, "Hamburger Gemeindeakten," in *Jüdisches Archivwesen*, 102.

30. For a critical view, see Rein, "Die Bestände der ehemaligen jüdischen Gemeinden Deutschlands," 323.

31. "Die Geschichte der Juden in Hamburg und die Geschichte der deutschen Juden überhaupt ist beendet. Für einen echten und lebendigen Neuanfang fehlt jede Voraussetzung." A. Landsberg, Jewish Trust Corporation, 1955, in "Schreiben vom 19.12.1955," in STH, 133-1III, 215-1/4/2, vol. 1, quoted in Sielemann, "Hamburger Gemeindeakten," in *Jüdisches Archivwesen*, 102.

32. In the words of Jewish Historical General Archives director Daniel J. Cohen, himself originally from Hamburg: "similar to the 'Ingathering of the Exiles,' the nation's archives are ingathered, in order to preserve for the people the memory of their past." Daniel J. Cohen, *The Jewish Historical General Archives* (Jerusalem: Central Press, 1964), 1.

33. Also in Worms the saved materials were microfilmed. See Rein, "Die Bestände der ehemaligen jüdischen Gemeinden Deutschlands," 325.

34. On this division, see the files in the State Archive of Hamburg (StAHH) on the collection 522-1 and the respective locating aid.

35. See Freimark, "Vom Hamburger Umgang," 103.

36. For the history of the institute and its theological focus on missionizing among the Jews, see Karl Heinrich Rengstorf, "85 Jahre Institutum Judaicum Delitzschianum," in *Zeugnis für Zion. Festschrift zur 100-Jahrfeier des Evangelisch-Lutherischen Zentralvereins für Mission unter Israel e. V.*, ed. Reinhard Dobbert (Erlangen: Verlag der Ev.-Luth. Mission, 1971), 30–68.

37. For a detailed account of this process, see Siegel, "Verworrene Wege," in *50 Jahre, 50 Quellen*, 34–44.

38. Erich Lüth to Dr. von Heppe, Hamburg, 17 January 1964, IGdJ Archive, file 47-033ff., folder 47-035. For a more detailed account of this specific debate and more details on Rengstorf, such as his involvement in National Socialism, see Siegel, "Verworrene Wege," in *50 Jahre, 50 Quellen*, 41–43.

39. As an example, the case study of Selma Stern, who fled to the U.S. in 1941 and stayed there as a scholar in the context of the Leo Baeck Institute in New York. Irene Aue-Ben-David, *Deutsch-jüdische Geschichtsschreibung im 20. Jahrhundert. Zu Werk und Rezeption von Selma Stern* (Göttingen: Vandenhoeck & Ruprecht, 2017).

40. His academic mentor, Hamburg historian Fritz Fischer (1908–1999), was well known for the international controversy surrounding his study on the causes of the outbreak of the First World War. On Fritz Fischer, see Rainer Nicolaysen, "Rebell wider Willen? Fritz Fischer und die Geschichte eines nationalen Tabubruchs," in *100 Jahre Geschichtswissenschaft in Hamburg*, ed. Rainer Nicolaysen and Axel Schildt (Berlin: Reimer, 2011), 197–236.

41. See Berg, *Der Holocaust und die westdeutschen Historiker*. See also Yfaat Weiss, "Kann es zu viel Geschichte geben?," in *Jüdische Geschichtsschreibung heute. Themen, Positionen, Kontroversen*, ed. Michael Brenner and David N. Myers (Munich: C. H. Beck, 2002), 229–246, here 236.

42. See Ulrich Herbert, "Deutsche und jüdische Geschichtsschreibung über den Holocaust," in *Jüdische Geschichtsschreibung heute*, 247–258, here 250.

43. Ursula Büttner, "Die Forschungsstelle für die Geschichte des Nationalsozialismus in Hamburg," *Zeitschrift des Vereins für Hamburgische Geschichte* 74/75 (1989): 81–96.

44. See Stefanie Schüler-Springorum, "Werner Jochmann und die deutsch-jüdische Geschichte," and "Werner Jochmann—ein Rückblick zum zehnten Todestag," *Zeitgeschichte in Hamburg 2004 [Jahresbericht der Forschungsstelle für Zeitgeschichte in Hamburg]* (Hamburg: Forschungsstelle für Zeitgeschichte in Hamburg, 2005), 14–20, and 11–13.

45. See Schüler-Springorum, "Jochmann," in *Zeitgeschichte in Hamburg 2004*, 16. She points out that Cohen even accused Graupe of plagiarism. Daniel Cohen, who was one of the two protagonists fighting for a transfer of the Jewish community files from Hamburg to Israel (along with Alex Bein), became a close friend of Jochmann.

46. In German: *böswillig entstellte Bild der Juden*. "Hamburg in der jüdischen Geschichte. Eröffnung des neuen Instituts," *Mitteilungsblatt des Irgun Olej Merkaz Europa*, 20 May 1966.

47. See Peter Freimark, "Das Institut für die Geschichte der deutschen Juden (Hamburg) und die deutsch-jüdische Geschichtswissenschaft heute," *Revue d'Allemagne* 13, no. 3 (1981): 589–596, here 593. See also Peter Freimark, "Geschichtswissenschaft und Schulbucharbeit. Ergebnisse, Tendenzen und Folgerungen am Beispiel der deutsch-jüdischen Geschichte (18.-20. Jh)," *Internationale Schulbuchforschung. Zeitschrift des Georg Eckert Instituts* 2 (1980): 11–37.

48. In German: "Lehrmeister der Menschheit." Wollheim, *Zum 9*, 4.

49. In German: ". . . , daß nicht zuletzt mit dem 9. November 1938 uns Juden in Deutschland unsere Geschichte genommen wurde, an der wie im alten Köln schon vor fast 1.600 Jahren unsere Vorfahren gebaut haben." Wollheim, *Zum 9*, 13.

50. See Stefan Rohrbacher, "Jüdische Geschichte," in *Wissenschaft vom Judentum. Annäherungen nach dem Holocaust*, ed. Stefan Rohrbacher and Michael Brenner (Göttingen: Vandenhoeck & Ruprecht, 2000), 164–176, here 166.

51. Heinz Mosche Graupe, *Die Entstehung des Modernen Judentums: Geistesgeschichte der Deutschen Juden, 1650–1942* (Hamburg: Leibniz-Verlag, 1969); English translation: *The Rise of Modern Judaism. An Intellectual History of German Jewry, 1650–1942*, trans. John Robinson (Huntington, N.Y.: R. E. Krieger, 1983).

52. Universitätsarchiv Hamburg (UAH), collection 105a Präsidentinnen und Präsidenten, no. 1. On honorary degrees at the University of Hamburg in general, see Angelika Schaser,

"Gabentausch. Eine Geschlechtergeschichte der Ehrenpromotionen von 1919 bis 1989 am Beispiel der Hamburger Universität," *Jahrbuch für Universitätsgeschichte* 20 (2017): 145–176.

53. On the importance of the History Workshop movement on German-Jewish contemporary history, see Beate Meyer, "Von der Alltagsgeschichte und der oral history zur deutsch-jüdischen Geschichte," *Transversal* 14 (2013): 14–28.

54. Another major research, the Institute for Contemporary History (Institut für Zeitgeschichte) in Munich, was founded in 1949. For the special role of the Jewish historian Joseph Wulf at this institute, see Berg, *Der Holocaust und die westdeutschen Historiker*, and Kempter, *Joseph Wulf*, 158.

CHAPTER 5

MIGRATION, MEMORY, AND NEW BEGINNINGS

THE POSTWAR JEWISH COMMUNITY IN FRANKFURT AM MAIN

Tobias Freimüller

In May 1957, the Jewish Community in Frankfurt am Main celebrated the ninth anniversary of the founding of the State of Israel. The ceremony took place in the Westend Synagogue, named after its location in the Westend quarter, which had been a predominantly Jewish neighborhood before 1933. Invited to give the main speech was Georg Salzberger, the former Liberal rabbi in the Westend Synagogue. Salzberger had been arrested after Kristallnacht in November 1938 and spent five months in the Dachau concentration camp near Munich. Afterward, he could leave Germany and went to London, where he became cofounder of a German-Jewish community in exile. Almost twenty years later, he still worked as a rabbi in London. For the postwar Jewish community in Frankfurt, Salzberger was an important figure. He personified a continuity of Jewish history in Frankfurt between the prewar era and the postwar period. Even if this continuity did not actually exist, it was extremely important for the founders of the postwar Jewish community that it be regarded as a successor to the older Jewish community.

Georg Salzberger gave his speech in the very same synagogue in which he had served as a rabbi for twenty-seven years, but he spoke to an audience that knew little or nothing about the local Jewish history. The Jewish community that Salzberger had been part of since 1910 had been almost completely expelled and annihilated between 1933 and 1945. Salzberger was aware of that paradoxical setting. The Jewish people remained a nation (*ein Volk*) unaffected by its geographical fragmentation, he declared. They were linked together as a consequence of their segregation by the Christians, because of their own self-concept, and because of the Bible. The Jewish nation now found a homeland in the State of Israel; it should find another homeland in its religious faith. Religion, said Salzberger, quoting Heinrich Heine, is a "portable homeland" for the Jews.[1]

Of course, Salzberger did not mention West Germany or the city of Frankfurt as a homeland for Jews. Jews all over the world strongly opposed any renewal of Jewish life in Germany after World War II and the Holocaust. However, a small group of Jews decided—for very different reasons—to stay in the "land of the perpetrators" and on the "bloodstained soil of Germany."[2] Many of them chose to live in Frankfurt. Their story is one of migration, memory, and new beginnings.

Migration

As a percentage of the overall population, Frankfurt am Main had been the most Jewish city in Germany. At the end of the Weimar Republic, about 5 percent of the total population in Frankfurt had been Jewish. Nationwide, only about 1 percent of the Germans was Jewish. The city was home to four synagogues, three Jewish schools, a Jewish orphanage, and numerous recreation homes and old people's homes before 1933. Moreover, there were approximately five hundred Jewish associations and foundations in Frankfurt. Probably the most prominent among them was the Institute for Social Research, founded by Felix Weil in 1923, at the University of Frankfurt. In 1933, Jews owned seventeen of the twenty-three department stores in Frankfurt. They played an important role in banking houses and at the Frankfurt stock exchange. The Free House of Jewish Learning (Freies Jüdisches Lehrhaus), founded by Franz Rosenzweig in 1920, offered adult education courses taught by Martin Buber, Siegfried Kracauer, and Erich Fromm, among many others.

Like Georg Salzberger, most Jewish men in Frankfurt were arrested after the November pogroms in 1938. Three of the four synagogues were destroyed. In 1941 and 1942, most of the Jews still living in the city—more than nine thousand people—were deported to the east. Less than two hundred of them survived. At the end of the year 1943, only 602 Jews still lived in Frankfurt, mostly in mixed marriages with non-Jewish partners. The majority of them, however, were also deported before the end of the war. When American troops arrived at the end of March 1945, a correspondent from the Jewish Telegraphic Agency (JTA) counted 106 Jews, most of them women, who lived in the ruins of the widely destroyed city.[3] Three weeks later, the newspaper *Aufbau* wrote that "less than one hundred" Jews remained in Frankfurt, though it also printed an index of one hundred and sixty "Jews in Frankfurt/M" in the same issue.[4]

When the Jewish community was re-created, its founding fathers were Jews of German origin who had survived because they lived in mixed marriages and could somehow evade the last deportations in early 1945. Some had lived in hiding for a while, including Max L. Cahn. Some survived in concentration camps and came back to Frankfurt after the liberation. About 350 Jews from Frankfurt survived in the concentration camp of Theresienstadt, and 336 of them returned to their hometown in June and July 1945.[5] Among them was Max Meyer, a merchandiser and former factory owner in Frankfurt. He was elected as the first chairman of the Jewish community. Returning from Theresienstadt was also Leopold Neuhaus, a former rabbi in Frankfurt who had been deported in 1942.

Cahn, Meyer, Neuhaus, and others did not build a new Jewish community; they wanted to continue the existence of the old one, which had only been disrupted during the Third Reich. Max L. Cahn stated, "The community is not the successor, it still exists."[6] Their hopes to establish new Jewish life and to renew the local community seemed to come true when several survivors from Buchenwald, Bergen-Belsen, and other liberated concentration camps returned to Frankfurt during the year 1945. In the summer of 1946, about 650 Jews were living in the city, and roughly half of them were actually "old Frankfurters." But this percentage was on the decline. By early 1947, only 30 percent of the members of the Jewish community originally came from Frankfurt.[7] The number of returnees was low, and it made little difference when Mayor Walter Kolb used his New Year's speech for 1947 to call for the expelled and deported Jews from Frankfurt to come back.

"We all know," Kolb declared, "that Frankfurt became rich and huge not least because of the work and the achievements of its Jewish fellow citizens. An unutterable flow of blessing and beneficence came from them. And I can only simply utter the hope and the appeal that some of the old Jewish Frankfurters who are still, in their hearts, citizens of our city to ask themselves seriously whether they want to return—in spite of all hardships and distrust. We promise wholeheartedly to welcome you, and we solemnly assure you to do our best to make you feel comfortable in your old hometown."[8] Kolb's statement was a very unusual move given the political climate in Germany at that time. While most Germans strongly insisted on bringing an end to denazification and saw themselves as the victims of both Hitler and the Allied occupation, it seemed to be extremely unpopular to call back the surviving victims to live among former perpetrators.

The vast majority of Jews coming to Frankfurt after the war were not former Frankfurters anyway. They were not even German Jews, but rather displaced persons (DPs) from Eastern Europe. For those survivors who wanted to immigrate to America or to Palestine as soon as possible, the U.S. occupation zone on German territory appeared as an "extraterritorial America."[9] Especially Frankfurt, the leading city in the German state of Hessen and the place where the American forces set up their headquarters in defeated Germany, appeared to be a safe haven for Jewish DPs. In Zeilsheim, a suburb of Frankfurt, a camp exclusively for Jewish DPs was established. During the three years of its existence, more than four thousand Jewish refugees lived in the Zeilsheim camp.

In the huge camp, a variety of Jewish institutions developed. The DPs had access not only to a provisional synagogue and a preschool but also to a secondary school, a vocational school, and a rabbinical school. A "people's university" even offered academic education. Outside the camp, a huge black market flourished and became a very controversial subject. The black market caused conflicts between the inhabitants of Zeilsheim, German police, American troops, and Jewish DPs for several years. The presence of the U.S. Army not only made the city of Frankfurt into the most "American" place in Germany but also had a strong influence on Jewish life in the entire area. When the first religious service was held in the Westend Synagogue in September 1945, the number of American soldiers attending was three times higher than the number of surviving Jews.

The founders of the postwar Jewish community quickly realized that they would not be able to reestablish Jewish life without—or even against—the Jewish DPs, who were mainly from Eastern Europe. They insisted on the historical continuity between the prewar Jewish community and the new Jewish community in Frankfurt. At the same time, however, Cahn, Neuhaus, and the other community leaders did not create organizational structures that would prohibit the DPs from becoming members of the Jewish community. Any open exclusion of DPs would have surely displeased not only Jews all over the world but also American officials in Frankfurt, who saw themselves as protectors of the Holocaust survivors and refugees.

For the time being, the DPs founded a "committee of liberated Jews in Frankfurt" in May 1946 and generally did not join the Frankfurt Jewish community. Therefore, community leaders did not face the dilemma of whether to openly exclude DPs. When most DPs finally left Germany after the foundation of the State of Israel and the passage of the Displaced Persons Act in the United States in June 1948, the so-called committee found its membership dramatically reduced. In 1949, the Jewish community officially incorporated the DP committee and its remaining members. With this fusion, the Jewish community became one of the "typical German–East European communities" that could also be found in other large cities in the Federal Republic of Germany.[10] In 1955, the new united community had 1,378 members, and its leaders assumed that approximately four hundred Jews lived in Frankfurt without being members of the community. When new statutes were enacted in 1955, it was stated that every Jew moving to Frankfurt would be automatically registered as a member of the Jewish community.[11] Even though former DPs easily outnumbered the members of German origin, leadership of the Jewish community was still dominated by German Jews. Among them, the group of "old Frankfurters" was vanishingly small.

In the late 1950s, about twenty-five thousand Jews lived in West Germany—roughly 5 percent of the Jewish population in Germany before 1933.[12] One in six of them lived in Frankfurt. The Jewish community in Frankfurt was not the largest Jewish community in the Federal Republic, but Frankfurt was often considered the most Jewish city in West Germany.[13] The notion of a "Jewish Frankfurt" referred to the city's prewar history, but it also made sense regarding the postwar period. Beginning with the foundation of the Deutsche Bundesbank's forerunner, the Bank of the German States (Bank deutscher Länder), in Frankfurt, the city had become the center of the West German financial system. The traditional fur trade business moved from Leipzig (located in the Soviet occupation zone) to Frankfurt. Since Frankfurt, thanks to its huge airport and its central location, was a transportation hub in the western part of Germany, the city also became the most important place for trade fairs.

The city's economic growth since the early 1950s provided opportunities, especially for businesses founded by immigrants.[14] Although Jews certainly could not continue their prewar economic success story in Frankfurt, the city offered better prospects than either Berlin or Munich. In the mid-1950s, the U.S. Army alone spent twenty to twenty-five million marks per month in Frankfurt. Many Jewish DPs were able to establish commercial firms, especially draper's shops, while others became the owners of bars and dance halls near the U.S. military bases. Word on the street was that the entire area around Frankfurt's main train station was in the hands of "the Jews." The real estate market was another field of activity for those who were ready to assume a risk. The city council, willing to rebuild the extensively bombed city as quickly as possible, projected ambitious urban expansion. Banks allowed easy credit to purchase real property. In this situation, courageous stakeholders were needed, "people who act fast, having no connection to the historic environment."[15]

In 1956, Hendrik van Dam, secretary general of the Central Council of Jews in Germany, stated, "Germany is no immigration country and no country of remigration for Jews."[16] In fact, the Federal Republic saw a wave of Jewish immigration, especially from Israel, beginning in the mid-1950s. Some came to retire; many had not been able to establish themselves in Israel and decided to return to their home country. A West German compensation law from 1956 ensured six thousand deutsche marks in "immediate aid" to all Jewish victims of the National Socialist regime. As a result, the number of members of the Jewish community in Frankfurt nearly doubled between 1956 and 1959 alone. At the same time, 14 percent of the Jewish community's members left Frankfurt, most of them probably leaving Germany for Israel or the United States. Overall, Frankfurt saw the highest fluctuation of Jewish population in West Germany.[17]

Notwithstanding the fact that the Jewish community had dramatically changed after 1945 as a result of economic growth and constant migration, Jewish community officials still insisted on its connection with the prewar community. This was the most substantial argument in its dispute with the Jewish Restitution Successor Organization (JRSO). The JRSO had the task of collecting the ownerless Jewish property in order to transfer it to the European Jews in exile. After long negotiations between the JRSO and the city of Frankfurt concerning the properties of the prewar Jewish community, city officials agreed to restitute fourteen properties originally owned by the prewar Jewish community to the postwar Jewish community. Moreover, the city of Frankfurt handled all claims of compensation by paying 3.2 million deutsche marks to the Jewish community. This payment rehabilitated the finances of the community and made it possible to establish a youth club in 1958 and an elementary school in 1966. Almost two thirds of the annual budget of the Jewish community was spent for social purposes, mostly for a home for the elderly.

"A new community arose from the ruins," the local newspaper *Frankfurter Rundschau* stated in 1953. "In 1943, this history seemed to be destroyed," it continued, but hard work created a Jewish community that could carry on the traditions of all the old Jewish communities in Frankfurt. In fact, the Frankfurt Jewish community had been going through a process of economic stabilization in the early 1950s. In 1951, a Central Welfare Center of the Jews in Germany was established, Jewish loan associations helped in setting up businesses, and the restitution of Jewish property began. In late 1949, 701 out of 752 male members of the Jewish community had been employed. In 1955, 35 percent of all male community members were self-employed, and 20 percent were public servants, employees, or workers. By contrast, however, the remaining 40 percent were retirees or unemployed. "Moreover," stated the *Frankfurter Rundschau*, "there is mental stress. Many of these people live in fear."[18]

Memory

When Georg Salzberger, a former rabbi of the prewar Jewish community of Frankfurt, gave his aforementioned speech in the Westend Synagogue in May 1957, he did not openly address the fear and horror that most people in the audience had experienced. The Holocaust was no subject of discussion. Salzberger also did not discuss the fact that his listeners had stayed in Germany rather than immigrate to Israel, the homeland for the Jewish people. He could not refer to the Jewish history of Frankfurt either, since most of the members of the Jewish community came to the city only after 1945. Memories of the Holocaust were repressed, and memories of the local history were nonexistent for most of the Jews in the city. This made the notion of religion as a "portable homeland" for Jews the only point of reference that Georg Salzberger could share with his audience.

Yet in public speeches about German-Jewish matters, politicians throughout not only Frankfurt but also the Federal Republic again and again evoked a German-Jewish past. They appreciated the enormous contribution Jews had made to Germany overall or to their respective cities or regions. One of the most common rhetorical tropes was the "loss" Germany had suffered when Jewish "fellow citizens" (*Mitbürger*) were expelled after 1933. The city of Frankfurt did in fact try to renew and rebuild Jewish life more than usual. Walter Kolb's previously mentioned New Year's address was only one initiative taken by German cities' officials.

After 1945, municipal authorities restored property that used to be in possession of the Jewish community in an unusually nonbureaucratic manner. From 1946 on, the city of Frankfurt, the state of Hessen, and the University of Frankfurt took great efforts to reestablish the Institute for Social Research in Frankfurt. It took some effort to convince Max Horkheimer to return to Germany, but in 1950 the institute was refounded as a sociology school closely linked to the Faculty of Philosophy at the university.[19] Since the foundational assets had been lost in exile, the city of Frankfurt and the state of Hessen provided the institute's basic funding. Max Horkheimer was appointed not only a full professor but also the rector of the University of Frankfurt. With Horkheimer, Oscar Ganz, and Fritz Neumark, the university chose three Jewish rectors between 1951 and 1955.

Max Horkheimer and Theodor W. Adorno, who followed Horkheimer from California to Frankfurt, not only dominated the city's intellectual sphere but also rose to "intellectual leading figures and icons of the Federal Republic."[20] And they were not the only Jewish intellectuals in Frankfurt after the war. The literary critic and author Hans Mayer, for example, was the leader of Radio Frankfurt's political department and campaigned for the local Communist Party branch, which organized lectures and other cultural events in cooperation with the Association of Victims of the Nazi Regime (Vereinigung der Verfolgten des Naziregimes, or VVN). At the same time, the author Stephan Hermlin led the cultural department of Radio Frankfurt, the forerunner of Hessischer Rundfunk. The historian Golo Mann came to Frankfurt as an officer of the U.S. Army. In 1956, the lawyer Fritz Bauer became attorney general of the state of Hessen. Bauer, who initiated the first Frankfurt Auschwitz Trial (1963–1965) and helped find Adolf Eichmann in Argentina, was promoted by the prime minister of Hessen, Georg August Zinn of the Social Democratic Party. Zinn wanted to turn Hessen into a model social democratic state and a socialist bastion against the conservative federal government led by Chancellor Konrad Adenauer. Frankfurt became the center of this network of leftist and critical intellectuals. Nowhere else in the young federal republic could so many personal and intellectual connections be found to the lost German-Jewish world of the Weimar Republic.

In this respect, Frankfurt was the place where memories of a Jewish past in Germany were much more present than anywhere else in West Germany. Strongly connected to this Jewish tradition were those of Freud and psychoanalysis. Beginning in the early 1960s, the psychoanalyst Alexander Mitscherlich, who founded the Sigmund Freud Institute, brought (mostly Jewish) psychoanalysts to Frankfurt who had left Germany after 1933. Not one of them, in fact, remigrated to Germany, but many came regularly to train young prospective German psychoanalysts.[21] A third connection to the intellectual sphere of the Weimar

Republic was Marxism. Indeed Marxism, psychoanalysis, and critical thought were blended together into "critical theory" and could be studied at the Institute for Social Research. Seminars and lectures held by Adorno, Horkheimer, and others inspired more than one generation of German students since the early 1950s and had a strong impact on the students' movement in the 1960s.

Such intellectual ties and memories did re-create a certain sphere of critical political and intellectual thought in Frankfurt with which many Jewish scholars could easily associate themselves. This specific intellectual sphere in Frankfurt during the early decades of the Federal Republic had almost no connection, however, to the lives of the members of the official Jewish community.

On 19 February 1951, the files of the Jewish community listed a new member: Max Horkheimer, born 14 February 1895 in Stuttgart, moved from America to Westendstraße 69 in Frankfurt, and having the profession "university professor." The Jewish community quickly learned that Horkheimer was an influential person who had and would continue to play "an important role in public life and in Jewish life."[22] Whenever possible, Horkheimer appeared in public lectures and discussions organized by the Jewish community. In January 1955, he took part in a roundtable discussion with two representatives of the Jewish community on the "cultural duties of Jewish communities." In November 1955 he gave a lecture on "prejudice," held in the auditorium of the Philantropin, the oldest and biggest Jewish school in Germany, which had been closed in 1942. When Horkheimer agreed to give a talk—on, for example, "The contributions of Judaism to the European culture"—the Jewish community asked all Jewish owners of restaurants and bars to promote the event and to tell their guests about it.

Horkheimer, however, could only sporadically take part in the life and activities of the Jewish community. In 1961, he wrote a letter to the community's directorate: "Dear Sirs, please excuse the delay in my answer to your friendly telegram on my birthday on 14 February. I returned from America only a few days ago, where I took part in the German-American consultations [*Freundschaftsgespräch*]. I was wholeheartedly pleased with your compliments. Unfortunately, during the last couple of years I could not stay in contact with the Jewish community in the way I would like to because I had to leave Frankfurt very often. Since my last journey was about Jewish matters, I hope you understand the reason."[23] Horkheimer's "Jewish matters"—that is, his close connections to the American Jewish Committee (AJC) and other international Jewish organizations—again did not affect the Jewish community in Frankfurt at all.

Not surprisingly, there were discussion contacts between Frankfurt and Jewish organizations abroad. The AJC, for example, preferred to correspond with government offices in Bonn or with important figures such as Bundestag representative Jakob Altmaier, lawyer Robert Kempner, professor and journalist Eugen Kogon, or Max Horkheimer rather than discuss Jewish matters with the Central Council of Jews in Germany. Isaac Emil Lichtigfeld, state rabbi of Hessen and a rabbi in Frankfurt from 1954 to 1967, was seen as "one of the outstanding rabbinical personalities of Europe," as the AJC noted. The American Jewish Joint Distribution Committee (JDC), for example, heard about plans to move the Central Council's headquarters from Düsseldorf to Cologne "from our loyal friends in the Hessian Landesverband, Dr. Alschoff and Mr. Willner."[24]

When Jewish institutions in New York wanted to learn more about the anti-Semitic incidents that happened all over the Federal Republic of Germany in early 1960, starting with an attack on the synagogue in Cologne on Christmas Eve 1959, they turned to the Institute of Social Research in Frankfurt. Horkheimer's institute carried out a quick pilot study on anti-Semitism. Whereas Max Horkheimer did not find much time to stay in contact with the Jewish community in Frankfurt, he was in constant exchange with the AJC, and he wrote letters and provided estimates of the political situation in West Germany. In the 1960s, he also organized "study trips" to the United States, which enabled West German opinion shapers in the fields of media, education, and politics to get to know not only about America itself but also about democracy and education methods.

In October 1955 the former German emigrant Hans Wallenberg took a trip to West Germany financed by the Ford Foundation. From Frankfurt he reported to America that the number of prominent Jewish personalities was not large but that all of them were highly regarded. Jewish university professors, in particular, had "a loyal and even enthusiastic following." The sixty-fifth birthday of actor Ernst Deutsch had been widely celebrated, and the conductor Georg Solti was the musical director of the Frankfurt Opera. When Martin Buber received the city's Goethe Prize in 1953, bookstores all over Frankfurt displayed his portrait in their shop windows. Prominent Jews, Wallenberg wrote, "are not only welcomed into the German community but any indication that they consider themselves part of that community is received with great satisfaction."[25] Then again, everyday lives of ordinary Jewish inhabitants of Frankfurt mostly had no connection to these spheres of Jewish intellectualism and local notables.

The vast majority of members of the Jewish community, who had come to Frankfurt after 1945, could not come to terms with the city's history—to speak nothing of Frankfurt's Jewish tradition. When efforts were made to link Jewish life in postwar Frankfurt to the city's Jewish history or to get in contact with Jewish Frankfurters in exile, it was the city council that provided that impetus, not the Jewish community. In 1961, a Research Commission for the History of Frankfurt Jewry was established. This institution's origins went back to a suggestion from the circle around Georg Salzberger in London. In the early 1960s, when city officials tried to find out more about the Jews expelled from Frankfurt after 1933, the Jewish community could not provide any information. To track down former Frankfurters, ads were placed in American and Israeli newspapers. Starting in the early 1980s, the city of Frankfurt invited its former Jewish citizens to visit their hometown and financed their trips from abroad. Again, this initiative did not come from the Jewish community.

In Frankfurt, very few people were able and willing to keep alive local Jewish memory. More than anyone, it was Paul Arnsberg, who personified the Jewish history of prewar Frankfurt. This journalist and publisher returned from exile in Palestine and Israel in 1958. He quickly became an important writer for national newspapers such as the *Frankfurter Allgemeine Zeitung*, and at the same time, he became a member of the Jewish community's managing committee. Arnsberg, who started to write several books on Frankfurt's Jewish history up to 1933, stood alone in his orientation toward local Jewish tradition, which he always combined with the hope for a self-confident Jewry in postwar Germany.

Officially, the Jewish community did not find its point of reference in the history of prewar Jewish life. Instead, its point of reference was Israel, the new homeland for Jews from all over the world. It was a paradox to see Jews living in Frankfurt who, apparently and for very different reasons, did not comply with the clear expectations of international Jewish institutions to leave Germany. On the contrary—West Germany saw increasing immigration from Israel in the second half of the 1950s. Between April 1955 and December 1958 alone, around 840 Jews from Israel came to Frankfurt, and very few of them had lived there ever before. At the same time, about 15 percent of the community members left the city. Therefore the Jewish population in Frankfurt was subject to a strong fluctuation of immigration and emigration, and since the late 1950s, a relatively large group of Jews with Israeli backgrounds formed a third relevant group alongside German Jews and former Eastern European Jewish DPs. The Jewish community in Frankfurt became an international community. In the late 1950s, it had about 2,400 members, and the number continued to grow to about 5,000 in later years. This growth of the Jewish population required the expansion of the city's Jewish infrastructure—that is, the establishment of as a youth club, an elementary school, and a new home for the elderly as noted above.

Israel, however, did remain the focus of many if not all cultural and educational programs set up by the Jewish community. Israel as a shared orientation, as a source of identity, or as an "*Identitätsersatz*," as Dan Diner puts it, was to bridge all gaps within the Frankfurt community itself. The ties to Israel were also very close insofar as Jews in West Germany gave more money per head in financial assistance to Israel than any other Diaspora community, as Anthony Kauders has shown. In Frankfurt, this led to bizarre practices in collecting funds that reached the point where the community passed a resolution in 1969 that asked those members who donated to the solidarity fund 1. "not to accept any invitation to social events (organized) by persons who did not participate in the Solidarity Action of 1968, 2. not to request these people's company, 3. not to attend gatherings to which these persons have been invited."[26]

Other than Israel, Jewish religion also could have been a source of collective identity, but this turned out to be challenging. The first rabbi in Frankfurt after the war was Leopold Neuhaus. Since he had been the last rabbi before the war, Neuhaus stood for the continuity of Jewish life in Frankfurt as no one else. But already he resigned in 1946 and immigrated to America. "There is not much left of the old Frankfurt," he said. "Many unknown people live here, who do not know Frankfurt, and Frankfurt does not know them."[27] It took the Jewish community two years to find a rabbi who was willing to come to Germany. In 1948, Wilhelm Weinberg, originally from Galicia, was appointed as Neuhaus's successor. Only three years later Weinberg, deeply frustrated at seeing former Nazis returning to key positions, left Germany with "bitterness."[28] His successor, Zwi Harry Levy, also stayed merely two years in Frankfurt.

Under these circumstances, rebuilding Jewish religious life was extremely difficult. Only in 1954, when Isaac Emil Lichtigfeld took the position as rabbi in Frankfurt, did the Jewish community see a stabilization of its religious life.[29] Lichtigfeld, born in Galicia but raised in Germany, was a stroke of luck and a figure of integration because he could talk to the "German" members of the Jewish community as well as to the former DPs from Eastern Europe. To enhance religious practice, Lichtigfeld broke with tradition in 1956 and no longer followed the historic religious rite specific to Frankfurt, the Frankfurt *minhag*. Instead, he arranged the service closer to traditions from Eastern Europe. Lichtigfeld was heavily criticized for this move, but he maintained the chosen course to reach out demonstratively to the former Eastern European Jewish DPs. This did not increase the Jewish community members' interest in religious life, though. Lichtigfeld constantly quarreled with the Eastern European Jews over their comportment in the synagogue, and the number of worshippers remained deplorable. In the early 1960s, less than 5 percent of the members of the Jewish community took part in the services on Shabbat. (This, however, was typical for Jewish communities in the Federal Republic of Germany at that time.)

It was equally hard to strengthen religious education. The religious school had to deal with many children from unreligious homes. The percentage of Jewish children who took part in religious instruction even sank from two thirds in 1957 to 45 percent in the early 1960s.[30] When Rabbi Lichtigfeld gave speeches on Judaism and Jewish religion in national broadcasts on the radio station Deutschlandfunk, he received many responses—and always positive reactions—but curiously "only from non-Jewish listeners."[31]

When the journalist William Frankel visited the Federal Republic as a representative of the AJC in 1960, he painted a pessimistic picture of Jewish life in postwar Germany. The communities were aging, and synagogues resembled museums more than houses of worship: "Official Germany takes great pains to behave decently to Jews . . . and Jewish leadership has extraordinarily free access to all leading German personalities." Germans were extremely interested in Judaism, Frankel wrote. Rabbis were overwhelmed with requests, and school classes regularly visited synagogues. The West German really wanted "to know something more about the people Hitler tried to exterminate." But Jewish life itself, Frankel noted, was "not very Jewish in a religious sense . . . but a communal social, huddling together."[32]

In the following year, the *New York Post* presented a similar picture of Jewish life in West Germany in a series of articles: no Jew considered Germany to be his or her homeland, and everybody shared photos of a daughter in San Francisco or a son in Canada. "Even Jewish officials of the organized community have caught themselves referring to *your* Finance Minister, and *your* parliament in public speeches," the newspaper reported.[33] Many Jews saw the presence of the U.S. Army as their only protection. An engineer from Frankfurt had told the *New York Post* that he would leave the country as soon as the American troops left Germany.

In 1959, the Jewish community in Frankfurt launched a survey among its older members to find out more about their life situations, worries, and needs. The results were written down in a "Report on the Examination of the Situation and the Needs of People over 60 Years Old in the Jewish Community Frankfurt." Contrary to expectation, the study revealed a profound opposition between the Jews born in Germany and those from Eastern Europe: "The vast majority of the respondents born in Germany again and again expressed their disapproval of the Jews from eastern Europe."[34] The "*Ostjuden*" were criticized because of their public behavior and because of their religious practices. Many German Jews explained their decision not to take part in Jewish communal life by saying that they did not want to come into contact with the former DPs. The alienation from the Jewish community and its institutions, both on the side of the German Jews and on the side of the DPs, was related to an international orientation. While the Jewish community was seen primarily as an institution of social welfare, social contact for many of its older members was limited to airmail letters.

New Beginnings

In view of the complicated situation of the generation of Holocaust survivors in postwar Germany, it is not surprising that high hopes were set on their children. It was the so-called second generation that should build new Jewish life, but it remained unclear *where* this should happen. Paradoxically, the Jewish community in Frankfurt constantly tried to strengthen the capacities of its social and educational institutions—and at the same time, younger Jews were confronted with the obligation to leave Frankfurt and Germany and go to Israel. The younger generation was expected to do what its parents had failed to do for very different reasons.

The youth work organized by the Jewish community, however, remained stereotypical. While the Federal Republic remained strange for many younger

Jews, Israel as an offer of Jewish identity remained formulaic. For instance, Micha Brumlik, born in 1947 and raised in Germany since 1952, felt irritated and confused by the "national romantic rituals" he experienced in the Zionist youth group he attended in Frankfurt: "Could a schoolboy easily raise a flag after having read Orwell's '1984' and Heinrich Böll's novel 'Stranger, Bear Word to the Spartans We . . .'?"[35] Brumlik and his peers became acculturated members of an increasingly liberal West German society, while at the same time they were confronted with the expectation to leave that country. In Frankfurt, the most American and international city in West Germany, this conflict was especially apparent. Young Jews grew up with the Amerika Haus, its library, and its cultural programs. They grew up with a club scene established around the U.S. Army barracks. They listened to the American Forces Network radio station and to records imported from America.

Dan Diner, born in 1946, has argued that the specific social and cultural environment in Frankfurt produced "a very special genre of Jewish adolescents." These young Jews distinguished themselves through "a high intellectual level, great public involvement, [and] subsequent careers that accompany that."[36] One of these young Jews growing up in postwar Frankfurt was Marek Lieberberg, born in the Jewish DP camp in Frankfurt Zeilsheim in 1946. Lieberberg later set up the concert agency Mama Concerts and brought international bands and rock stars to German stages beginning in the early 1970s. His parents came from Poland, and neither one could ever really gain a foothold in Frankfurt. His father obtained a license from the U.S. occupation authorities to produce chocolate, and later he ran a coffee-roasting house. Marek's mother gambled most of the family's money away. "My parents were broken," Lieberberg says. They did not openly live as Jews, but they sent their son to a boarding school in England, where he should learn about Jewish history.[37]

Micha Brumlik has similar memories about his parents: "They never were deported to concentration camps or to death camps, but National Socialism has done serious damage to their lives."[38] The Brumliks had left Germany in 1933, and they could not feel at home anywhere after 1945. Brumlik reflected that "the loss could not be replaced elsewhere. Returning to the country that had taken everything from them could not bring back the loss either. Their wish to see me finding a home in a faraway, ideal country remained unfulfilled. It took several attempts for me to finally find a place that I could come to terms with." His own life, Brumlik wrote, was "the story of multiple losses and of multiple approaches to regain what was lost."[39]

Sammy Speier was born in Palestine in 1944. He came to Frankfurt with his parents in the 1950s. "The memory of leaving Israel is connected to strong senses of guilt," Speier remembers. "My parents left in a cloak-and-dagger-operation. Not even my best friend was supposed to know about it. It was a betrayal of the Jewish, Israeli nation and state."[40] When Sammy visited the youth club of the Jewish community in Frankfurt, he found "Israelis, a familiar language and familiarity, but also many unknown, strange things." He saw himself as a Zionist, and he continued to speak Hebrew to his brothers to avoid losing his language skills. At the same time, he visited the parental homes of his non-Jewish schoolmates—even after hearing that one father had been a member of the SS. Sammy Speier felt as if he were living in "two worlds."[41]

Speier spent years living in Israel, but he returned to Frankfurt in order not to be drafted into the Israeli army. In 1967, Micha Brumlik also immigrated to Israel and started studying at the Hebrew University of Jerusalem. He quickly realized that this experience would not familiarize him with the State of Israel, but rather with American counterculture and an academic anti-Zionism.[42] In 1969 Brumlik returned to Frankfurt. Cilly Kugelmann, born in Frankfurt in 1947, also left Germany and enrolled at the Hebrew University in 1966. She arrived in a country that had not much in common with the idealized portrait of Israel that was provided in Frankfurt. It was an "authoritarian society, very hard, very uncharming, and not playful."[43] In 1971 Cilly Kugelmann returned to Frankfurt.

Many of the younger Jews—whether or not they had spent some time in Israel—found themselves on the left side of the political spectrum in the 1960s and 1970s. Marek Lieberberg studied sociology for one year at the University of Frankfurt and came into close contact with the local leftist scene. Micha Brumlik also joined the student revolution movement and tried to leave everything behind—the world of his parents' experiences, Judaism, Zionism, and "the oath I had sworn at the campfires of our summer camps."[44] Dan Diner remembers Club Voltaire as the place where the second generation of Jews in Frankfurt could get closer to the non-Jewish majority society. The bar and event location, founded in 1962 in the city center, became the meeting point for Frankfurt's leftist scene. For young Jews, Club Voltaire was a "place of conversion," as Diner puts it. After attending synagogue, parents met together in the Opera Café while their children went to Club Voltaire. By doing so they went from a private sphere into a public sphere, from the Jewish world into the non-Jewish world. The young Jews would change their language and their habitus. They performed a "cultural acculturation." Their Jewish heritage became insignificant. Club Voltaire, Diner remembers, was no place of the German society of perpetrators but rather a place of the political left. Both the Jewish and the non-Jewish sixty-eighters could distance themselves from their parents and from their parents' history. As Diner wrote, "Both, Jews and Germans, left the past behind, as leftists."[45]

Young Jewish leftists also caused some unrest in the Jewish community itself. Earlier than elsewhere in West German Jewish communities, there was a generational conflict between the Frankfurt community officials and some rebellious youth representatives. In the mid-1960s, some exponents of the second generation fought for more liberal and less restrictive authorization procedures concerning the articles published in the local Jewish youth newspaper *Regew*. In 1971, some members of the second generation stood for election to the board of the Jewish community. To their own surprise, five of them were elected as board members. Even if their political commitment did not last long, the young functionaries tried to burst old structures and organized public round table talks on controversial topics such as Jewish youth, drugs, and sexuality.

The core group of young Jews from Frankfurt continued to be active in the political left in the 1970s. Some of them were part of the Socialist Bureau (Sozialistisches Büro) in Offenbach, near Frankfurt, and participated in the newspaper *links* (Left). In 1980, a group called Jüdische Gruppe formed in Frankfurt and served as a discussion group for members of the second generation who were wrestling with key questions: "The relationship between German and Jewish leftists, our relation to our parents and to their decision to raise us in Germany, their ability or inability to share their experiences of persecution. Not least we discussed again and again about the state of Israel and its policy towards the Palestinians to which we stood in strict opposition."[46] The feeling of homelessness, however, did not go away. The "cultural acculturation" within the milieu of the political left, which Dan Diner had hoped for, was made difficult by the West German student movement's radical turn and its attitude toward Israel after 1967. After the Six-Day War, leftist German students would no longer support Israel in solidarity, but rather the "liberation struggle" of the Palestinians. During the 1970s, anti-Semitic undertones were unmistakable in the heated debate about the demolition and new construction of the Westend neighborhood in Frankfurt when Jewish building contractors and investors were denunciated as speculators.

The 1980s finally saw a new dimension of the heated debates on German-Jewish topics. In 1985, leading figures in Frankfurt's Jewish community stopped the premiere of Rainer Werner Fassbinder's highly controversial play *Garbage, the City, and Death*—which dealt with the story of the Frankfurt *Häuserkampf*, a battle against redevelopment and gentrification of the Westend in the 1970s—by literally occupying the stage of the theater. Shortly thereafter, young Jews and non-Jews occupied a building site in Frankfurt's city center where ruins of the medieval Judengasse had been discovered during construction works. The question was: Should these ruins be saved, or should they again be buried under a new office building?

Both debates took place in the context of Chancellor Helmut Kohl's new politics of memory (*Geschichtspolitik*) and after the miniseries *Holocaust* had been shown on German television in 1979. Both debates, however, dealt above all with the position of Jews in West German society. Jews now took center stage in public debates. It is no coincidence that this "coming out" of Jews in postwar Germany took place in Frankfurt. Many of those younger Jews from Frankfurt who had started to question the world around them in the 1960s established themselves in the West German elite during the 1980s: as university professors like Micha Brumlik and Dan Diner or as museum organizers and designers like

Cilly Kugelmann. These critical intellectuals did not feel bound anymore to the demand of inconspicuousness that had shaped Jewish life in postwar Germany for decades.

In this respect, the history of Jews in Frankfurt am Main was in many ways a typical example of the rebuilding of Jewish life in postwar West Germany. At the same time, it was a special case insofar as conditions in Frankfurt were more favorable than elsewhere in the Federal Republic of Germany for laying the foundations of a more controversial—but also more lively and visible—Jewish life starting in the 1960s.

NOTES

1. "Die Hoffnung war immer da," *Frankfurter Rundschau*, 8 May 1957.

2. World Jewish Congress, "Germany," in *Resolutions Adopted by the Second Plenary Assembly of the World Jewish Congress, Montreux, Switzerland, June 27th–July 6th, 1948* (London: Odhams Press, [1948]), 7. Quoted after Jay Howard Geller, *Jews in Post-Holocaust Germany, 1945–1953* (Cambridge: Cambridge University Press 2005), 62.

3. "Die Letzten in Frankfurt a.M.," *Der Aufbau*, 6 April 1945, 1.

4. "Juden in Frankfurt a. M. und München-Gladbach," *Der Aufbau*, 27 April 1945, 1; cf. *Der Aufbau*, 27 April 1945, 19.

5. Alon Tauber, *Zwischen Kontinuität und Neuanfang. Die Entstehung der jüdischen Nachkriegsgemeinde in Frankfurt am Main 1945–1949* (Wiesbaden: Kommission für die Geschichte der Juden in Hessen, 2008), 26.

6. "Protokoll der Sitzung der Interessenvertretung der Jüdischen Gemeinden und Kultusvereinigungen," 2 March 1947. Zentralarchiv zur Erforschung der Geschichte der Juden in Deutschland (ZA). B 1/13, A 412.

7. Tauber, *Kontinuität*, 99.

8. "Oberbürgermeister Kolb zum neuen Jahr," *Frankfurter Rundschau*, 12 January 1947.

9. Cilly Kugelmann, "Zur Identität osteuropäischer Juden in der Bundesrepublik," in *Reichspogromnacht. Vergangenheitsbewältigung aus jüdischer Sicht*, ed. Micha Brumlik and Petra Kunik (Frankfurt am Main, Brandes und Apsel: 1988), 178.

10. Cilly Kugelmann, "Befreiung—und dann? Zur Situation der Juden in Frankfurt am Main im Jahr 1945," in *"Nach der Kristallnacht." Jüdisches Leben und antijüdische Politik in Frankfurt am Main 1938–1945*, ed. Monica Kingreen (Frankfurt am Main: Campus, 1999), 455.

11. Tauber, *Kontinuität*, 44–45.

12. Tauber, 44–45.

13. Cilly Kugelmann, "Frankfurter Nachkriegskarrieren," in *Ignatz Bubis. Ein jüdisches Leben in Deutschland*, ed. Fritz Backhaus, Raphael Gross and Michael Lenarz (Frankfurt am Main: Suhrkamp, 2007), 46.

14. Kugelmann, *Nachkriegskarrieren*, 51.

15. Kugelmann, 51.

16. Hendrik G. van Dam, "Rückkehr nach Deutschland? Zur Frage der Rückwanderung," *Allgemeine Wochenzeitung der Juden in Deutschland*, 21 September 1956, 1.

17. Harry Maor, "Über den Wiederaufbau der Jüdischen Gemeinden in Deutschland seit 1945" (PhD thesis, Universität Mainz, 1961), 44, 55, 257.

18. "Aus Trümmern entstand eine neue Gemeinde," *Frankfurter Rundschau*, 6 March 1953.

19. *Die Frankfurter Schule und Frankfurt. Eine Rückkehr nach Deutschland*, ed. Monika Boll and Raphael Gross, Jüdisches Museum Frankfurt (Göttingen: Wallstein, 2009).

20. Clemens Albrecht, Günther C. Behrmann, and Michael Bock, *Die intellektuelle Gründung der Bundesrepublik. Eine Wirkungsgeschichte der Frankfurter Schule* (Frankfurt am Main: Campus, 1999), 13.

21. Tobias Freimüller, *Alexander Mitscherlich. Psychoanalyse und Gesellschaftsdiagnosen nach Hitler* (Göttingen: Wallstein, 2007).

22. "Zu- und Abgänge, Aufstellung und Statistik 1946–1954," ZA 1/13, 02, 3609, A 844.

23. Max Horkheimer to Jüdische Gemeinde Frankfurt, 3 March 1961, ZA 1/13, 2925.

24. Irving M. Engel to Isaac Emil Lichtigfeld, 29 January 1959, ZA 1/13, 463.

25. Memorandum by Kurt R. Grossmann, "Report of Hans Wallenberg on Democratic Institutions in Germany," 14 May 1956, YIVO Archives, FAD 41, AJC Paris Office, box 30.

26. Anthony Kauders, *Unmögliche Heimat. Eine deutsch-jüdische Geschichte der Bundesrepublik* (München: Deutsche Verlags-Anstalt, 2007), 115.

27. Tauber, *Kontinuität*, 165.

28. Walter Leiske to Walter Kolb, 12 November 1951, Institut für Stadtgeschichte Frankfurt, Magistratsakten, 5.800, Israelitische Gemeinde: Rabbiner, Synagogen.

29. Andreas Brämer and Julius Carlebach, "Continuity or New Beginning? Isaac Emil Lichtigfeld, Rabbi in Frankfurt," *Leo Baeck Institute Year Book* 42 (1997): 275–302.

30. Andreas Brämer, "Das Frankfurter Rabbinat nach 1945," in *Wer ein Haus baut, will bleiben. 50 Jahre Jüdische Gemeinde in Frankfurt a. M. Anfänge und Gegenwart*, ed. Jüdisches Museum Frankfurt am Main (Frankfurt am Main: Societäts-Verlag, 1998), 125.

31. "Bericht Dr. Pick über seine Tätigkeit im Rundfunkrat des Deutschlandfunks," 1965, ZA B 1/13, 1963.

32. William Frankel, "Report on a Visit to Germany," May 1960, YIVO Archives, FAD 41 AJC Paris Office, box 30.

33. Harry Golden, "The Jews in Germany 1961," *New York Post*, 14 June 1961.

34. "Bericht über die Untersuchung der Lage und der Bedürfnisse der Personen über 60 Jahre in der Jüdischen Gemeinde Frankfurt," Joint Distribution Committee Archives Jerusalem, Geneva I/II, 447/29.

35. Micha Brumlik, *Kein Weg als Deutscher und Jude. Eine bundesrepublikanische Erfahrung* (München: Ullstein, 2000), 38.

36. Dan Diner, "Man hat mit der Sache eigentlich nichts mehr zu tun (Interview)," in *Wir sind da! Die Geschichte der Juden in Deutschland von 1945 bis heute*, ed. Richard Chaim Schneider (Berlin: Ullstein, 2000), 242.

37. "Der einzige wirkliche Charakter bei den Stones ist Keith Richards," interview with Marek Lieberberg, *Süddeutsche Zeitung*, 2/3 July 2005.

38. Brumlik, *Kein Weg*, 10.

39. Brumlik, 10.

40. Sammy Speier, "Von der Pubertät zum Erwachsenendasein. Bericht einer Bewußtseinswerdung," in *Reichspogromnacht. Vergangenheitsbewältigung aus jüdischer Sicht*, ed. Micha Brumlik and Petra Kunik (Frankfurt am Main: Brandes und Apsel, 1988), 182.

41. Speier, 184.

42. Brumlik, *Kein Weg*, 86.

43. Cilly Kugelmann, "Kindergartensandkastenperspektive vom polnischen Stetl (Interview)," in *Wir sind da! Die Geschichte der Juden in Deutschland von 1945 bis heute*, ed. Richard Chaim Schneider (Berlin: Ullstein, 2000), 287.

44. Brumlik, *Kein Weg*, 91–92.

45. Diner, "Man hat mit der Sache," in *Wir sind da!*, 243.

46. Brumlik, *Kein Weg*, 141.

CHAPTER 6

HELMUT ESCHWEGE AND JEWISH LIFE IN THE GERMAN DEMOCRATIC REPUBLIC

Alexander Walther

On 30 October 1948, Helmut Eschwege sent a letter to the writer Arnold Zweig, who was preparing to return to Germany, painting a grim picture of postwar society: "The German people in its entirety is still strongly influenced by fascist ideology. . . . Maybe because it was not even roughly called to account for the damages it caused. Restitution has become a farce as well. The Germans still consider themselves innocent, be it of the atrocities, their benefit, or the war as such. . . . The shadow of fascism keeps blighting today's life. The best friend may suddenly turn out to be a Nazi in disguise, leading to distrust of everything and everyone."[1] Eschwege's portrayal was not meant to discourage Zweig but was rather an expression of his skepticism toward German society, a skepticism that was shared by many returned Jewish émigrés and survivors.

When the war ended in Germany in May 1945, only a few imagined that Jewish life could ever be possible in the country again. Since the Soviet military administration did not allow camps for displaced persons (DPs) in their area, the bulk of Jewish former concentration camp inmates and forced laborers were moved to the zones of the Western Allies, mostly to the American zone. Despite this great shift, Jewish life was forming right from the beginning in various cities and places throughout the country.

Jewish life in the German Democratic Republic (GDR) has been analyzed ever since the state collapsed, and to some degree also before that. The first authors to do so described the Jewish communities mostly from the perspective of the state. While the regime was always suspicious of the communities throughout the GDR, it chose to make use of them whenever it seemed beneficial. Yet these works commonly neglected an inside perspective of the communities themselves, presenting them as mainly willful subjects of the Socialist Unity Party of Germany (SED).[2] Helmut Eschwege has been described in a similar manner, as both a victim of censorship and a collaborator with the GDR's Ministry of State Security (Stasi).[3] In this, he served as a prime example of the discussion surrounding Jews in the GDR, with his autobiography being a frequently, and often uncritically, cited reference.[4] His own intentions remained mostly obscure, however, and his views on Jewish life unnoticed. Yet many key aspects of what it meant to be Jewish in postwar Eastern Germany can be discussed based on Eschwege's activities. This chapter will ask how Helmut Eschwege shaped Jewish life after the Shoah in Germany and how he himself lived as a member of the Jewish communities in the GDR.

Reestablishing Jewish Life

After the war, it seemed only natural to many Jewish survivors to join forces and reorganize community structures. While the provision of religious services was one of the concerns, the more pressing one dealt with the supply of food and shelter. The new communities consisted mostly of two rather different groups: DPs and those who had remained in Germany during the war. Members of the latter had been able to survive in Germany either in hiding or due to their non-Jewish spouses. Though they had not belonged to the most respected members of the community before the war, they now felt the urge to reestablish Jewish institutions in their cities. Since most of the former members either had gone into exile or had been deported during the war, the number of those remaining was scarce. Yet the communities soon grew at least slightly, as some DPs had managed to attain permission to stay, commonly through marriage with a German.[5]

The reaction toward these establishments from Jewish institutions and individuals outside Germany was mostly dismissive. The editor of the Israeli paper *Ha'aretz*, Gershom Schocken, born in the East German city of Zwickau, deemed the (re)settlement of Jews in Germany an "undignified behavior," heavily criticizing the choice to live "amongst the murderers of their brothers."[6] In fact, a ban seemed to have been imposed on Germany as a whole by most Jews outside of it. The decision not to return to the "bloodstained soil of Germany" and to boycott everything German was adamant and was officially enunciated in the resolution of the World Jewish Congress during its meeting in summer 1948.[7]

Yet there were Jews migrating to Germany, and quite a number of them. The Soviet Occupation Zone (SBZ) in particular was the aim of predominantly Communist returnees who had fled National Socialism. At least several hundred of them were of Jewish origin.[8] However, most were not religious and did not regard themselves as Jews. Being born in the 1910s and 1920s, they came mostly from bourgeois homes but had joined the Communist Party or similarly affiliated youth groups at an early stage. They opted for a different life than their families lived, often by denouncing their Jewish origins partially or totally. This "red assimilation" seemed to satisfy a need for "safety and clarity," as Karin Hartewig has described.[9] The returned émigrés soon participated prominently in the building of a new, Communist Germany, firmly believing in the existence—or at least possibility—of a "German-Jewish symbiosis," a vision for which most Jews outside of Germany had lost all hope.[10]

Surprisingly, this vision was mostly shared by those from religious Jewish families, quite often born in Eastern Europe, who had to negotiate between their belief, recent experiences, and their decision to stay in post-Nazi Germany. Only the possibility of an improvement in German-Jewish relations seemed to justify such a decision. Still, the persecution that they had endured shaped their understanding of a future Jewish life in Germany. The Jewish community of Berlin stated in a letter to the municipal authorities that "the term 'Jew' is again to be understood in a religious sense only," defining Jews specifically as members of a Jewish congregation.[11] Being Jewish was exclusively seen as a matter of faith rather than as a matter of origin or ethnicity. This is an obvious reaction to National Socialism and its racist anti-Semitism that had affected even the nonreligious, converted, and assimilated. Still, being Jewish also implied being German at the same time, a right that Jews had been denied only a short time ago.

The need to restore dignity and overcome anti-Semitic stereotypes ingrained in the German population was vital to the founders of the reestablished communities. Yet the new authorities were suspicious and not at all eager to accept these new communities as the legal successor of the old communities especially in terms of reparations. When the community in Chemnitz attempted to retrieve its former possessions, the authorities denied it at first due to its new name, "Jewish Community," rather than the old "Israelite Religious Community." The community argued that "especially since the term Jew was a curse word and meant discrimination during the Hitler regime, did we, as conscious Jews, choose the name Jewish community."[12]

Helmut Eschwege considered himself to be a "conscious Jew." Yet his role within the communities in the GDR deviated from the way the regime wanted members of the Jewish population to behave. Born in a Jewish family in Hannover in 1913, Eschwege enjoyed both a religious Jewish upbringing and a leftist socialization. The family moved to Hamburg to ensure a religious education. Later, Eschwege became a member of the Socialist Workers Youth and the Social Democratic Party. He rebelled against the orthodox lifestyle of his parents but became a devoted Zionist. In 1934, he emigrated to Denmark with the help of the local Hashomer Hatzair group. Due to his political activities in Denmark, Eschwege was forced to leave the country and sought help from a pro-Soviet group, which suggested moving to the Jewish autonomous region Birobidzhan in the far east of the Soviet Union.[13] He ended up living in an Estonian kibbutz for two years before attaining a visa for Palestine. There, he joined the local Communist Party, which soon proved to be inimical, as he was forced to switch jobs frequently. In 1942, he was engaged as a civil worker in the British Army. In his time in Palestine, Eschwege enjoyed the friendship of other German émigrés and was already establishing contacts that would prove useful to him in the future.[14] Despite his Zionist belief, Eschwege decided to return to Germany, as did many other Communists in Palestine. In 1946, he was able to gain a visa to go to Czechoslovakia. From there he made his way to Dresden, arriving in September. Like many other Jewish returned émigrés, Eschwege was lured by the promises uttered by the Communist Party, and later the SED, to build a better, antifascist Germany in which anti-Semitism would have no place.[15]

The majority of Jewish Communists in the GDR did not join a Jewish community after their return. Yet there were some who firmly believed that being Communist and Jewish at the same time were not mutually exclusive. Due to his experiences, Eschwege "felt" Jewish as he told it later.[16] Accordingly, filling in a form, he selected "Jewish" as his nationality, which put him in conflict with the authorities.[17] In 1951, the SED surveyed its members and refused Eschwege's form due to his answers. The party ordered him to change it, pressuring him in talks, and he yielded only grudgingly. In a letter to the party's regional commission, Eschwege complained about this, stating that a number of party members were "afraid of detriments that may be caused by their profession of the Jewish people with which they had suffered only yesterday. I am proud of my nationality, and of my people, and consider it shameful . . . to have succumbed to the commission's decision."[18]

Despite his feelings and beliefs, Eschwege was not a devoted member of the Jewish community, at least in the early years. He had waited for some months before applying for a membership and was refused by the community initially. Eschwege complained to the American Joint Distribution Committee ("Joint") about this in March 1948, stating that he had been refused "since I am a freethinker, and they only accept religious people."[19] The community replied that Eschwege was only allowed in if he professed the "mosaic religion," underlining the religious nature of their community.[20] The clash between the two views is obvious. While the community was eager to think of itself solely as a congregation and (mostly) disregarded the notion of a Jewish people, Eschwege saw himself as a Jew by birth and upbringing rather than by religion. Though he eventually joined the community only a few weeks later, this dissension shaped his relationship to the community for years.[21]

In 1947, Eschwege was assigned to re-collect large quantities of books that the Nazis had banned and that had often been confiscated from Jewish households and then sold to collectors or libraries in Prague or elsewhere. Shuffling through libraries and piles of books and regaining lost literary treasures became Eschwege's work and dedication for the rest of his life. Retrieving these stocks and collections appeared vital to him, and handing them back to their previous owners or legal successors seemed only natural.

Restitution of previously deprived property—or "Aryanization"—soon became a hotly debated issue. Since the SED's leaders regarded themselves as victims as well—quite fittingly so—rather than the successors of the perpetrators, they did not accept responsibility regarding recompense. The GDR struggled with the harsh reparations imposed by the Soviet Union, which were usually called *Wiedergutmachung* (rectification) and were presented as the only suitable form of recompense in order that private claims would seem unwarranted. Furthermore, National Socialism was perceived as the rule of monopoly capitalists with the Nazis as their henchmen. Thus incorporating large amounts of the Third Reich's capital in order to erect a Communist state seemed morally justified to SED leadership. While the Jewish communities were mostly compensated and received at least parts of their previous estates, private claims were denied on a large scale. By retaining these assets, however, the SED perpetuated the Nazis' seizure and discrimination.[22]

This caused distress and protests by mostly Jewish politicians and citizens, with Paul Merker (though being gentile) and Leo Zuckermann as the most prominent voices.[23] Eschwege contributed to this issue as well. In late 1946, Paul Merker, at the time a member of the Politbüro (the inner circle of the party) wrote to Eschwege asking for his thoughts on Communist policy toward Jews. Eschwege listed several points in his reply. First, the German people should acknowledge its active or passive participation in National Socialism and its guilt toward the Jews. Second, he advocated restitution not as a substitute for destroyed Jewish life but as an "act of justice." Third, Eschwege denounced anti-Semitism as unworthy for a "cultured people," endorsing a legal prohibition on it.[24]

Eschwege presented his views as the most basic foundation for the possibility of Jewish life in Germany after the Shoah. Only if the Germans were held to these standards, he claimed, could the Jews trust them again. Eschwege's letter summarized the thoughts of many Jews who had returned to Germany. Moreover, he implicitly denounced assimilation, urging that the German Jews should be entitled to "rights of a national minority." Although Stalin denounced that right in 1913, as he stated in a footnote, the "development since 1933" would require a reconsideration of the problem. Though it is unclear if Merker received a copy of the letter including this sentence, Eschwege kept arguing in this manner from a Marxist-Leninist point of view, renouncing Stalin's view on the "National Question" and instead referring to the situation of Soviet Jews in his frequent disagreements with the party.[25]

The terms of restitution, and the failure to compensate especially former Jewish persecutees, kept upsetting Eschwege. Questions of restitution were absent from the law regulating the status of the Persecutees of the Nazi Regime (Verfolgte des Naziregimes) in 1949. Instead, the SED chose a form of privileged social welfare, paying higher pensions, and granting certain benefits to the victims. Right from the beginning the Communist leadership had opted for a division of this group, distinguishing between "fighters" and "victims." Jewish victims were commonly sorted into the latter category. Jews could be considered "fighters" as well but were then primarily regarded as political victims rather than "racial" ones. After the law was enacted in 1950, the SED initiated a process of vetting Nazi victims living in the GDR. Social welfare was granted due to the alleged political reliability of the individual.[26]

These commissions included members of the Jewish communities as they were interested in exposing recipients with dubious or made-up background stories as well. Due to the harsh supply situation after the war, the communities meticulously examined the applications of potential new members. Since they were receiving some additional support from the Joint, being a member of a Jewish community implied extra provisions. Acts of fraud were bound to appear. This delimiting strategy was kept up in the following years, enhanced by the self-definition of being a strictly religious community. Eschwege represented the community's interests in the local commission in Dresden.[27]

In sorting out seemingly unsuitable candidates, he participated in the party's strive to enforce their definition. While the commission sorted out former Nazis who had given false information, they also discarded some who had been interned as so-called *Berufsverbrecher* (habitual offenders). These previous convicts were sent to concentration camps as an alleged matter of "precaution" to prohibit them from committing any further crimes. Since the definition of this term was deliberately held vague, the crimes committed by the internees beforehand could include also minor ones.[28] Still, the SED, supported by the Communist-dominated Union of Persecutees of the Nazi Regime (Vereinigung der Verfolgten des Naziregimes), was eager to neglect the suffering of various groups in order to establish a caste of ostensible superior victims, mostly formed by previous political inmates.[29]

Eschwege, however, never forgot the focus of his work, and kept arguing for a revision of the restitution guidelines, thereby also trying to achieve a proper acknowledgment of Jewish persecution under National Socialism. The Dresden community sent him their thoughts on a possible revision in 1951 and asked Eschwege to ensure that their views were considered in the guidelines review by the local and central commission.[30]

His work in the community did not last long, though. In November 1952, the Communist Party of Czechoslovakia tried its own general secretary, Rudolf Slánský, for allegedly participating in a "Trotskyite-Titoite-Zionist conspiracy." Eleven of the fourteen accused were Jewish, most of them hanged shortly afterward. The trial spurred a series of arrests, show trials or silent imprisonment and exclusion from the party throughout Eastern Europe, with especially harsh situations in the GDR. Leading Jewish politicians and prominent representatives of the Jewish communities hastily fled the country while some were interrogated by the Stasi and ended up in jail subsequently. Paul Merker, being the most prominent case, was tried and only vindicated in 1957.[31]

At the time, Eschwege was working at the Museum for German History in East Berlin. He was eagerly collecting artifacts of German-Jewish history, sparking conflicts with the director. In order to prevent a dismissal issued by the museum, Eschwege handed in his notice on 5 March 1953, the day Stalin died.[32] Simultaneously, the SED had initiated an investigation with the aim of excluding him from the party due to his "Zionist" belief.[33] Beforehand, Eschwege left the Jewish community in Dresden.[34]

Though never cutting all ties, he only applied for a new membership in the community in November 1957. In his application, he stated that his exit four years earlier "happened due to the press releases and comments about the Slánský trial. . . . In these reports, the Jewish communities . . . were libelled in strongest terms. I fell victim to these calumnies." He ended the letter "with Jewish greetings!"[35] By leaving the community, it seems, Eschwege tried to forestall a trial, and not just a suspension from the SED as he claimed later.[36] Also, he had reasons to worry, as his profile and history matched the criteria of others tried at the same time. An informant of the Stasi within the community had blackened his name, stating that Paul Merker had instructed him to convince Jewish SED members to join their respective communities.[37] Eschwege's withdrawal must, thus, be seen as a sheer act of self-defense and precaution.

The Stasi initiated their surveillance of Eschwege in March 1953, keeping a close eye on him for almost three years. Then they successfully blackmailed Eschwege into becoming an informant. His first period as an informant lasted for about two years during which he provided several reports.[38] The Stasi was eager to receive information from him due to his contacts to Jewish institutions abroad, and to some of the former leading members of the communities who had fled the GDR in 1953 such as Leon Löwenkopf, the former head of the Dresden community.[39]

In 1956, Eschwege was sent to Western Germany to meet Löwenkopf in order to convince him to return. His results were meager, though. His report from the talk with him was merely an account of Löwenkopf's deep dismay, disappointment, and desire for Dresden, hardly usable for the Stasi. While Eschwege depicted himself trying to talk Löwenkopf into returning, it is highly doubtful whether he really did so given his personal experience only three years earlier.[40] It seems more plausible that Eschwege simply wanted to meet Löwenkopf again. Later, Eschwege approached the Stasi offering them a report on Israel in exchange for a trip there. They gladly accepted, and Eschwege was able to meet with his family after years of separation.[41] Afterward, the Stasi, despite being pleased with his reports, ended its cooperation with him. They accused Eschwege of lying since the SED, having converted his exclusion to a mere reprimand in 1953, had prohibited him from this trip. In suggesting the reports to the Stasi in exchange for the permission to travel, Eschwege found a way to circumvent the party's refusal. On return, the SED was furious with him, finally excluding him in January 1958. Eschwege's attempts to revoke this decision in the following years proved unsuccessful.[42]

The State Association and Jewish Life in the GDR

Eschwege's dual membership in the SED and a Jewish community was not a rare combination in the early years of the GDR. Most chairmen of the communities were party members, such as Julius Meyer (Berlin) or Leon Löwenkopf (Dresden). Still, the community, as a religious association, treaded with caution and attempted to remain separate from the state. After the exodus of virtually all leading Jewish figures from the GDR in 1953, the situation changed drastically. Now dual memberships were hardly considered problematic.

The State Association of Jewish Communities in the GDR (Verband der Jüdischen Gemeinden in der DDR), which had tried to remain independent of the party as much as possible, was now run by people who had not been willing to flee but were still aware of their uncertain situation. After the death of Hermann Baden in 1962, Helmut Aris became the new president of the association, heading also the Dresden community until his death in 1987. During this time, the Jewish communities and the association moved closer to the party and the responsible State Secretary for Church Affairs (Staatssekretariat für Kirchenfragen). The SED tended to abuse the association and the Jews in the GDR as a bargaining chip in their contention with Western Germany. It perpetually claimed that anti-Semitism had been wiped out, with the GDR forming a true home (*Heimstatt*) for its Jews.[43] Yet the Jewish communities were not as passive and submissive as often depicted. Rather, the chairmen had realized that in order to survive and to secure their position and Jewish life as such they would have to make compromises with the regime.[44] Their public support for the state must be seen in this context, especially following the events of 1953. Still, the frequent statements favoring and praising the GDR and the SED were a constant source of offense to some community members, particularly to Helmut Eschwege.

His relationship to the association and other chairmen was reserved, and Eschwege never held a position within the community or the association after 1953. From his return onward, Eschwege, though not a trained historian, engaged in collecting archival material, and finally started writing the first monograph on the Shoah in the GDR. He asked for a letter of support to gain access to the GDR's central archive in Potsdam. Yet the community in Berlin denied him such a letter in 1959, and Eschwege, also due to the general restriction of sources on

Jewish history, was never granted access to the archive.[45] His book was never published in its original form, and various other projects suffered a similar fate.[46]

His relationship to Aris grew worse throughout the years. In 1964, Eschwege's third wife applied for membership in the community. Her application was denied by both the GDR's chief rabbi, Martin Riesenburger, and the chairmen of all communities. She and her husband kept insisting that she, a daughter of a Jewish mother, was Jewish herself, granting her access to the community. Yet Aris insisted on her taking lessons with the cantor Werner Sander (Leipzig), which still infuriated Eschwege years afterward.[47]

Eschwege decided to act against Aris, pushing for reforms and elections in the community, and sought the support of others. His first letter to all chairmen was sent in November 1965. Eschwege suggested a more open policy of accepting those who had left the communities in 1953, argued for an improvement in child and youth care, and demanded a more active cultural life, also for nonreligious (potential) members.[48]

Eschwege provided an overview of his points of criticism in a report for the Stasi already in 1957. He disapproved of the community's self-conception as solely religious groups. Furthermore, the Jews in the GDR suffered from not being able to contact Jews from abroad. Also, cultural work was absent within the communities. Instead, he suggested a newsletter on national and international Jewish life and culture.[49]

Over the years, Eschwege repeated his plea for improved education of the youth. Worried about the bond of his children to the community, he proposed organizing talks about Jewish history and culture, and would gladly help in this matter as he wrote to the community in 1968.[50] While it is doubtful whether such talks would in fact have strengthened the adolescents' Jewish heritage, Eschwege's suggestion exemplifies his devotion to Jewish history. Early on the association established a yearly summer camp for its youth members, enabling them to enjoy a vacation with proper food supplies—a bitterly needed necessity in the postwar years—and to foster their ties to the Jewish community. However, attendance at these trips declined over the years, and Jewish education was scarce, as Eschwege remarked. The only Jewish thing in these camps, he wrote in 1971, was "hearing a *Kiddush* (a blessing recited at Shabbat) and eating a slice of kosher sausage."[51] While the communities in Leipzig and Berlin started to offer cultural events to a slightly broader public in the 1970s, albeit with initially scarce attendance, Aris prevented such events in Dresden.[52]

Even the religious services were difficult to uphold due to the small number of registered members and those attending ceremonies. Already in 1963, the association ruled that the *minyan* (quorum of ten male adults necessary for service) could be lowered to just three if required.[53] After the death of Martin Riesenburger in 1965 and the departure of his successor Ödön Singer shortly afterward, the GDR had no rabbi until 1987. Religious services were organized by cantors like Werner Sander (Leipzig) and Oljean Ingster (Berlin-East) or by the chairmen themselves. Kosher food and matzot had to be imported and were sometimes only available to the community in Berlin. Most members were not raised in religious households and only joined the community due to nostalgic reasons, matters of identity, and the need to feel part of a group. For the most part, they were comfortable with their situation in the GDR, being East German citizens while also retaining a fraction of their Jewish identity. This, however, was also the reason religious life remained marginal.[54]

Despite being raised in an orthodox household, Eschwege was more interested in Jewish culture and history than religion. This also spurred conflict with Helmut Aris. While he kept insisting on the solely religious constitution of the community, Eschwege dismissed this, criticizing that Aris himself would hardly live a religious Jewish life. Eschwege meticulously noted Aris's lapses, such as driving his car to Shabbat prayers, and reported them to other chairmen. The "personality cult" of Aris must come to an end, he wrote to Peter Kirchner, head of the Berlin community, in 1980.[55] Eschwege did not leave it at that but took matters in his own hands. Besides pushing for an election of a new president, he kept asking Peter Kirchner to replace Aris. Also, when Aris died in 1987, Eschwege tried to prevent Siegmund Rotstein from becoming his successor—to no avail.[56]

Eschwege did not recoil from cooperating with the Stasi in order to advance his own interests. For years, a rumor had been spread that the head of the community in Halle, Karin Mylius, was of non-Jewish origin. In fact, Mylius was the daughter of a Christian couple, converted only in 1961, successfully conspired against the chairman of the community, and succeeded him in 1968. The Stasi was first informed about these allegations in 1961, but ignored documents and accounts up until 1985. Mylius kept changing her life story and even compelled her son to stage fake anti-Semitic attacks on the family. Aris dismissed all criticism as calumny so that Mylius could continue as head. Eschwege received information about this by an employee of the community's archive in 1982. Three years later, the rumors became louder so that the Stasi approached Eschwege with a request. They wanted him to find proof of Mylius's non-Jewish origin. Angered by Aris's protection and driven by his indignation, Eschwege accepted. During a trip to Mylius's birthplace in Münster in Western Germany, he attained a copy of her birth certificate. Despite this evidence, Aris tried to protect Mylius but finally filed an indictment accusing her of fraud.[57]

Eschwege pressured Aris to dismiss Mylius, threatening publication of the allegations. He kept pushing Aris so that finally the Stasi felt compelled to intervene, urging Eschwege not to contact them in that matter again.[58] Eschwege, however, could not care less. He had informed the American paper *Aufbau* about the allegations months before, which had finally compelled the Stasi to act.[59] Mylius died of cancer before she could resign in late 1986. Despite the association's and the regime's interest in concealing this affair, Eschwege published an article about the history of the Jews in Halle in 1988 describing Mylius, though anonymously, as the daughter of a Nazi policeman.[60] The Stasi was alarmed and tried to stop the distribution of the journal but only managed to obtain half of the copies.[61] Eschwege had successfully asserted his intentions.

Due to his quarrels with the association, Eschwege tried to implement his views on Jewish culture elsewhere. He found an ally in Arnold Zweig who himself was concerned with the place of Jews in post-Shoah Germany. They had discussed the publication of a journal for the Jews in the GDR, but Zweig rejected the idea eventually given the small readership.[62] Moreover, Zweig was reworking his account of the Jewish contributions to the German nation, *Bilanz der deutschen Judenheit*. Eschwege suggested a broadening of the focus in order to include the European countries. He was eager to find representative scientists from every country and encouraged Zweig to write the chapter on Germany. As in the letter to Paul Merker, Eschwege again stressed that Jews should be granted national minority rights. Zweig was hesitant, and Eschwege kept suggesting the project for well over two years. Zweig never managed to finish the additional chapters on the Shoah and Eastern Europe, which he wanted to include into the new edition. Moreover, he denied Eschwege's request due to his impaired eyesight. Both agreed, however, that an account of the state of German Jewry after the Shoah was necessary, and that the Jewish culture of Eastern Europe had to put in contrast to that.[63]

Both Zweig and Eschwege contemplated what it meant to be Jewish after the Shoah, yet neither really managed to put it into words. While Zweig was struggling with the idea of a Jewish people and his place in it, Eschwege was firm in his belief. To him, Jewish existence after the Shoah negated the possibility of a "German-Jewish symbiosis." He kept referring to himself as a Jew domiciled in Germany, rather than a German Jew.

Anti-Semitism and Anti-Zionism

While Eschwege took a clear stance on Zionism, other community members felt trapped at times, torn between their allegiance to the party and the GDR, and their Jewish origin, linking them to Israel. The SED, following the Soviet Union's example, initially supported the foundation of the state. Yet from 1949 onward, the regime established strong ties with Israel's neighboring Arab countries. Israel was commonly depicted as an imperialist agent of the United States, and official rhetoric often linked Israeli policy to National Socialist crimes. The SED forced the communities to issue negative statements especially in times of war, but the association never gave in.[64]

Following the Six-Day War in 1967, though, Alfred Scheidemann (Schwerin) and Abraham Glanz (Magdeburg) succumbed to the pressure and critiqued the war. When Heinz Schenk (Berlin) heard about this he was furious, stating that

Scheidemann had "betrayed all Jews."[65] The two chairmen were questioned by the others shortly afterward. The reluctance to join the party in its damnation of Israel continued during the Yom Kippur war in 1973, although Helmut Aris issued a statement criticizing the war as such. Yet he underlined the special relationship of Jews with Israel. During a meeting with a group of party officials earlier that year, Aris explained, "We are Jews first of all."[66]

Eschwege supported this view, retaining a special fondness of the state ever since his time in exile there. He managed to visit his family four times in Israel but was denied several requests for additional trips. Eschwege used his time there for archival research as well and usually handed in an analysis of the state for the Stasi. In fact, he advanced to become one of the leading sources on Israel for the secret police, thereby trying to alter the regime's rigid image of the state.[67]

Furthermore, Eschwege was eager to defend Israel when, for example, a blatantly anti-Semitic fairy tale was printed in a children's paper in 1984. The story titled "Fire Dragon Zion" described how a small, starving dragon was fed by the "children of Palestine." The dragon grew stronger, devouring more and more food until everything was gone, which infuriated the dragon. The children concluded that "a dragon will always be a dragon" and expelled him "from their land."[68] In his letter to the editors, Eschwege scolded the author, pointing out that the history of Palestine was entirely different than suggested in the story while also stressing that "anti-Zionism always leads to a baiting of Jews." The editors promised to print a more nuanced tale about the friendship between Palestinian and Jewish children.[69]

During the Lebanon war in 1982, the president of the Technical University of Dresden, Eschwege's workplace, asked him to provide a written statement condemning Israeli policy. In his reply, he supported a two-state solution, concluding, "Neither my family nor any member of a Jewish community will agree to the destruction of Israel, a country which saved my family in need."[70] Shortly before, the head of Eschwege's department suggested granting him the university's award. Following the statement, however, Eschwege was not considered, and the professor suggesting him was scolded. He was finally honored in 1990.[71]

Eschwege not only did confront anti-Semitism in letters but also strove to educate the public via lectures. As in Western Germany, the broader East German public began to take an interest in Jewish culture from the 1960s onward. Church groups were particularly keen to strengthen their members' knowledge of and ties to the Jewish community. Eschwege soon became a sought after historian who was frequently invited for talks, especially since most of the established historians hardly took an interest in the matter. He traveled within both German states, supported the founding of a church group "Encounters with Judaism" in Dresden, and contributed to their work by giving lectures on Jewish history, the Shoah, and Israel. The efforts made in the GDR did not remain unnoticed. Eschwege and the minister Siegfried Theodor Arndt were awarded the Buber

Figure 6.1. Helmut Eschwege (second from right) celebrating Helmut Aris's twenty-fifth anniversary as chairman of the association, 24 June 1987. Photographer: Erhardt Freund. Source: Archive of the Jewish Community, Dresden.

Rosenzweig Medal in Western Germany in 1984.[72] Again, the Stasi took an interest in Eschwege's connections, resulting first in years of surveillance, and then in his second unofficial collaboration with them. Eschwege managed to satisfy his own interests with the help of the Stasi while supplying it with mostly trivial facts.[73]

In sum, Helmut Eschwege must be considered one of the most active and controversial Jewish citizens of the GDR. He did not refrain from collaborating with the Stasi, yet his reports were much less informative than often assumed. At times, he deliberately fooled the authorities, but gladly accepted the benefits of his relations with them. More important, Eschwege helped shape the rebuilding of Jewish life in the GDR, though his views often clashed with those of the party and the communities. Due to harsh restrictions, but also his often stubborn and unflinching manner, he failed in many of his attempts, and his actual influence within the communities was rather benign. Yet he is one of only few who were engaging passionately in Jewish life in the GDR. Oscillating between his Socialist conviction, Jewish origin, and experiences of anti-Semitic persecution, Eschwege was constantly struggling to reestablish Jewish culture in East Germany and finding aspects where his different perspectives could align. Unlike the chairmen of the communities, he did not define Jewishness as a matter of religion only but insisted on the existence of a Jewish people. Eschwege never quite believed in a "German-Jewish symbiosis," and, although he was concerned with the dissemination of Jewish culture to the subsequent generation, he remained deeply rooted in the prewar German-Jewish world, essentially failing to modernize his views.

NOTES

1. Helmut Eschwege to Arnold Zweig, 30 October 1948, Akademie der Künste Berlin (AdK), Arnold-Zweig-Archiv, 12436.

2. As an overview, see Constantin Goschler, "Die DDR und die Juden—Neue Literatur und Perspektiven," *H-Soz-Kult*, 1 January 1999, accessed 1 February 2018, https://www.hsozkult.de/publicationreview/id/rezbuecher-5122.

3. Cf. Peter Maser, "Helmut Eschwege: Ein jüdischer Historiker in der DDR," *Horch und Guck* 44 (2003); Stefan Meining, *Kommunistische Judenpolitik: Die DDR, die Juden und Israel* (Hamburg: Lit, 2002), 205–215. For a nunanced view cf. Karin Hartewig, *Zurückgekehrt. Die Geschichte der jüdischen Kommunisten in der DDR* (Cologne: Böhlau, 2000), 186–194.

4. Helmut Eschwege, *Fremd unter meinesgleichen: Erinnerungen eines Dresdner Juden* (Berlin: Ch. Links, 1991).

5. Cf. Hendrik Niether, *Leipziger Juden und die DDR: Eine Existenzerfahrung im Kalten Krieg* (Göttingen: Vandenhoeck & Ruprecht, 2014), 33–34; Nora Goldenbogen, "Jüdisches Leben in Sachsen 1945 bis 1989," in *Juden in Sachsen*, ed. Gunda Ulbricht and Olaf Glöckner (Leipzig: Edition Leipzig, 2013), 177–189.

6. Gershom Schocken, "We and the Germans," *Ha'aretz*, September 2, 1949, cited in Tamara Anthony, "Ins Land der Väter oder der Täter? Israel und die Juden in Deutschland nach der Schoah" (Berlin: Metropol, 2004), 151.

7. Cited in Jay Howard Geller, *Jews in Post-Holocaust Germany, 1945–1953* (New York: Cambridge University Press, 2005), 62; also cf. Dan Diner, "Im Zeichen des Banns," in *Geschichte der Juden in Deutschland von 1945 bis zur Gegenwart: Politik, Kultur und Gesellschaft*, ed. Michael Brenner (Munich: C. H. Beck, 2012), 21.

8. Hartewig estimates about 1,000 to 3,500, though some 34,000 former racially persecuted people lived in Berlin alone in summer 1946. Cf. Hartewig, *Zurückgekehrt*, 2–3.

9. Hartewig, *Zurückgekehrt*, 104–106, quote 105.

10. Cf. Wolfgang Benz, "Die Legende von der deutsch-jüdischen Symbiose," *Merkur* 45, no. 2 (1991).

11. Jewish Community Berlin to Magistrat of Berlin, 11 February 1946, Centrum Judaicum Berlin Archive (CJA), 5 A 1, Nr. 1.

12. Jewish Community Chemnitz to State Government of Saxony, 3 August 1948, cited in Jürgen Nitsche, *Juden in Chemnitz: Die Geschichte der Gemeinde und ihrer Mitglieder mit einer Dokumentation des jüdischen Friedhofs* (Dresden: Sandstein, 2002), 178–179.

13. Cf. Eschwege, *Fremd*, 12–32.

14. Cf. Eschwege, 33–50; Hajo Funke and Robin Ostow, "The Unorthodox Approach to Jewish History in the German Democratic Republic: An Interview with Helmut Eschwege," *New German Critique* 38 (1986).

15. Cf. Olaf Groehler, "Antifaschismus und jüdische Problematik in der SBZ und der frühen DDR," *Die SED-Politik, der Antifaschismus und die Juden in der SBZ und der frühen DDR*, ed. Olaf Groehler and Mario Keßler (Berlin: Gesellschaftswissenschaftliches Forum, 1995).

16. Eschwege, *Fremd*, 66.

17. See the questionnaire, dated 1952, in Archive of the Jewish Community of Dresden (AJGD), A03-02-02.

18. Eschwege to the regional control commission, 4 August 1951, cited in Eschwege, *Fremd*, 66–67.

19. American Joint Distribution Committee (Joint) to Jewish Community of Dresden, 9 March 1948, AJGD, A03-01-48.

20. Jewish Community of Dresden to Joint, 1 April 1948, AJGD, A03-01-48.

21. Jewish Community of Dresden to Helmut Eschwege, 17 April 1948, AJGD, A03-01-48.

22. Hartewig, *Zurückgekehrt*, 274–314; Geller, *Jews*, 112–118.

23. Jeffrey Herf, "East German Communists and the Jewish Question: The Case of Paul Merker," *Journal of Contemporary History* 29, no. 4 (1994).

24. Helmut Eschwege to Paul Merker, 10 February 1946, Bundesarchiv Berlin (BArch), DY 30/68820, 4–6, quote on 4. Eschwege's plea to outlaw anti-Semitism almost became realized when the regional parliament in Saxony approved a draft bill against the "Avowal of Hatred against People, Faith, or Race," proposing up to five years in prison for anti-Semitic utterances. The bill was eventually dismissed. Cf. Angelika Timm, *Hammer, Zirkel, Davidstern: Das gestörte Verhältnis der DDR zu Zionismus und Staat Israel* (Bonn: Bouvier, 1997), 106–110.

25. Two versions of this letter exist, dated 1946 and 1947 (BArch, DY 30/68821, 31–35). Hartewig is right in assessing that 1947 is correct rather than 1946 as Jeffrey Herf states (Hartewig, *Zurückgekehrt*, 285); Jeffrey Herf, *Divided Memory: The Nazi Past in the Two Germanys* (Cambridge, Mass.: Harvard University Press, 1997), 85. The copy dated 1946 contains the additional, crucial sentence on minority rights, combined with a footnote on Stalin's dismissal of this right, which Eschwege seems to have added afterward. The 1947 version lacking the sentence seems to be the fair copy. How both letters ended up in the party archive is unclear. Cf. also Graham Smith, ed. *The Nationalities Question in the Soviet Union* (London: Longman, 1990).

26. Cf. Hartewig, *Zurückgekehrt*, 274–314; Niether, *Leipziger Juden*, 82–94.

27. Jewish Community of Dresden to Eschwege, 6 December 1951, AJGD, A03-01-51; cf. Eschwege, *Fremd*, 62.

28. Cf. Nikolaus Wachsmann, *KL: A History of the Nazi Concentration Camps* (London: Little, Brown, 2015), 140–151.

29. Cf. Mary Fulbrook, "East Germans in a Post-Nazi State: Communities of Experience, Connection, and Identification," in *Becoming East German: Socialist Structures and Sensibilities after Hitler*, ed. Mary Fulbrook and Andrew Port (New York: Berghahn Books, 2013), 35–41.

30. Jewish Community of Dresden to Eschwege, 25 October 1951, AJGD, A03-01-51.

31. Cf. Geller, *Jews*, 169–176.

32. Zentralarchiv zur Erforschung der Geschichte der Juden in Deutschland (ZA), B. 2/11, Nr. 4 and 10.

33. Cf. Eschwege, *Fremd*, 76.

34. Jewish Community of Dresden to State Association of Jewish Communities in the GDR, 20 April 1953, AJGD, A03-01-53.

35. Helmut Eschwege to Jewish Community of Dresden, 18 November 1957, AJGD, A03-01-57.

36. Eschwege, *Fremd*, 154.

37. Report by "Irene Müller," 16 January 1953, Der Bundesbeauftragte für die Unterlagen des Staatssicherheitsdienstes der ehemaligen Deutschen Demokratischen Republik (BStU), MfS, BV Dresden, AIM Nr. 448/58, Handakte, 3.

38. BStU, MfS, BV Dresden, AIM Nr. 448/58, Personalakte, 27; BStU, MfS, BV Dresden, AIM Nr. 448/58, Bd. 1.

39. Cf. Nora Goldenbogen, "Leon Löwenkopf, erster Vorsitzender der Jüdischen Gemeinde zu Dresden nach der Shoah," in *Zwischen Erinnerung und Neubeginn. Zur deutsch-jüdischen Geschichte nach 1945*, ed. Susanne Schönborn (Munich: Meidenbauer, 2006).

40. Cf. BStU, MfS, BV Dresden, AIM Nr. 448/58, Bd. 1, 24, 32, 48–50.

41. Cf. Eschwege, *Fremd*, 85 (although Eschwege trivializes his relationship with the Stasi).

42. Cf. Eschwege, 87–89. See also several letters by and to the party, 1956–1958, ZA, B. 2/11, Nr. 4.3.

43. Cf. Herf, *Divided Memory*, 106–200. The term was frequently used in speeches by both community and party officials. See Hartewig, *Zurückgekehrt*, 5.

44. Cf. Geller, *Jews*, 182.

45. Cf. Heinz Schenk, Jewish Community Berlin, to Eschwege, 3 December 1959, AJGD, A03-01-59. Although they granted him access to their own archive, Eschwege's main interest was the *Gesamtarchiv der deutschen Juden*, parts of which were confiscated by the SED and moved to Potsdam in 1958.

46. ZA, B. 2/11, Nr. 6–9 and Nr. 13. Cf. Eschwege, *Fremd*, 184–277. He could only publish a collection of sources: Helmut Eschwege, ed. *Kennzeichen J: Bilder, Dokumente, Berichte zur Geschichte der Verbrechen des Hitlerfaschismus an den deutschen Juden 1933–1945* (Berlin: Deutscher Verlag der Wissenschaften, 1966).

47. Cf. the letters in AJGD, A03-01-64, and Eschwege, *Fremd*, 158.

48. Cf. Eschwege, 157–158.

49. Eschwege, *Antwort auf einige Fragen*, 2 February 1957, BStU MfS BV Dresden AIM Nr. 448/58, Personalakte, 57–59, and ZA, B. 2/11, 4.8.

50. Eschwege to Jewish Community of Dresden, 1 January 1968, AJGD, A03-01-68.

51. Eschwege to Israelite Religious Community Leipzig, 5 July 1971, ZA, B. 2/11, Nr. 15, and in CJA, 5 B 1, Nr. 179, 13–15.

52. Cf. Niether, *Leipziger Juden*, 236–238.

53. Association to the communities, 17 June 1963, cited in Erica Burgauer, *Zwischen Erinnerung und Verdrängung: Juden in Deutschland nach 1945* (Reinbeck: Rowohlt, 1993), 149.

54. An exception was the chairman of the Leipzig community, Eugen Gollomb; cf. Burgauer, *Erinnerung*, 137–152, 202–208.

55. Eschwege to Peter Kirchner, 18 February 1980, ZA, B. 2/11, Nr. 15, and his letters to other chairmen, ZA, B. 2/11, Nr. 15, and in CJA, 5 B 1, Nr. 179.

56. See the letters in ZA, B. 2/11, Nr. 15.

57. BStU, MfS, BV Dresden, AIM 5010/90, Bd. I/I, 71–79; BStU, MfS, BV Dresden, AIM 5010/90, Bd. II/I, 9–21; BStU, MfS, HA XX/4, Nr. 605, 162–176. Cf. Frank Hirschinger, *Fälschung und Instrumentalisierung antifaschistischer Biographien: Das Beispiel Halle/Saale 1945–2005* (Göttingen: v&r unipress, 2007), 113–136.

58. BStU, MfS, HA XX/4, Nr. 605, 177–179; BStU, MfS, BV Dresden, AIM 5010/90, Bd. I/I, 79.

59. Hermann Pichler, "Kontroverse um Gemeindevorsitzende von Halle," *Aufbau*, 12 April 1985, 5.

60. Helmut Eschwege, "Geschichte der Juden in Halle/Saale," *Wissenschaftliche Zeitschrift der Universität Halle* 37, no. 5 (1988), 37. Mylius's father was a policeman during National Socialism, yet it is unclear whether he actually joined a battalion engaged in killing Jews in Eastern Europe as Eschwege suggested. Cf. Hirschinger, *Fälschung*, 116; Eschwege, *Fremd*, 162; Burgauer, *Erinnerung*, 208–221.

61. BStU, MfS, HA XX/4, Nr. 605, 78.

62. See the letters in AdK, Arnold-Zweig-Archiv, Nr. 14692 and 14693.

63. AdK, Arnold-Zweig-Archiv, Nr. 13803, 13804, 14074, 14414, and 14415.

64. Cf. Timm, *Hammer*, 171–332.

65. BStU, MfS, ZA 14719/69, Bd. 3, 73–74.

66. Meeting of the chairmen with staff of the state secretary, 30 January 1973, BArch, DO 4, 1341. See a copy in Timm, *Hammer*, 541–545. Eugen Gollomb scolded Aris for this statement, resulting in a boycott of the association's journal by the Leipzig community. Cf. Niether, *Leipziger Juden*, 224–227.

67. BStU, MfS, BV Dresden, AIM 5010/90, Bd. II/1, 81–88, 196–224. Cf. Hartewig, *Zurückgekehrt*, 191, 194.

68. Paul Horst Basedow, "Der Feuerdrache Zion," *Die ABC-Zeitung* 11 (1984), 18.

69. ZA, B. 2/11, Nr. 5. Eschwege was not alone in this matter as the story had provoked several reactions. Other than that it was usually only Eugen Gollomb who was similarly eager to protest anti-Semitism. Cf. Niether, *Leipziger Juden*, 223–234; Christian Gaubert, "Der Nahostkonflikt und die Wahrnehmung Israels in Kinder- und Jugendzeitschriften der DDR," in *Antisemitismus in der DDR. Manifestationen und Folgen des Feindbildes Israel*, ed. Wolfgang Benz (Berlin: Metropol, 2018), 42–43, 60–62.

70. BStU, MfS, BV Dresden, APO 2222/84, Bd. 3, 217–218.

71. BStU, MfS, BV Dresden, OD TU/H 1284, 147–148. Cf. Eschwege, *Fremd*, 278–279.

72. Cf. Eschwege, 167–179; Niether, *Leipziger Juden*, 239–250. See the certificate ZA, B. 2/11, Nr. 45.

73. BStU, MfS, BV Dresden, AIM 5010/90, Bd. I/1, 152–154; BStU, MfS, BV Dresden, AIM 5010/90, Bd. II/1, 11.

CHAPTER 7

LEARNING YEARS ON THE PATH TO DISSIDENCE

STEFAN HEYM'S FRIENDSHIP WITH ROBERT HAVEMANN AND WOLF BIERMANN

Cathy S. Gelbin

As near-destitute refugees, Stefan Heym and his American wife Gertrude Gelbin arrived in the GDR in 1952 with shattered illusions and freshly minted hope. Behind them lay an almost unprecedented odyssey through a broken Europe, which had indirectly led them back through the stations of Heym's exile from National Socialism—the United States, Czechoslovakia, Germany. Before them lay a series of events that would forever change their view of socialism: the Stalinist Slánský trials in Czechoslovakia in 1952, in which the majority of those executed were Jews; the Paul Merker trial in the GDR in 1953, which, although not fatal, still took place under similar circumstances; the uprising in East Berlin on 17 June 1953; the Soviet military suppression of the Hungarian uprising of 1956; the construction of the Berlin Wall in 1961; and last but not least the invasion of Soviet troops in Czechoslovakia in 1968, which shattered the idea of "socialism with a human face." This long period of disillusionment had begun with an escape from the anti-Communist pursuits of Senator McCarthy in the United States; it would end with the death of Heym's wife, my grandmother, in the gloomy East Berlin of January 1969. In this foreign land, she was eventually broken by the impossibility of keeping her socialist dream in the face of real-world circumstances.

Stefan Heym (1913–2001), whose life spans all five political systems in twentieth-century Germany—the Empire, the Weimar Republic, National Socialism, the divided German states of the Cold War, and German and European unity after 1990, became one of the most versatile and widely read German-speaking authors of the postwar era on both sides of the German-German divide. Like no other individual in divided Germany, Heym united literary meaning with real political commitment and thus became a prominent moral and politically symbolic figure. Even in the GDR, whose politics attained increasingly dictatorial traits after 1953, Heym derived his sustained literary and political credentials from his exemplary embodiment of the "Good Germany," whose democratic traditions had been evoked by Thomas Mann in his famous speech at the American Library of Congress in May 1945.

Heym was born the son of a Jewish merchant family in Chemnitz in 1913. As the author of an antiwar poem, the high school student had already by 1932 been forced to flee Chemnitz by a gang of Brownshirts. He traveled to Berlin and emigrated from there to Prague in 1933. From 1935 he lived in the United States, where he got by as a dishwasher and editor of the expatriate newspaper *Deutsches Volksecho* (*German People's Echo*). While in exile in New York, he got to know Gertrude, who was thirteen years his elder and used her first married name Gelbin throughout her life. Through her advertising work at Metro-Goldwyn-Mayer Hollywood Studios, she helped Heym to establish himself as a writer in the United States, as well as to connect with other intellectuals. From 1943, after becoming a U.S. citizen, Heym served in the U.S. Army in the Ritchie Boys reconnaissance unit and from there advanced to sergeant for psychological warfare.[1] In the GDR, Heym was immediately courted with material benefits for intellectuals. He acquired a villa in a quarter of Grünau erected specifically for his purposes, in which he lived and wrote until his death. Gertrude Gelbin founded the sub-publication Panther Books with Liszt Verlag Leipzig, in which she published the original works of English-speaking authors. From 1958, a series of works under the new title "Seven Seas" appeared through Volk & Welt Verlag. This is where the early works of Stefan Heym appeared—until Gelbin's death, he initially wrote in English before translating his material into German himself—alongside authors from the United States, the United Kingdom, Australia, and South Africa.

According to Heym's self-portrayal, his personality was often described as being in a state of permanent dissent against all the political systems in which he lived.[2] In fact, Heym continually took an oppositional stance in relation to the powers that be as they were determined by the way of the world. Yet Heym's development into the most significant GDR dissenter of the 1980s is anything but monolithic. Such a description would be too smooth, too simple, and would barely correspond to the checkered life of its protagonist; it relies too much upon a claim derived from the irreconcilable dichotomies of National Socialism and the Cold War, with its clear lines, ideological unambiguity, and moral absoluteness. The following analysis of the important steps in Heym's development into dissidence in the 1960s, exemplified through his friendship with two prominent GDR dissenters in Robert Havemann and Wolf Biermann, is conducted in the context of a broadly based biographical project that seeks to reveal anew the character of Heym via previously understudied biographical evidence—including biographical texts, secret service files and previously unpublished image sources.[3] In particular, this chapter will accentuate the Jewish aspect of Heym's life and work, as well as Heym's self-determination as a cosmopolitan whose interactions ultimately catalyzed his emergence as the most significant dissenter of the GDR.

Such a reading of Heym allows new conclusions on the role of Jews in GDR culture and politics by scrutinizing the established argument of the generally loyal Jewish population within the GDR. This cliché has until now culminated in Michael Wolffsohn's depiction of Jews in the GDR as "criminals and victims, villains and useful idiots, hangers-on and collaborators."[4] "Some of them were apparent, not real disturbers of the peace, most notably Stefan Heym," so Wolffsohn[5] concludes, invoking Marcel Reich-Ranicki's postulation that Jews are "disturbers of the peace" in German literature.[6] Regarding accusations of collaboration with the GDR regime, Wolffsohn predominantly exempts authors of Jewish heritage who moved to the West, such as Jurek Becker, Wolf Biermann, and Barbara Honigmann, yet does not sufficiently illuminate the individual routes of these authors. Such an undifferentiated view may serve as a good example of Robin Ostow's observation from 1988 that the majority of investigations into Jews within the GDR support a considerably polarized character and are "not much more than primitive communist or anti-communist propaganda."[7] The present study seeks to expand this constricted view concerning the issue of openly expressed Jewish particularity as political provocation, as viewed by GDR leaders—a strategy that Heym also increasingly deployed.

By contrast, apart from some helpful small-scale investigations into Heym's work in the context of his biography,[8] as well as a series of individual depictions of the person and his work,[9] no comprehensive academic biography of Stefan Heym exists to this day. In addition, there has been broader research on Jews in the history, politics, and culture of the GDR and in the unified Federal Republic of Germany since 1990, offering relevant insight into both the position of Jews in GDR politics and culture as well as the function of Jews in national political discourse.[10] This body of workplaces the history of Jews in the GDR in the context of the history of Jewish communities, which nonetheless only covered a small proportion of Jews living there, as well as official discourse on National Socialism and Israel.[11] Currently, there are also various investigations into the depiction of Jewish individuals, specifically in GDR literature and film, as well as the relationship of individual Jewish authors and artists to their Jewish heritage.

However, such investigations often struggle to comprehend the Communist and often radically assimilated attitudes of their subjects, even under Jewish auspices. During the Weimar Republic, in which Heym also grew up, many left-leaning Jews had subsumed these aspects of their self-presentation under the term *cosmopolitanism*, which was also posited as internationalism in accordance with Communist Party policy in the 1920s.[12] However, in the wake of the Stalinist terror, internationalism gradually retreated behind Soviet nationalism, until it became an anti-Semitic epithet analogous to Nazi ideology. Nevertheless, a cosmopolitan foundation remained in the self-determination of many Jews, particularly those who had come from all over the world to the "better Germany" during the early postwar era. Many of them would once again leave this land in the mid-1960s in order to save themselves from Stalinist persecution or at least to escape political pressure.

Others, such as Heym and his wife, stayed, although they felt Germany—even its Eastern side—to be enemy territory due to the Holocaust. They assembled an international circle, which has received little attention from researchers until now, in which they saw their Jewish sensibilities subsumed. Under the auspices of cosmopolitanism, they created a sphere characterized by their understanding of Jewish values and history, such as the struggle for social justice and against "racial oppression," which may be viewed as a sign of their "Jewish sensibilities"[13] and which they also passed on to their familial and social environment. Moreover, Heym became aware of aspects of an ethnic-Jewish self-image that he had observed in American Jews, predominantly immigrants from Eastern Europe, during his exile. Indeed, his wife Gertrude Gelbin also came from this environment. In the context of Jewish friendships, or those forged from National Socialist persecution, which Heym made particularly during his phase of disillusionment with state socialism between 1952 and 1968, this chapter will trace and investigate the formation of these Jewish sensibilities in relation to the GDR, insofar as they were also mutually dependent on Heym's emergence as a dissenter.

"A Kind of Emergency Group": Heym, Havemann, Zuckermann, and Hollitscher

By the beginning of the 1960s, his friendship with Robert Havemann (1910–1982) would become the decisive political and personal alliance for Heym outside of his marital and working relationship with Gertrude Gelbin. His association with Havemann was based on close political agreements relating to their fundamental approval of the socialist idea and their simultaneously increasing criticism of the SED state. Even on a personal level, there were deep affinities, which cemented their association until its sudden termination by Heym in 1966. In his recently published autobiography, Wolf Biermann (born 1936), who became the third member of this friendship group from 1963, accuses Heym implicitly of cowardice. Heym, consistently referred to as a "scaredy-cat" with the occasional addition of "cheeky," was said to have buckled under the pressure of the GDR regime after the Eleventh Plenum.

Heym's account of Havemann in *Nachruf* (Obituary) begins with a distancing from his former friends, by which Heym simultaneously also implicitly modifies his own role as an opponent of the GDR at that time: "There was never a Havemann-Biermann-Heym Group whose members, the first a balladeer, the second a publicist and the third a spiritus rector, had planned to subvert the Republic."[14] Contrary to claims at the Eleventh Plenum of the SED Central Committee in 1965, there had been no subversive element, but merely the "symbol and voice" of subliminally constructed oppositional movements in the GDR.[15] Nevertheless, Heym's friendship with Havemann, albeit circuitously, was to become the pivotal moment in his development into dissent.

Heym's relationship with Havemann was marked by deep admiration as well as gratitude for the resistant role taken when Havemann had risked his life for Jews facing persecution. As early as the summer of 1952, shortly after arriving in the GDR, Heym had encountered the, in his eyes, already "legendary Professor Havemann [. . .], who had helped to organize the resistance in Brandenburg Prison from death row" at Bertolt Brecht's house, where the "eternally cheerful" Viennese philosopher and psychoanalyst Walter Hollitscher had introduced him.[16] However, Havemann was an ambivalent political hero, far more than Heym may have known. As we know today, after the National Socialists seized power, the young Communist Havemann had made occasional dubious remarks about the Jews before he transformed himself into an insurgent. In 1943, Havemann qualified for the Kaiser Wilhelm Institut (KWI) at the University of Berlin with "a poison gas project for the Army Ordinance Office." Also in 1943, he founded the European Union Resistance Group with three other men, which chiefly supplied persecuted Jews with concealment and forged papers.[17] For these supporting efforts, Havemann was posthumously honored with the title "Righteous Among the Nations" by Yad Vashem in 2005. Allegedly, of those affected, only one woman had ultimately survived.[18]

In the summer of 1943, the four founding members of this group were accused by Roland Freisler, chair of the People's Court, of "Communist conspiracy," "espionage," and "supporting Jews living illegally" and were sentenced to death.[19] As his knowledge as a chemist was vital to the war effort, Havemann alone was spared execution. While still imprisoned at Brandenburg-Görden, where he had been given a laboratory especially equipped for him, he wrote a flyer for the underground.[20] After his release, Havemann returned to the KWI, now situated in the American zone of West Berlin; in 1946, he also attained a professorship in physical chemistry at Humboldt University in the Soviet zone of occupation. In 1950, after his abrupt release from the KWI on the grounds of his protests against the American hydrogen bomb, he was relocated to the GDR. There, he was appointed Director of the Institute for Physical Chemistry at Humboldt University and obtained a series of high political offices.

Havemann's interest in the overlap between science and Marxist theory coincided with the interests of Walter Hollitscher, through whom he became acquainted with Heym, from the opposite perspective. Much like Heym, Hollitscher had come to the GDR as a Jewish Western emigrant, although he was now a Lutheran convert.[21] Returning from British exile first to Vienna, he had been studying the relationship between Marxist theory and physics as director of the Institute for Philosophy at Humboldt University since 1949.[22] Also on the panel was Leo Zuckermann, whom Heym also knew from his exile in New York and who now worked together with Havemann at the university. In his 1978 interview with Eckart Boege in Mexico City, Zuckermann remembers the "circle" that comprised Heym, Hollitscher, and "Havermann" (obviously meaning Havemann) alongside the attractive wives of Hollitscher and Heym. This, according to Zuckermann, had been a kind of international emergency group in which they could let off steam about the state of the GDR in private company. According to Zuckermann, Heym had already launched heavy criticisms of the current situation in the GDR from the beginning of his time there.

> We came together and discussed anything and everything. The boldest of us, of course, was Stefan Heym, who didn't much care about anything. He would go on rants. . . . And then Stefan began, "but I heard something today" . . . , that was awful. . . . Basically, it was awful that people who had other things to discuss were discussing such rot. It was also an internationally mixed society. At the time, Hollitscher's wife was an Italian, . . . she was so beautiful and Heym's wife was an American and American women can be beautiful, and how. And it was a very nice circle, but we were more thrown together, it was more a kind of emergency group.[23]

Indeed, Heym's previous circle soon fell apart due to burgeoning political and purges with anti-Semitic motivators within the GDR. "By night and fog (not a metaphor)," as it was reported in February 1953 by Alfred Kantorowicz, himself a Jewish Western emigrant and professor of modern German literature at Humboldt University, Leo Zuckermann fled from his villa in Niederschönhausen with his wife and child.[24] This had happened previously in December 1952, after the infamous decision of the SED Central Committee in the Slánský trial, when Zuckermann crossed the border to West Berlin. His journey took him via France to Mexico, where he had already spent his exile from National Socialism. Walter Hollitscher was arrested by the Stasi in 1953 and turned up again later, under mysterious circumstances, in his home city of Vienna. Much like Zuckermann, Kantorowicz also eventually escaped the looming political persecution for West Berlin in 1957.

Heym and Havemann: A Political Friendship between Men

In the subsequent years until the end of 1965, Havemann, now almost twenty years older, had become Heym's closest personal friend and an important political adviser. Heym's ongoing admiration for Havemann is also presented in an almost unequaled description of Havemann's remarkable physical presence: "Were it not for his ears, which were too large and stuck out to boot, and his wide, thin mouth, Havemann might have been considered a handsome man," Heym remembers in *Nachruf.*[25] To this end, Havemann had "a fine, manly laugh" that could "reduce even the profoundest of verbose declarations by the powers that be to their true size."[26] Heym evidently felt attracted to Havemann's rarely consistent attributes as a resistance fighter and intellectual, in which he, as a writer and victorious war veteran, could, in a way, probably also see himself reflected. For Heym, who by his own account had always shown an inclination toward heroes, Havemann started out as precisely that. As Heym wrote, "There is the cell on death row from which he always supplied the entire prison with news, [. . .] there is the position he took towards the strikers on the day of June 17, there are his scientific achievements."[27]

Even in the early days of their friendship, Heym's literary work was inspired by Havemann. In July 1953, Heym started work on his new novel about the East Berlin uprising of 17 June 1953, under the title *Der Tag X* (*Day X*). To that end, he also consulted Havemann, who as an insider of the GDR nomenclatura could provide him with important internal details.[28] However, in 1956 Khrushchev revealed Stalin's crimes at the Twentieth Congress of the CPSU and then bloodily suppressed the Hungarian Uprising, strengthening the voice of the GDR against intellectuals. In 1957, Heym lost his column in the *Berliner Zeitung*, "Offen gesagt" (Speaking frankly), in which he had publicly denounced the economic inequalities that had led to the 1953 East Berlin Uprising. By 1960, *Day X* was finally completed. In 1961, the Ministry of Culture ultimately forbade its publication, despite Heym's repeated revisions to the novel and his concessions to the official GDR interpretation of the Uprising. In this respect, Havemann launched a clear broadside against Heym. Their friendship had meanwhile broken down when he wrote in a book published in West Germany in 1970 that Heym should be grateful to the Party that "Day X" was never published. After all, Heym accepts the fundamentally incorrect official interpretation in which the "June 17" incident was a counterrevolutionary affair organized by Western secret services.[29]

State Security Service [Stasi] documents demonstrate Heym's continual attempts throughout the 1960s to attain a GDR publication of his novel through perseverance, humor, and guile. He produced writings from memory and hauled a tape recorder along with him to debates and events in order to hold functionaries to their word. He sneaked into events of socialist writers' associations, from which he had been excluded, in order to take the floor. And he responded to rejections of his manuscript and the public attacks by functionaries with indignant letters that he addressed personally to those involved. He fought with the typewritten word, but in vain: the novel was not accepted for publication in the GDR. Only in 1974 was *Der Tag X* published in the West for the first time under the title *Five Days in June*; in 1989, the book was finally released in the then collapsing GDR.

Almost in parallel to this in the mid-1960s, Havemann began his transition to dissent. In the autumn of 1963, Havemann, who had meanwhile been judged an ideological enemy by the Stasi, began his public lectures at Humboldt University on "Scientific Aspects of Philosophical Problems," in which he spoke on questions of freedom and democracy in revolutionary socialism. Together with an audience from across the Republic, Heym and Havemann's new friend Wolf Biermann attended these lectures. Soon, Havemann's lectures were branded revisionist by the Party. In 1964, Havemann was expelled from the SED; in 1965, he lost his professorship. Also in 1965, after the West German publication of his first volume of poetry, *Die Drahtharfe* (*The Wire Harp*)—then widely hushed up in the GDR—Biermann was also blacklisted from the GDR. Heym and Havemann's friendship reached its zenith at this time in which both provided moral and practical support for each other in their struggle against increasing ostracism. Havemann maintained "a very intense connection to Heym," as summarized by the Stasi at the beginning of 1966.[30] "It is probable that Heym is the true spiritus rector of Havemann's political-ideological activities,"[31] so they argued, concluding that "the scribblings of HEYM are essentially nothing more than HAVEMANN's proclaimed philosophy transposed into writing."[32]

Heym relied on Havemann, among other things, in his efforts with *Day X*. In 1961, according to an undated report from the Stasi, he sent a manuscript, likely *Day X*, to a series of high-ranking personalities in the GDR, including Walter Ulbricht, Walter Grotewohl, and Albert Norden. Robert Havemann also received a copy.[33] Heym clearly wished to disseminate this manuscript among these people to cause the functionaries to change their minds. On 19 January 1961, Heym was summoned by Alfred Kurella, head of the Cultural Commission of the SED Central Committee Politburo, to make a verbal statement on *Day X*. Heym, however, offered a written reply refusing Kurella. Subsequently, Heym invited Kurella together with his co-workers and their wives to an informal "cognac" or "dinner evening" at his home, so that "we can then talk reasonably with one another." Obviously struck by Heym's offer, Kurella grudgingly agreed. The phone call recorded by the Stasi was not without its unintentionally comical moments, as Kurella weakly added that this would be "no matter for women. Heym: No matter for women? Kurella: No. Heym: Well, well. Many beautiful women appear in the book. (Long pause)."[34] Kurella clearly could not counter Heym's ironic-erotic allusion.

The discussion took place in May 1961 when Kurella appeared at Heym's villa in Grünau with one colleague as backup. However, to his surprise, it emerged that Heym had also invited reinforcement, arriving in the form of Havemann. "Under these circumstances, the discussion was declined by Comrade KURELLA," the Stasi noted.[35] In a later report, the Stasi recorded that Arnold Zweig had also been invited and was present at this meeting, because "HEYM clearly wanted to force an acceptance or concrete statement from the comrades of the Central Committee before witnesses."[36] In January 1964, Heym delivered an additional manuscript to Havemann only a few days before the latter traveled to West Germany; it was likely to do with *Day X*, which Havemann was to bring along to discussions with interested Western parties.[37]

But these men were also connected via close personal interests, which, among other things, consisted of their tendency toward whiling away hours in the country. The Stasi reported reciprocal visits between both men as well as the close friendship between their wives, Gertrude Gelbin and Karin Havemann, which even survived after the Havemanns' divorce in 1966. In *Nachruf*, Heym recalls, "Still, they were nice, the hours in the cottage by the lake in Grünheide behind Erkner, in which both of them, S.H. and the professor, talked of so much that was subversive; but what was not subversive at that time? Sometimes, S.H. came in his motorboat, which was moored, on the Langer lake, alongside ferries from Grünau to Wendenschloss."[38]

Even Wolf Biermann fondly remembered these summer days spent together, when Heym "would race up beside Robert in an elegant two-seater motorboat. His clever wife Gertrude always beside him [. . .]. They reached a waterway from Grünau via the canals and lakes of the Mark region as far as Erkner, sailed further and then moored alongside Kuddeldaddeldu [Robert's boat] at Robert's own dock. . . . Sociable conversations took place in Robert's dacha, as well as summer parties, Bacchanalian eating, drinking and lovemaking. Belligerence, spirit, an appetite for contradiction, a hunger for truth. . . . I supplied these friends with fresh *Seelenbrot* [soul bread] and erotic desserts to the delicious sound of my guitar."[39]

This is a generation that has much catching up to do following persecution and war. This particularly applies to Havemann, Heym, and Biermann, who all experienced a loss of rights, powerlessness, and probably also damaged manhood due to this persecution. They met with a response from German women who had often spent a damaged childhood and youth in a shower of bombings, had lost their fathers and, in their view, have something to catch up on and something to forget. Only a few years after the construction of the Wall, this "Bohemia of the East," as Jutta Voigt has recently termed it,[40] arose with its excessive lifestyle and objection to the increasing feeling of imprisonment by the dry, humorless functionaries of the GDR.

Damaged Father Figures in the Name of the Holocaust

The portrayal of wounds inflicted by the Holocaust in relation to fathers is among the most moving passages in the autobiographies of Heym and Biermann. From Havemann, in contrast, there is only a cursory glimpse of his nationally disposed yet apolitical parents. Similar to the age difference between Gertrude Gelbin and Stefan Heym, Havemann's mother was also thirteen years older than his father. Originating from a noble military family, she was a painter and the dominant influence on her son. Havemann's father had initially been a teacher; later, as a magazine editor before 1933, he had a large circle of Jewish acquaintances. In his autobiography, Havemann, having become a radical Communist after the National Socialists' accession to power, evidently wished to stand out from this bourgeois environment.[41] Heym also constructed his beginnings in a similar way. He was the only one in his family to become a Communist, and he also saw his father as a person marked by an "otherness"[42] in the sense that he was shaped by Prussian fulfillment of duty and found it difficult to display emotions and physical affection toward his two sons. But in the wake of Nazi persecution, a fundamental change occurred in Heym's relationship with his father, whom his son now painfully saw as the vulnerable one in need of protection. And yet this new view of his father also allowed for hitherto unexperienced facets of tenderness and vulnerability.

In *Nachruf*, Heym recalls feelings of "pity, love, an anticipation of death, or all three in one,"[43] which had befallen him during his final encounter with his father. At this time, Heym was already living in exile in Prague; after his escape from Germany, his father, now fifty-three years old, was taken in his place into Gestapo custody, from which he, already a depressed man, returned broken. After his release, he visited his son in Prague. There, Heym noticed while his father was shaving in the morning "the white patterns of scarred-over cuts"[44] on his wrists, the signs of past suicide attempts. At their farewell, at the train window, Daniel Flieg gripped "the hands of his son once again [. . .], who once more ha[d] the scars on the wrists before his eyes and sobs."[45] A few months later, Heym, having reached Chicago, heard of his father's successful suicide. "This time," Heym wrote, "he had brought it to an end."[46] Heym illustrates the profound turning point of this experience stylistically by letting his autobiography suddenly lapse from a third-person to a first-person narrative: "I have sometimes asked myself if I share any guilt in the death of my father."[47]

Even in Biermann's overall characteristically casual narrative tone, the memory of his father becomes one of the most touching moments in his autobiography. Biermann writes about the imprisonment of the Hamburg dockyard worker Dagobert Biermann, who remained for him an "intimately close, strange man."[48] As Biermann recalled, "My father was torn from me when I was four months old. . . . Grief for the Communist, the worker, the Jew Biermann is my fateful influence, my good and my evil spirit. He is the law by which I stand. . . . This political-genetic grief became all my vegetative hate, but also my semi-skilled lust for life. Grief for my father remained my desolate hope, my endangered love."[49]

As the child of a "privileged mixed marriage," Wolf Biermann spent his early years in the shadow of the Nuremberg Laws. His father, Dagobert Biermann, was killed in Auschwitz as a Jew; his grandparents and other relatives died after deportation to the Minsk ghetto. His non-Jewish mother, who met his father in the Communist Party, pushed him through, according to Biermann, so that he may some day later avenge his father and establish Communism.[50] Biermann sees himself as dutiful to this legacy when he migrates from Hamburg to the GDR in 1953, becoming an actor and singer. But he, "the natural-born child of Communism,"[51] began to criticize his leaders out of a feeling of rightful personal inheritance. By 1964, he was subjected to intensified repression. Biermann's description of his growing critical awareness of the GDR is portrayed against the backdrop of National Socialism. In "Mortal Fear," he sought new friends for himself, such as "the fearless Robert Havemann, the cheeky worrywart Stefan Heym and the Stalinist anti-Stalinist Walter Janka."[52]

Biermann's public commitment to the Jewish part of his family history, which can be traced, at the latest, to his German translation of Yiddish Holocaust epics by Itzhak Lejb Katzenelson in 1994 (Katzenelson died in Auschwitz in 1944), must be read in the context of the postunification discourse about the murder of European Jewry. The Berlin Memorial to the Murdered Jews of Europe is probably the most impressive example of this discourse, which is also reflected in the biographies of those involved. In the Eastern side of the country, Jewish narratives could be freely expressed for the first time without falling subject to political pressure; in addition, the identity vacuum that resided in the majority of the Left after the downfall of Communism could be filled with a newly (re)located Jewish identity. In 1989, the very year of transition, Marcel Reich-Ranicki had polemically formulated this in relation to Barbara Honigmann: in her life following her departure to the West, "one faith replaced the others, in place of the dogma of Marxism emerged the commandments of the Mosaic religion, and instead of the red flag, there now glowed the Star of David."[53] The fiftieth anniversary of the end of the war in 1995 finally catalyzed the search for a historical narrative in the newly united Germany, which sought to break free of the stigma of a nation of perpetrators, and has since then imagined the German-Jewish past anew. In this discourse, German-Jewish interspaces could also be newly articulated, such as Biermann's defiant self-determination at the end of his autobiography: "I remain what I always was: half Jew-brat and half goy."[54]

However, it is clear that Biermann had been traumatized since childhood by his father's murder, even if the Jewish aspect of it may have remained hidden for a long time. This also corresponded with official GDR discourse in which the persecution of the Jews, if not simply excluded, was nevertheless superimposed by the image of Communist resistance and thus underwent reinterpretation. Such conflation and superimposition of Jewish and political facets are not least expressed by Biermann's trio of elected father figures—Havemann, Heym, and Janka—who opposed National Socialism with each of their different stories of persecution and resistance. Since the death of his father in the concentration camp, as Heym also mentions in *Nachruf*, Biermann searched for a paternal replacement and Havemann eventually accepted him.[55] Heym's mostly tolerant approach toward Biermann possibly also stemmed from their separate experiences of paternal loss, through which he tried to decode Biermann's motivations.

"Battle for Cleanliness and Morality": The Eleventh Plenum of the SED Central Committee

There is strong evidence to suggest that GDR functionaries immediately attempted to sever Heym's friendship with Havemann and Biermann. In August 1965, the Chair of the Council of Ministers, Alexander Abusch, invited Heym to a discussion of *Day X*. At the moment, Abusch said, it would not be appropriate to publish the book. Heym pointed out that he had been constrained and monitored since 1956 and that he had already postponed the publication of *Day X* for four years at the behest of the party; by this, he clearly meant that he had not circumvented the GDR's prohibition via a publication in the West. Heym signaled that he would be "prepared to work closer with you, but the book 'Day X' must be released"; he is "convinced that we must find a modus vivendi, but I cannot change my opinion." Abusch made it clear that the government desired a conversation with him, but "in your actions, you really must regard the government of our Republic as your own." Others "such as Prof. Havemann or Biermann" would "cause lasting damage to the laws of our Republic" by "duplicating [their works] without licences and disseminating these duplications." Heym offered to mediate with Havemann, which Abusch rejected because he had "neither interest nor objective in talking with Havemann." At the end of the conversation, with Abusch clearly not prepared to make any concession for *Day X*, Heym concedes: he "respects" the reasons for this and "will continue to wait." As a result, Abusch repeated that the reason for the conversation was "to clarify if contact between us [. . .] may be improved." To this, Heym responded that he understood and saw the conversation as a beginning: "But that does not mean that I will unconditionally agree to everything."[56]

Following Heym's public refusal to separate himself from Havemann and Biermann, the three friends were subject to radical political exclusion by the end of 1965. In a conversation with artists and literary figures in the GDR State Council on November 25, 1965, GDR State Council chair Walter Ulbricht referred to sexually explicit images on television and rhetorically asked whether the party must set "certain moral standards."[57] Kurt Hager, Head of the Ideology Committee of the Politburo, spoke intensely of a "battle for cleanliness and morality—and in literature and film, the boundaries between literature and pornography are transgressed."[58] In his article "Does Our Time Need Prophets? Who Speaks the Truth?" in the November 28 edition of the *Neues Deutschland* newspaper, chief editor and Politburo candidate Hermann Axen, who had survived Auschwitz and Buchenwald as a Jewish Communist, launched an indirect attack against Stefan Heym's piece "The Boredom of Minsk," which first appeared in a Czechoslovakian magazine and was soon published in the West German *Zeit*. In this article, Heym cited a personal conversation from 1955 in which Brecht had demanded, when necessary, a critical realism in literature, writing, "I will tell you when there will be literature in the Soviet Union again. When a novel is published there which begins with words along the lines of—he pondered—along the lines of: Minsk is one of the most boring cities in the world."[59]

"Every era has its speakers who express the fears and hopes of the people," Heym goes on to state.[60] In ancient times, these would have been prophets, Heym says, making an obvious reference to the Jewish Bible; today "it is writers and scientists who seem to undertake this role."[61] Because of this, Heym claims, the ruling classes have committed "censorship which works via economic pressure or fear, or both."[62] However, the "truth" is "revolutionary," and only by insisting upon it may socialist writers measure up to their colleagues and "claim and win the right to moral leadership."[63] To this claim, the Party then answered with its attack on the pornographic elements, which allegedly defile "cleanliness and morality."

"Every era has its speakers. In the grey ancient times, these would have been the prophets. Today . . . writers and scientists undertake this role. One writer has recently made such claims." Axen opens his article with an almost verbatim quotation of Heym, although he does not refer to the disfavored writer by name. Axen almost appears conciliatory toward the biblical tradition for a moment: "We do not wish to argue about the role of the ancient prophets here." Then he goes on the attack: he is far more interested in the new prophets who would emerge here. Axen assigns a subversive tendency to Heym's words since they "proclaim a leading role for writers and scientists" and "negate the leading role of the working class," headed by the SED.[64]

This is the prelude to the Eleventh Plenum of the SED Central Committee three weeks later, from 16 to 18 December 1965, in which the GDR government launched an unprecedented attack on its artists. They could, as the future GDR leader Erich Honecker threatened, no longer "continue to increase productivity and thus living standards" and at the same time "spread nihilistic, hopeless and morally corrosive philosophy in literature, film, theatre, television and journals."[65] In light of the fact that two authors of Jewish heritage in Heym and Biermann were charged, these words remind us, not coincidentally, of the anti-Semitic cliché of a culturally and morally corrosive Jewish intellect that was fashionable under National Socialism. In his closing words, Walter Ulbricht stated to the plenum that they must "once again clarify positions" with regard to the "development of socialist ethics and regarding the laws of socialist morality."[66] Ulbricht spoke of a "line of filth," into which the "circle of Havemann, Heym, Biermann" had slid and that as a group "purposefully waged and continues to wage a political battle against worker-peasant power."[67]

Over the "Bridge of Sighs": Summons from the Ministry of the Interior

The verbal declaration of war by the state at the Eleventh Plenum was shortly followed by the threat of detention. Only days after the Eleventh Plenum, at dawn on December 22, 1965, Havemann, Heym, and Biermann, without warning or mutual knowledge, received a summons from Interior Minister Major General Friedrich Dickel. At the gate, Biermann stated "a stuffed uniform" collected him and led him over a glass bridge into a side building. In the lightless corridor, he encountered Heym, who was "also escorted by a uniformed figure":[68]

> Heym walked along more hunched than usual. His coat and jacket open, he looked like a broken old Jew following his people on the ramp. This look made me fearful. . . . he kept his head down, starred at his feet and muttered a word which I didn't hear. Now I no longer had fear, fear had me.[69]

Regarding the content of the summons, as Biermann later learned, Dickel had also recited "a stilted explanation" and a "standardized empty threat" verbatim to Havemann and, as he suspected, also to Heym. Yet he did not know this exactly, "because Heym hid"[70] from him and Havemann from then on. Havemann, at least, merely laughed at that episode: "They are at a loss, they don't know what to do with us."[71] According to his autobiography, Biermann seemed to also adopt this reaction toward the "Sermon of the Minister."[72] In contrast to Heym, a short while later, before Christmas, Biermann gossiped to Havemann that Heym had called them to break up their friendship and to forbid future visits, writing, "And nor do I wish you to visit Gertrud (sic) and myself at home, not even under the pretext of a Christmas present."[73]

There are many reasons to believe that this course of events essentially took place. However, Biermann's rendition remains problematic, above all in contrasting the unbowed Havemann, resistance hero, with the broken Heym who, as an old Jew, passively walked toward the gas chamber. Here, Biermann draws on the repertoire of anti-Semitism after Auschwitz with precisely the depiction that was current in the GDR, according to which the Jews went like lambs to the slaughter. With this image, Biermann disavows the image of Heym, which remains despite Wolffsohn's defamatory study, as the leading opponent of the

GDR until the 1980s, never bowing down to the regime. In doing so, Biermann simultaneously enhances his own role and that of Havemann in opposition to the GDR.

Equally problematic is Biermann's broad acceptance of Havemann's version of other events. The question, then, is to what extent is the contrast Biermann made between Heym and Havemann correct? Indeed, the differing assessments of those days spent with Havemann and Heym are evident. In Havemann's autobiographical work *Fragen Antworten Fragen* (*Questions Answers Questions*) (1970), 22 December 1965 is not mentioned, yet the book is nonetheless structured around a series of further summons, which Havemann received from May 1966 from State Security headquarters on Magdalenenstraße. During the third summons on 18 May 1966, the conversation is said to open with the question of Havemann's friendship with Stefan Heym. To this, he responded that he was friends with Stefan Heym but that "Stefan Heym is one of those people whom you are never quite sure if they really are your friends."[74]

To this cryptic statement, Havemann adds the reflection that "my friend Stefan . . . thought almost entirely about what was to come, and unfortunately sometimes too much on that which actually came."[75] In contrast, he depicts his interrogations at the State Security headquarters in May 1966 against the backdrop of previously experienced interrogations and arrests during National Socialism and his first postwar years in West Berlin where he was engaged in opposition to American nuclear politics. These experiences, he suggests, had given him the tools to remain confident during State Security interrogations, since only through betrayal was one susceptible to blackmail by the system. On the imprisonment of another person known to the GDR, he argues:

> Terms of imprisonment are times of great psychological strain. They never fail to leave their mark on a person. Some have their spines broken in prison. Particularly vulnerable are those people induced by the secret police to betray their friends under the pressure of interrogation. Thus they often enjoy benefits, are released early and quickly get decent work again and other material benefits. But in return they are also blackmailed by the secret police to serve as a systematic informant for them. Whoever goes down this path soon realizes that it is the path to their downfall. Most of the time, however, it is too late by then. The supposed benefits and conveniences prove to be terrible chains of slavery which demean and morally destroy the victim.[76]

Had Heym made himself susceptible to blackmail? That the interrogation on 22 December 1965 signified a turning point for him is obvious from the fact that he publicly addressed that morning on four occasions: in a speech at the Deutscher Schriftstellerverband in February 1966, during a conversation with Politburo candidate Werner Lamberz in November 1976, in *Nachruf* in 1988 and in *Der Winter unsers Mißvergnügens* (*The Winter of Our Discontent*) in 1996. With some variations, these versions subsequently depict the same course of events. But first, Heym writes in 1996, he paid a visit in December 1965 to his friend Walter Janka, who had read about the speeches of Honecker and Sindermann at the Eleventh Plenum in *Neues Deutschland.* There was talk of a "Havemann-Biermann-Heym" group; it was "the language of trials,"[77] no doubt a reference to Stalinist show trials. Janka was a former member of the International Brigade and survivor of the Le Vernet internment camp in France; he had survived his later imprisonment by the GDR in Bautzen from 1957–1960 while seriously ill. Now he wished to give Heym "a few tips. [. . .] How one survives in detention, in prison."[78] Upon hearing these suggestions, Heym writes, he felt "a chill up his spine."[79]

In his first public version of the events of 22 December 1965, Heym reports to the Deutscher Schriftstellerverband in February 1966 that a plainclothes man rang his doorbell at 7:30 on 22 December and ordered him to the Ministry of the Interior at 9:15 "for the purposes of explaining an offence." There he was received by the Interior Minister, who issued him with the order to cease his "comments . . . against the Republic and worker-peasant power." He responded to the Interior Minister, Heym stated in 1966, that he had "not once" made such comments and that it would therefore not be difficult for him "to fulfill the obligation you have imposed on me. I see no reason to start saying things now that I have not said previously."[80]

Heym chronicles that morning a second time in *Nachruf*, where a man appeared at his doorstep at 7:30 and ordered him to the Ministry of the Interior at 9:15. In the watch room, which he now mentions, he was received by "two officials in green, both the required height of guards and, judging by their epaulettes, the rank of majors; they positioned themselves to his right and left so that he could not escape."[81] Trapped in this manner, he is brought over the "Bridge of Sighs," which he mentions for the first time here, to the Minister's Office, from which two men in uniform lead out Havemann in the same manner. He "grins at him. S.H. now considers standing still and greeting Havemann, or at least yelling yoo-hoo, but he is then seized by his escort and pushed onward."[82] At the end of the interview, he bumps into Biermann at the door, flanked by two officials and currently being led in.

The incident appears a third time in Manfred Krug's 1996 reprint of an unofficial conversation, secretly recorded on audiotape by Krug, between writers and artists and Politburo member Werner Lamberz, who was widely touted as Erich Honecker's crown prince and whom the critical intellectuals associated with the hope of liberalization. This meeting took place at Krug's house on 20 November 1976, only a few days after Biermann's deprivation of citizenship, which been protested by the artists present who now wanted to intercede with Lamberz. Here, Heym also tells of his summons by the Ministry of the Interior in 1965.

Here, however, there are three men at once, still in leather coats, who appeared at his home as early as by 6 o'clock and ordered him to the Ministry for 7 o'clock. In the ministerial building, he was then led "by a police officer to his right and a police officer to his left over the famous Bridge of Sighs" to Interior Minister Dickel, who falsely accused him of slandering the GDR. In this version, Heym also refutes Dickel's allegations and encounters Biermann afterward "on the Bridge of Sighs, also accompanied by two people."[83]

In *Winter of Our Discontent* in 1996, Heym reports that, on a December day that year (obviously referring to 22 December), two men "correctly dressed" rang forcefully at his door at 6 o'clock in the morning.[84] He was summoned to the Ministry of the Interior exactly one hour later. He shaved, noticed that his knees were not shaking and then said good-bye to Gertrude: "'I'll be back soon,' I say. 'I hope so,' she says." At the Ministry, two policemen take him "in the middle" and lead him along intertwined paths and eventually over the "Bridge of Sighs." After the interview, which follows the same pattern as before, he encounters "shortly before the Bridge of Sighs [. . .] Wolf Biermann, like me escorted by two police officers. We nodded to each other."[85]

In none of these versions, nor those of Biermann, does Havemann play a role as the subject of discussion. The astounding proliferation of Heym's versions suggests one thing above all: it is not so much that factual truth is to be found in them, but that the events of 22 December bore a symbolic character; they were a form of key event, which Heym had gone over again and again. The impression of detention, the faceless uniforms, and men in leather coats suggest that Heym is describing this summons using the template of a Gestapo summons and that he symbolically lived through the Gestapo detention of his father at first hand. The richly associative phrase "Bridge of Sighs" seems particularly meaningful, especially since Heym's *Nachruf* explicitly refers to the iconic significance of this choice of words: the bridge within the GDR Ministry of the Interior discussed here resembles "the famous Bridge of Sighs in Venice,"[86] which led from the Doge's Palace to the city prison. Prisoners were led over this historic bridge from court to jail or to execution; according to this idea, it is here that they breathe their last sighs as free humans.

Behind this web of associations, it can be assumed, lies grief for the father who was shattered by imprisonment by the Gestapo and for whose death Heym always felt guilt. However, his father's suicide may also have tormented him in the form of a fear of repeating the act upon himself. In December 1965, Heym was fifty-three years old; his father had been fifty-three years old when the Gestapo arrested him. Did these fears go beyond a fear of persecution? *Nachruf* implies that Heym came from an "a family rich in suicides"[87] in both parental lineages: his maternal grandmother had also committed suicide in 1914; Heym's brother Werner, who followed him during his emigration to the United States, would voluntarily take his own life at the age of fifty-one. In his youth, Heym writes, he came across personal feelings of failure and subsequent depression, in which he fantasized himself in the role of a winner. Werner was, as Heym recalls, "also full of self-doubt which he strived to cover up through achievement or through feigning superiority that he did not possess in truth; when things went wrong and an unavoidable depression came, he learned to overcome this by pulling his fantasies over himself like a plastic raincoat and conceiving a new role-play in which he still remained victorious."[88]

One thing is certain: the Eleventh Plenum and the summons from Interior Minister Dickel signified a grave turning point in Heym's life. It was clear at this juncture that his current strategy against GDR leaders was not enough to continue to reach his GDR public and thus change GDR society. The publication of *Day X* was aborted; his following novel *Die Papiere des Andreas Lenz* (*The Lenz Papers*) was only published in 1963 under the guise of a historical text. Since 1963, Heym had been working on a subsequent novel, *Die Architekten* (*The Architects*),[89] which had been banished to a drawer after the hostilities at the Eleventh Plenum and would only be released after the fall of the Wall. In 1965, moreover, Heym had begun the manuscript for *Lassalle* (*Uncertain Friend*), his first Jewish historical novel, which he conceptualized in the spirit of Lion Feuchtwanger's idea of historical novels. Feuchtwanger placed at the center of his idea the ancient Jewish historian Flavius Josephus, whose work "really had nothing to do with what we call history" but was a means "of facing up to oneself and to history."[90] After some setbacks, Heym's *Lassalle* was published in 1969 in both German states almost simultaneously.

In this respect, the biographical texts of our three protagonists, Heym, Havemann, and Biermann, are not historical evidence in the sense of possible verisimilitude but must be considered evidence of self-representation in which their roles with regard to historical events and to each other are reconsidered. In part, their biographies may illustrate the different personal skills that these three friends brought to their political opposition and used for that purpose in a way that effectively raised their public profile. Read in this way, the texts of this unique trio assert the respective priority of each individual protagonist to their role of the most important GDR dissenter, which Heym's account of the "Bridge of Sighs" impressively seeks to highlight as the point of culmination on this path.

With this in mind, Biermann's descriptions of Heym must also be read as polemic exaggerations assisted by the "cudgel of Auschwitz"—that is, in the sense of a moral charge against the backdrop of Auschwitz, under the weight of which Biermann himself suffered throughout his lifetime. According to Biermann, even in his school days, his mother had literally reprimanded him for poor grades with a "cudgel of Auschwitz": "Your father died in Auschwitz so that you could get a Five in Maths!"[91] At the same time, Heym's "Bridge of Sighs" becomes a contradictory metaphor for the themes of persecution, guilt, and resistance that accompanied the writer throughout National Socialism and the GDR regime and that he will make fruitful in both literary and political terms. In this respect, the bridge is a symbol of transformation through which Heym, having reached the other side, redetermines the parameters of rebellion, now without Havemann.

Break with Havemann

After the Eleventh Plenum, Heym must have been aware that his previous strategy against the State had backfired, required changes and that offering his work for publication in the GDR would henceforth interfere with his relationship with Havemann. Time preyed on Heym's mind: he was certain of his literary importance, but he had not published a major work since *The Crusaders* (*Die Kreuzfahrer*), his great work of exile literature. However, a new beginning in the West was closed to him and his wife. In early 1965, Gertrude Gelbin traveled to the United States for four weeks to visit friends and relatives.[92] She was also determining the possibility of a return to her homeland. However, already sixty-five years old at the time, she was suffering from a severe heart condition and thus a resettlement could not be realized. Heym's own bridges in the United States were burned, while emigration to the conservative 1960s Federal Republic with its leaders incriminated by National Socialism was out of the question for both partners. Furthermore, Heym was also vilified by the West German press as a GDR loyalist author. Writing about Heym's "Writing in the Zone" shortly after the construction of the Wall in 1961, *Die Welt* states that he is "no natural fighter. Stefan Heym is no rebel. Stefan Heym is an honorary citizen of the Soviet Zone. As audaciously as Stefan Heym tells the truth, so audaciously does Stefan Heym lie."

Thus the author probably had only one way forward: to attempt to come to terms with GDR leaders again by ending his contact with Havemann in late summer 1966. But to what extent is this, in fact, betrayal, as Biermann suggests? The available sources suggest that Heym's decision to end his friendship with Havemann proved more complex than Biermann admits. On Heym's appearance at the plenary of the Deutscher Schriftstellerverband on 25 February 1966, the State Security reported that a critical discussion took place with Heym and Biermann at which Heym had lost all sympathy of those present. Heym began with a "drastic, dramatic depiction of a 'summons'" to Interior Minister Friedrich Dickel, which he had contradicted with the claim that "the minister's information was incorrect" and that since he "had never made such claims, it would be easy for him to refrain from doing so."[93]

With this speech, Heym had aimed to portray the accusations against his person as unjustified because they allegedly "rested on false information or bureaucratic misjudgements" and that he was, in contrast, "a staunch socialist and had also always stood up for the GDR in the West."[94] The State Security obtained the latter statement from Heym's citation in West German press reports.[95] However, Heym's speech found "little favor" with those present; both functionaries and fellow writers "opposed it decisively." In light of this, Heym also prompted both the association and the GDR government to "put right the injustice committed" against him.[96] Evidently, pressure had been put on Heym at this meeting with regard to Havemann. Thus the association reported to the State Security in late March 1966 that, following the recent discussion, it was now up to Heym "to abandon his ties to Havemann."[97]

This speech to the association, with which Heym thwarted methods of intimidation based on silence and isolation, was the last straw. Together with Biermann and Havemann, the Stasi wrote in early March 1966, Heym was to be "muzzled."[98] Parallel to this, Heym expressed his feelings of uncertainty in private circles. An informant of the State Security reports in early March 1966 that, according to Heym, Gertrude, already in hospital following a cardiac infection, could lose her job due to his political problems and be forced onto minimum pension. He emphasizes "that he is against capitalism and against West Germany and that he supports socialism."[99] Naturally he felt existential fear, which he went through during his fundamental experience of exile: "In this context he told me that he would not mind if he were to lose everything. In his life, he had often done very simple jobs, including working as a dishwasher in the USA."[100] This contact person was unable to report anything further, as she had indulged in Heym's cognac.

In a further private conversation in August 1966, Heym lamented that he has been equated with Biermann and Havemann, and yet his stance fundamentally differed from theirs. According to this secret informant, he had shown "a quite abnormal degree of caution and also a certain fear" that day; he assumed there were listening devices in his apartment and had insisted on conducting the conversation on a walk in the open air.[101] Heym had also wanted to obtain information about criminal procedure from him and would picture the perilous situation for himself. According to the report, "He is crazy with this excessive caution." The report continued that Heym was feeling confined and "unsafe in his current life" because "he cannot write what he wants and thus sees himself as completely unfree." Here, Heym alludes to his efforts concerning *Day X*.[102] In this conversation, Heym also mentioned certain material shortages, according to the informant.

Only in June 1968 did the Stasi retrospectively report that Heym had dissolved his "good connections" to Havemann and allegedly did so "because HAVEMANN had published his adversarial theses in the foreign and West German press. According to H.[eym], this was counterrevolutionary. He was only in favor of internal dispute. This attitude from H.[eym] shows that he works with great caution; because in reality he himself publishes his negative concoctions abroad."[103]

For the State Security, Heym's termination of his relationship with Havemann was deemed a diversionary tactic "for calculating reasons"[104] and "to cover himself."[105] Heym's esteem for Havemann would continue, he was "not hostile" toward him but "considered him a smart person and valued his thoughts."[106] According to the Stasi, he continued to maintain an "indirect relationship with Havemann" through mutual acquaintances as well as through the holiday resort of Ahrenshoop,[107] while Gertrude Gelbin also had "good contacts" with Havemann's divorced wife Karin.[108] As Havemann also wrote more generally, contact with him after his exclusion from the Party and his employment ban was "risky": "The majority of people who were good friends with me or were, at any rate, on friendly terms, had to be very careful."[109]

The fact that Heym did not break off his relationship with Havemann outright through fear or calculation seems to indicate that his rather "loose ties to Biermann,"[110] according to the State Security, persisted even if they took a more sporadic form from then on. Also a crucial factor in Heym's decision regarding Havemann was likely the troubled relationship between Gertrude Gelbin and Robert Havemann. Heym reports in *Nachruf* Gelbin's attempts to restrict contact between the two men because she "sensed the danger that would have arisen if two long-time recalcitrant and self-absorbed characters such as S.H. and Havemann continued to snipe at each other."[111] The State Security, although they saw Gelbin, too, as unreliable, suspected that she was the driving force behind Heym's break with Havemann because she "judges Havemann to be a morally degenerate person and wants nothing more to do with him."[112] According to reports, she had ceased contact with Havemann out of personal antipathy as late as March 1965.[113] Of course, the State Security's concept of morality was dubious, given that it also used sexually active informants without reservation. Gelbin's statement presumably refers to Havemann's relationships with women, yet it is possible that she at least also sensed far more problematic aspects of Havemann's personality. This obviously tense relationship possibly informed Biermann's description of Gelbin as "a sharp-tongued old trout."[114]

Havemann's "Errors of a Serious Nature"

Biermann's ambivalent evaluation of Heym seems to essentially follow that of Havemann from the 1970s onward, and must be read in relation to Heym's break with his former friend. In his autobiographical work *Ein Deutscher Kommunist* (A German Communist), published in 1978, Havemann argues that it had only ever been Biermann and himself who had expressed "an unequivocal criticism of the politics of the SED." The "bourgeois intellectuals" of the GDR, although almost all of them concurred with him and Biermann, had until the latter's expatriation consistently tried "to escape scot free from Party criticism, to remain just within the bounds of what was permissible and to provide an ideological outlet for opposition in the GDR."[115] This was obviously aimed at Heym, whom Havemann only mentions in a section of the book dealing with Biermann's expatriation.

From the historical simplifications and distortions resulting from such polarizations, it becomes apparent that even Havemann's role in the GDR remained ambivalent for a long time. For Havemann, this was also true of Heym's strategy in the early 1960s of combining fundamental assent to the socialist GDR project with a need for self-realization strengthened by the deprivations of the National Socialist era. Similar can be suggested of Biermann, who stood as a candidate for the SED in 1962 and only took up the role of dissenter after his rejection, which in 1963 was likely due to his personal lifestyle. Relating to Havemann, Hurwitz notes, for example, an "art of survival and at the same time an extraordinary striving for autonomy in determining the direction of one's own life through time constraints and conditions of the system."[116] Similar to Heym at first, Havemann also increasingly used the initial privileges of the state's highly valued intelligentsia to popularize his critical views of GDR politics. In the course of this strategy, both men went through partially parallel stages of disillusionment with the State.

Unlike Heym, however, as became apparent in 1989, Havemann was also not afraid of getting rid of personal competitors with the help of the State Security. It only became known after the collapse of the GDR that, between 1946 and 1963 and deep into his friendship with Heym, Havemann served as a secret informant to the KGB, the Ministry for State Security and GDR army reconnaissance, particularly reporting on other academics.[117] Havemann researcher Harold Hurwitz has thus already inquired as to what extent Havemann took it upon himself to make "fateful decisions about other people" after the war.[118] Among other things, this manifested itself in his actions against the aforementioned Walter Hollitscher, whom he knew through Heym. At that time, the erstwhile friends Havemann and Hollitscher were likely already enemies, yet continued to maintain personal contact.[119] By this stage, Havemann's academic work was already suffering due to his vast number of political roles in the GDR. Now he began to wage a smear campaign against Hollitscher, who represented psychoanalysis, which was deemed undesirable to the GDR authorities. In one review, Havemann reproached Hollitscher for "a collection of ideological shortcomings" and "a lack of partiality and an irreconcilability towards reactionary ideologies" and labeled Freud's psychoanalysis itself an "antihumanist, barbaric ideology" that had already been dealt with in the Soviet Union in the 1930s—an only thinly veiled reference to the Stalinist purges.[120]

By means of an obvious lie, Havemann implied Hollitscher's cooperation with the British Secret Service in a report to the SED Central Committee in February 1952, resulting in Hollitscher's arrest under the orders of the SED Central Committee in 1953. The Central Committee had already published their *Lessons from the Proceedings against the Slansky Conspirator Center*, and Hollitscher, via death threats, was blackmailed to return to Vienna in order to report from there to the State Security and later the KGB.[121] Probably as a cynical reward for this extorted cooperation, Hollitscher later received high GDR honors, remaining a regular visiting professor at the Karl Marx University in Leipzig for the last twenty years of his life. Havemann's quoted remark above, according to which anyone who gave the finger to the State Security while in prison would soon have to shake hands with them, appears especially infamous in this context.

Havemann himself also cryptically admitted to his long-standing and ambiguous role in the GDR, without going into specific examples. As Havemann wrote in an unpublished manuscript about his early affirmation of the GDR, obtained via State files, he made

> errors at that time of . . . a serious nature. . . . I was raised to show unconditional humility before the collective wisdom of the Party. For me, the truth was: the Party was always right. . . . However, at the time I often had difficulty understanding the wisdom of the Party to the last detail.[122]

Did Heym know of this entanglement, or at least suspect it? His *Nachruf* does not mention it at least, although Heym never shies away from openly naming other friends and acquaintances who collaborated with the secret service, and is also definitely critical of Havemann in his writing. He had once openly admired Havemann, but after the loss of his professorship, he noticed "with horror,"

> it is becoming increasingly clear how the personality of the man is changing. It begins with a growing disinterest in things to do with physics. . . . The ground has been taken from under him, he now only speaks as a politician, and indeed one whose power base are the occasional visitors of an improved summer house in a village near Erkner, all of his thoughts and, however right they may be, all of his words turn to empty clamor. By this he probably really thinks that the parties in his home, where he can show off in front of two or three dozen mostly young people, are significant.[123]

This is, Heym muses, what Biermann's importance to Havemann was about. Havemann had taken on a father figure role with Biermann, partly due to "true feelings" and partly through a calculated measure since he was "clever enough to simultaneously see the advantages that Biermann's loyal entourage bring him."[124] Biermann was not able to knock his father figure Havemann from his pedestal until his autobiography in 2016; regarding his unsettling double role in the GDR, there is only a persistent silence. Instead, Biermann attacks Heym, whose "patriarchal attacks"[125] likely felt to him as if he were being pushed back into the past. Heym's rather sarcastic manner toward Biermann also appears in *Nachruf*, according to which everyone knew that Biermann was "a veritable bundle of talents, equally gifted as a poet and composer, as a singer and actor, and, so that he could also express these gifts properly, totally extroverted."[126] The fact that Heym was ambivalent about a paternal role can also be seen in other biographical constellations of his life. However, it is also conceivable that Heym felt somewhat excluded from the triumvirate as the friendship between Havemann and Biermann deepened, and that this also motivated the breakup of his friendship with Havemann.

Denaturalization as a National Socialist Practice: Heym and the Biermann Protests

These personal constellations did not prevent Heym from maintaining contact with Biermann after 1966, nor from repeatedly offering him support. As the State Security reported in 1968, Heym had encouraged Biermann to join the international PEN Center, despite a narrow majority vote, and to carry out "strong public promotion of his election."[127] Heym sporadically crossed paths with Biermann, particularly after the death of Gelbin. In 1971, the State Security reported that Heym had reactivated personal contact with Havemann and Biermann. "Through an unofficial source," the report says, "it has become known that Wolf Biermann and Robert Havemann visited Stefan Heym at his apartment in March 1971. H.[eym] was both very surprised and pleased about it" and even invited Biermann to his marriage with the DEFA practitioner Inge Wüste, for which Biermann would nevertheless be indisposed.[128] From then on, Biermann would stay on good personal terms with Inge Wüste-Heym, which likely improved his rapport with Heym.

In 1973 Heym, albeit in vain, attended a meeting with the head of the Department of Culture of the SED's Central Committee, Hans-Joachim Hoffmann, about an appearance by Biermann at the Tenth World Festival of Youth in East Berlin. In the interim, Heym had been able to publish two novels in the historical style. *Die Schmähschrift* (*The Queen against Defoe*) and *Der König David Bericht* (*The King David Report*) were published almost simultaneously in 1972. *Der König David Bericht* became the biggest selling novel both in Heym's GDR career as well as in all GDR oppositional literature. This was his second historical Jewish novel in which he articulated criticism of the Stalinist terror through the figure of the biblical King David. With *Der König David Bericht*, immediately published in West Germany and only afterward in a minor edition in the GDR, Heym also celebrated his first success in both Germanies.[129] The book was translated into many languages and is his most renowned book internationally even today.

With *Der König David Bericht*, Heym had found his own voice on the GDR that only increased in topicality after his separation from Havemann. Following Havemann and Biermann, he also received an occupational ban in the GDR because of this, which would stand until 1989. In 1974, the Ministry for State Security even formed a special force for the three archenemies in their own country, Biermann, Havemann, and Heym, dubbed the Operative Group of the XX Main Department, which would then monitor the trio over several operations.[130] But even constant surveillance, a publication ban, and several threats of prosecution did not prevent Heym from continuing to work in the GDR. Alongside a multitude of smaller pieces, he added two more major novels to the collection, *Collin* (1979) and *Ahasver* (1983), lending a Jewish voice to GDR oppositional literature. His novel *Schwarzenberg* (1984) would also be refused publication in the GDR.

By the mid-1970s at the latest, Heym had taken on the role of spokesperson for the GDR opposition. This is especially clear in the protests against the denaturalization of Wolf Biermann on 16 November 1976. By November 17, Heym, alongside Stephan Hermlin, had already gathered a band of twelve GDR authors and artists whose public appeal against the denaturalization of Wolf Biermann went global on the same day via the French news agency AFP. Many other artists signed up to the appeal in the days that followed. This was the first public protest in the GDR since 17 June 1953. On 20 November 1976, three days after the first publication of the appeal, a group of signatories were gathered together in the house of singer and actor Manfred Krug for an unofficial interview with the head of the Department of Agitation and Propaganda of the SED's Central Committee, Werner Lamberz. This interview, which Krug secretly recorded on tape and published as a transcript in 1996, was predominantly conducted by Heym, who made a courageous plea on behalf of Biermann.

In the conversation with Lamberz, Heym positions the aforementioned story of the "Bridge of Sighs" as one of the core parts of his argument. "It was the second time that I encountered him in such a situation," Heym said of Biermann. The first time was in 1956, when Biermann had come to him "as a young student" and asked him for help since finally "something was now happening in '56," by which Heym meant the unrest in Hungary that had spread to the GDR. Biermann had attempted to retaliate with him.[131] "That was Biermann," Heym summarizes to Lamberz. "If Biermann has become what he is today, so critical, then it is, Comrade Lamberz, not the fault of Biermann."[132] The "extraordinarily talented" Biermann "with his products made specifically for **us** [sic],"[133] Heym wanted to tell Lamberz, had been falsely made into an enemy by the state.

In this interview with Lamberz, Heym implicitly mobilizes the image of a defenseless orphan by whose side he diligently stood. Although he does not explicitly mention Biermann's father murdered in Auschwitz, he uses Biermann's Jewish heritage associatively as a symbol of his victim status also in the GDR in the space. In particular, Heym utilizes the narrative of the "Bridge of Sighs" in order to accuse the GDR of National Socialist practices in relation to Biermann's denaturalization. With this argument, he presumably wanted to hold GDR leaders to their own antifascist credo and thus put them under moral pressure. Heym therefore references a polemic against Biermann published a few days previously in *Neues Deutschland*, whose author was a former member of the NSDAP. The terminology of the author and acting editor of *Neues Deutschland*, Günter Kertzscher, is "obtained verbatim [. . .] from the denaturalization documents of the National Socialist state"; the denaturalization itself "is namely a Nazi practice."[134] The author Jurek Becker, who belonged to Heym's inner circle together with Krug from the 1970s, added a comment that the West German broadcaster SBF had announced Kertzscher's NSDAP member number. "This is a[n] embarrassing matter," Becker states. "I could weep with shame."[135] Without a doubt, Heym and Becker not only operated strategically here, but they themselves also felt extremely affected and impassioned as Jewish survivors of the Nazi regime: Becker had survived the Lodz ghetto as a child, while Heym had experienced a Nazi denaturalization directly as a young expatriate.

In fact, Kertzscher's article evokes a series of anti-Semitic clichés such as the parasite—"A Herr Biermann could even live here for over ten years without working"—and the morally depraved liar and exploiter: "The labor movement has constantly had to do with people who were completely black inside but had put on a red cap."[136] In particular, Kertzscher's reference to a "duty of loyalty to the state" that Biermann "consciously, consistently and grossly violated" (bringing the denaturalization on himself) is borrowed from the citizenship law of the GDR, according to which, the preceding ND article states, "citizens can be denied their GDR citizenship due to gross violation of their citizen's duty."[137] Heym also refers to this passage. Heym's insistence to Lamberz that it was "precisely the wording of Nazi commentators"[138] is corroborated by the almost literal correspondence between the GDR and Nazi legislature. As the GDR Citizenship Law of 1967 stated that citizenship may be denied to "citizens who reside or remain outside of the German Democratic Republic due to gross violation of their citizen's duty," so does the Nazi "Law on the Revocation of Naturalization and the Deprivation of German Citizenship" passed in July 1933 and applied primarily to East European Jews: "German citizenship may be stripped from Germans who reside abroad and damage German interests through their demeanor there."[139]

Ironically, Lamberz's slate was also not entirely clean with regard to National Socialism. As *Der Spiegel* had reported in May 1976, he had attended the elite Nazi institution, the Adolf Hitler School.[140] Heym was, at the very least, a keen reader of the Western press and so this may have been well known to him; possibly, he was also hoping to appeal to Lamberz's conscience with this argument. However, Lamberz downplayed the issue with the remark, this is "standard international law in every state."[141] He did not want to confront the particularly German lines of tradition in hounding Biermann, and Heym's appeal for leniency with his description of a poignantly naive Biermann who first came to him asking for advice as a "young student"[142] in 1956 fell upon Lamberz's deaf ears. Naturally, he could not show any sympathy for the dissenter Biermann; even speaking with Heym was distinctly inconvenient to him. Through this unofficial conversation with Biermann's supporters alone, he had likely hung himself too far out of the window. Only fifteen months later, in March 1978, according to official reports, Lamberz died in a helicopter crash in Libya, but his body was never discovered.[143]

Jewish Dissent in the GDR: A Perspective

Through his experiences in the 1960s, Heym had developed into an effective voice of GDR opposition by the 1970s. Based on Heym's example but also that of a series of other GDR artists with Jewish family histories—including Jurek Becker, Wolf Biermann, Thomas Brasch, Günter Kunert, and Monika Maron—questions arise not only about the often noted affinity of this group with the GDR but also about how their connection to their Jewishness catalyzed conflict with the official GDR narrative, as well as how this mobilized them consciously toward their dissent. For example, Monika Maron's rather ambiguously titled first novel *Flight of Ashes* (1981), about pollution in the GDR, begins with the burning of the first-person narrator's Polish-Jewish grandfather before her birth: "My grandfather Pawel, they had driven him to a Polish cornfield the year before. When my grandfather and the other Jews had arrived at the center of the cornfield, they set it alight on all sides."[144] Jurek Becker's *Bronstein's Children* (1986), contrastingly, turns a Jewish survivor who keeps his tormentor from his concentration camp captive into a successful metonymy for the GDR regime and its wall.[145]

It could also be asked to what extent Stefan Heym's Jewish novels provided an important impulse for contemporary Jewish writing among young authors of oppositional literature and how far this literature formed itself under the precept of a resolutely Jewish dissent akin to the Jewish dissenters of the Soviet Union. Of Heym, at least, this can be claimed convincingly. After attempts to determine a position against the GDR, Heym emerged as a firmly critical and Jewish voice with his novel *Lassalle* at the end of the 1960s; he finally established his development as a dissenter firmly in the context of his Jewish biography in *Nachruf*, beginning with his circumcision. At the end, he questions how his "memory will live on"; to know this, he would have to wait "until I have been carried onto the final part of my journey."[146] Even on this topic, Heym was awkward. The Jewish atheist and dissenter who had asked himself about Israel in *Nachruf* and whether "this land [was] his land" and "these Jews his people"[147] died on 16 December 2001 after a swimming accident in the Dead Sea at En Bokek.

Notes

1. Christian Bauer and Rebekka Göpfert, *Die Ritchie Boys. Deutsche Emigranten beim US-Geheimdienst* (Hamburg: Hoffmann und Campe, 2005).
2. Peter Hutchinson, *Stefan Heym: The Perpetual Dissident* (Cambridge: Cambridge University Press, 1992).
3. Valentina Glajar, Alison Lewis, and Corina L. Petrescu, eds., *Secret Police Files from the Eastern Bloc: Between Surveillance and Life Writing* (Rochester, N.Y.: Camden House, 2016).

4. Michael Wolffsohn, *Die Deutschland Akte. Tatsachen und Legenden* (Munich: edition ferenczy bei Bruckmann, 1995), 13.

5. Wolffsohn, *Die Deutschland Akte*, 23.

6. Marcel Reich-Ranicki, *Über Ruhestörer. Juden in der deutschen Literatur* (Munich: dtv, 1993).

7. Robin Ostow, *Jüdisches Leben in der DDR* (Athenäum Verlag, 1988). 21.

8. Peter Hutchinson and Reinhard K. Zachau, eds., *Stefan Heym: Socialist, Dissenter, Jew. Stefan Heym: Sozialist, Dissident, Jude* (Oxford: Peter Lang, 2003); Regina U. Hahn, *The Democratic Dream: Stefan Heym in America* (Oxford: Peter Lang, 2003).

9. Stephan Braese, "Ahasver im Bauernstaat—Stefan Heyms Bibel-Lektüren," in *Zwischen Politik und Kultur—Juden in der DDR*, ed. Moshe Zuckermann (Göttingen: Wallstein Verlag, 2002); Therese Hörnigk, ed., *Ich habe mich immer eingemischt: Erinnerungen an Stefan Heym* (Berlin: Verlag für Berlin-Brandenburg, 2013); Bernadette Malinowski and Ulrike Uhlig, eds., *Der Jahrhundertzeuge: Geschichtsschreibung und Geschichtsentwürfe im Werk von Stefan Heym* (Würzburg: Königshausen & Neumann, 2013).

10. Jeffrey Herf, *Divided Memory: The Nazi Past in the Two Germanys* (Cambridge, Mass.: Harvard University Press, 1997); Thomas C. Fox, *Stated Memory: East Germany and the Holocaust* (Rochester, N.Y.: Camden House, 1999); Paul O'Doherty, *The Portrayal of Jews in GDR Prose Fiction* (Amsterdam: Rodopi, 1997).

11. Erica Burgauer, *Zwischen Erinnerung und Verdrängung. Juden in Deutschland nach 1945* (Reinbek bei Hamburg: rororo, 1993); Jay Howard Geller, *Jews in Post-Holocaust Germany, 1945–1953* (Cambridge: Cambridge University Press, 2005); Angelika Timm, *Hammer Zirkel Davidstern. Das gestörte Verhältnis der DDR zu Zionismus und Staat Israel* (Bonn: Bouvier Verlag, 1997).

12. Cathy S. Gelbin and Sander L. Gilman, *Cosmopolitanisms and the Jews* (Ann Arbor: University of Michigan Press, 2017).

13. Mark Gelber coined the term *Jewish sensibilities* in reference to the assimilated Jewish writer Stefan Zweig. Mark Gelber, *Stefan Zweig, Judentum und Zionismus* (Innsbruck: Studienverlag, 2014).

14. Stefan Heym, *Nachruf* (Munich: C. Bertelsmann, 1988), 669.

15. Heym, 669.

16. Heym, 547.

17. Simone Hannemann, *Robert Havemann und die Widerstandsgruppe "Europäische Union." Eine Darstellung der Ereignisse und deren Interpretation nach 1945* (Berlin: Robert-Havemann-Gesellschaft e.V., 2001). 52ff.

18. Yad Vashem, "The Righteous among the Nations," accessed 1 October 2019, http://db.yadvashem.org/righteous/family.html?language=en&itemId=5419422.

19. Quoted in Hannemann, *Robert Havemann*, 82.

20. Yad Vashem, "The Righteous among the Nations."

21. Hollitscher was considered a Jew by Nazi laws according to more recent research into the forced explusion of Jewish students from the University of Vienna in 1938. See Katharina Kniefacz and Herbert Posch, "Emigration/Remigration in den Bildungsbiographien der 1938 vertriebenen Studierenden. Das Gedenkbuch für die Opfer des Nationalsozialismus an der Universität Wien 1938," in *Bilderbuch-Heimkehr. Remigration im Kontext*, ed. Katharina Prager and Wolfgang Straub (Wuppertal: Arco Verlag, 2017), 231–242; on Hollitscher, see esp. 235.

22. See the contribution of Walter Hollitscher, "Der dialektische Materialismus und die Physiker," *Physikalische Blätter* 8, no. 7 (1952).

23. Interview by Eckart Boege with Leo Zuckermann (1978), Casette 4, mins. 25–28. My thanks to Philipp Graf (Leipzig) for the reference and interview.

24. Alfred Kantorowicz, *Deutsches Tagebuch. Zweiter Teil* (Berlin: Verlag Klaus Suhl, 1979), 341.

25. Heym, *Nachruf*, 670.
26. Heym, 670.
27. Heym, 670.
28. Heym, 583.
29. Robert Havemann, *Fragen Antworten Fragen. Aus der Biographie eines deutschen Marxisten* (Munich: R. Piper, 1970), 142.
30. Der Bundesbeauftragte für die Unterlagen des Staatssicherheitsdienstes der ehemaligen Deutschen Demokratischen Republik (BStU), Ministerium für Staatssicherheit (MfS), HA XX/1, OV "Diversant," AOP 25507/91, vol. 3, 1, 11 January 1966.
31. BStU, MfS, HA XVIII/5, OV "Diversant," AOP 1066/91, vol. 6, 66, undated.
32. BStU, MfS, OV "Diversant," AOP 1066/91, undated.
33. BStU, MfS, OV "Diversant," AOP, 25507/91, vol. 1, 32, undated.
34. BStU, MfS, OV "Diversant"; BStU, MfS, AOP 25507/91, vol. 1, 47, 18 January 1961.
35. BStU, MfS, HA V/1/4, OV "Diversant," AOP 25507/91, vol. 1, 80, 17 May 1961.
36. BStU, MfS, HA XX/1, OV "Diversant," AOP 25507/91, vol. 1, 167, 27 December 1965.
37. BStU, MfS, III/6/ Ref S, OV "Diversant," AOP 1066/91, vol. 6, 50, 22 January 1964.
38. Heym, *Nachruf*, 669.
39. Wolf Biermann, *Warte nicht auf bessre Zeiten! Die Autobiographie* (Berlin: Ullstein Buchverlage, 2016), 136–137.
40. Jutta Voigt, *Stierblutjahre. Die Boheme des Ostens* (Berlin: Aufbau Verlag, 2016).
41. Robert Havemann, *Ein deutscher Kommunist. Rückblicke und Perspektiven aus der Isolation* (Reinbek bei Hamburg: Rowohlt, 1978), 33ff.
42. Heym, *Nachruf*, 6.
43. Heym, 134.
44. Heym, 116.
45. Heym, 118.
46. Heym, 134.
47. Heym, 75.
48. Biermann, *Warte nicht auf bessre Zeiten!*, 23.
49. Biermann, 7.
50. Biermann, 50.
51. Biermann, 142.
52. Biermann, 142.
53. Reich-Ranicki, *Über Ruhestörer*, 196.
54. Biermann, *Warte nicht auf bessre Zeiten!*, 53.
55. Heym, *Nachruf*, 674.
56. Heavily edited transcript, 3 August 1965; OV "Diversant"; BStU, MfS, AOP 1066/91, Bd. 1, Bl. 157, 159, 160.
57. Quoted from Günter Agde, "Zur Anatomie eines Tests. Das Gespräch Walter Ulbrichts mit Schrifstellern und Künstlern am 25. November 1965 im Staatsrat der DDR," in *Kahlschlag. Das 11. Plenum des ZK der SED 1965. Studien und Dokumente*, ed. Günter Agde (Berlin: Aufbau Taschenbuch Verlag, 1991), 136.
58. Agde, *Kahlschlag*, 140.
59. Stefan Heym, "Die Langeweile von Minsk," in *Wege und Umwege. Streitbare Schriften aus fünf Jahrzehnten*, ed. Peter Mallwitz (Berlin: btb, 1998), 353.
60. Heym, "Die Langeweile von Minsk," 354.
61. Heym, 354.
62. Heym, 356.
63. Heym, 358.
64. Hermann Axen, "Braucht unsere Zeit Propheten? Wer spricht das wahre Wort?," *Neues Deutschland*, 28 November 1965.
65. Agde, *Kahlschlag*, 141.

66. Agde, 349.
67. Agde, 349.
68. Biermann, *Warte nicht auf bessre Zeiten!*, 170.
69. Biermann, 170.
70. Biermann, 171.
71. Biermann, 171.
72. Biermann, 171.
73. Biermann, 171.
74. Havemann, *Fragen Antworten Fragen. Aus der Biographie eines deutschen Marxisten*, 159.
75. Havemann, 160.
76. Havemann, 203.
77. Heym, *Nachruf*, 88.
78. Heym, 88.
79. Heym, 88.
80. "Tatsachen und Dokumente. Rede vor der Vollversammlung des Berliner Schriftstellerverbandes," 367.
81. Heym, *Nachruf*, 710.
82. Heym, 710.
83. Manfred Krug, *Abgehauen* (Berlin: Ullstein Taschenbuch, 2016), 40.
84. Stefan Heym, *Der Winter unsers Mißvergnügens: Aus den Aufzeichnungen des OV Diversant* (Berlin: btb, 1998), 89.
85. Heym, 91.
86. Heym, *Nachruf*, 710.
87. Heym, 9.
88. Heym, 9.
89. Peter Hutchinson, foreword to *The Architects*, by Stefan Heym (Evanston, Ill.: Northwestern University Press, 2006).
90. Lion Feuchtwanger, "Was ist Wahrheit?," *Unterhaltungsblatt der Vossischen Zeitung*, 21 October 1932.
91. Biermann, *Warte nicht auf bessre Zeiten!*, 59.
92. BStU, MfS, HA XX/1/III, OV "Diversant," AOP Nr. 1066/91, vol. 8, 31, 15. April 1965.
93. BStU, MfS, HVA/II (300), OV "Diversant," AOP 1066/91, vol. 10, 47, 25 February 1966.
94. BStU, MfS, HVA/II (300), OV "Diversant," AOP 1066/91, vol. 10, 47, 25 February 1966.
95. According to Heym's speech, the *Darmstädter Tagblatt* reported on 26 December 1965 that "Heym . . . verteidigte den Sozialismus als seine ureigene Angelegenheit" ("Heym . . . defended Socialism as his very own matter"), while on 2 December 1965 the *Hannoverische Presse* wrote, "Er ist ein überzeugter Bürger seines Staates, den er jedoch keineswegs für vollkommen hält" ("He is a staunch citizen of his state which he by no means considers perfect"). "Tatsachen und Dokumente. Rede vor der Vollversammlung des Berliner Schriftstellerverbandes," in *Wege und Umwege. Einmischung*, ed. Peter Mallwitz (Munich: btb, 1998), 367–378; for these quotes, see 372 and 373.
96. BStU, MfS, HA XX/1/III, OV "Diversant," AOP 1066/91, vol. 10, 52, 26 February 1966.
97. BStU, MfS, Deutscher Schriftstellerverband, OV "Diversant," AOP 1066/91, vol. 10, 111, 31 March 1966.
98. BStU, MfS, HA XX/1, OV "Diversant," AOP 1066/91, vol. 10, 64, 3 March 1966.
99. BStU, MfS, "Simone," OV "Diversant," AOP 1066/91, vol. 10, 56 and 57, 1 March 1966.
100. BStU, MfS, "Simone," OV "Diversant," AOP 1066/91, vol. 10, 56 and 57, 1 March 1966.
101. BStU, MfS, "GI Cube," OV "Diversant," AOP 25507/91, vol. 3, 23 and 24, 10 August 1966.
102. BStU, MfS, "GI Cube," OV "Diversant," AOP 25507/91, vol. 3, 23 and 24, 10 August 1966.
103. BStU, MfS, HA XX/1, OV "Diversant," AOP 1066/91, vol. 12, 128, 10 June 1968.
104. BStU, MfS, HA XX, OV "Diversant," Nr. 22708, 88, 27 July 1966.

105. BStU; MfS, HA XX/1, OV "Diversant," BStU, MfS, AOP 25507/91, vol. 3, 31, 13 September 1966.

106. BStU; MfS, HA XX/1, OV "Diversant," BStU, MfS, AOP 25507/91, vol. 3, 31, 13 September 1966.

107. BStU; MfS, HA XX/1, OV "Diversant," BStU, MfS, AOP 25507/91, vol. 3, 31, 13 September 1966.

108. BStU; MfS, HA XX/1, OV "Diversant," AOP 1066/91, vol. 12, 128, 10 June 1968.

109. Havemann, *Ein deutscher Kommunist*, 23.

110. BStU, MfS, HA XX/1, OV "Diversant," AOP 25507/91, vol. 1, 174, 27 December 1965.

111. Heym, *Nachruf*, 670.

112. BStU, MfS, HA XX/1, OV "Diversant," AOP 25507/91, vol. 3, 21, 27 July 1966.

113. BStU, MfS, HA XX/1/III, OV "Diversant," AOP 1066/91, vol. 8, 32, 15 April 1965.

114. Biermann, *Warte nicht auf bessre Zeiten!*, 136.

115. Havemann, *Ein deutscher Kommunist*, 23–24.

116. Quoted in Hannemann, *Robert Havemann*, 125.

117. Arno Polzin, *Der Wandel Robert Havemanns vom Inoffiziellen Mitarbeiter zum Dissidenten im Spiegel der MfS-Akten*, BF informiert 26/2005, accessed 18 April 2018, http://www.bstu.bund.de/DE/Wissen/Publikationen/Publikationen/E_polzin_havemann.pdf?__blob=publicationFile.

118. Harold Hurwitz, "Die Widerstandsgruppe 'Neu Beginnen' und Robert Havemann in den Jahren von 1933 bis 1948," Paper for the Robert Havemann Conference at the Evangelist Academy and the Robert Havemann Society, Berlin 1994. Quoted in Hannemann, *Robert Havemann*, 128.

119. See the biography of Havemann by Ingeborg Rapoport, *My First Three Lives* (Berlin, 1998), quoted in Hannemann, *Robert Havemann*, 126.

120. See Hannemann, *Robert Havemann*, 118, 122, and 131.

121. Hannemann, *Robert Havemann*, 127.

122. Quoted in Polzin, *Der Wandel Robert Havemanns*, 21.

123. Heym, *Nachruf*, 672–673.

124. Heym, 674.

125. Biermann, *Warte nicht auf bessre Zeiten!*, 318.

126. Heym, *Nachruf*, 673.

127. BStU, MfS, HA XX/1, OV "Diversant," AOP 1066/91, vol. 12, 128, 10 June 1968.

128. BStU, MfS, HA XX/7, OV "Diversant," AOP 1066/91, vol. 1, 135, 9 August 1971.

129. Hutchinson, *Stefan Heym*, 161–162.

130. Joachim Walther, *Sicherungsbereich Literatur. Schriftsteller und Staatssicherheit in der Deutschen Demokratischen Republik* (Berlin: Ch. Links, 1996), 84.

131. Krug, *Abgehauen*, 40. See also Biermann, *Warte nicht auf bessre Zeiten!*, 136.

132. Krug, 41.

133. Krug, 41.

134. Krug, 42.

135. Krug, 42.

136. Günter Kertzscher, "Angemessene Antwort auf feindseliges Auftreten gegen die DDR," *Neues Deutschland*, 17 November 1976.

137. N.n., *Neues Deutschland*, 17 November 1976.

138. Krug, *Abgehauen*, 42.

139. Joseph Walk, ed. *Das Sonderrecht für die Juden im NS-Staat. Eine Sammlung der gesetzlichen Maßnahmen und Richtlinien—Inhalt und Bedeutung* (Heidelberg: C. F. Müller Verlag, 1996), 36.

140. "Der war der geborene Führer," *Spiegel* online, 24 May 1976, accessed 1 October 2019, https://www.spiegel.de/spiegel/print/d-41213407.html.

141. Krug, *Abgehauen*, 42.

142. Krug, *Abgehauen*, 43.

143. See the interview with specialist in forensic medicine Wolfgang Keil who investigated the GDR delegates who were victims of the crash at the Charité. *FOCUS Magazine*, 26 July 2010, accessed 1 October 2019, https://www.focus.de/magazin/archiv/menschen-wahrheit-gibt-zufriedenheit_aid_534250.html.

144. Monika Maron, *Flugasche* (Berlin: Welt Edition, 2009), 9.

145. Jurek Becker, *Bronsteins Kinder* (Munich: Süddeutsche Zeitung, 1986).

146. Heym, *Nachruf*, 843, 844.

147. Heym, *Nachruf*, 448.

CHAPTER 8

ERNST BLOCH'S ESCHATOLOGICAL MARXISM

Michael Meng

Like its Western competitor, the German Democratic Republic (GDR) emerged from the cauldron that was the Weimar Republic. Its stalwart leaders—Walter Ulbricht and Erich Honecker—both became diehard Communists in the interwar years, as did many other Germans who made a mark on the history of East Germany. Prominent among these was Ernst Bloch, the country's most famous and significant Marxist thinker, who returned to the GDR from exile in 1949 to teach at the University of Leipzig before defecting for the West in 1961. Bloch shared little in common with his party leaders other than owing his formative experience to the Weimar Republic, and perhaps not even that.[1] For Bloch emerged from the Weimar Germany that produced not only Communist agitators but also a number of thinkers, many of Jewish origin, who thought about eschatology, about what is outermost, most mysterious; about what seems farthest from yet nearest to each of us: death, the end of time (*chronos ouketi estai*).[2]

Marxists do not typically think about death, at least not in public, and especially not bureaucrats like Ulbricht and Honecker. This is partly because Marx, unlike Hegel, rarely wrote about death and partly because death, as Bloch understood, poses a problem to the Marxist project of human emancipation.[3] Bloch, however, was an unusual Marxist thinker who wrote about death at length, prompting Theodor W. Adorno to praise Bloch for getting "to the heart of the matter."[4]

Bloch gets to the heart of matter because he believes that freedom, equality, and peace cannot be achieved without accepting or overcoming death. Unlike Marx, who suggests that the equalization of material resources and self-realization through labor in the Communist utopia will satisfy the human being, Bloch does not believe that distributive justice and labor will usher in human satisfaction.[5] To be sure, Bloch remains committed to overthrowing capitalism, but its overthrow alone is not enough, for something else ails the human—the metaphysical pain of death, the pain that we face like no other living beings do:

> The dying ego has always before it that pulverizing, annihilating dread so peculiar to man, for animals fear dying, not death. They have no self-conscious ego that can foresee its own annihilation, and can fear the plain and final fact of death even more than it fears the act of dying. Where then can man find strength to face this outright and immediate devaluation?[6]

Bloch asks in this passage, How does one "deal" with death? In his magnum opus, *The Principle of Hope*, Bloch sought to combat death through a philosophy of hope, through a philosophy of overcoming the despair of mortality that he expressed by invoking the Latin expression *non omnis confundar* (let me not be utterly destroyed). While inspired by the religious orientation toward salvation from death as manifested particularly in the Judeo-Christian tradition, Bloch insisted that true freedom from death must be atheistic in the sense that it must be envisioned and realized in the world. Otherwise it will fail to free us from fearful subservience to death, "the absolute master," and the various regimes of authority that depend on that fear, not least the regime of theism that locates salvation in a heavenly realm and thus enslaves humans to a higher authority.[7]

In what follows, I explore these arguments in three sections. The first section focuses on death as an impediment to human freedom, specifically Bloch's claim that the interpretation of death as "something" frightening and mysterious underpins regimes of domination, as exemplified in the case of Nazism. The second section discusses Bloch's utopian project of hope as centered on overcoming death. The third section briefly brings these two parts together to underscore the distinctiveness of Bloch's ostensibly "Jewish" contribution to the political rebuilding of post-Nazi Germany, a distinctiveness that consists in his concern with death and the eschatological tradition of the Jewish and Christian religions.[8]

Bloch's focus on death might seem like an unusual chapter in the postwar history of Jews and Jewish life in Germany even within the particular history of German Communists of Jewish heritage who became attracted to Communism.[9] Bloch is indeed unusual as a philosopher in general and as a Marxist in particular. Yet therein consists his intervention as an eschatological thinker whose focus on death calls into question the notion of freedom dominant on both sides of the Berlin Wall. His religious sensitivity to metaphysical suffering brings him to argue that the standard way of thinking about freedom in postwar

Germany—namely, the capitalist alignment of freedom with the satisfaction of material desires—will not yield human freedom and satisfaction.[10] For Bloch, there can be no political freedom without freedom from death.[11]

Death and Nazism

One of the most original aspects of Bloch's interpretation of Nazism lies in his exploration of the centrality of death to Hitler's movement. While Bloch's elliptical, poetic style of philosophical reflection never brings him to offer a concise expression of his argument, the most fundamental elements of his position can nevertheless be pieced together from his corpus. The starting point of his exploration into the relationship between death and Nazism consists in his basic understanding of authority as originating from vulnerability and fear—the most basic of which pertaining to death: people turn to regimes of authority in the face of suffering and death. They seek authority to be saved from a threat. That authoritarianism arises from insecurity and fear is hardly a new thought; one thinks of Sophocles, who draws a connection between death and authority in *Oedipus the King*, or of G. W. F. Hegel, who does so in his master-slave narrative in *The Phenomenology of Spirit*.

The latter, as the most obvious source for Bloch, warrants a brief discussion. In the master-slave narrative, Hegel suggests that a fight for prestige or recognition breaks out between two persons who both desire to be acknowledged by the other as the particular individual (*Einzelnes*) that they conceive themselves to be. This fight to the death ends with one of them capitulating to the other. The one who capitulates, the slave, trembles in the face of death and thus becomes enslaved to the master, who does not succumb to the fear of death.

Hence, authoritarianism (*Herrschaft*) rests on fear for Hegel. And yet fear, as what enslaves, also frees insofar as it reveals to the slave what he or she must overcome to achieve genuine and radical freedom: the slave must be freed from death to be fully free. Specifically, the slave realizes that freedom comes through working for the survival of the community.[12] The slave becomes conscious of his true humanity as a communal being who lives and works for the higher end of the community and, in so doing, becomes freed of the egoistic attachment to his own particular life, which compelled the slave to fight for recognition in the first place.

Hegel's master-slave narrative can be boiled down to two claims: first, that domination depends on the fear of death; and second, that liberation from death is the necessary and sufficient condition for human freedom from domination. Bloch affirms these two claims, though he gives his own interpretations of them through his understanding of Nazism and his philosophy of hope, respectively. Let us begin with the former.

By thinking about the relationship between death and Nazism, Bloch focuses on the way in which Nazism glorified the "heroic" struggle against death on the battlefield. Vainglory was the greatest and most noble promise Nazism had to offer; the only consolation for death it could come up with was the age-old Achillean hope for immortal glory (*kleos*), a hope that has animated warriors and authoritarians for centuries. The famous quote by Napoleon comes to mind here: "I live only for posterity," he said. "Death is nothing, but to live defeated and without glory is to die every day."[13]

Bloch himself cites Ernst Jünger, who, perhaps more than any other German writer, affirmed the excitement and glory of war in *Storm of Steel*:

> Over the ruins, as over all the most dangerous parts of the terrain, lay a heavy smell of death, because the fire was so intense that no one could bother with the corpses. You really did have to run for your life in these places, and when I caught the smell of it as I ran, I was hardly surprised—it belonged there. Moreover, this heavy sweetish atmosphere was not merely disgusting; it also, in association with the piercing fogs of gunpowder, brought about an almost visionary excitement, that otherwise only the extreme nearness of death is able to produce.[14]

For Bloch, Jünger's glorification of struggling against death with manly fortitude betrays the impoverishment and vapidity of bourgeois life, a life of boredom that, in desperation, becomes attracted to death as a "wild ending."[15]

While this characterization of Jünger might be dismissed as a bland assertion of Marxist orthodoxy, to do so would be to miss the more penetrating philosophical point that lies behind it, a point that Bloch makes in his polemic with Martin Heidegger. Bloch views Heidegger as a bourgeois philosopher of death who beckons us to embrace the mystery and loneliness of death. For Heidegger, death is one's *ownmost* possibility. It "belongs" to the individual and to the individual alone. One's own death cannot be exchanged with anyone else; in Heidegger's words, death is nonrelational (*unbezüglich*). There is thus no common experience of death, since death is a burden that each *Dasein* (being-there, or there-being) confronts on its own. What is most "mine," my death, I cannot share with anyone.

The consequence of Heidegger's insistence on death as nonrelational is that any attempt to create a society around what might be said to bring humans together must fail in the face of death as one's ownmost, nonrelational possibility. Death pulls asunder any and all social relations as illusory attempts to bridge a divide that cannot be bridged. By making this claim, Heidegger challenges not only Hegel's argument that human reality is inherently social but also Hegel's insistence on the possibility of overcoming death in and through the community.

For Heidegger, Hegel's attempt to overcome death is yet another inauthentic evasion of death as one's ownmost possibility. Indeed, any and all forms of sociality hide our essential solitude as being-towards-death (*Sein zum Tode*); sociality evades death as what individuates us and separates us from others.

Few claims by Heidegger are more destructive of sociality, as Bloch understood.[16] For Bloch, a Hegelian-Marxist thinker, there is only one life: the social life. Thus to think of sociality as an illusion or evasion is to embrace the bourgeois valorization of the individual as completely and radically isolated or, as Bloch puts it, to think of the human as completely and radically alone in the world, as *solus ipse*.[17] In Heidegger, Bloch sees a petit bourgeois thinker whose insistence on death as the most individuating of possibilities advances a destructive politics of asociality in the guise of ontology; a politics that condemns rational relations with others to the realm of inauthenticity.[18] Moreover, Bloch recognizes that Heidegger undermines any notion of salvation from death, be it the theistic belief in the immortality of the soul or the atheistic overcoming of death through the community. There is no salvation from death for Heidegger. As Bloch puts it, "There is no consolation against death as the positively recognized and acknowledged 'downright nullity' of existence itself."[19] Finally, Bloch argues that Heidegger turns death into a source of authority that bears an affinity with the theistic creation of God as an authority that compels unquestioned compliance through fear.[20] For Bloch, Heidegger is a theist whose insistence on the mystery of death establishes death as an authority outside what the human can know absolutely and master finally. In so doing, he affirms the hegemony of nature—of death—over any and all strivings for human freedom. Heidegger's philosophy of death blocks the utopian freedom that Bloch envisions as possible.[21]

In this respect, Bloch characterizes Heidegger as espousing a "pro-fascist nihilism."[22] What makes Heidegger both a nihilist and a fascist? With regards first to nihilism, the central issue for Bloch is Heidegger's denial of the possibility of communality in the face of the loneliness and individuality of death.[23] Heidegger's insistence on the solitary individual is nihilistic for Bloch because it challenges one of the bedrock claims of the Hegelian-Marxist tradition: that the human is essentially a communal being. Hegel develops this claim in *The Phenomenology of Spirit*, where he demonstrates that the realization of the self depends essentially on the other (the "I" cannot be an ego or an "I" without being social; i.e., without being recognized as such in and by language by the other). The Hegelian scholar Michael Forster summarizes this point as follows: "[The] Hegelian man, through coming to recognize in these ways that his very existence and identity, and also the realization of all his deepest aspirations, depend essentially on his community and his conformity with it, loses all sense of himself as a being ontologically or practically autonomous of his community."[24]

This basic insight informs Marx's understanding of the human as essentially communal. As for Hegel, so too for Marx—we can never be completely alone in the world insofar as we live and interact in it with others.[25] To say otherwise is to deny the essence of the human as a social being or "species-being" (*Gattungswesen*), to invoke Marx's term.[26] This denial lies at the heart of the capitalist system, which alienates the individual from its essence as a social being. As Marx explains in the *Economic and Philosophic Manuscripts of 1844*:

> In estranging from man . . . his own active functions, his life activity, estranged labor estranges the *species* from man. It changes for him the *life of the species* into a means of individual life. First it estranges the life of the species and individual life, and secondly it makes individual life in its abstract form the purpose of the life of the species, likewise in its abstract and estranged form.[27]

By aligning labor solely with the individualistic end of pursuing one's own interests, capitalism alienates us from ourselves, from our very humanity, because what we truly are is social. Put in the terms Bloch employs, capitalism is nihilistic because it rejects the essential sociality of the human being.

The same is the case with fascism. According to Bloch, fascism is nihilistic in its glorification of the individualistic, egoistic rule of the master and the warrior as evident in the example of Hitler, who asserted himself over others and aimed to win "immortal glory" through war and empire. Hitler's claim to be acting for the greater glory of the German nation merely masked his true, egoistic motives. Heidegger, on this score, is more complicated insofar as he finds consolation neither in the impulse to dominate nor in the striving to be remembered, since he finds no consolation for death. Nothing saves one from death, not action, not hierarchy, not commemoration—nothing at all. Nevertheless, Heidegger's emphasis on the individuality and loneliness of death brings him into the fascist camp for Bloch because he not only denies but blocks the possibility of building an egalitarian and peaceful society in his philosophy of death.

Death and Salvation

Bloch counters Heidegger with a philosophy of hope that hinges on overcoming the fear of death, "the power of the strongest non-utopia."[28] This focus on death makes Bloch an unusual Marxist thinker; indeed, one would be hard pressed to come up with another Marxist thinker of Bloch's stature who connects freedom with overcoming the fear of death as he does.[29] In a conversation with Bloch, Theodor W. Adorno came to the same conclusion:

> It moved me very much, Ernst, that *you* were the one who touched on this, for my own thinking has been circling around this point in recent times—that

> the question about the elimination of death is indeed the crucial point. This is the heart of the matter. . . . I believe that without the notion of an unfettered life, freed from death, the idea of utopia, the idea of *the* utopia, *cannot* even be thought at all.[30]

This comment might prompt one to wonder if it even makes sense to characterize Bloch as a Marxist thinker, since Marx takes such a different approach to the issue of human freedom. To review briefly, Marx suggests that the central impediment to freedom lies in the capitalist system, which valorizes the individual, egoistic pursuit of wealth and thus alienates the human from his or her "social existence" (*gesellschaftliches Dasein*). Under capitalism one interacts and lives in the world purely for the sake of advancing one's own individual existence (*individuelle Existenz*) at the expense of others. This enslavement to naked self-interest is pernicious for Marx not only because it leads to domination and oppression but also because it alienates the human from its essence as a social being.

If self-interest is the central problem for Marx, the panacea is overcoming it in one of two ways. The first is through the revolutionary establishment of a society oriented toward the flourishing of the whole over the selfish pursuit of one's own interests; in this purely selfless society, one would labor for the sake of the community. The second is through the revolutionary establishment of a society that enables creative activity to flourish with, as its aim, self-realization; in this society, one would labor for one's own fulfillment in full consciousness of one's essential dependence on others for that fulfillment. The former leads to self-abnegation, the latter to the enrichment of individuality within and through the community.[31]

While these two possibilities could not be more different, they both offer a resolution to the same problem of self-interest as understood narrowly by Marx in materialistic terms.[32] Marx aligns self-interest with the capitalistic pursuit of money and the commodification of labor, not with the selfish struggle for prestige and recognition as Hegel does. Indeed, Marx rewrites Hegel's master-slave narrative as pertaining to the domination of the laborer by the capitalist.[33] While one could interpret the capitalist pursuit of money as a form of recognition—as a vain and selfish response to death—Marx does not advance that interpretation himself. Rather, he argues that capitalism has transformed us into self-interested beings habituated to the pursuit of wealth.

But is this so? Is selfishness a product of capitalism? And can it therefore be overcome through a revolutionary change in the material conditions of human life? While Bloch does not offer a direct answer to these questions, he intimates in a passage on self-preservation in *The Principle of Hope* that the inherently self-interested "drive" to preserve oneself—though it courses through all history, not just the capitalist era—need not necessarily be egoistic and selfish. There can be, for Bloch, a universal form of self-interest oriented toward communal solidarity and freedom. If this position aligns him with the Marxist camp, he departs from it in claiming that communal solidarity and freedom can only come into realization, if it can be realized at all, by resolving the perplexity of death.[34]

How might the perplexity of death be resolved? It is not clear that Bloch thinks it can be resolved *pace* Hegel, though he appreciates human efforts to resist death as he makes clear in his discussion of various beliefs in immortality. One might be tempted, therefore, to conclude that Bloch offers little more than praising salvation as a "noble" yet futile act of resistance against mortality; if so, then utopia turns out to be a hope and nothing more in the face of "the Jaws of death [that] grind everything."[35] When one comes across phrases such as this, it is difficult not to view Bloch as offering nothing more than Sisyphean protests against death, protests that are vain but noble insofar as they demonstrate the strength of human resistance. Yet this characterization of Bloch's position is not entirely fair because he seems to be grasping for something different, at least in the most suggestive passages of *The Principle of Hope* and *The Spirit of Utopia*.[36] In those passages, Bloch develops a notion of salvation around overcoming the fear of death.

Bloch asks, "How do we shake off the final fear?"[37] We cannot shake it off, he insists, by evading death, for evasion is the bourgeois solution to death:

> Men have never been anxious to count their ever dwindling years, yet what is bourgeois and merely lives from one day to the next is encouraged, among many other things, not to look to the end at all. . . . Dying is pushed away . . . Thus we live from one day to the next and into the night, no thought must ever be given to the worst end which is yet to come. This wish is simply to hear and to see nothing of it, even when the end is here. Thus fear at least shrinks, becomes flat, like so much else.[38]

The bourgeois evasion of death manifests itself above all in the superficiality of American culture, which turns away from the suffering of life and thus of life itself by elevating material success and comfort as the highest goal of human striving.[39]

If Bloch rejects this response to death, it is difficult to pinpoint what he prefers as an alternative, since he explores several possibilities in his work, two of which stand out as noteworthy. The first comes from Bloch's early work, *The Spirit of Utopia* (1918), where he envisions the overcoming of bourgeois superficiality by the creation of a radically new society that embraces death and suffering rather than evading it. According to this possibility, the goal of socialism would be to accept suffering, a most unconventional thought in the context of Western Marxism; indeed, one might say it is not "Western" but "Eastern," as Bloch suggests in his invocation of Fyodor Dostoevsky to describe what the new life, the new communitarian society, will inaugurate:

> Then human beings will finally be free for those concerns and questions which alone are practical, which otherwise only await them at their hour of death after their entire restless life up to then had done nothing but seal them off from everything essential.... We are not becoming free for ourselves, as should already have been evident, just to fall asleep more easily, or to universalize the agreeable idleness of a particular upper class; we are not struggling to regain Dickens at best, or Victorian England's cozy fireplace; rather, this is the goal, the eminently practical goal, the basic motif of socialist ideology: to bestow on every human time outside of work, his own need, boredom, wretchedness, privation and gloom, his own submerged light calling, a life in the Dostoevskyan sense.[40]

This passage suggests that the Communist utopia will not offer salvation from human suffering but rather freedom from salvation so as to allow each individual to face his or her own suffering. Bloch imagines the creation of a community born of sober respect for suffering in which one's solidarity with others and one's work in the community takes on a richness not experienced hitherto. This richness comes from an awareness of the fragility of life, an awareness that enables one to engage in the world and with others in a profoundly different way. While Bloch does not describe what precisely this new way of interacting in the world would entail, his reference to Dostoevsky provides a clue. In *The Brothers Karamazov*, Dostoevsky discusses, among other themes, communal solidarity as a response to the loneliness and solitude of death, a response that rejects the conventional, egoistic reaction to death centered on the selfish valorization of one's own suffering over and against the suffering of the other. Whereas the valorization of one's own suffering encourages one to accord preference to oneself over another, the relinquishment of that valorization allows one to live and work for others. One responds to the solitude of death not by isolating oneself from society but by living in it for oneself and for others. Dostoevsky elegantly makes this point in the following passage:

> In order to make the world over anew, people themselves must turn onto a different path psychically. Until one has indeed become the brother of all, there will be no brotherhood. No science or self-interest will ever enable people to share their property and their rights among themselves without offense. Each will always think his share too small, and they will keep murmuring, they will envy and destroy one another. You ask when it will come true. It will come true, but first the period of human *isolation* must conclude. . . . [The isolation] which is now reigning everywhere, especially in our age, but it is not all concluded yet, its term has not come. For everyone now strives most of all to separate his person, wishing to experience the fullness of life within himself, and yet what comes of all his efforts is not the fullness of life but full suicide,

> for instead of the fullness of self-definition, they fall into complete isolation. For all men in our age are separated into units, each seeks seclusion in his own hole, each withdraws from the others, hides himself, and hides what he has, and ends by pushing himself away from people and pushing people away from himself. He accumulates wealth in solitude, thinking: how strong, how secure I am now; and does not see, madman as he is, that the more he accumulates, the more he sinks into suicidal impotence. For he is accustomed to relying only on himself, he has separated his unit from the whole, he has accustomed his soul to not believing in people's help, in people or mankind, and now only trembles lest his money and his acquired privileges perish.[41]

Dostoevsky argues that death can bring a community together only if people give up their selfishness to live for others. Bloch tends to agree with this point,[42] though he equivocates insofar as he also envisions the flourishing of the individual through work.[43]

This equivocation on Bloch's part brings up the second alternative to bourgeois superficiality that he explores, chiefly in *The Principle of Hope*, where he advances a different notion of salvation from death.[44] Rather than embracing suffering à la Dostoevsky, Bloch celebrates the futural orientation of our being-towards-death as opening up the possibility of hope, of the new, of the "not-yet-become." Bloch views our finite, unfinished condition as salutary; he embraces the "astonishment" and "exuberance" of life as the always inexhaustible unfolding of what has not yet been realized, achieved, and become.[45] The future possibility of the new staves off the despair of death—the ebullience of the change that finitude inevitably brings takes away the sting of death.

Bloch seems to be gesturing at a new way of living afforded by the revolutionary overcoming of bourgeois life, a new way of interacting in the world that embraces the immediacy of the moment freed from the need to preserve that moment in some kind of regime of permanency. In the Communist utopia, then, one would create not for the purpose of preserving something of oneself—of leaving a trace after one's death—but rather in exuberant and joyful protest against death: "Now it is precisely this joy and this form of astonishment which seek to look forward to death with strange certainty: *not only as a journey of the extremest order but as a setting-free precisely of the—exuberance of life*."[46] Although Bloch does not develop this claim in much detail, he seems to be offering here an interpretation of Marx's understanding of the human as a self-consciously free and creative being—that is, a being aware of the fact that it creates not only to satisfy immediate physical needs but also in freedom therefrom.[47] That freedom comes for Bloch above all from awareness of death: we become aware of the fact that we create to satisfy the human desire for salvation or what Bloch refers to as the imperative of *non omnis confundar* (let me not be utterly destroyed). This desire for salvation leads to creative protests against death that Bloch celebrates as distinctly human. To be human for Bloch is to act, to produce, to create in rebellion against the limitations and injustice of nature.

It is not fully clear how Bloch squares this affirmation of creativity with his Hegelian-Marxist commitment to egalitarianism. The problem lies in the basic Hegelian understanding of action as arising from the selfish desire to be recognized by others as a particular individual (*Einzelnes*). This desire leads to inequality, violence, and the propensity to accord preference to one's own interests above those of others. To find a way out of this problem, Hegel supports the ancient Greek fusion of individual and communal interest. If Bloch embraces a similar solution, then his Communist utopia would recast individual action against death in communal terms such that one acts in solidarity with others who also face the loneliness of death. Bloch does not directly suggest such a solution, but it seems to be the most plausible one available in light of his political commitment to egalitarianism.

Bloch and Building a New Germany

By according such significant attention to death, Bloch is an untimely thinker, now and in the postwar era in which he wrote and taught, both in East Germany (where he worked until 1961) and in West Germany (where he lived until his death in 1977). There is no other thinker in the postwar era who writes as directly about death as Bloch, aside from his philosophical counterpart, Martin Heidegger, who challenges the need for salvation from death that Bloch, for the most part, elevates as human and beautiful. This striking focus on salvation and death can be understood within the historical-cultural setting in which Bloch emerged as an intellectual—namely, the Weimar Republic. The historian Paul R. Mendes-Flohr astutely situates Bloch within the Weimar renaissance of Jewish culture and thought, which was concerned with, among other things, eschatological questions about death and redemption. Recall the first lines of Franz Rosenzweig's *The Star of Redemption*, a book partly written while Rosenzweig fought in World War I:

> From death, it is from the fear of death that all cognition of the All begins. Philosophy has the audacity to cast off the fear of the earthly, to remove from death its poisonous sting, from Hades his pestilential breath. All that is mortal lives in this fear of death; every new birth multiples the fear for a new reason, for it multiples that which is mortal. The womb of the inexhaustible earth ceaselessly gives birth to what is new, and each one is subject to death; each newly born waits with fear and trembling for the day of its passage into the dark.[48]

That Rosenzweig's—and Bloch's—concerns with death and salvation partly come from the serious attention they paid to the Jewish and Christian religious traditions is an obvious and pedantic point; less obvious and more interesting is the political importance of their focus on death and salvation in the context of postwar German-Jewish history.

Bloch's contribution to the rebuilding of Jewish life in Germany can be characterized as political, albeit not in the conventional sense of Jewish engagement in state policies but rather in the sense of the fundamental questions he raises about freedom and equality.[49] Bloch suggests that freedom and equality can only be achieved in a community that addresses the pain and suffering of death. While this view might be dismissed as eccentric, Bloch is convinced that the standard, materialist notion of freedom will not establish the peaceful, free, and egalitarian society it promises to create. The overcoming of capitalism is a necessary but not sufficient condition for freedom and equality, since it fails to confront death—the deepest origin of human anguish, suffering, and violence. A great deal is at stake for Bloch. For if we fail to confront death, we open the door to resigned submission to and violent protest against death; we let in Heidegger and Jünger, the bourgeois philosopher who teaches impotence in the face of death and the fascist warrior who bravely welcomes death.[50] If we fail to confront death, then we accept death as the basic limiting condition of human life that permanently blocks a truly free and utopian society from ever coming into existence.

Bloch believes that the left must offer a different response to death. But what is that response exactly? Should the left offer Dostoyevskian acceptance of suffering and death as the basis of communal solidarity? Or should it strive to overcome death or, at minimum, diminish the pain it brings? Should it argue for accepting mortality or overcoming it? In the main, Bloch sides with overcoming death in the metaphorical sense of combatting mortality through some notion of salvation in the world (e.g., achieving permanency through work for the community or sacrificing oneself for the Communist cause).[51] In this respect, he sees the revolutionary message of Christianity in its admission of the likeness between God and man: "Christianity triumphed in the early centuries with the call, 'I am the resurrection and the life!' It triumphed with the Sermon on the Mount and with eschatology."[52] By recovering utopian hopes of eternal life, albeit in the world, Bloch ultimately gave Marxism a new and different form—a distinctly religious form that underscored the central importance of metaphysical suffering to building a new Germany and to constructing a new world of equality and freedom; a world freed from the fear of death.

NOTES

1. On the importance of the Weimar context for understanding the GDR, see Catherine Epstein, *The Last Revolutionaries: German Communists and Their Century* (Cambridge, Mass.: Harvard University Press, 2003).

2. Revelations 10:6. Among other thinkers of Jewish origin, Theodor W. Adorno, Walter Benjamin, and Franz Rosenzweig wrote about death (and suffering). Perhaps the most

notable philosopher of death, however, was hardly Jewish but in fact an anti-Semite: Martin Heidegger. I will return to Heidegger because Bloch engages with him extensively.

3. While I think this generalization fairly applies to German Communists, a fascinating counterexample is the case of Russian Communists who made overcoming death central to the Communist project of human emancipation. As a start, see Nikolai Krementsov, *Revolutionary Experiments: The Quest for Immortality in Bolshevik Science* (New York: Oxford University Press, 2014).

4. "Something's Missing: A Discussion between Ernst Bloch and Theodor W. Adorno on the Contradictions of Utopian Longing," in Ernst Bloch, *The Utopian Function of Art and Literature: Selected Essays*, trans. Jack Zipes and Frank Mecklenburg (Cambridge, Mass.: MIT Press, 1988), 1–17. For a basic overview of Bloch's interest in death, see Emmanuel Levinas, *God, Death, and Time*, trans. Bettina Bergo, ed. Jacques Rolland (Stanford, Calif.: Stanford University Press, 2000), 92–105.

5. As Bloch puts it, death "disturbs one constantly so that one cannot be satisfied, no matter how great the satisfaction is and no matter how many economic miracles and welfare states there are" (Bloch, "Something's Missing," 11).

6. Ernst Bloch, *Atheism in Christianity*, intro. Peter Thompson, trans. J. T. Swann (New York: Verso, 2009), 240.

7. G. W. F. Hegel, *Phenomenology of Spirit*, trans. A. V. Miller (New York: Oxford University Press, 1977), 117; Ernst Bloch, *The Principle of Hope*, trans. Neville Plaice, Stephen Plaice, and Paul Knight (Cambridge, Mass.: MIT Press, 1986), 1104.

8. For the Judeo-Christian context of Bloch's eschatology, see Paul R. Mendes-Flohr, "'To Brush History against the Grain:' The Eschatology of the Frankfurt School and Ernst Bloch," *Journal of the American Academy of Religion* 51, no. 4 (1983): 631–650.

9. Karin Hartewig, *Zurückgekehrt. Die Geschichte der jüdischen Kommunisten in der DDR* (Cologne: Böhlau, 2000); Mario Keßler, *Die SED und die Juden—Zwischen Repression und Toleranz. Politische Entwicklungen bis 1967* (Berlin: Akademie Verlag, 1996).

10. Although East Germany claimed that it offered its citizens a different, "socialist" notion of freedom, its own policies were oriented toward the satisfaction of material desires, partly in response to the dominance of consumerist capitalism in West Germany. That the East German regime sought to satisfy material, consumerist needs raises the broader issue of material satisfaction in Marxist thought. If Marx's paradise is the satisfaction of material needs, then Marxism would seem to embrace, rather than overcome, the bourgeois claim that material satisfaction is paradise. See Paul Betts, *Within Walls: Private Life in the German Democratic Republic* (New York: Oxford University Press, 2010).

11. To put Bloch's argument in theological terms, moral evil cannot be eliminated without eliminating metaphysical evil. The connection between moral and metaphysical evil was developed most lucidly by Gottfried Wilhelm Leibniz, who described three kinds of evil: *metaphysical* evil refers to the defects of the human as an imperfect being (i.e., as a mortal being); *moral* evil pertains to the sins that humans, as rational and free creatures, choose to commit and that are made possible by their necessary limitation as creatures qua creatures; and *physical* evil relates to the sufferings that arise from the moral evils that humans voluntarily carry out. Leibniz views death as potentially evil insofar as imperfection is a necessary, but not sufficient, condition of moral evil, in that death makes it possible for free creatures to choose to commit evil actions. In other words, moral evil arises from the free choice to act, and all forms of action—from the most ordinary to the most grandiose, from eating to pursuing "glory"—are oriented toward countering death. And since death only afflicts individuals, countering death entails the advancement of one's own interests above those of others unless one takes up the universal, Promethean project of countering death for all humanity.

12. As Charles Taylor puts it, "For Hegel, a crucial factor in the education of men, in the transformation which brings them to the universal, is the fear of death. The prospect of

death shakes them lose, as it were, from all the particularities of their life." Charles Taylor, *Hegel* (New York: Cambridge University Press, 1975), 155.

13. Georges Lefebvre, *Napoleon*, trans. Henry F. Stockhold and J. E. Anderson (New York: Routledge Classics, 2011), 58.

14. Ernst Jünger, *Storm of Steel*, trans. Michael Hofmann (New York: Penguin, 2003), 93.

15. Bloch, *Principle of Hope*, vol. 3, 1157.

16. See also George Lukács, *The Destruction of Reason*, trans. Peter Palmer (Atlantic Highlands, N.J.: Humanities Press, 1980); Alexandre Kojève, *Atheism*, trans. Jeff Love (New York: Columbia University Press, 2018).

17. Ernst Bloch, *Principle of Hope*, vol. 1, 109.

18. As Bloch writes, "the grasped death as the grasped being-to-the-end is radical individuation." Ernst Bloch, *Heritage of Our Times*, trans. Neville and Stephen Plaice (Cambridge: Polity, 1991), 282.

19. Bloch, 283.

20. Bloch, *Principle of Hope*, vol. 3, 1161.

21. While Bloch's reading of Heidegger is astute, I think his interpretation of Heidegger as a theist might underplay Heidegger's radicality by folding him into the metaphysical tradition that he otherwise endeavors to upend. If Heidegger insists on failure and impossibility—on finitude—then the question becomes: *Why* does he insist on impossibility and finitude? One might argue, as Bloch does, that Heidegger wishes to retain the authority of the strange, the unassailable, the mysterious in terms of either being-towards-death or of Being itself, so as to advance a politics of domination under the pretext of "scientific ontology." In short, Heidegger condemns us to servitude by affirming the hegemony of death over us. This interpretation of Heidegger strikes me as very plausible, but I hasten to add that Heidegger seeks to recast servitude to an unsurpassable authority as driven not by "Jewish" fear but rather by a "Greek" sense of wonder and courage in the face of death. Heidegger insists that each *Dasein* accept its being-towards-death rather than fearfully fleeing from it. All forms of flight are castigated by Heidegger as inauthentic, nihilistic, and "Jewish"; herein lies the core of Heidegger's anti-Semitic attack against the slave revolt of "Jewish Christianity" as essentially nihilistic and misanthropic.

22. Bloch, *Principle of Hope*, vol. 3, 1161.

23. To emphasize, this point strikes me as fundamental to Heidegger's thought, as can now be confirmed by a number of texts not available to Bloch, not least the *Black Notebooks*.

24. Michael N. Forster, *Hegel's Idea of a Phenomenology of Spirit* (Chicago: University of Chicago Press, 1998), 85.

25. Marx gives the example of property to demonstrate his point. Property is a social relation among (1) an object, (2) its owner, and (3) the society that recognizes the relation between (1) and (2). As Marx puts it in the *Grundrisse*, "An isolated individual could no more have property in land and soil than he could speak. . . . As regards the individual, it is clear e.g. that he relates even to language itself *as his own* only as the natural member of a human community. Language as the product of an individual is an impossibility. But the same holds for property." Karl Marx, *Grundrisse*, trans. Martin Nicolaus (New York: Penguin, 1993), 485, 490.

26. This awkward locution comes from Ludwig Feuerbach where it refers to sociality as the essence (*Wesen*) of the human: "The inner life of man is the life which has relation to his species, to his general, as distinguished from his individual nature. . . . Man can perform the functions of thought and speech, which strictly imply such a relation, apart from another individual. Man is himself at once I and thou; he can put himself in the place of another, for this reason, that to him his species, his essential nature, and not merely his individuality, is an object of thought." Ludwig Feuerbach, *The Essence of Christianity*, trans. Marian Evans (London: Trübner, 1881), 2.

27. *Karl Marx Frederick Engels Collected Works*, vol. 3 (New York: International Publishers, 1975), 276.

28. Bloch, *Principle of Hope*, vol. 3, 1103.

29. Herbert Marcuse comes to mind, but he does not discuss death with the frankness that Bloch does. See Herbert Marcuse, *Eros and Civilization: A Philosophical Inquiry into Freud* (Boston: Beacon Press, 1955); Herbert Marcuse, "The Ideology of Death," in *The Meaning of Death*, ed. Herman Feifel (New York: McGraw-Hill, 1959), 64–76.

30. Bloch, "Something's Missing," 7–8 and 10.

31. These two possibilities course through a number of Marx's writings, especially the *Economic and Philosophic Manuscripts of* 1844. See also *The German Ideology*, *Grundrisse*, and *The Communist Manifesto*.

32. Here one might suspect he affirms Adam Smith. See Smith, *The Wealth of Nations*, ed. Edwin Cannan (New York: Modern Library, 1994), 15.

33. Marx rewrites Hegel's master-slave narrative in a single paragraph: "If the product of [man's] labour, his labour objectified, is for him an *alien, hostile*, powerful object independent of him, then his position towards it is such that someone else is master of this object, someone who is alien, hostile, and independent of him. If he treats his own activity as an unfree activity, then he treats it as activity performed in the service, under the dominion, the coercion, and the yoke of another man." *Karl Marx Frederick Engels Collected Works*, vol. 3, 278–279.

34. One could claim that Marx addresses death in a similar manner through his notion of species-being; that is, the recognition of oneself as a communal or universal being that labors for the sake of the community—which survives the individual—diminishes the pain and fear of individual death. See *Karl Marx Frederick Engels Collected Works*, vol. 3, 299.

35. Bloch, *Principle of Hope*, vol. 3, 1107.

36. Ernst Bloch, *The Spirit of Utopia*, trans. Anthony A. Nassar (Stanford, Calif.: Stanford University Press, 2000), 233–278; *The Principle of Hope*, vol. 3, 1178–1182. Elsewhere in *The Principle of Hope*, Bloch offers more conventional notions of salvation from death through work or self-sacrifice for the community. See *The Principle of Hope*, vol. 3, 1161–1167 and 1172–1176. See also *Spirit of Utopia*, 245.

37. Bloch, *Principle of Hope*, vol. 3, 1104.

38. Bloch, 1105.

39. Bloch, 1156–1158; Bloch, *Spirit of Utopia*, 267.

40. Bloch, 246, 268.

41. Fyodor Dostoevsky, *The Brothers Karamazov*, trans. Richard Pevear and Larissa Volokhonsky (New York: Farrar, Straus and Giroux, 1990), 303.

42. See Bloch, *Spirit of Utopia*, 245.

43. Bloch, *Principle of Hope*, vol. 3, 1162.

44. Bloch, vol. 3, 1178–1182.

45. Bloch, vol. 3, 1180.

46. Bloch, vol. 3, 1180 (emphasis in original).

47. *Karl Marx Frederick Engels Collected Works*, vol. 3, 276.

48. Franz Rosenzweig, *The Star of Redemption*, trans. William W. Hallo (Notre Dame, Ind.: University of Notre Dame Press, 1985), 9.

49. This kind of engagement of Jewish leaders in German politics has been explored by others. See, among others, Jay Howard Geller, *Jews in Post-Holocaust Germany* (New York: Cambridge University Press, 2005).

50. As we have discussed, Heidegger is the central target of Bloch's critique insofar as his philosophy of death undermines the utopian striving to overcome mortality by insisting on human weakness and frailty. Heidegger beckons one to accept death, an acceptance that stands in opposition to the modern drive for freedom from death through technological mastery. As Bloch puts it,

There is a picture by Voltaire of despair—the total despair of a shipwrecked man who is swimming in the waves and struggling and squirming for his life when he receives the message that this ocean in which he finds himself does not have a shore but that death is completely in the now in which the shipwrecked man finds himself. That is why the striving of the swimmer will lead to nothing, for he will never land. It will always remain the same. To be sure, this strongest counterutopia exists, and that must be said to make things more difficult. Otherwise, there would not be that Heideggerian "creature" (*Wesen*) at all, if there were not something here in the reality that is unavoidable and has no history up till now and no change in the real process—thus, if this reality itself did not ward itself so extraordinarily from the test case. (Bloch, "Something's Missing," 9)

51. Bloch, *Principle of Hope*, vol. 3, 1161–1167; 1172–1176.
52. Bloch, "Something's Missing," 9.

CHAPTER 9

DIASPORIC PLACE-MAKING IN BARBARA HONIGMANN

Katja Garloff

It may seem odd to include an essay on Barbara Honigmann in a volume that explores the rebuilding of Jewish life in postwar Germany, as Honigmann appears to have done the opposite when she abandoned the life that her Jewish parents had tried to build after arriving in East Berlin in 1946, following years of exile in London. Her mother, Litzi Friedmann, was a Viennese Communist of Hungarian Jewish origins and her father, Georg Honigmann, was a German Jew who after his return to Germany worked as an editor, journalist, film producer, and cabaret director. While Judaism in a religious or cultural sense seems to have played no role in her parents' home, Honigmann herself began in the 1970s what she described as a "search for a minimum of Jewish identity in my life."[1] She started learning Hebrew, got married in a Jewish ceremony, and in 1984 left the GDR for Strasbourg, a French city close to the German border that is home to a sizable and vibrant Jewish community.[2] It is here that she wrote her first collection of prose texts, *Roman von einem Kinde*, which upon its publication in 1986 became an instant success on the German book market. Honigmann would stage and restage this central fact of her life—that she became a German-language writer at the moment she left Germany to live a more consciously Jewish life—in a series of literary and essayistic texts. One of the main motives of her oeuvre, one may say, is the birth of writing from the spirit of departure.

In this essay I suggest that in all her emphasis on departure and exile, Barbara Honigmann also invites us to rethink concepts such as "return" and "rebuilding." Like much contemporary German-Jewish literature, Honigmann's writing is characterized by a tension between displacement and (re)settlement. Displacement is a central theme in many recent German-Jewish writers, whose experiences of migration and diaspora inform their literary works. At the same time, they emphatically depict scenes of arrival, dwell on locations, and turn spaces into places by investing them with personal meaning and emotional significance. Honigmann's 2015 *Chronik meiner Straße* (Chronicle of my street), which relates how a run-down street in Strasbourg becomes the narrator's permanent home as she retells the stories of the street's residents, is one example of such diasporic place-making. I propose to read this form of place-making together with two other spatial motifs frequently encountered in Honigmann's work: her parents' return to Germany, which she scrutinizes quite critically, and her own visits to Jewish cemeteries, which help her reconnect to the Jewish past and imagine a Jewish future.

Honigmann's work hovers between history, autobiography, and fiction in a way that marks it as autofiction, a term that has been applied to this work by critics and by the author herself. Autofiction is a form of autobiographical writing that emerged toward the end of the twentieth century at a time when postmodern aesthetics had called into question the unity of the self and the stability of linguistic reference. Honigmann used the term in a 2002 lecture, in which she criticized the attempt to reduce her literary work to her biography and emphasized the at least partially fictitious character of all autobiographical writing: "*Autofiction*. Autobiographical writing lies somewhere in the middle between diary and novel. It is fiction not only because every transformation of reality into writing is fiction but also because its project of self-examination, self-discovery, and self-revelation is to at least the same degree always also self-staging and self-fictionalization, a transformation of one's life into a novel, sometimes in fact a self-mythologization. In this sense autobiographical writing can be more novelistic than a novel."[3] The historian Yfaat Weiss has suggested that Honigmann's autofiction allows for the constant variation of a life story that has historical significance; that the genre enables the author to wrest her stories away from the specific historical context and give them a universal meaning.[4] My essay continues this line of thought and proposes that as Honigmann narrates experiences that are at their core historical but not tied to a single meaning, she elaborates new possibilities out of the concepts of displacement, return, and settlement. She offers her own and unique vision of what it might mean to rebuild Jewish life—on French territory, to be sure, but also in German literature and culture.

Returning to Germany

The decision of her parents, who were Communists and refugees from Nazism, to move to East Germany and help build a new socialist state after the Second World War is an important reference point throughout the work of Honigmann. She repeatedly criticizes the blind spots and self-delusions that informed this decision, which ultimately left her parents with an exacerbated sense of displacement. Her own development into a practicing Jew and a German-language author living in France emerges as an alternative to her parents' precarious settlement in East Germany. In pitting her own departure against her parents' return, I argue, Honigmann ends up reworking the very meaning of return.

The dialectic between departure and return already plays out in Honigmann's 1991 *A Love Made Out of Nothing*. The book's narrator, a young Jewish woman working at a theater, leaves the GDR for Paris in the hope of gaining new experiences and perspectives. But she soon finds that by going to Paris she involuntarily repeats the journey of her parents, who during the Third Reich were persecuted both as Jews and as socialists and forced into Parisian exile. The book never fully resolves the tension between these two different conceptions of exile—of exile as a grand awakening to new possibilities and of exile as the result of persecution and expulsion—leaving us with a peculiar sense of circularity and "stuckness." As the narrator states at one point, "Perhaps more than anything else, I've been running away from my parents and yet still go on trotting along behind them."[5] Only at the very end does the narrator stand a certain chance of breaking the cycle of repetitions. After attending her father's funeral in Berlin, she departs a second time for Paris, and while sitting on the train, she closes the window curtains because she cannot endure seeing the scenery "once again."[6] Significantly, the narrator's refusal to reenact her parents' past "once again" coincides with the beginning of her own writing. Among the belongings of her deceased father she had found a notebook he had kept after the end of the war, and now, while leaving Germany for good, she decides to fill the remaining empty pages with her own entries.

Throughout the book, the narrator suggests that her parents' return to Germany did not lead to a more settled life but rather created a sense of permanent displacement. Thus they moved in social circles composed of former emigrants and kept their distance from most Germans, yet they did not identify with Jews and Judaism in any positive way. At one point she speculates that the parents, who escaped Nazi persecution during the war yet afterward were haunted by images of the Holocaust, suffered from survivor's guilt and desperately sought to distance themselves from the past:

> That must have been a heavy burden—so heavy that they always acted as if they hadn't had anything to do with all that. . . . And in the end, they'd come to Berlin to build a new Germany, one which was to be entirely different from the old one, and, for that reason, it would be better not to talk about the Jews at all anymore [deshalb wollte man von den Juden besser gar nicht mehr sprechen]. But somehow things didn't work out and the day came when they even had to justify their choice of the country where they'd spent their exile—why was it a Western country and not the Soviet Union?[7]

The use of the indefinite personal pronoun *man* (you) in this passage creates some ambiguity. To whom does *man* refer—that is, who no longer wants to talk about the Jews? While the narrator appears to refer to her parents' desire for a radically new beginning, *man* also alludes to the GDR at large, which glorified political resistance to Nazism and eschewed a commemoration of the Jewish victims of the Holocaust.[8] The mention of subsequent discrimination against remigrants from Western countries vaguely evokes the ideological opposition between political and "racial" refugees. Beyond survivor's guilt and public silencing, there are additional reasons for the parents' persistent sense of displacement. The mother never felt at home in Berlin because she was not from Germany to begin with (in the novel she is from Bulgaria; in reality, Honigmann's mother was born in Vienna to Hungarian Jewish parents). The father's rather abrupt adoption of a Communist worldview and identity intensified his sense of displacement and disorientation, of which his multiple failed marriages seem to be a corollary. As he himself states, "Actually I don't know where I'm from and don't even know where I belong now."[9] As we have seen, the narrator both reenacts this model and distances herself from it. Ultimately, *A Love Made Out of Nothing* shows how the narrator becomes a writer while thinking through her parents' fraught attempt at resettlement.

A Love Made Out of Nothing is a prime example of autofiction. The book carries no subtitle or genre designation, yet its paratexts help establish what Philippe Lejeune has called the "autobiographical pact"—that is, they set up readers' expectations that the events relayed in the text reflect the author's experience.[10] The German jacket copy announces the book's autobiographical character—"Barbara Honigmann reports on her childhood in East Berlin"[11]—and provides details of the author's background that correspond to the narrator's life as depicted in the literary text. A closer reading, however, reveals some differences between the lives of author and narrator, suggesting the presence of other fictitious elements in the text. For example, in *A Love Made Out of Nothing* the narrator's mother is from Bulgaria rather than Hungary; the narrator moves to Paris rather than Strasbourg; the narrator is single and childless rather than a married mother of two. The book also lacks a pivotal feature of autobiography—namely, the homonymy of author, narrator, and protagonist (who in *A Love Made Out of Nothing* remains unnamed), which creates a further ambiguity about the autobiographical nature of the work. This ambiguity, I argue, sets into motion an experiment with various forms of settlement and displacement. In subsequent essayistic and autobiographical works, Honigmann elaborates the critique of Jewish emigrants returning to East Germany first advanced in *A Love Made Out of Nothing*.

Throughout her work, Honigmann would add new facets to the nonarrival of her parents. "Selbstporträt als Jüdin," for example, suggests the existence of a vibrant network of former emigrants in the GDR that constitutes the family's primary social circle. Yet this does not shield them from feelings of coldness and emptiness that result, the narrator suspects, from a pervasive sense of nonbelonging: "Perhaps this coolness and emptiness arose not only because nothing came of the socialism that my parents wanted to build, but also because they were caught in the middle: they no longer belonged to the Jews and had not become German."[12] The life trajectory of the narrator—who resettles in France, embraces her Jewishness, and intermittently returns to Germany through her writing—offers an alternative model of return: "As a Jew I left Germany, but in my work, in my very strong attachment to the German language, I return again and again."[13]

One effect of Honigmann's juxtapositions of her parents' return to Germany and her own departure to France is that the very concept of "return" undergoes a revision and redefinition. According to Honigmann, we do not necessarily return to a place in which we have lived before but to a place that allows us to resume, retrieve, or reimagine a strand of past experience. In another piece from *Damals, dann und danach*, entitled "Hinter der Grande School," Honigmann imagines her emigration to Strasbourg as a form of return. To be sure, her remarks are a bit tongue-in-cheek—she admits that she has construed a legend—yet at least partially based in reality because she can trace her family genealogy back to the Rhine Valley: "For my new Strasbourg life I had concocted a legend according to which I had not come to, but had rather returned to this place, since one of my grandmothers had been born a Weil and everyone knows that all the Weils, however spelled, come from the Rhine valley, and I therefore come from there through this line of my family."[14]

This new concept of return may also explain the curious subtitle of another work by Honigmann, *Das überirdische Licht: Rückkehr nach New York*, which she wrote while on a writing fellowship in New York City. Why did she conceive of her stay as a form of return (*Rückkehr*)? To be sure, there are several possible reasons: she has visited the city before; she meets there an old friend from Berlin who moved to New York decades ago as well as a distant relative she never knew in person; she frequently encounters traces of German-Jewish immigration of the past. Furthermore, the idea that America is not only a place of arrival but also one of return echoes a statement made earlier in *A Love Made Out of Nothing*: "Ellis Island is my home."[15] Still, the position of the word *return* in the subtitle of *Das überirdische Licht* raises a broader question, What does one need to find in a place—or what does one need to make of a place—so that one's arrival there can be considered a form of return? Tellingly, Honigmann revisits her father's profoundly unsettled life once more in *Das überirdische Licht*, inspired by a dream that she had about him. She now locates the reasons for the father's unsettlement in the early losses he incurred in childhood, including the death of his mother and brother, to explain why his most natural environment is the hotel room. She also remembers a scene in which the father, after learning that his daughter was about to emigrate to France, enjoined her to go to America: "You have to go to America. There you will find your place . . . Go far away. As far as possible! Go to America. Wrest yourself free!"[16] Read in conjunction with the book's subtitle, this scene implies that in going to New York City, Honigmann belatedly responds to her father's injunction and finds her own place—or more precisely, that she *returns* to a place that has always already been her own.

Visiting Jewish Cemeteries

In several of Honigmann's works, a defunct Jewish cemetery serves to illustrate the dislocation and discontinuity of Jewish life. *A Love Made Out of Nothing* opens with just such an image. The narrator's father, who never identified with Jews and Judaism, is buried in Weimar in a tiny Jewish cemetery that has been out of use for decades. (This is another instance in which Honigmann takes poetic license with reality; the real Georg Honigmann was buried in the Weißensee cemetery in Berlin, a pivotal place for Honigmann that I will discuss below.) The father's funeral is depicted as a strange and jarring ceremony, which highlights the inner heterogeneity of Jewish culture and religion and undermines the sense that a religious ritual might restore a sense of home, tradition, or identity. Among other things, the Saloniki-born cantor, who had to be brought in from another city, continues to mispronounce the father's German name with his Sephardic accent, the narrator notices with dismay. When the narrator enters her father's room after the funeral in search for a memento, she finds that his clothes are lying around "forlornly" (*verloren*)—a word that connotes both loss and dispersion, which helps her realize "that the memories had fallen out of those objects."[17] In other words, even in his death the narrator's father cannot find a place. Nor do cemeteries establish a connection to the past at any other point in the story. When the narrator makes a stopover en route to France in Hesse to see the places in which her father's German-Jewish ancestors lived, she searches for the gravestones of her relatives in the local Jewish cemeteries—in vain, it turns out, not because the gravestones are gone but because there are too many similar names and the narrator lacks the knowledge of her ancestors' lives and deaths that would enable her to identify them.[18]

At the same time, the visits to Jewish cemeteries provide an impetus for the narrator to reconnect to the German-Jewish past and to restore a sense of place and continuity. A powerful imperative seems to issue from these cemeteries—an imperative to recover, to retrieve, to retell. In her first prose collection, *Roman von einem Kinde*, Honigmann recounts how Gershom Scholem, the famous historian of Jewish mysticism, came to East Berlin and how she accompanied him to his family grave on the Jewish cemetery Weißensee. While standing at the grave, Scholem began to tell stories about his parents and his brothers; summing up the life of each of them and ending on a moment of silence and a short prayer.

Scholem's visit to Berlin is a form of return ("He had again retraced the journey of his life, once again Berlin–Jerusalem, in the reverse direction"[19]) that stands in clear contrast to the return of Honigmann's parents. It is a temporary return that occasions acts of commemoration and reaffirms his commitment to Judaism. When he dies shortly later, an epitaph is added to the family grave, so he ends up having two graves: one in Jerusalem and one in Berlin. Scholem's visit leaves a deep impression on the narrator both because his writings on Jewish history and religion come alive for her and, we can infer, because his double grave exemplifies the duality she would ultimately choose for herself. *Roman von einem Kinde* further suggests that the encounter with Scholem marks a turning point in the narrator's development; that the older scholar's advice to immigrate to a country in which the teaching of the Torah is still alive motivates her own move to France, which is recounted in the last story of the collection.

The Jewish cemetery is the site where the differences between the first two generations of post-Holocaust German Jews crystallize: between the survivors who want to cut all ties with the past and their children who wish to reconnect to it. This becomes especially clear in a story entitled "Gräber in London," which Honigmann included in her prose collection *Damals, dann und danach*. Nestled in this story about the narrator's visit to her grandparents' graves in London are memories of her earlier excursions to the Weißensee cemetery in East Berlin. At the time, the narrator had a circle of friends who, though mostly of Jewish descent, were ignorant about Judaism before they collectively began to rediscover and reimagine the German-Jewish past. It is during her lonely walks through the vast, overgrown, labyrinthine Weißensee cemetery that the narrator first gets an inkling of the existence of an extensive network of Jewish families that also encompasses herself. This recognition occurs not only because the names on the gravestones resemble her parents' names but also because she encounters something unfamiliar, even illegible—namely, Hebrew characters that she cannot decipher: "I stared at the Hebrew letters, which I could not read, as if they contained, perhaps, a secret and very important message for me, a message that would reveal the riddle of my origin and break the silence of my parents."[20] The text implies that the riddle posed by the Hebrew characters propels the narrator toward the rediscovery of Judaism, or what she calls "the recapture of our Judaism out of nothingness."[21] She begins to attend a synagogue, marries in a Jewish ceremony, and reads the Bible in Hebrew.

As in many of Honigmann's writings, the Jewish cemeteries depicted in this piece are bleak, forsaken places. If the narrator found neglect and overgrowth in Weißensee, she later encounters absence and emptiness in the Jewish cemetery in London. And yet, these cemeteries harbor a message, one that is all the more imperative because of its obscurity. "Gräber in London" begins with a 1942 letter in which the narrator's grandmother enjoins her daughter (the narrator's mother) to take care of the grave of her father (the narrator's grandfather). This letter is the only thing the narrator's mother, who throughout her life showed a marked disinterest in genealogical continuity, bequeathed to her daughter.[22] Over the course of the text, it becomes clear that the narrator's mother had completely ignored the grandmother's request: she had buried her parents in London "like dogs, without tombstone and without name."[23] Why then did she pass the written request, this proof of her own failure, on to her daughter? Was the bequeathal an admission of guilt, a plea to the daughter to fulfill the request in her place? The narrator's visit to London can indeed be read as a response to her grandmother's request, an attempt to take care of the grave not by saying the *kaddish* or erecting a gravestone but by telling the story of the absent gravestone and the unfulfilled request. That storytelling has this power becomes clear in the passages that reflect on the effect of the narrator's writing. Thus she describes how the book she wrote about her father's life (*A Love Made Out of Nothing*, though the book's title is not mentioned in the passage) effectively restored a sense of continuity and of belonging as lost relatives from all over the world have begun to contact her: "Suddenly past generations had resurrected themselves after the death of my father, generations that told a coherent story and that mitigated the state of total homelessness my father had bequeathed to me."[24]

Diasporic Place-Making in *Chronik meiner Straße*

As I have shown, Barbara Honigmann describes her parent generation's return to East Germany as fraught with problems and her own visits to Jewish cemeteries as excursions that, while ultimately motivating her to reconnect to Judaism, initially reinforce a sense of loss and exile. Her own 1984 move to Strasbourg offers an alternative to the sense of displacement and rootlessness that characterize her parents' lives. Honigmann revisits her settlement in France in one of her recent works, *Chronik meiner Straße* (2015). The subject of the book is the Rue Edel, a run-down street in Strasbourg onto which new immigrants often first move but in which they seldom reside for long. While the Rue Edel is for most immigrants a mere stopover on the route to better neighborhoods, the narrator still lives there thirty years after her arrival. In what follows, I will argue that *Chronik meiner Straße* transforms a *space* of transition into a *place* of dwelling. I take my inspiration from Barbara Mann's *Place and Space in Jewish Studies*, which among other things draws attention to the duality of diasporic existence: if uprootedness is the condition of diaspora, actual life in a diaspora enables people to put down new roots and make new homes, all the while sustaining imaginative relations with other places. Literature can be part and parcel of this diasporic place-making. For example, travel narratives that closely attend to the physical details of the sites visited and remembered are a way of inhabiting a place imaginatively.[25] Analogously, I will argue that Honigmann's narration of the Rue Edel and the lives of its residents is a form of literary place-making.

In *Chronik meiner Straße*, Honigmann seizes upon an existing chronotope—that is, a literary time-space configuration that organizes the narrative of a particular motif or genre. The chronotope of the street, which is closely related to those of the path and the road, has been a structuring principle of the Western novel since antiquity.[26] Its three most prominent features can still be found in *Chronik meiner Straße*:

1. The street signifies both physical movement and individual development. In fact, the one is often mapped on the other as the literary image of the street overlaps with the metaphor of the *Lebensweg* (journey through life). In *Chronik meiner Straße*, this meaning resonates in the social mobility associated with the Rue Edel, whose immigrant residents are in the process of assimilating to French culture and moving to fancier neighborhoods. Although never described in detail, these "better" neighborhoods are the vanishing point of the street, the horizon to which the immigrants are moving.
2. The street is a site of chance encounters, an opportunity to meet and interact with a wide variety of people. In the Rue Edel, immigrants and French citizens from different ethnic, religious, and cultural backgrounds find themselves as next-door neighbors. There is no plan behind these living arrangements, they just continue to evolve and shape the narrator's experience and narration.
3. Finally, even though it signifies movement and mobility, the street always leads through a homeland, describing a path that is already carved out and therefore familiar. As I will argue, this sense of familiarity is an effect rather than a precondition of *Chronik meiner Straße*, which claims the Rue Edel as the narrator's own—not necessarily as her homeland in an emphatic sense, but as a place of permanent residence and reassuring familiarity.

Any given street can be considered a place in the sense of Yi-Fu Tuan's famous distinction between place and space, on which Barbara Mann draws: "If we think of space as that which allows movement, place is a pause."[27] A street is a segment of space that has been given a proper name and visible contours, that has been carved out of the infinite space of possibilities into something definite. Over the course of *Chronik meiner Straße*, the Rue Edel is gradually endowed with meaning and value in a way that makes it more fully a place in Mann's sense. The first act of place-making is the choice of the possessive adjective *meine* (my) in the title of the book (and the plural form, *unsere*, in the first chapter), which, in combination with a blurb on the jacket copy that encourages us to read the text as autobiographical, associates the street with Honigmann and establishes a relationship of belonging. The first chapter expands this gesture of appropriation into scenes of inhabitation. The narrator begins by emphasizing the street's state of neglect, its emptiness and desolation. Referring to the gardens, beautiful parks, and notable buildings that surround houses in fancier neighborhoods, she states laconically, "Our street has nothing of all that."[28] Instead the street features ugly houses, which were often built rather quickly to fill in construction gaps. At this point the narrator mentions how a friend of hers as a child used to play ball in just such a construction gap in the Rue Edel. The image of a child's play filling an empty space with activity is, I would argue, an allegory of the act of narration: the narrator's depiction of the street and the lives of its residents turns a space into a place by furnishing it with particulars and endowing it with significance.

The narrator initially bestows on the street a sense of particularity by providing specific geographical and historical information. Not coincidentally, the first of these facts is one that would matter to her personally—namely, the location of the Rue Edel on the Eastern edge of Strasbourg and in close proximity to Germany. The nicknames that the narrator's family has given to different elements of the street, such as a false driveway and a restaurant called "Tomate," and that in some cases draw on their memory of buildings in East Germany,[29] further shows how they inhabit the Rue Edel by attaching a personal meaning to it. If the first chapter positions the narrator at the center of the street, subsequent chapters extrapolate her bodily location, posture, and perspective onto the surrounding space. The chapters often begin with an explicit description of the narrator's location—at her desk, in the brasserie next door, on the balcony—before shifting to the things and people she sees from, or encounters in, that location, such as an errant tree, a Kurdish man from Turkey, or a rabbi from Kovno (Kaunas). At other times, the narrator's location is implied in deictic expressions such as "next door" and "on our floor,"[30] by which she introduces her stories of others. It is her own presence and orientation in the street that determines what comes into view and enters the narrative.

The text further creates a sense of particularity by oscillating between plural and singular, between groups and individuals. The narrator initially focuses on the different *Völker* that inhabit the Rue Edel—that is, she subsumes individuals in the ethnic groups to which they belong: "Many peoples [Völker] are living in our street, and one hears them speaking in many languages."[31] Whether she registers the chaos of languages on the street—"In our street there is calling, talking, speaking, yelling and screaming in countless foreign languages"[32]—or the separateness of different ethnic groups who actively avoid each other, she creates an impression of deindividualized multitudes. However, the focus on ethnic groups (the depiction of which often borders on stereotypes) gradually gives way to the stories of individual people and families. By resting her gaze on a specific site and her memory on a specific ritual, the narrator enables the individual to emerge from the group and a particular life story from the street's general history. Witness the story of the Kurdish man in whose store people from different ethnic backgrounds meet and interact. The narrator highlights the man's exceptional status—he is unassimilated, speaks poor French, and disregards the Sunday rest order—and it is perhaps for this reason that he serves as a cultural mediator and the first resting place of the narrator's gaze. In the narrator, the image of this man triggers memories of two Kurdish brothers who had previously operated the store and offered her special deals, and it finally leads to reflections on the regular rhythm in which the store changes owners and on the chain of Kurdish relatives in which the current owner is only one link. The effect of this oscillation between the general and the particular is that the street appears inhabited by particular people, its chronicle filled with life stories.

The place-making in *Chronik meiner Straße* culminates in an account of how the narrator's husband Peter erects a sukkah in their courtyard in order to celebrate the Jewish holiday of Sukkot. The erection of the sukkah is a quintessential example of diasporic place-making. The temporary hut in which Jews are traditionally required to eat and sleep during the seven or eight days of Sukkot is by definition a transient, porous, open place—or more precisely, it superimposes in one specific site several real and imagined places, including the land of Israel and the presence of God. If celebrated in the Diaspora, the sukkah may engage in various ways with the non-Jewish environment. It may incorporate elements from local architecture and its three-walled structure may offer a view into the non-Jewish surroundings.[33] The celebration of Sukkot marks a place as temporarily Jewish while exposing its participants to the gaze, or sometimes even to the attacks, of their non-Jewish neighbors—as the narrator of *Chronik meiner Straße* remembers from her first Sukkot in Strasbourg, when rotten tomatoes were thrown through the permeable roof of the sukkah. Over the course of the text, the sukkah becomes a signifier of openness as such. The narrator contemplates how its structure is meant to remind the Jews of "the fragility and uncertainty of their existence, for which they have to compensate by tenacity and adaptability, just as back then, after the Exodus from Egypt, when they lived in huts in the desert, this empty and undefined place where the newly acquired freedom meant mostly that nobody knew where to go, what to do, and what would happen next."[34]

By the end of *Chronik meiner Straße*, the narrator's own environment is no longer as "empty and undefined" as the desert into which the Israelites escaped during Exodus. The erection of the sukkah and other acts of place-making recounted throughout the text have endowed the Rue Edel with personal meaning and communal significance and have thereby transformed it into a viable place of residence. The Rue Edel, the "street of arrival and beginning and of getting stuck,"[35] does not necessarily become a final destination or a permanent home. Rather, it is a place in which the narrator can dwell in a state of preliminary permanence, fully aware of the other places from which people may hail and to which they may move.

Literary critic Andreas Kilcher has distinguished between two forms of exterritoriality in contemporary German-Jewish literature: self-defined Jewish authors who reside in Germany or Austria (such as Maxim Biller, Esther Dischereit, Doron Rabinovici, and Robert Schindel) tend to deconstruct the German language from within and emphasize the difference between their own works and those of non-Jewish German and Austrian writers. In contrast, authors who have left Germany and write in German from a deliberate geographical distance (such as Chaim Noll and Barbara Honigmann) often situate their writing within German cultural traditions, especially of the *Goethezeit* (Age of Goethe), and choose a classical writing style marked by linearity and readability.[36] In this chapter, I have argued that Honigmann claims not only past traditions but also present-day places. In order to understand the dialectic between displacement and settlement in contemporary German-Jewish writers, I suggest we need to pay attention to the literary places they claim or create while relaying their (often autobiographical) stories of exile and migration. In addition to the Rue Edel depicted in Honigmann's *Chronik meiner Straße*, such places include the ancient *mikveh*, or ritual bath, on which Benjamin Stein's 2010 *Die Leinwand* ends as well as the Viennese *Naschmarkt* on which Doron Rabinovici's *Ohnehin* is partly set. Another case in point would be Vladimir Vertlib's 1999 *Zwischenstationen*, which recounts his family's odyssey from Russia to Austria via several transit stations. What the family fails to achieve—the firm establishment in a place—the novel itself accomplishes through its careful accumulation of descriptive and narrative detail. Like Barbara Honigmann, these contemporary German-Jewish authors engage in a literary place-making that allows displaced subjects to put down new roots in the Diaspora.

NOTES

1. Barbara Honigmann, "Selbstporträt als Jüdin," in *Damals, dann und danach* (Munich: Carl Hanser, 1999), 11–18, here 15.

2. On the heterogeneous character of Strasbourg's Jewish community and Honigmann's conception of diasporic writing, see also Christina Günther, "Exile and the Construction of Identity in Barbara Honigmann's Trilogy of the Diaspora," *Comparative Literature Studies* 40, no. 2 (2003): 215–231.

3. "*Autofiktion.* Das autobiographische Schreiben liegt irgendwo in der Mitte zwischen Tagebuch und Roman, und es ist nicht nur deshalb Fiktion, weil alle Verwandlung von Wirklichkeit in Schreiben Fiktion ist, sondern auch, weil sein Projekt der Selbsterforschung, Selbstentdeckung und Selbstoffenbarung mindestens in dem gleichen Maß immer auch Selbstinszenierung, Selbstfiktionalisierung, Verwandlung des Lebens in einen Roman, manchmal sogar Selbstmythologisierung ist. In diesem Sinn kann autobiographisches Schreiben romanhafter sein als ein Roman." Barbara Honigmann, "'Wenn mir die Leute vorwerfen, daß ich zuviel von mir spreche, so werfe ich ihnen vor, daß sie überhaupt nicht über sich selbst nachdenken': Zürcher Poetikvorlesung (I): Über autobiographisches Schreiben," in *Das Gesicht wiederfinden: Über Schreiben, Schriftsteller und Judentum* (Munich: Hanser,

2006), 31–60, here 39 (emphasis by Honigmann). Unless otherwise noted, all translations are mine.

4. "Die leicht variierenden Wiederholungen setzen die einmalige persönliche in der kollektiv erscheinenden Geschichte frei und verleihen ihnen einen prinzipiellen, universalen Status." Yfaat Weiss, "Im Schreiben das Leben verändern—Barbara Honigmann als Chronistin des jüdischen Lebens in Deutschland," in *Kurz hinter der Wahrheit und dicht neben der Lüge: Zum Werk Barbara Honigmanns*, ed. Amir Eshel and Yfaat Weiss (Munich: Fink, 2013), 17–28, here 20. Weiss draws special attention to Honigmann's GDR background and the prejudices and anti-Semitism encountered by former Jewish refugees, especially those who had spent their exile in Western Europe: "Durch die Augen der Kinder dokumentiert Barbara Honigmann die Geschicke der wenigen Juden, die es vorzogen, aus ihren Exilorten nach Ostdeutschland zurückzukehren, und dort trotz der politischen Repressionen zu bleiben, die gegen sie als Individuen und als Gruppe Anfang der fünfziger Jahre ausgeübt wurden" (Weiss, "*Im Schreiben das Leben verändern*," 21).

5. Barbara Honigmann, *A Love Made Out of Nothing* and *Zohara's Journey*, trans. John Barrett (Jaffrey, N.H.: Godine, 2003), 22. "Mehr als von allem anderen bin ich vielleicht von meinen Eltern weggelaufen und lief ihnen doch hinterher." Barbara Honigmann, *Eine Liebe aus nichts* (Reinbek: Rowohlt, 1993), 31.

6. "noch einmal," Honigmann, *A Love Made Out of Nothing*, 76; *Eine Liebe aus nichts*, 106.

7. Honigmann, *A Love Made Out of Nothing*, 24; "das muß eine schwere Last gewesen sein, so schwer, daß sie immer so taten, als hätten sie damit gar nichts zu tun gehabt. . . . Und schließlich waren sie nach Berlin gekommen, um ein neues Deutschland aufzubauen, es sollte ja ganz anders werden als das alte, deshalb wollte man von den Juden besser gar nicht mehr sprechen. Aber irgendwie war alles nicht geglückt, und eines Tages mussten sie sich sogar für das Land ihres Exils rechtfertigen, warum es ein westliches Land war und nicht die Sowjetunion." Honigmann, *Eine Liebe aus nichts*, 34.

8. See Jeffrey Herf, *Divided Memory: The Nazi Past in the Two Germanys* (Cambridge, Mass.: Harvard University Press, 1997).

9. Honigmann, *A Love Made Out of Nothing*, 25; "eigentlich weiß ich nicht, wo ich herstamme, weiß auch nicht, wo ich jetzt hingehöre," Honigmann, *Eine Liebe aus nichts*, 35.

10. See Philippe Lejeune, *On Autobiography*, trans. Katherine Leary (Minneapolis: University of Minnesota Press, 1989), esp. 3–31.

11. "Barbara Honigmann *berichtet* von *ihrer* Kindheit in Ost-Berlin" (my emphasis).

12. "Vielleicht kam diese Kühle und Leere nicht nur davon, daß aus dem Sozialismus, den meine Eltern aufbauen wollten, nichts wurde, sondern auch davon, daß sie vollkommen zwischen den Stühlen saßen, nicht mehr zu den Juden gehörten und keine Deutschen geworden waren." Honigmann, "Selbstporträt als Jüdin," 14.

13. "Als Jude bin ich aus Deutschland weggegangen, aber in meiner Arbeit, in meiner sehr starken Bindung an die deutsche Sprache, kehre ich immer wieder zurück." Honigmann, "Selbstporträt als Jüdin," 18.

14. "Für mein neues Straßburger Leben hatte ich mir eine Legende zurechtgelegt, nach der ich nämlich gar nicht her-, sondern vielmehr hierher zurückgekommen bin, da eine meiner Großmütter eine geborene Weil war, und ja jeder weiß, daß alle Weils in allen Schreibweisen aus dem Rheintal kommen, und ich also in dieser Linie meiner Familie von dort stamme." Honigmann, "Selbstporträt als Jüdin," 59.

15. Honigmann, *A Love Made Out of Nothing*, 40; "Ellis Island ist meine Heimat," Honigmann, *Eine Liebe aus nichts*, 57. As Emily Jeremiah observes, the potential "pathos of this statement" is cut short right away, as a friend "informs her that it no longer exists." Emily Jeremiah, *Nomadic Ethics in Contemporary Women's Writing in German: Strange Subjects* (Rochester, N.Y.: Camden, 2012), 178.

16. "Nach Amerika mußt du gehen. Dort wirst du deinen Platz finden . . . Geh weit weg. So weit wie möglich! Geh nach Amerika. Reiß dich los!" Barbara Honigmann, *Das überirdische Licht: Rückkehr nach New York* (Munich: Hanser, 2008), 64.

17. Honigmann, *A Love Made Out of Nothing*, 6f.; "daß die Erinnerung aus den Dingen herausgefallen war," Honigmann, *Eine Liebe aus nichts*, 9.

18. See Honigmann, *A Love Made Out of Nothing*, 49; Honigmann, *Eine Liebe aus nichts*, 68.

19. "Er hatte die Reise seines Lebens noch einmal zurückgelegt, noch einmal Berlin–Jerusalem retour," Barbara Honigmann, *Roman von einem Kinde: Sechs Erzählungen* (Frankfurt am Main: Luchterhand, 1989 [1986]), 96.

20. "Auf die hebräischen Buchstaben, die ich nicht lesen konnte, starrte ich, als ob sie vielleicht eine geheime, sehr wichtige Botschaft für mich enthielten, durch die sich das Rätsel meiner Herkunft offenbaren würde und das Schweigen meiner Eltern gebrochen werden könnte." Honigmann, "Gräber in London," in *Damals, dann und danach*, 19–37, here 28.

21. "die Wiedereroberung unseres Judentums aus dem nichts," Honigmann, "Gräber in London," 29.

22. The mother's profound disinterest in genealogical continuity also transpires in her indifference to the loss of a necklace that was the only memento from her female ancestors (26) and in her general conviction that the past has no bearing on the present: "Meine Eltern aber sagen: die Geschlechter sind tot, die Vergangenheit ist vorbei und die Gräber sind leere Orte." Honigmann, "Gräber in London," 31.

23. "wie Hunde, ohne Grabstein und ohne Namen," Honigmann, *Damals, dann und danach*, 37.

24. "Plötzlich waren nach dem Tod meines Vaters vergangene Generationen wieder auferstanden, die eine zusammenhängende Geschichte erzählten und den Zustand der völligen Unbehaustheit, den mein Vater mir hinterlassen hat, milderten." Honigmann, "Gräber in London," 34. In another story in *Damals, dann und danach*, titled "Der Untergang von Wien," the Jewish cemetery similarly provides an opportunity to reconnect with the past, an opportunity that is realized not in funeral rituals but in the narrator's own spatial movement and storytelling. The text opens with a description of the Viennese Jewish cemetery in which mother was buried. Once again we learn that the mother is uninterested in remembering the past; for example, she refuses to revisit the Viennese places that mattered to her as a child. It is her daughter who attempts to get a sense of the Viennese past by visiting the cemetery and other significant places: "nach ihrem Tod erst habe ich das in ihren Augen Ungerhörige getan und bin selbst an die alten Orte gegangen, die sie, wie ich mir einbildete, vor mir verheimlichte" (101).

25. See Barbara E. Mann, *Space and Place in Jewish Studies* (New Brunswick, N.J.: Rutgers University Press, 2012), 98–115.

26. See Mikhail M. Bakhtin, "Forms of Time and Chronotope in the Novel," in *The Dialogic Imagination: Four Essays*, trans. Caryl Emerson and Michael Holquist (Austin: University of Texas Press, 1994 [1981]), 84–258, esp. 243–245.

27. Cited in Mann, *Space and Place*, 5. The original quote is in Yi-Fu Tuan, *Space and Place: The Perspective of Experience* (Minneapolis: University of Minnesota Press, 2014 [1977]), 6.

28. "Von alldem hat unsere Straße gar nichts." Barbara Honigmann, *Chronik meiner Straße* (Munich: Hanser, 2015), 5.

29. See, for example, Honigmann, *Chronik meiner Straße*, 9: "Wiwifak."

30. "im Nebenhaus," "auf unserer Etage," Honigmann, *Chronik meiner Straße*, 51, 58.

31. "Viele Völker wohnen in unserer Straße, und man hört sie in vielerlei Sprachen sprechen." Honigmann, *Chronik meiner Straße*, 9.

32. "Es ruft, redet, spricht, brüllt und schreit in unserer Straße in unzähligen fremden Sprachen," Honigmann, *Chronik meiner Straße*, 13.

33. See Miriam Lipis, "A Hybrid Place of Belonging: Constructing and Siting the Sukkah," *Jewish Topographies: Visions of Space, Traditions of Place*, ed. Julia Brauch, Anna Lipphardt, and Alexandra Nocke (Burlington, Vt.: Ashgate, 2008), 27–41. See also Sonja Dickow, "Unbehaustes Wohnen: Zum Chronotopos der Laubhütte in Michal Govrins *Hevzekim* (2002) und Barbara Honigmanns *Chronik meiner Straße* (2015)," in *Figurations of Mobile Identities in Contemporary European Jewish Literature: Yearbook for European Jewish Literature Studies* 5 (2018): 156–171.

34. "die Zerbrechlichkeit und Unsicherheit ihrer Existenz, die sie durch Zähigkeit und Anpassungsfähigkeit kompensieren müssen, wie damals, nach dem Auszug aus Ägypten, als sie in Hütten in der Wüste wohnten, diesem leeren, unbestimmten Ort, wo die neuerworbene Freiheit hauptsächlich darin bestand, daß keiner wußte, wohin jetzt, was tun und wie es weitergehen wird," Honigmann, *Chronik meiner Straße*, 136.

35. "Straße des Ankommens und Anfangens und des Hängenbleibens," Honigmann, *Chronik meiner Straße*, 13.

36. See Andreas B. Kilcher, "Exterritorialitäten: Zur kulturellen Selbstreflexion der aktuellen deutsch-jüdischen Literatur," in *Deutsch-jüdische Literatur der neunziger Jahre: Die Generation nach der Shoah*, ed. Sander L. Gilman and Hartmut Steinecke (Berlin: Frankfurt am Main, 2002), 131–146.

CHAPTER 10

TUR TUR'S LANTERN ON A TINY ISLAND

NEW HISTORIOGRAPHICAL PERSPECTIVES ON EAST GERMAN JEWISH HISTORY

Constantin Goschler

In 1960, German author Michael Ende published his book *Jim Button and Luke the Engine Driver* (*Jim Knopf und Lukas der Lokomotivführer*). The central setting of the book is Lummerland, a tiny island in the ocean, about twice the size of an apartment. Since there is not enough space on the island for a lighthouse, the two main protagonists, Jim Button and Luke, hire the illusionary giant Tur Tur, who has a unique feature: seen from a short distance, he appears normally sized, but his appearance increases from the farther away one looks at him. Standing on the island with a lantern, Tur Tur can be seen from far away, while he does not take up much space on the island itself.

Michael Ende not only wrote a wonderful children's book but also delivered a great metaphor for the role of Jews in contemporary historical research on the German Democratic Republic (GDR). The GDR rapidly dwindled from its role as allegedly the seventh-largest economy in the world to a "footnote of history," as writer Stefan Heym had already warned during a protest rally in East Berlin in 1989. Later, German historian Hans-Ulrich Wehler also labeled the GDR a footnote of history and marginalized the East German state as a "Soviet satrapy," which for him did not warrant historical inquiry.[1] In 2003, his colleague Jürgen Kocka contended that due to a temporary research boom since 1990, the history of the GDR finally had been exhaustively researched and, moreover, had suffered from notorious self-isolation.[2] And in fact, it seems that historical research on the GDR today is mostly fueled by programs with vast financial resources from the German federal budget, which sponsors literally hundreds of scholarships for PhD students working in this field. By doing so, conservative politicians aim at strengthening in the East German population a negative remembrance of the socialist dictatorship.

In the same year when Jürgen Kocka stated that the history of the GDR might not be the next big thing in historiography, Peter Maser made a similar statement with respect to the history of Jews in the GDR: "In the meantime, the investigation of the Jews in the GDR, at least concerning the facts, can be considered as mostly completed, but that does not mean of course, that there has already been reached a consensus with respect to all assessments."[3] And who might wonder about that, given the tiny number of Jews in the GDR, at least since the Jewish exodus from East Germany to the West following the wave of anti-Semitism in the Eastern bloc in 1952? In 1985, the late days of the GDR, there were no more than four hundred and fifty active members of the Jewish communities in that country, with two hundred and forty of them in East Berlin alone. Additionally, there existed seven thousand so-called victims of fascism, who had suffered anti-Jewish persecution and thus at least were considered as connected to Jewishness from the outside in one way or other, though we cannot automatically say how they regarded themselves. In any event, while the number of Jewish community members in the GDR did not match those in the Federal Republic of Germany (i.e., West Germany) by far, the role of persons with a Jewish background in the political and cultural elite was very significant in East Germany.[4]

Apparently, the cycles of interest in the history of the GDR in general and in the history of Jews in the East German state follow a different logic. While interest in the former has very much declined and nowadays is mostly kept alive by politically inspired research funding, interest in the latter has remained sturdy and even contributed to a substantial widening of historiographic perspectives. As in Michael Ende's book, where the illusionary giant Tur Tur, with his lantern in his hand, allows the tiny island of Lummerland to be seen from a great distance, just a few Jews in this country make for a much higher visibility of the GDR in historiography. The following essay will try to describe some major tendencies of research on the history of Jews in the GDR—or rather, of Jewish history in East Germany. As a first step, it will briefly look at publications in the first decade after German unification, which took place in 1990. As a second step, which will form the main part of the article, it will assess newer research produced since 2000. As a third step, some concluding remarks on potential future fields of inquiry with respect to Jewish history in the GDR will be presented.

The GDR and the Jews: The First Wave of Research after 1990

In the first years after German reunification, when the Jews in the GDR were discovered to be an important object of research, the Cold War still reverberated. The

GDR always had claimed that it was the "better Germany" in the sense that, due to its antifascist self-understanding, it had broken more profoundly with the Nazi past than its Western counterpart. Therefore, the Jewish population in Germany has always been considered a litmus test for the political claim regarding which part of Germany had done better in breaking with its Nazi past. The main impetus for historical inquiry into Jews in East Germany after 1990 was to deal with these Cold War assumptions—not least since, even after 1990, sympathies with the older notion of the GDR as the "better Germany" still existed in some leftist intellectual milieus outside of Germany. The order of the battle followed a simple pattern. On the one hand, some authors looked at Jews in the GDR to prove that antifascism in East Germany had been a good thing—in theory, if not in practice.[5] On the other hand, several authors decried antifascism as a big swindle from the very beginning, and the history of Jews in the GDR was considered as major proof for that political assertion.[6] Consequently, early postreunification research on Jews in the GDR mostly shared a focus on the triangle between Jewish communities, the East German state, and Israel.[7] In essence, the dispute in the 1990s mostly referred to the legitimization or delegitimization of the political system of the GDR, and so Jews in East Germany were foremost analyzed from a functionalist perspective.

The bonanza of newly opened state archives in the former GDR also produced a very one-sided picture of Jews in East Germany. The focus on material from agencies of the state and the party, including the infamous *Stasi* (Ministry for State Security), very much reproduced the hegemonic perspective of the East German authorities. At the same time, most of the research done in this decade also was marked at least by an implicit normativity: scholars favored either acculturation or leaving Germany as valid options, while they did not consider the issue of the legitimacy of Jewish life and identity in Germany as an object of historical investigation. Ultimately, these pioneer works on Jews in the GDR were also marked by a certain monotony. Mostly scholars simply applied the old questions from the Cold War era to the newly accessible sources. Again and again, they discussed to what extent Jews and Jewish organizations had been instrumentalized by the East German state and the ruling Communist Party, the Sozialistische Einheitpartei Deutschlands (SED), for their purposes and to what extent Jews and Jewish groups had resisted or not.

Jewish History in the GDR: New Approaches since 2000

Since 2000, a substantial shift of perspective has taken place. One might say that while the focus of historical research was previously on the GDR and the Jews, since then the focus has shifted to Jewish history in the GDR. No longer is the organizational perspective, which prevailed in the 1990s, dominant so to speak, but rather interest has moved to the plurality of Jewish groups, individuals, and identities in a transnationally enhanced East German environment. At the same time, it seems that the history of the GDR in general and Jewish history in East Germany have become rather independent subdisciplines.[8] While the former is mostly interested in the relationship of power, state, and society, the latter is mostly related to the context of the history of the Holocaust, post-Holocaust memory, and Jewish identity.

A systematic overview of the main directions of investigation in the field of Jewish history in the GDR since 2000 can identify at least five major trends. The first centers around the role of anti-Semitism and the relationship of the GDR to Israel, which carries on earlier historiographical trends. In this area, the old struggle between advocates and critics of "real socialism" continues. On the one hand, there are those who want to defend the image of the GDR as a beacon of antifascism and to rebut accusations of anti-Semitism, to the effect that sometimes defense crosses the border to apologia.[9] On the other hand, there are those who try to blame the official anti-Zionism of the East German state on (at least latent) anti-Semitism, and this perspective is preferentially sponsored by public agencies of political education in the Federal Republic of Germany.[10] But while the battles of the Cold War are still raging to some degree, a more sober strain of research has also emerged. As a convincing example, Monika Schmidt systematically investigated the desecration of Jewish cemeteries in the GDR and related it to the issue of popular anti-Semitism in East Germany.[11]

A second line of inquiry into Jewish history has evolved from earlier studies of the interrelationship of culture and politics and since then has moved forward to the issue of Jews as both actors and objects of the media. An important bridge between the old and new tendencies was a collection of essays edited by Moshe Zuckermann and published in 2002.[12] This volume no longer simply refers to the old notion of "instrumentalization" of Jews through culture but instead displays a higher sensitivity for the inherent logic of media and art—not the least by presenting Jews as not only objects but also actors in the field of culture. The collection of essays has also inspired several subsequent studies on the role of Jews in East German media and arts, studies that at least partly continued the volume's work on issues of Jewish identity.[13]

A third research trend clearly overcomes the old focus on Jewish communities in the GDR and their interrelationship with state and party authorities by addressing Jewish biographies and life courses. This historiography also highlights the activity of Jewish individuals outside the Jewish communities, as they often played an overlooked role in East German politics and society. While Robert Allen Willingham's study on the politics and identity of Jews in Leipzig in the twentieth century takes some cautious steps in that direction, it still sticks to a more traditional approach of combining local history with a strong biographical impetus.[14] In contrast, Karin Hartewig's trailblazing study on the history of Jewish Communists in the GDR who had returned from exile after 1945 widens the scope beyond traditional notions of Jewishness.[15] The general postmodern interest in the fashioning of identities has thus had a considerable impact in the field of Jewish history in the GDR, looking mostly at tensions, contingencies, and shifts of Jewish identities.[16]

A fourth trend in the research is also closely related to a postmodern sense of dissolution or transgression of boundaries. As part of a general trend for transnational history in recent years, several studies have widened the spatial perspective and investigated the tensions between the local and the global and also looked closely at acts of negotiation of belonging, which take place between different localities. This also implies a wider notion of Jewishness, which is no longer primarily limited to Jews in a traditional, religious sense, but now also includes a variety of opportunities to look at how people identify themselves as Jewish. Hendrik Niether also wrote a book on Jews from Leipzig, but unlike Willingham, he uses the perspective of transnational history, aiming to analyze processes of negotiation, scopes of action, and also opportunities to influence Jewish life under the circumstances of "real socialism" in the GDR.[17] Thus the transnational widening of space also expands the scope of what comes to be considered as Jewish. An outstanding example of this trend is Michael Meng's superb study *Shattered Spaces*, where he compares how societies in East and West Germany and Poland dealt with the spatial remnant of destroyed Jewish communities after 1945.[18] So while Willingham writes on Jews in Leipzig and Niether extends the view to Jews formerly from Leipzig, Meng brings the shadows of once-Leipziger Jews into the picture.[19]

Finally, a last major trend concerns new overall presentations of the history of Jews in Germany after 1945, which include the story of the Jews in East Germany. In 2016, the Irish scholar Pól Ó Dochartaigh published a short comprehensive survey on Germans and Jews since the Holocaust, which also devotes two chapters to the GDR.[20] Also recently, a multiauthor, comprehensive history of Jews in Germany after 1945, edited by Michael Brenner and originally published in German in 2012, was released in English.[21] While Ó Dochartaigh offers a synthesis of previously published research literature, the volume edited by Brenner is based on extensive archival research and pools the expertise of authorities in the field. Since the author of this essay also contributed to Brenner's volume, my comments might hardly be accepted as unbiased. However, at least this allows me to report that the integration of the GDR in a comprehensive German postwar history was considered quite challenging during the collective research and editing process. While the volume has a focus on politics, culture, and society, it mostly operates with a focus on members of Jewish communities, which leads to a serious mismatch between East and West Germany. However, the volume also considers the dramatic changes that took place in the structure of Jewish life in Germany as a result of the massive influx of Jews from the former Soviet Union. Nevertheless, in both aforementioned comprehensive studies, the story of Jews in the GDR mostly appears as an appendix to the story of Jews in the Federal Republic of Germany.

What then are the historiographic strategies to expand the topic of Jews in the GDR, which otherwise might be considered limited to the story of several hundred or maybe several thousand persons and ultimately might be completely covered by a limited series of group or individual biographies? Three main strategies came to the fore during the previous short survey on recent research trends. First, Jewish identities are extended by widening the scope of Jewish belonging, especially by transcending the narrow bounds of community membership and including so-called crypto-Jews (i.e., Jews in the GDR who hid their Jewish identities) as well as by including aspects of intergenerationality. In doing so, belonging to Jewry is considered as a historical problem in itself, which moves into the focus of research. Thus the history of Jews in the GDR becomes part of a much wider field of historical inquiry, which touches fundamental questions regarding minorities, difference, and cosmopolitanism.

A second strategy to widen the field of the history of Jews in the GDR is to extend the time period under study—namely, by transcending the thresholds of 1945 and 1990 in both directions. Another important option to widen the timeframe is to include those Jews who were absent after 1945 by studying various aspects of Jewish legacy ranging from tombs to buildings. By doing so, a general shift from the history of Jews in the GDR to the history of Jewish memory takes place.

Finally, a third strategy is to widen the limited space of the GDR by applying perspectives of transnational history and thus connecting the local with the global. One might even say that there has been a trend to consider Jewish history as transnational history *per se*, which also might raise some concern. Such an approach might involve a tendency to adopt the old metaphor of Jewish *Luftmenschen*[22] and to shift the traditional external ascription of "placeless" Jews into a social reality. At a time when—particularly in Eastern and East-Central Europe—the juxtapositions of space and place and of cosmopolitanism and localisms have had strong effects on contemporary political discourses,[23] this might become potentially threatening.

Some Perspectives for Future Research: A Jewish or a German History of Jews in Germany after 1945?

Finally, what might be perspectives for future research on Jewish history in the GDR, and how might they be related to future trends in referring to the history of the GDR in general? With respect to the latter, Ulrich Mählert optimistically asserted, "There's life in the old dog yet." According to him, the sclerosis that has characterized this field for some time should be overcome by abandoning its traditionally prevalent combination of positivism and normativity.[24] Alternatively, Mählert and other authors call for eliminating the narrow boundaries of the subject in terms of time and space.[25] It seems that the magic phrase "transnational history" also helps salvage the historiographical misery afflicting the study of the GDR. But it is an open question whether the future of Jewish history in East Germany might be related to this possible revival of the history of the GDR in general. An essay by Dan Diner titled "An Outline of a Jewish History of Jews in Germany after 1945" takes a different direction. The slightly baroque title of this essay programmatically articulates the bifurcation of the history of the GDR and the history of Jews in Germany. Here "Jewish" describes not only the object but also the subject and the perspective of investigation. Diner argues that despite its small size, the Jewish community in Germany had been of considerable symbolic importance for Jews in the world; yet he limits this statement to Jews living in the Federal Republic of Germany since the 1950s,[26] while Jews in the GDR are not mentioned by him in this context. According to Diner, Jewish history in Germany must be written as a history of the gradual cancelation of the spell that had been imposed on this country after the Shoah. The history of Jews living in Germany after the war, he argues, may not be properly narrated from within itself but must be contextualized in micro- and macrohistorical constellations. From this perspective, Germany acquires for Jews worldwide the role of a magnifying glass for their historical perception.[27] Ultimately, this leads to a divided historical consciousness between Jews and non-Jews resulting from the Shoah and thus moves away from the idea of a universal historical consciousness. One might argue about the theoretical implications of such an assumption; however, from an institutional perspective, this division has largely taken place anyway.

What then might be future tasks for a Jewish—or possibly also non-Jewish—history of Jews in the GDR? Two premises seem especially important to me. First, we should think in terms of a history of relations between Jews and non-Jews, which has also to take into account that the boundaries between the two groups are themselves an object of historical investigation. Second, we should proceed in our attempts to widen the spatiotemporal framework of future research on Jews in East Germany. That brings me to five concluding suggestions:

First, we should no longer consider the role of Jews in East Germany—and of course also in West Germany—as a litmus test for democratic behavior, but rather we should inquire about the transformations of this example of historical moral economy. In the case of the Federal Republic of Germany, such an investigation has already been convincingly attempted by Anthony Kauders, who applied the model of gift exchange, developed by French sociologist and ethnologist Marcel Mauss in 1925, to analyze the relationship between Jewish institutions and the West German political system since 1945.[28]

Second, we should carefully avoid falling into the trap of the metaphor of *Luftmenschen* in analyzing real Jews in the GDR and rather strive for a social-historical demystification of the idea of placeless, uprooted Jews. This seems to be particularly important with regard to the current conflict between *space* and *place* (i.e., between the liberal, cosmopolitan and the antiliberal, identitary concepts of identity).

Third, we should investigate the multiple waves of construction of Jewish identity in East Germany, which several times repeated a process that already had taken place in the nineteenth century. As a characteristic feature of German-Jewish history, repeated processes of amalgamation between "German" and "non-German" Jews took place, which eventually led to the emergence of a new "German Jewishness." After some time, the latter encountered new waves of non-German Jewish immigration, and so the game started again. With respect to East Germany, the years after 1945 and 1990 are of special importance, particularly because this process is still ongoing in the present time.

Fourth, we should inquire into the effects of collective experiences of rupture on individual biographical constructions. This leads to the question, what exactly does it mean when we speak of Jewish identities?

Hence a *fifth* field of historical inquiry might be East Germany as a compression zone, where competing models of Jewish identity may be studied, ranging from religion to ethnicity to a community of fate to "Jewish spaces." Coining the latter term, Diana Pinto described the emergence of urban spaces in Europe after 1990—and namely, in Berlin—which contain "things Jewish," thus creating an ambient substitute for the loss of former Jewish culture.[29] Yet the recent wave of anti-Semitism, and in particular of frequent violent attacks on Jews in the public area, raises serious doubts as to whether the idea of Jewish spaces might have been a case of post–Cold War optimism.[30]

By tracing these questions, we might not only better understand some crucial aspects of Jewish history but also learn something about current problems of German society, where we necessarily need to think about West and East together. Perhaps the crucial questions are no longer to what extent Germany has learned lessons regarding the Shoah and the Jewish minority and which part of Germany might have outperformed the other in doing so. Studying Jewish history in East Germany—and also in West Germany—might become important with respect to understanding the ambivalences of the "reconciliatory cosmopolitanism,"[31] which for some time has become the standard German state of mind whenever issues of Jewish history and Jewish presence are touched. Thus Tur Tur's lantern might shed light far beyond Lummerland.

NOTES

1. Hans-Ulrich Wehler, *Deutsche Gesellschaftsgeschichte*, vol. 5, *Bundesrepublik und DDR: 1949–1990* (Munich: C. H. Beck, 2008), xv; cf. also Patrick Bahners, ed., *Bundesrepublik und DDR. Die Debatte um Hans-Ulrich Wehlers "Deutsche Gesellschaftsgeschichte"* (Munich: C. H. Beck, 2009).

2. Jürgen Kocka, "Der Blick über den Tellerrand fehlt," *Frankfurter Rundschau*, 22 August 2003.

3. Peter Maser, "Juden in der DDR," in *Bilanz und Perspektiven der DDR-Forschung*, ed. Rainer Eppelmann, Bernd Faulenbach, and Ulrich Mählert (Paderborn: Schöningh, 2013), 217–225, quote on 224.

4. Michael Brenner, "Introduction," *A History of Jews in Germany after 1945: Politics, Culture, and Society*, ed. Michael Brenner (Bloomington: Indiana University Press, 2018), 3.

5. See especially Mario Keßler, *Die SED und die Juden—zwischen Repression und Toleranz. Politische Entwicklungen bis 1967* (Berlin: Akademie, 1995); Angelika Timm, *Hammer, Zirkel, Davidstern. Das gestörte Verhältnis der DDR zu Zionismus und Staat Israel* (Bonn: Bouvier, 1997).

6. See especially Michael Wolffsohn, *Die Deutschland-Akte. Juden und Deutsche in Ost und West. Tatsachen und Legenden*, 2nd ed. (Munich: edition ferenczy bei Bruckmann, 1996); Jutta Illichmann, *Die DDR und die Juden. Die deutschlandpolitische Instrumentalisierung von Juden und Judentum durch die Partei- und Staatsführung der SBZ/DDR von 1945 bis 1990* (Frankfurt am Main: Peter Lang, 1997); Ulrike Offenberg, *"Seid vorsichtig gegen die Machthaber." Die jüdischen Gemeinden in der SBZ und der DDR 1945–1990* (Berlin: Aufbau, 1998).

7. Keßler, *Die SED und die Juden*; Lothar Mertens, *Davidstern unter Hammer und Zirkel. Die Jüdischen Gemeinden in der SBZ/DDR und ihre Behandlung durch Partei und Staat 1945–1990* (Hildesheim: Georg Olms, 1997); Timm, *Hammer, Zirkel, Davidstern*; Yeshayahu A. Jelinek, ed., *Zwischen Moral und Realpolitik. Deutsch-israelische Beziehungen 1945–1965. Eine Dokumentensammlung* (Gerlingen: Bleicher 1997); Offenberg, *"Seid vorsichtig gegen die Machthaber."*

8. A recent survey on possible fields of future research on the history of the GDR does not discuss the role of Jews or Jewish history. See Ulrich Mählert, ed., *Die DDR als Chance. Neue Perspektiven auf ein altes Thema* (Berlin: Metropol, 2016).

9. Detlef Joseph, *Die DDR und die Juden. Eine kritische Untersuchung* (Berlin: Das neue Berlin, 2010). The subtitle of the book, "a critical examination," might be considered poorly deserved.

10. Solvejg Höppner, ed., *Antisemitismus in Sachsen im 19. und 20. Jahrhundert* (Dresden: Sächsische Landeszentrale für politische Bildung, 2004); Andreas H. Apelt and Maria Hufenreuter, eds., *Antisemitismus in der DDR und die Folgen*, on behalf of Deutsche Gesellschaft e. V. and Deutsch-Israelische Gesellschaft e.V. in cooperation with the Bundesstiftung zur Aufarbeitung der SED-Diktatur (Halle a. d. Saale: Mitteldeutscher Verlag, 2016).

11. Monika Schmidt, *Übergriffe auf verwaiste jüdische Gräber. Friedhofsschändungen in der SBZ und der DDR* (Berlin: Metropol, 2016).

12. Moshe Zuckermann, ed., *Zwischen Politik und Kultur—Juden in der DDR* (Göttingen: Wallstein, 2002).

13. See Chaim Noll, "Juden und Judentum in der Literatur der DDR," *Deutschland-Archiv* 42, no. 6 (2009): 1033–1040; Karsten Fritz, "Juden im Spielfilm der DDR," *Medaon. Magazin für jüdisches Leben in Forschung und Bildung* 4, no. 6 (2010): 1–5; Lisa Schoß, "Politik, Unterhaltung und Romantisierung. Juden und 'Juden' im DDR-Fernsehen," in *Das war Spitze. Jüdisches in der deutschen Fernsehunterhaltung der DDR*, ed. Ulrike Heikaus (Essen: Klartext, 2011), 115–125; Lisa Schoß, "Ein Jiddenfilm im Fernsehen der DDR," in *Aus einem Land vor unserer Zeit. Eine Lesereise durch die DDR-Geschichte*, ed. Marcus Böick, Anja Hertel, and Franziska Kuschel (Berlin: Metropol, 2012), 165–176; Elke Schieber, *Tangenten. Holocaust und jüdisches Leben im Spiegel audiovisueller Medien der SBZ und der DDR 1946 bis 1990—eine Dokumentation* (Berlin: DEFA Stiftung, 2016).

14. Robert Allen Willingham, *Jews in Leipzig, Germany under Nazism, Communism, and Democracy: Politics and Identity in the 20th Century* (Lewiston, N.Y.: Edwin Mellen, 2011).

15. Karin Hartewig, *Zurückgekehrt. Die Geschichte der jüdischen Kommunisten in der DDR* (Cologne: Böhlau, 2000).

16. Stephanie Tauchert, *Jüdische Identitäten in Deutschland. Das Selbstverständnis von Juden in der Bundesrepublik und der DDR 1950 bis 2000* (Berlin: Metropol, 2007); Cora A. Granata,

"Political Upheaval and Shifting Identities: Holocaust Survivors in the Soviet Occupied Zone of Germany, 1945–1949," in *Lessons and Legacies*, vol. 10, *Back to the Sources. Reexamining Perpetrators, Victims, and Bystanders*, ed. Sara R. Horowitz (Evanston, Ill.: Northwestern University Press, 2012), 213–140; Cora A. Granata, "The Cold War Politics of Cultural Minorities: Jews and Sorbs in the German Democratic Republic, 1976–1989," *German History* 27, no. 1 (2009): 60–83; Mike Dennis and Norman LaPorte, *State and Minorities in Communist East Germany* (Oxford: Berghahn, 2011).

17. Hendrik Niether, *Leipziger Juden und die DDR. Eine Existenzerfahrung im Kalten Krieg* (Göttingen: Vandenhoeck & Ruprecht, 2015), 23.

18. Michael Meng, *Shattered Space: Encountering Jewish Ruins in Postwar Germany and Poland* (Cambridge, Mass.: Harvard University Press, 2011); Michael Meng, "East Germany's Jewish Question: The Return and Preservation of Jewish Sites in East Berlin and Potsdam, 1945–1989," *Central European History* 38, no. 4 (2005): 606–636; Michael Meng, "(Trans)National Spaces: Jewish Sites in Contemporary Germany," *Three-Way Street: Jews, Germans, and the Transnational*, ed. Jay Howard Geller and Leslie Morris (Ann Arbor: University of Michigan Press, 2016), 321–340.

19. See also Anton Legerer, *Tatort: Versöhnung. Aktion Sühnezeichen in der BRD und in der DDR und Gedenkdienst in Österreich* (Leipzig: Evangelische Verlagsanstalt, 2011).

20. Pól Ó Dochartaigh, *Germans and Jews since the Holocaust* (Basingstoke, U.K.: Palgrave Macmillan, 2016).

21. Michael Brenner, ed., *A History of Jews in Germany after 1945: Politics, Culture, and Society* (Bloomington: Indiana University Press, 2018), originally *Geschichte der Juden in Deutschland von 1945 bis zur Gegenwart. Politik, Kultur und Gesellschaft* (Munich: C. H. Beck, 2012).

22. Nicolas Berg, *Luftmenschen. Zur Geschichte einer Metapher*, 2nd ed. (Göttingen: Vandenhoeck & Ruprecht, 2014).

23. See Ivan Krastev, *After Europe* (Philadelphia: University of Pennsylvania Press, 2017).

24. Ulrich Mählert, "Totgesagte leben länger. Oder: Konjunkturen der DDR-Forschung vor und nach 1989. Eine Einführung," in *Die DDR als Chance. Neue Perspektiven auf ein altes Thema*, ed. Ulrich Mählert (Berlin: Metropol, 2016), 9–21.

25. Mählert, "Totgesagte leben länger"; Thomas Lindenberger, "Ist die DDR ausgeforscht? Phasen, Trends und ein optimistischer Ausblick," *Aus Politik und Zeitgeschichte* 64, no. 24–26 (2014): 27–32; Frank Bösch, "Geteilte Geschichte. Plädoyer für eine deutsch-deutsche Perspektive auf die jüngere Zeitgeschichte," *Zeithistorische Forschungen* 12, no. 1 (2015): 98–114; Frank Bösch, "Geteilt und verbunden. Perspektiven auf die deutsche Geschichte seit den 1970er Jahren," in *Geteilte Geschichte. Ost- und Westdeutschland 1970–2000*, ed. Frank Bösch (Göttingen: Vandenhoeck & Ruprecht, 2015).

26. Dan Diner, "Skizze zu einer jüdischen Geschichte der Juden in Deutschland nach '45," *Münchner Beiträge zur jüdischen Geschichte und Kultur* 4, no. 1 (2010): 8–16, esp. 8.

27. Diner, 9–10.

28. Anthony Kauders, *Unmögliche Heimat. Eine deutsch-jüdische Geschichte der Bundesrepublik* (Munich: Deutsche Verlags-Anstalt, 2007).

29. Diana Pinto, "A New Jewish Identity for Post-1989 Europe," *JPR Policy Paper* 1 (1996).

30. Cf. also Eszter Brigitta Gantner and Koby Oppenheim, "Jewish Space Reloaded: An Introduction," *Anthropological Journal of European Cultures* 23, No. 2 (2014): 1–10.

31. Meng, *Shattered Spaces*, esp. 263–270.

CHAPTER 11

COMMUNITY RESPONSES TO THE IMMIGRATION OF RUSSIAN-SPEAKING JEWS TO GERMANY, 1990–2006

Joseph Cronin

In January 1991, the federal government of the newly reunited Germany finally agreed to continue a policy that had first been inaugurated by the East German government in July 1990—granting Jews from the Soviet Union a right of residence. This immigration had been halted in October 1990 when East Germany ceased to exist as a state. When it was reinstated by the Federal Republic of Germany, it was placed under a legal framework called the *Kontingentflüchtlingsgesetz* (quota refugee law), which had originally been devised in 1980 for refugees fleeing political instability and violence in mainland Southeast Asia. Ironically, one of the modifications made to this law for Jews emigrating from the Soviet Union was that there would be no quota on numbers.[1]

For Jewish *Kontingentflüchtlinge* (quota refugees), the German authorities decided to admit anyone who had at least one Jewish parent as defined by the Soviet authorities. The right of residence was offered as an act of humanitarian aid, and the primary reason given by the German government was that Jews living in the Soviet states were experiencing a rise in anti-Semitic incidents. During Bundestag debates held in October 1990 to decide whether to resume the East German policy of accepting Soviet Jews, all members agreed that Germany had a "historical responsibility" to help Jews who were in danger of persecution.[2]

Upon arrival in Germany, Jewish immigrants' destinations were assigned according to the *Königsteiner Schlüssel*, a geographic formula that distributed immigrants across Germany's sixteen states according to their tax revenues and population size.[3] Jewish immigrants were then encouraged to register with their local Jewish community. There were two reasons for this. The first was that German politicians had preconceptions about the Jews who were arriving in Germany. Some, such as parliamentary state secretary Horst Waffenschmidt of the conservative Christian Democratic Union, hoped that the immigration would lead "to a revitalization of the Jewish element in German cultural and spiritual life, which in the past has played such an important role."[4] At this point in time, however, this was a far less important reason for allowing immigration than Germany's historical responsibility toward Jews. The second reason was that the Jewish communities had been given funding by the federal government to provide welfare services to the newcomers, such as language training and help with finding accommodation.[5]

All of Germany's Jewish communities follow Jewish religious law (*Halakhah*) in deciding who is to be considered a Jew.[6] According to the *Halakhah*, a person is a Jew if he or she was born to a Jewish mother or has converted to Judaism. However, not all Jewish communities across the world adhere to the halakhic definition. In the United States, for example, Reform communities also accept those who only have a Jewish father, so long as they have been raised in the Jewish tradition and identify themselves as Jewish.[7] However, German communities' strict adherence to the halakhic definition caused problems because a large percentage of the Jewish quota refugees were not Jews according to the *Halakhah*. There was a high rate of intermarriage between Jews and non-Jews in the Soviet Union, partly due to the Soviet Union's atheist and "internationalist" principles (Jews were defined as a nationality by the Soviet authorities).[8] Furthermore, of these intermarriages, more involved Jewish men marrying non-Jewish women than the other way around. Mark Tolts has shown that of all Jews who married in the Soviet Union in 1988, 58.3 percent of Jewish men married non-Jewish women, compared to 47.6 percent of Jewish women marrying non-Jewish men.[9] The children of marriages between Jewish men and non-Jewish women would not be considered halakhically Jewish, since their mothers were not Jewish.

Another dimension to this situation is that anti-Semitic discrimination in the Soviet Union operated (as elsewhere) on the basis of whether a person was identifiably Jewish. The most reliable way of identifying whether a person had a Jewish background was his or her family name. Accounting for exceptions in cases where the family name had been changed, the situation for Jews in the Soviet Union would therefore be as follows: If you had two Jewish parents, then of course you would be a halakhic Jew and have a Jewish last name. If you had a Jewish mother and a non-Jewish father, you would be a Jew according to halakhic law but have a non-Jewish family name. Finally, if you had a Jewish father and a non-Jewish mother, then you would not be a halakhic Jew but would have a

Jewish last name. You would therefore (as with those who had two Jewish parents) be an easier target for anti-Semitism.

This chapter will be divided into two parts. The first will explore how nonhalakhic Jews from the former Soviet Union were received by Germany's Jewish communities, and the second will examine the legislative process whereby the regulations governing the immigration of Jews from the former Soviet Union were ultimately brought into line with halakhic criteria. It will therefore investigate how a policy designed to help Jews who were facing persecution changed over time to become one that was aimed specifically at "strengthening" Germany's Jewish communities.

The Reception of Nonhalakhic Jews in Germany's Jewish Communities

Most scholars estimate that the number of nonhalakhic Jewish immigrants to Germany was between 25 and 50 percent of all Jewish quota refugees.[10] Jeffrey Peck has put the figure much higher at 80 percent of all immigrants,[11] but his statistic appears to be an anomaly. The figure also varies depending on whether non-Jewish relatives, who were also allowed to migrate as quota refugees, are included or not. Whatever the actual figure, the number of nonhalakhic Jewish immigrants to Germany was large, and this caused considerable difficulties for Jewish communities, since they were forced to decide whether to turn away potential new members—thereby endangering their long-term survival prospects—or whether they should welcome them, which would require the communities to reconsider their adherence to halakhic law.

Although all Jewish communities in Germany adhered to the halakhic definition, different communities adopted different policies toward nonhalakhic Jews. Nadine Fügner's 2007 study of Jewish immigration to the state of Brandenburg has shown that the communities there remained open to those who did not qualify as members.[12] By contrast, Helga Krohn has stated that the community in Frankfurt am Main made it clear from the outset that only halakhic Jews were allowed to become members and thereby participate in community life.[13] In a study from 2009, Karen Körber stated that the position adopted by many communities was that nonhalakhic Jews could take part in community activities (e.g., youth clubs) but were not allowed to become members, have a bar or bat mitzvah, and so on.[14] This appears to correspond to the attitude of the Brandenburg communities outlined by Fügner.

As such, the only solution for many nonhalakhic Jews who wanted to join a community was to formally convert to Judaism. However, for a number of reasons, conversion was difficult in Germany, and particularly so for Russian-speaking Jews. First, Germany's rabbis deferred to the chief rabbinate in Israel in matters of conversion. This was primarily due to the relatively small size and, consequently, low critical mass of the Jewish community in Germany.[15] Consequently, the chief rabbinate in Israel effectively controlled the process of conversion to Judaism in Germany. This meant that, when communities faced the problem of large numbers of Russian-speaking nonhalakhic Jews who wanted to become members, Germany's rabbis were unable to expand the infrastructure for dealing with converts to Judaism. From a sympathetic perspective, their hands were tied. However, Moritz Neumann has argued that German rabbis were not "self-conscious enough to free themselves from the tutelage of the Chief Rabbinate in Israel."[16]

The most striking symbol of the Jewish communities' incapacity was that, until 2004, there was no Beth Din (rabbinical court) in Germany that could oversee conversions. The nearest was in Basel, Switzerland. Until 2010, there were also no seminars or courses to prepare nonhalakhic Jews who wanted to convert, because German rabbis were not able to provide these without the consent of the chief rabbinate in Israel.[17] Before 2004, therefore, converting to Judaism for those living in Germany required at least one trip abroad (to formally convert) and others to undertake the preparatory course required for conversion that Germany's Jewish communities were not in a position to provide. For Russian-speaking Jews, many of whom lacked time and money, this was not a feasible option.

In 1994, reports about Jewish quota refugees being refused entry into Jewish communities reached the attention of the German press. *Der Spiegel* quickly sought the opinion of Germany's most senior Jewish representative, the president of the Central Council of Jews in Germany (*Zentralrat der Juden in Deutschland*), Ignatz Bubis. Bubis made it clear that he was incontrovertibly in favor of the communities' use of halakhic admission criteria. "I truly see myself as a liberal," he said, "but even for me the Jewish religious law is the basis. Whoever is not a Jew according to this law will not be accepted [into the communities]."[18] Two years later he reaffirmed his position: "When only the father is Jewish and the mother is not and then there is a child, according to our religious principles the mother and child are not Jewish. Therefore they cannot be accepted into the communities unless they convert to Judaism."[19] Bubis did have a reputation as a liberal and a modernizer, particularly in terms of his engagement with the German public. However, his refusal to compromise on the halakhic issue is not surprising. Like his predecessors, Bubis was religiously conservative and wanted to preserve the traditional character of Germany's "unified community" (*Einheitsgemeinde*).[20]

Already by the mid-1990s, discussions were taking place between senior Jewish representatives and the German government about whether the immigration regulations for Russian-speaking Jews could be altered so that only halakhic Jews would be admitted to Germany. In late 1994, publicist Leibl Rosenberg reported in the *Allgemeine Jüdische Wochenzeitung* (the main Jewish newspaper in Germany, affiliated with the Central Council of Jews in Germany and henceforth referred to as *Allgemeine*) that representatives of the Central Welfare Office of Jews in Germany had met in Frankfurt with immigration experts from the

Federal Administrative Office to "exchange their experiences" about the immigration of Russian-speaking Jews. One proposal that arose from this meeting was to bring the immigration in line with halakhic criteria. This would require that "the mother must be or have been Jewish—or, if only the father was a Jew, it must be proved that the immigrant suffered serious disadvantages for this reason."[21]

Bundestag members also debated whether the immigration regulations for Jews from the former Soviet Union should be made more restrictive in two sessions in 1996. Amke Dietert-Scheuer of political party the Greens noted at one debate that "only 20 percent" of immigrants were eligible to join a Jewish community,[22] while at another, Social Democrat Horst Sielaff asked whether Germany's immigration policy for Jews should follow Israel's, which, he noted erroneously, "follows only the female line of descent."[23] However, at this point in time, it appears that German politicians had no desire to restrict Jewish immigration. It was only after the Central Council applied pressure that things began to change.

Jewish newspapers in Germany rarely presented Russian-Jewish perspectives on the "halakhic issue." One exception is an article in Düsseldorf's community newspaper from August 1996, which featured eight short accounts from Russian-speaking Jews on the subject of religion. Two mentioned the halakhic issue. One of them, an unnamed female immigrant, described the frustration she felt when she had tried to register with the Düsseldorf community:

> They said to me: "You are not Jewish." And I said: "How so? I was beaten up at school, I couldn't enter university, I couldn't do this and that, I had no rights, all because I was Jewish." "It makes no difference to us," they said to me. "You are not a Jew. Your mother is a Russian." And that was exactly how it was back then. "You are a Jew." And here, also, it was as if they had to touch something dirty: "You are not a Jew." And so I said to myself, what am I doing in the community? The community doesn't need me at all.[24]

In an article from 2003, Judith Kessler focused on the psychological impact a rejection by a Jewish community could have on nonhalakhic Russian-speaking Jews, writing that this was "the straw that broke the camel's back" for those who had been invited to Germany as Jews, tried to join a community, and were then told that they were not Jewish.[25] Julius Schoeps and Olaf Glöckner argued in 2008 that Russian-speaking Jews, whose Jewish self-understanding was primarily ethnic and who often had little knowledge of religion, simply could not understand why the German communities would not accept those who "only" had a Jewish father.[26]

In December 1997, Anna Sokhrina, a writer and Russian-Jewish immigrant, published an account of her first three years in Germany in the *Allgemeine*. Sokhrina explained that the rate of intermarriage between Jews and non-Jews was high in the Soviet Union because "we Jews lived amongst Russians, Ukrainians, Belarussians, Kazakhs," and therefore "it was only natural that people didn't stay 'amongst themselves.' We worked, lived and celebrated together—and sometimes people married outside of their own group."[27] Sokhrina then went on to tell the story of one such "mixed" family, with whom she had shared lodgings after their arrival in Germany: "The woman was Russian. She was big and loud. Originally she came from Ukraine. Her husband was a Jew, both her in-laws too, but the children didn't count as Jews. So say our laws." The phrase "so say our laws" (*so sind unsere Gesetze*), which is common among German-speaking Jews, was probably meant ironically. These laws were not familiar to most Russian-speaking Jews, and many had first encountered them only when they went to register with a Jewish community after they had arrived. In relation to this, Körber has argued that these exclusionary practices caused Russian-speaking Jews to view the communities' halakhic entrance criteria as a form of arbitrariness as opposed to something religiously proscribed.[28]

Sokhrina continued her account by describing the "big and loud" Russian woman:

> [She] felt her lack of belonging and developed complexes as a result. These complexes expressed themselves in an unusual way: "If I am a Russian, why should I have to clear up after you Jews?," she bellowed in the communal kitchen. "Why should I have to take the rubbish out?" When the cleaning list was put out, she was allocated fewer days.[29]

But Sokhrina juxtaposed this unreasonableness with another story: the woman was told that her children were not allowed to take part in a summer camp organized by the synagogue, though another boy, who had a Jewish mother and a Russian father, was allowed. When Sokhrina heard the woman shout, "Where is the justice here?" she was reminded of the time her aunt's son was not accepted into a prestigious institute in the Soviet Union on the basis of his Jewish surname, while another boy, whose mother was Jewish but who bore his father's Russian surname, was accepted.[30] The point Sokhrina wanted to make was that, of the children born from mixed marriages, it was those with Jewish fathers, and hence Jewish last names, who received the brunt of Soviet anti-Semitism. And yet it was they who were now unable to join the Jewish communities.

Legislative Changes to Bring the Immigration of Russian-Speaking Jews into Line with Halakhic Criteria

In mid-2001, Jewish newspapers began to report on legislative proposals that aimed to bring the immigration of Russian-speaking Jews in line with halakhic law. In 2000, an immigration commission was convened under the leadership of Christian Democratic politician Rita Süssmuth. Its mission was to investigate current immigration policy in Germany with a view to improving immigrants' integration prospects. One of its twenty-one-member team was Central Council president Paul Spiegel, who was included because of the significant number of Jews from the former Soviet Union entering Germany at this time.

A year later, in July 2001, they published their findings and recommendations in a document called *Zuwanderung gestalten—Integration fördern* (Organize Immigration—Promote Integration). This document turned out to be an important milestone in the history of postwar Germany, as it was the first time that Germany's status as a "country of immigration" (*Einwanderungsland*) was officially acknowledged.

The report made recommendations for Germany's entire immigration policy and contained a section relating to the immigration of Jews from the former Soviet Union.[31] It stated, "The regulated immigration of Jews from the former Soviet Union should contribute to the further strengthening of the Jewish communities in Germany."[32] With this statement, the immigration commission changed the original and primary reason for the immigration of Russian-speaking Jews: Germany's historical responsibility toward Jews who were being persecuted.[33] This instigating factor was not mentioned anywhere in the immigration commission's report. By changing the primary reason for the Russian-Jewish immigration, the commission made the regulations governing the entry of Russian-speaking Jews look unsuitable. From this point it was easy to argue that "Jewish religious law will be the basis for assessing applicants' entitlement to immigrate. That means that only persons with a Jewish mother or who have converted according to the rules of the rabbinical court are entitled."[34] Thus the commission's report followed the communities' position that a Jew was someone born to a Jewish mother or who had converted to Judaism. Furthermore, it did not acknowledge the difficulties faced by nonhalakhic Jews who wanted to convert, since there were at this time no rabbinical courts in Germany.

In the weeks preceding and following the publication of the immigration commission's report, Spiegel gave interviews to several newspapers in which he justified the recommendations pertaining to the Russian-Jewish immigration. He told *Der Spiegel* that, since quota immigration had begun, thirty thousand Jews had come to Germany "who are not real Jews according to our halakhic religious law."[35] He told *Zukunft*, a dual-language newspaper set up by the Central Council in 2001 and aimed specifically at Russian-speaking Jews, that immigration should "concern Jews and not persons with a mere Jewish background in a broad sense."[36] However, Spiegel wanted to assure Russian-speaking Jews already living in Germany that the new regulations would apply only to prospective immigrants—that is, those who had not yet submitted their applications to the German authorities in their respective countries. "Not a single quota refugee will be sent back!" he stated in an interview.[37]

Spiegel also emphasized in these interviews that the quota immigration's purpose was, and always had been, to strengthen the Jewish communities. He told *Zukunft*, "The immigration program was created at the time to improve the membership structure of the Jewish communities in Germany and to save them from extinction."[38] Spiegel may have believed by this point that the threat facing Jews in the former Soviet Union from anti-Semitic organizations such as Pamyat had largely subsided.[39] Yet Spiegel did not mention this issue and instead insisted that strengthening the Jewish communities had always been the aim of allowing Russian-speaking Jews to come to Germany. Spiegel thereby downplayed the seriousness of the situation Jews had faced in the collapsing Soviet Union and ignored Germany's historical responsibility toward them.

Spiegel also used the literal meaning of the designation "quota refugee" in his justification of the new recommendations. He stated that there was a specific quota for the incoming Jewish immigrants, which there never had been. The quota refugee law had been used by the German government as a framework for accepting Jewish immigrants simply because it already existed. Nonetheless, Spiegel argued that "the term 'quota refugee' denotes a certain quantity of refugees. Therefore we must point out that half of the refugees who have been able to immigrate so far are not Jews according to halakhic principles. The quota would therefore be met with a considerable portion of non-Jews, and halakhic Jews would no longer have the chance to immigrate to Germany."[40] Since Spiegel was surely aware that no quota for the Russian-speaking Jews had ever been put in place, this argument must have been aimed at those who did not know the real terms of the quota refugee law.

Spiegel did have a point in arguing that Jewish communities should not be responsible for determining who was a halakhic Jew and who was not, since the immigration had been initiated by the state, not by the communities. However, the logical corollary of this was not that nonhalakhic Jews should not be allowed to immigrate at all. Under Spiegel's recommendations, the German authorities in the former Soviet states would check the identity papers of applicants and would only allow halakhic Jews (i.e., those who could prove that their mother was Jewish) to obtain visas for Germany. However, an alternative solution would have been to keep the existing regulations in place but pass the responsibility for identifying halakhic Jews on to the German authorities upon the immigrants' arrival. Halakhic Jews could then be encouraged to join Jewish communities, while nonhalakhic Jews would receive their welfare support from the state. This way the German government could continue to fulfill its responsibility to those persecuted as Jews, while the Jewish communities would receive a contingent of halakhic Jews. The fact that this possibility was never raised might be explained by sensitivity about the Nazi past. The German government was hesitant to be seen as performing a "selection" of any kind on Jews. This was probably why, from the outset, it had passed the responsibility on to the Jewish communities. However, the complications arising from this decision ultimately led to the curtailment of Jewish immigration altogether.

German politicians were generally less enthusiastic than the Central Council about changing the immigration regulations to serve primarily religious ends. Werner Hoyer of the liberal Free Democrats commented in a Bundestag debate in June 1996 that while it was "understandable" for Jewish communities to complain that "of the X number of people who live in their community district, only a few commit to or even register with the community," he nonetheless maintained that every immigrant should be able to decide "whether or not he wishes to profess his religious belonging" upon arrival in Germany and that this should not be a factor in deciding applicants' eligibility.[41] Hoyer therefore highlighted the difference between two types of immigration policy with regard to the Russian-speaking Jews: one that focused exclusively on conditions in immigrants' countries of origin, and one that aimed to achieve a particular goal in the destination country—in this case, the revival of the Jewish communities in a religious sense. It was Spiegel's advocacy of the latter that determined the immigration commission's recommendations.

In December 2001, the immigration commission's proposals were debated in the Bundestag, and it was at this time that media coverage of the recommendations for Russian-Jewish immigration reached its peak. Spiegel's position was broadly supported by Jewish community leaders. Michael Fürst, head of the Jewish communities in Lower Saxony, stated that after the new regulations were put in place, they hoped to be able to "bind" new members "closer to the Jewish community."[42] Such responses were understandable. Given their communities' adherence to the halakhic definition, Jewish leaders naturally did not want to have to deal with large numbers of nonhalakhic Jews. However, they did not countenance the possibility that there were other solutions that could have allowed the quota immigration to continue without placing the responsibility for nonhalakhic Jews on the communities.

Spiegel's recommendations were, however, criticized by some communities. Members of the Jewish community in Aachen warned of a "restriction" on numbers if the proposals became law. They stated that the immigration had not originally been initiated to strengthen the communities and pointed to Germany's historical responsibility to protect persecuted Jews regardless of their halakhic status. Part of their statement read, "In the Third Reich, as is well known, it was not only Jews according to halakhic religious law who were persecuted and killed. In the ex-Soviet Union, Judeophobia threatens all those who are perceived as Jews."[43] John March, a board member of the Liberal Jewish community in Cologne, also criticized the idea that the Jewish immigration policy was only in place to strengthen the communities. He argued that the problem with the immigration was not that nonhalakhic Jews were coming to Germany and trying to join communities, but rather that efforts to educate all Jewish immigrants in religious matters were woefully inadequate. Filtering out nonhalakhic Jews in their countries of origin, March argued, would do nothing to solve the communities' integration problems. The only solution was to religiously integrate all immigrants who wanted to join the communities.[44] However, this led back to the issue of conversion, which, as described above, was by no means an easy solution.

Samson Madievski, a Jewish immigrant from Moldova to Germany, became a leading campaigner against the proposals. "We do not understand," he told the *Süddeutsche Zeitung* in August 2001, "how the Central Council can exclude such a large part of the Jewish immigrants."[45] His first argument was that prohibiting the immigration of nonhalakhic Jews would make no difference to the religious composition of the communities, which, after all, was the main reason given by supporters of the proposals. As Madievski put it, "What changes for the communities if only halakhic Jews come? They are not much more religious."[46] Four months later, in the *Neue Zürcher Zeitung*, Madievski raised three additional points against the recommendations. The first was that Germany's constitution, the Basic Law (*Grundgesetz*), forbade the state from making religious norms the basis for legislation; the second, that neither the Nazis nor the Soviets cared whether their victims were halakhic Jews or not; and the third, that the Central Council was acting out of self-interested motives and not looking at the broader humanitarian picture.[47]

At some point between December 2001 and March 2002, during the debates surrounding the immigration commission's proposals for a new immigration law, the federal government decided that Spiegel's recommendations—to accept only halakhic Russian-speaking Jews—were indeed unconstitutional. Although the documentation surrounding this decision is not currently available,[48] a comment made by parliamentary state secretary Fritz Rudolf Körper in July 2001 offers some insight into why the decision was made. Körper stated that the "ethical standard" of the German constitution was "openness towards the plurality of ideological and religious beliefs." Therefore, the state had to maintain "religious and ideological neutrality."[49] In April 2002, Stephan J. Kramer, then managing director of the Central Council, commented that Spiegel's recommendation had "no support at the present time" from the federal government, which had cited "the separation of church and state" as well as "other political objections" in their rejection of it.[50]

Despite this setback, Spiegel did not give up his campaign for the immigration regulations to be changed. He reiterated his main argument to *Zukunft* in July 2002 that the immigration "was initiated with the aim of permanently securing the existence of Jewish communities in Germany."[51] He also described the question "who is a Jew" as "indisputably defined, namely someone who was born to a Jewish mother or who has converted to Judaism."[52]

The period between the failure of the Central Council's recommendations in early 2002 and the eventual decision to revise the regulatory framework for the immigration of Jews from the former Soviet Union in June 2005 saw a high level of criticism of the *Einheitsgemeinde* communities' treatment of nonhalakhic Jews. During this period, there was a widespread feeling that the communities would have to find a way of dealing with nonhalakhic Jews, since they were not able to prevent them from entering Germany. At the end of 2002, a seminar was held at the Liberal community in Oldenburg to discuss integration strategies for Russian-speaking Jews. The British rabbi Jonathan Magonet, who believed in the halakhic definition, expressed his dilemma: "What is to be done with those for whom the state dictated: a Jew is someone who has a Jewish father? They are—politically speaking—obviously Jewish."[53] In an August 2003 interview with *Das Parlament*, a political newspaper published by the Bundestag, Julius Schoeps, professor of German-Jewish studies at the University of Potsdam, was asked, "Does the *Einheitsgemeinde* have to become more liberal? Should it not simply turn a blind eye and say: It doesn't matter if you are a Jew according to halakhic law or not—we consider you as Jewish because you see yourself as Jewish?"[54] Schoeps admitted that this possibility needed to be considered and, at the very least, a better infrastructure was needed for conversion in Germany.

The new immigration law for Germany was finally ratified in August 2004 after three years of negotiations. Although it did not include the "halakhic stipulation," one small component of this comprehensive new law—which came into effect on 1 January 2005—was to repeal the decision made by the Ministerial Conference (Ministerpräsidentenkonferenz) on 9 January 1991 to apply the quota refugee law to Jews in the Soviet Union. However, the German government decided that it wanted the immigration of Jews from the former Soviet Union to continue, and so the same regulations that had been in place since 1991 were continued under article 3 of the Residence Act (Aufenthaltsgesetz).[55] Then, in June 2005, the Conference of the Ministers of the Interior (Konferenz der Innenminister und -senatoren der Länder) drafted a resolution that put the immigration of Jews from the former Soviet Union on a new legal basis. These new regulations were in fact more restrictive than those proposed by the immigration commission in 2001, as they made the immigration contingent on not one but three extra factors: first, that prospective immigrants could show that they would be able to support themselves financially in Germany and would not be dependent on social welfare; second, that they could demonstrate a basic knowledge of the German language; and third, that they would be able to join a Jewish community.[56]

The final criterion allowed the federal government to circumvent the constitutional stipulation, which forbade the intrusion of religious matters into state law: Jews did not have to prove that they were halakhically Jewish in their countries of origin, but they did have to prove that they were eligible to join one of Germany's Jewish communities, and since all of these followed the halakhic definition, this meant in effect the same thing.[57] When members of Alliance 90 / The Greens asked in the Bundestag in September 2006 whether the new admission criteria would ensure "that secular [*sic*] Jews will still be accepted into Germany in the future," a government spokesperson replied by outlining the three criteria mentioned above and concluded, "Whether an individual is to be accepted into a Jewish community is exclusively a matter for the Jewish community [*Gemeinschaft*]."[58] In this way, the federal government managed to absolve itself of all responsibility for the content of the immigration, while at the same time making it appear as though it was merely deferring to the Central Council's wishes.

The new regulations for the Jewish immigration were ratified in November 2005 and came into effect in July 2006. Paul Spiegel described them in a press statement in late June 2005 as a "fair compromise."[59] Responses to the new regulations in the Jewish press were minimal. The absence of any criticism in the *Allgemeine* and in community publications can be explained by the Central Council's support of—and indeed active role in determining—the new measures. One of the few Jewish newspapers that did discuss the implications of the new regulations was the *Jüdische Korrespondenz*, published by the Jüdische Kulturverein Berlin, a Jewish cultural association with a liberal outlook. In the February 2005 issue, Pavel Polian, a Russian-Jewish historian, expressed his frustration with the way the new regulations were being negotiated, stating, "When the Bundestag originally decided on the admission of Jewish refugees from the former Soviet Union, the government received unanimous support from parliament. Today the government decides in secret and consults 'interested parties' behind closed doors." Polian believed that the new regulations would have a negative impact on Jewish life in Germany and that the current situation had been caused by the complete lack of Russian-Jewish representatives in the Central Council. What was needed now, he argued, was "an open dialogue with those whose fate it concerns, with representatives from the Russian-speaking press and with independent experts."[60] However, it appears that this did not take place.

The Central Council and the Jewish communities had their own motivations for implementing more restrictive, halakhically based immigration regulations for Russian-speaking Jews. But the new regulations also changed the meaning of such immigration. In a Bundestag debate in October 1992, politicians from various parties had agreed that the immigration was a "sign of reconciliation" and a product of Germany's "historical responsibility toward the Jewish people" and, resulting from this, a response to the "aggressive anti-Semitism" on the rise in the states of the former Soviet Union.[61] In contrast, by June 2006, a government statement described the "goal" of the immigration as being "to strengthen the Jewish communities in Germany" and stated that the new regulations were intended to facilitate the integration of new immigrants into the communities.[62] By changing the terms of the immigration in this way, the new entrance criteria appeared justified.

It is not clear why Germany's historical responsibility toward persecuted Jews was sidelined when the immigration regulations were revised in 2005. Although the immediate threat of anti-Semitic attacks in the former Soviet states had subsided by this point, there was no guarantee that this threat would not flare up again in the future. Yet the German government complied with the Central Council's requests and did not press the need to uphold Germany's historical responsibility. It is possible that the government recognized that it had mismanaged the immigration from the outset; first, by not realizing that there was a discrepancy between its admission criteria and that of the Jewish communities, and second, by placing the responsibility for the "selection" of halakhic Jews on individual communities. In view of its mistakes, the government was now prepared to let the Central Council take the lead in determining the new regulations. However, it is also possible that the government itself now wanted to limit the overall number of Jews migrating to Germany, since between 2002 and 2004, the number of Jewish immigrants arriving in Germany was greater than the number migrating to Israel.[63] Taken together with the Central Council's complaints about the large number of nonhalakhic Jews, the prospect of diplomatic tension with Israel may have led the German government to decide that the current regulations were now doing more harm than good and that the immigration should be curtailed.

NOTES

1. Susanne Schönborn, *Im Wandel—Entwürfe jüdischer Identität in den 1980er und 1990er Jahren* (Munich: Martin Medienbauer, 2010), 221.

2. See: Deutscher Bundestag, legislative period 11, sitting 231, 25 October 1990, 18359–18364; Deutscher Bundestag, legislative period 11, sitting 234, 31 October 1990, 18740–18747.

3. Yfaat Weiss and Lena Gorelik, "Die russisch-jüdische Zuwanderung," in *Geschichte der Juden in Deutschland von 1945 bis zur Gegenwart. Politik, Kultur und Gesellschaft*, ed. Michael Brenner (Munich: C. H. Beck, 2012), 394.

4. Bundestag, 11/231, 18363.

5. Madeleine Tress, "Soviet Jews in the Federal Republic of Germany: The Rebuilding of a Community," *Jewish Journal of Sociology* 37, no. 1 (1995): 48.

6. This also applies to Liberal Jewish communities in Germany. The preamble to the constitution of the Union of Progressive Jews in Germany, which was established in 1997, states: "A Jew is someone who was born to a Jewish mother or has converted to Judaism under halakhic law." See "Gibt es religiöse Freiheit unter den Juden in Deutschland?," *Jüdische Zeitung*, 4 March 2011.

7. This became practice after a landmark ruling of March 1983, known as the "Reform Movement's Resolution on Patrilineal Descent," though this has been the source of considerable controversy within the Reform movement. See: http://www.jewishvirtuallibrary.org/reform-movement-s-resolution-on-patrilineal-descent-march-1983.

8. In the Soviet Union, Judaism was regarded as a nationality, not as a religion, and as such it was listed on the fifth line ("Nationality") of a person's internal passport. See: Lothar Mertens, *Alija. Die Emigration der sowjetischen Juden aus der UdSSR/GUS* (Bochum: Brockmeyer, 1993), 43.

9. Mark Tolts, "Trends in Soviet Jewish Demography since the Second World War," in *Jews and Jewish Life in Russia and the Soviet Union*, ed. Yaacov Ro'i (Ilford, U.K.: Frank Cass, 1995), 371–372.

10. See, for example: Julius H. Schoeps, Willi Jasper and Bernhard Vogt, "Jüdische Zuwanderer aus der GUS—zur Problematik von sozio-kultureller und generationsspezifischer

Integration. Eine empirische Studie des Moses Mendelssohn Zentrum 1997–1999," in *Ein neues Judentum in Deutschland? Fremd- und Eigenbilder der russisch-jüdischen Einwanderer*, ed. Julius H. Schoeps, Willi Jasper, and Bernhard Vogt (Potsdam: Verlag für Berlin Brandenburg, 1999), 14–15; Barbara Dietz, Uwe Lebok and Pavel Polian, "The Jewish Emigration from the Former Soviet Union to Germany," *International Migration* 40, no. 2 (2002): 37.

11. Jeffrey M. Peck, *Being Jewish in the New Germany* (New Brunswick, N.J.: Rutgers University Press, 2006), 44.

12. Nadine Fügner, *Jüdische Zuwanderung im Land Brandenburg* (Potsdam: RAA Brandenburg, 2007), 96.

13. Helga Krohn, *"Es war richtig, wieder anzufangen": Juden in Frankfurt am Main seit 1945* (Frankfurt: Brandes & Apsel, 2011), 232.

14. Karen Körber, "Puschkin oder Thora? Der Wandel der jüdischen Gemeinden in Deutschland," in *Juden und Muslime in Deutschland: Recht, Religion, Identität*, ed. José Brunner and Shai Lavi (Göttingen: Wallstein, 2009), 244.

15. See: Moritz Neumann, "Secular or Religious Community? Jews in Contemporary Germany," in *Jews in Germany after 1945: Citizens or "Fellow" Citizens?*, ed. Otto R. Romberg and Susanne Urban-Fahr (Frankfurt: Tribüne-Verlag, 2000), 180.

16. Moritz Neumann, "Secular or Religious Community?," 180.

17. In October 2010, a notice for nonhalakhic Jews interested in converting to Judaism ("Angebot für Gijurinteressierte—deren Väter jüdisch sind") appeared in Jewish publications across Germany. It advertised a pilot project to be held in Bad Sobernheim that would prepare nonhalakhic Jews for a conversion that would be recognized by the chief rabbinate in Israel. The seminar course was provided by the main Jewish institutions in Germany (the Central Council of Jews in Germany, the Central Welfare Office of Jews in Germany, and the Rabbinical Conference) "in cooperation with the chief rabbinate of the State of Israel." (See: "Angebot für Gijurinteressierte," *Gemeindeblatt Köln*, October 2010, 57.) It is unclear whether the delay in providing such a course was due to the recalcitrance of the chief rabbinate.

18. "Eine neue Ausreisewelle," *Der Spiegel*, 24 January 1994, 54.

19. "Eine gewisse Unsicherheit," *Der Spiegel*, 27 May 1996, 24.

20. *Einheitsgemeinde* (unified community) is the designation applied to all Jewish communities affiliated with the Central Council of Jews in Germany, the organization that represents most Jewish communities in Germany.

21. Leibl Rosenberg, "Hilfe zur Selbsthilfe für Umsiedler," *Allgemeine Jüdische Wochenzeitung*, 29 December 1994, 10.

22. Deutscher Bundestag, legislative period 13, sitting 115, 26 June 1996, 10316.

23. Deutscher Bundestag, legislative period 13, sitting 130, 16 October 1996, 11720.

24. "Judentum bedeutet für uns etwas völlig anderes," *Unsere Jüdische Gemeinde Düsseldorf*, August 1996, 2.

25. Judith Kessler, "Kränkungen im Integrationsprozess," in "Kränkung und Krankheit: Psychische und psychosomatische Folgen der Migration von aus der ehemaligen Sowjetunion ausgewanderten Juden. Tagung am 8./9.12. 2003 in der Jüdischen Gemeinde Frankfurt/M.," ed. Heike von Bassewitz (unpublished conference proceedings, 2003), 80.

26. Julius H. Schoeps and Olaf Glöckner, "Fifteen Years of Russian-Jewish Immigration to Germany: Successes and Setbacks," in *The New German Jewry and the European Context: The Return of the European Jewish Diaspora*, ed. Y. Michal Bodemann (Basingstoke, U.K.: Palgrave, 2008), 148.

27. Anna Sokhrina, "Willkommen in Deutschland," *Allgemeine Jüdische Wochenzeitung*, 11 December 1997, 16.

28. Karen Körber, "Synagoge, Samowarverein, Veteranenclub? Jüdische Gemeinden in Deutschland heute," in *Die Achte Joseph Carlebach-Konferenz. Becoming Visible. Jüdisches Leben in Deutschland seit 1990*, ed. Miriam Gillis-Carlebach and Barbara Vogel (Munich: Dölling und Galitz, 2011), 128.

29. Sokhrina, "Willkommen," 16.

30. Sokhrina, 16.

31. Unabhängigen Kommission "Zuwanderung," *Zuwanderung gestalten—Integration fördern* (Berlin: Zeitbild, 2001), 185–188.

32. Unabhängigen Kommission, *Zuwanderung*, 185.

33. For evidence of this, see the comments made by Bundestag members from a debate in 1992: Deutscher Bundestag, legislative period 12, sitting 111, 9 October 1992, 9487–9489.

34. Unabhängigen Kommission, *Zuwanderung*, 188.

35. "Deutschkurse für Juden," *Der Spiegel*, 25 June 2001, 19.

36. "Die Gemeinden stehen Juden offen," *Zukunft*, September/October 2001, 3.

37. "Zentralratspräsident Paul Spiegel zur Zuwanderung," *Unsere Jüdische Gemeinde Düsseldorf*, November 2001, 7.

38. "Die Gemeinden," *Zukunft*, 3.

39. This issue had arisen in a Bundestag debate in June 1996, in which Cem Özdemir from Alliance 90 / The Greens argued that the decreased threat level was just a convenient excuse to limit the immigration (Bundestag, 13/115, 10316).

40. "Zentralratspräsident," *Unsere Jüdische Gemeinde*, 7.

41. Bundestag, 13/115, 10316.

42. "Jude sein," *Süddeutsche Zeitung*, 13 December 2001, 17.

43. "Jude sein," 17.

44. Susanne Spahn, "Die Mutter entscheidet: Jüdische Gemeinden streiten, welche Juden nach Deutschland einwandern dürfen," *Süddeutsche Zeitung*, 4 August 2001, 5.

45. Spahn, 5.

46. Spahn, 5.

47. "Konflikt um Zuwanderung von Juden aus der einstigen UdSSR," *Neue Zürcher Zeitung*, 14 December 2001, 8.

48. This is due to the *Schutzfrist*, a thirty or in some cases seventy-year period of protection for government documents under German law.

49. Deutscher Bundestag, legislative period 14, printed papers 6720, 20 July 2001, 10.

50. Stephan J. Kramer, "Das neue Zuwanderungsgesetz," *Zukunft*, 1 April 2002, 3.

51. "In Einwanderer investieren," *Zukunft*, 10 July 2002, 2.

52. "In Einwanderer investieren," 2.

53. Heide Sobotka, "Gelungene Annäherung," *Zukunft*, February 2003, 4.

54. "Mehr Juden kommen nach Deutschland als nach Israel," *Das Parlament*, 28 July / 4 August 2003, 11.

55. Deutscher Bundestag, legislative period 16, printed papers 1318, 14 June 2006, 1.

56. Bundestag, 16/1318, 1–2.

57. Bundestag, 16/1318, 2.

58. Deutscher Bundestag, legislative period 16, printed papers 2516, 5 September 2006, 7.

59. See: Deutscher Bundestag, legislative period 16, printed papers 2097, 30 June 2006, 3.

60. Pavel Polian, "Sprecht mit uns!," *Jüdische Korrespondenz*, February 2005, 2.

61. Bundestag, 12/111, 9487–9490.

62. Bundestag, 16/2097, 8 and 3.

63. During these years, Germany's intake of Russian-speaking Jews remained steady at around twenty thousand per year, while the number entering Israel dropped below twenty thousand for the first time since 1989. See: Yinon Cohen and Irena Kogan, "Jewish Immigration from the Former Soviet Union to Germany and Israel in the 1990s," *Leo Baeck Institute Year Book* 50 (2005): 251; Barbara Dietz, "Jewish Immigrants from the Former Soviet Union in Germany: History, Politics and Social Integration," *East European Jewish Affairs* 33, no. 2 (2003): 11.

CHAPTER 12

POLICING THE EAST

THE NEW JEWISH HERO IN DOMINIK GRAF'S CRIME DRAMA *IM ANGESICHT DES VERBRECHENS*

Jill Suzanne Smith

The German film and television director Dominik Graf's 2010 miniseries *Im Angesicht des Verbrechens* (*Face to Face with the Crime*) is a crime drama about the Russian Mafia and the German police who struggle to bring them to justice in the capital city of Berlin, and yet the opening images of the series are not of Berlin but of a woodland lake in Ukraine. It is there that viewers are introduced to the young Ukrainian woman Jelena (Alina Levshin), who by the end of the first episode is transported to Berlin under false pretenses, stripped of her passport, and forced to work as a prostitute for the brutal Mafia boss Andrej (Mark Ivanir). In the opening moments of the series—moments that will be repeated at the start of every subsequent episode—Jelena is presented to the audience as a naked nixie who yearns for love just as much as she yearns to leave her Ukrainian village. Wearing nothing but a silver cross around her neck, she dives into the depths of the lake, and in Ukrainian-accented German, her voiceover begins, "Grandmother said, 'Lenotschka, child, under water you will see the man you love.' . . . But all I ever saw was a German tank from the Great Patriotic War."[1] Diving into the water again, she swims past the tank and past ghostly faces of dead men until the softly lit image of a man's face, her future lover and the hero of the series, Marek Gorsky (Max Riemelt), becomes visible in the water. The mystical, dreamlike quality of the image evokes the vision of a clairvoyant, and it provides a sharp contrast to what follows the opening sequence. As Jelena smiles and reaches her face forward as if to kiss the underwater image, the camera cuts abruptly to four establishing aerial shots of Berlin and then cuts to a close-up of the policeman Gorsky, who is standing in the sterile, steel box of an elevator with his colleagues and preparing to make an arrest. As the director Graf himself

Figure 12.1. Max Riemelt as Marek Gorsky in *Im Angesicht des Verbrechens* (*Face to Face with the Crime*). Source: Screenshot, Ascot Elite Home Entertainment.

has claimed, the decision to open the series with Gorsky's apparition gives both Jelena and the audience a "glimpse at the men of the future."[2] What makes this particular man of the future different from other leading men in German crime series is that he is Jewish.

Marek Gorsky is the son of Latvian Jews who settled in Berlin after the dissolution of the Soviet Union in the early 1990s, and Graf's series brings its viewers into repeated contact with the post-Soviet Jewish milieu, from the large family gathering in the first episode to the humble shoe-repair shop run by the benevolent Ukrainian "Uncle" Sascha (Ryszard Ronczewski) to observations of the Sabbath and visits to the Jewish cemetery at Berlin Weißensee. By showing how post-Soviet Jews navigate a myriad of spaces, relations, and languages in postunification Berlin, Graf and screenwriter Rolf Basedow draw inspiration from contemporary Jewish life in the German capital, where Jews are more likely to hail from the former Soviet Union than anywhere else.[3] Basedow has cited Gorsky's Jewish migrant background as the spark of inspiration for the screenplay, and Graf has repeatedly claimed that the figure of Marek Gorsky as a young policeman who is not "ethnically German, but Jewish-Latvian" was what drew him to Basedow's screenplay in the first place.[4] Despite the series' deliberate marking of Jewishness and the creators' stated desire to present viewers with a new type of protagonist for the crime genre (a genre that has been historically devoid of Jewish characters, especially when it comes to depicting police), existing reviews and scholarly analyses of *Face to Face with the Crime* tend to ignore or gloss over the representation of Jewishness in the series.[5] More often than not, reviews in the press focus on the conflicts and connections between the world of the police, which is coded as German, and the world of the criminals, which is coded as Russian, despite the fact that the series depicts the world of organized crime as a mixture of ethnicities, all of them Eastern—Russian, Turkish, Ukrainian, Vietnamese—yet fully supported by German money. German film scholars Britta Hartmann and Peter Körte rather anxiously write about the series as if it were an exposé on the criminal underworld in Berlin. Körte admits that it gave him a more jaded view of his home city, and Hartmann ends her analysis of urban spaces in the series with the ominous claim that Berlin's "*inner erosion* is hiding beneath the surface."[6] Even Brad Prager's nuanced reading of Graf's miniseries delivers a surprisingly dismissive interpretation of Gorsky's Jewish identity, which Prager reads as "primarily an ornamental factor meant to differentiate him from the non-Jewish criminals he is fighting" and "to underscore . . . his general desire to respect the law."[7] Gorsky's Jewishness, thereby, becomes a one-dimensional adherence to ritual, which in turn becomes a symbol for his work in law enforcement.

In contrast to existing scholarship on Graf's miniseries, this essay engages with its multilayered figurations of Jewishness, looking primarily at Marek Gorsky himself but also at the representation of his elder sister, Stella (Marie Bäumer), and of Uncle Sascha in order to show how Basedow and Graf mobilize both historical and contemporary narratives of European Jewishness in order to pose critical questions about Germany's future. The reading of Gorsky I offer serves to both correct and explain why previous analyses of Graf's series dismiss or ignore Gorsky's Jewishness. It does so by arguing that Jewish masculinity in the form of the "muscle Jew" gets reconstructed in the figure of Gorsky, whose taut body and unshakable demeanor recall the "elegant posture, decisive confidence, and most of all, physical strength" promoted by Zionist thinkers like Max Nordau and Theodor Herzl and embodied by German-Jewish athletes and soldiers around the turn of the last century.[8] Meant at the time to serve as an antidote to the "weak, frail," and feminized Jew of the European Diaspora, the image of the muscle Jew provided hope for those who were, to quote Moshe Zimmermann, "looking for new horizons for Jewish life" beyond the increasingly anti-Semitic political and social climate of late nineteenth-century Europe.[9] And yet, as Todd Presner argues, Jewish "physical rejuvenation cannot in any way be limited to a Zionist project"; rather, the vision of a muscle Jew was part of "multiple discourses concerning the corporeal politics of regeneration" that often supported the German nationalist project.[10] Graf's series gives voice to contemporary German anxieties regarding the "inner erosion" (to recall Hartmann's formulation) of the newly unified nation due to the influx of large migrant populations, particularly from the former Soviet Union, but it also posits the idea that the future of Germany depends on people like Gorsky, who have migrant backgrounds yet can successfully and convincingly assimilate into German culture. As I will show (and I suspect that this is one reason that scholars like Prager are reluctant to give Gorsky's Jewishness too much emphasis), in the final episodes of the series Gorsky's Jewishness completely fades from view, and he is repeatedly called "the German man." By staging Gorsky's assimilation, the miniseries hints that, if post-Soviet Jews relinquish certain elements of their Eastern identities and embrace their civic responsibilities, they can become model Germans for the new millennium—Germans who can in turn rescue newer Eastern migrants, like the noble Ukrainian prostitute Jelena, from crime and corruption.

While an interpretation of Graf's series through the figure of the muscle Jew may end with a full integration of the post-Soviet Jewish man into the German nation, an alternate reading of the crime drama contends with figures who are less easily assimilated: Gorsky's sister, Stella, and the mischievous-yet-principled family friend, Uncle Sascha. Stella's ability to play both the "Jewish mama" while in her family's apartment and the cunning wife of the Russian Mafia boss Mischa (Mišel Matičević) when viewed alongside her affectionate yet antagonistic relationship with her younger brother allows her to expose the conflicts that exist between Jewish and non-Jewish Russians and to maintain an ambivalent position in regard to German culture. As a self-proclaimed and proud "Jew from Odessa," Uncle Sascha at first seems like an old jokester, and yet as the series progresses, he is revealed to be an influential figure within the world of organized crime, one who can sit in judgment over the warring Mafia bosses and police them from the inside. Both Uncle Sascha, as a Jew and former street bandit from Odessa, and Stella, who manages the restaurant Odessa as a legitimate cover for her husband's illegal activities, evoke a different historical image of Eastern European Jewry: that of Old Odessa, a city where Jewish thieves and rogues thrived.[11] By weaving the myth of Old Odessa as a city of Jews and a city of sin with that of Berlin, a city that still likes to flaunt its reputation as a modern Babylon, *Face to Face with the Crime* offers viewers a more playful view of the German capital—of, in Graf's words, a "less inhibited German world, . . . a dream world of gangsters with an attitude and a code of honour that never existed."[12] To look at multilayered representations of Jews, therefore, is to present Graf's miniseries not simply as a sociological study of post-Soviet migrant populations in Berlin and the competing familial and cultural allegiances with which they struggle but also as a more fantastical representation of lovers, siblings, heroes, and antiheroes that weaves a rich tapestry of Russian, German, and Jewish stories and histories.

The Muscle Jew Saves Germany

In a 1903 article published in the *Juedische Turnzeitung* (*Journal of Jewish Gymnastics*), the physician, writer, and cultural critic Max Nordau praises the Berlin Jewish gymnastic club for naming itself after the leader of an ancient Jewish revolt, Bar Kokhba, "a hero who refused to know defeat." Nordau repeats his 1898 call for the creation of "a Jewry of muscles" and calls on his readers to become like Bar Kokhba and "once more become deep chested, sturdy, sharp-eyed men."[13] By strengthening their bodies, honing their reflexes, and hardening their resolve, a Jewry of muscles could remedy the adverse effects of life in modern Europe, a life that deprived them of "light, air, water and earth" and made them into weak, timid, "unmanly" beings who were often blamed for the physical, mental, and moral decline, or "degeneration," of European culture.[14] Increased physical strength and masculine prowess would ready Jewish men for the Zionist project of leaving Europe and settling in Palestine, but paradoxically, in its praise of sunlight and toned bodies, the ideal of the muscle Jew also helped them conform to German ideals of masculinity and contribute to the project of building a strong German nation.[15] Germans and Jews of the nineteenth century embraced the idea of healthy corporeality as a means toward both individual and national regeneration; as Presner cogently states, "Strong, robust, and vital individuals would form a strong, robust, and vital body politic."[16] The idea of the muscle Jew is, therefore, as much about assimilation into German culture as it is about separation from it; indeed, Nordau, its main advocate, was himself an assimilated Jew who embodied the desire both to belong to German culture and to leave it, and his works reveal what Jay Geller has aptly called "the irresolvable antinomy between assimilationist desire and anti-Semitic repudiation."[17] While the muscle Jew as German patriot—both real and imagined—reached his pinnacle in the First World War and continued to resonate throughout the Weimar Republic, the era of the muscle Jew ended definitively with the rise of National Socialism and the murder of European Jews in the Shoah. In their study *Jewish Masculinities*, Paul Lerner, Benjamin Maria Baader, and Sharon Gillerman contend that Nazis' disenfranchisement and defamation of Jews, followed by their deportation and death, could be seen as a "systematic emasculation of Jewish men."[18] This emasculated image of Jewish men has had tremendous staying power in postwar and even post-Wall German visual culture, in which viewers are much more likely to find images of Jewish men as victims of Nazi persecution or, in more recent years, as figures of comic relief or as bookish, feminized objects of desire. While muscle Jews abound in Israeli visual culture, the muscle Jew was absent from German visual culture until Graf's *Face to Face with the Crime* premiered at the Berlin Film Festival in 2010.[19]

As the main protagonist and hero of Graf's crime series, Marek Gorsky has all the qualities of the muscle Jew: he is alert and quick to act; he is physically agile with a chiseled body and penetrating blue-gray eyes. In his role as a policeman, he always manages to outrun his more lumbering German partner, Sven Lottner (Ronald Zehrfeld), a charming East Berliner who provides welcome moments of comic relief to counter Gorsky's earnestness. In his role as the son of Latvian Jewish immigrants, he shows his devotion to family religious rituals and to the memory of his murdered brother, Grischa (Kai Michael Müller), who was shot ten years before the action of the series begins. There is perhaps no better representation of Gorsky as a muscle Jew than the image of him mourning at Grischa's grave in the Jewish cemetery at Berlin Weißensee, wearing a yarmulke and a short-sleeved shirt that accentuates his biceps. At the start of the series, Gorsky nimbly moves between spaces, social configurations, and languages. His language of choice is German with a Berlin accent, a mode of expression that shows his allegiance to his home city and allows him to establish a convincing buddy dynamic with partner Lottner, a key element of most police crime series. In the course of the first episode, however, we also see Gorsky praying in Hebrew at the family dinner table, and we hear him speak in fluent Russian at a Berlin club frequented by the Mafia brigades. The arrest sequence that introduces viewers to Gorsky cannily reveals all three of his linguistic and ethnic allegiances: when Gorsky and his team of cops enter the apartment of a Russian immigrant family, the camera cuts repeatedly to a close-up of Gorsky, who listens intently to the Russian parents and gleans valuable information about their son's whereabouts; when the younger son, Boris, pulls out a pistol and points it at Gorsky, he quickly yet calmly disarms the boy and just as quickly gives him a slap in the face. The brief confrontation with the armed boy, however, triggers the first of many flashbacks tinted in red—flashbacks that give viewers glimpses of Marek, Stella, and Grischa as teens. Although most of the red flashbacks show Grischa's grim death at the hands of the Ukrainian gangster Sergij Sokolov (Georgiy Povolotsiy), this first flashback focuses more on the siblings' dynamic as Stella points disapprovingly at Grischa while he cavalierly plays with a handgun. This is the only flashback that is set in the Gorskys' home, and it subtly yet clearly marks the family as Jewish long before we see them praying and mourning together. It does so by showing extinguished Sabbath candles and a candleholder with Hebrew letters on the living room table in front of Grischa, and when Grischa places his pistol on the table next to the candles, the camera zooms in on the two discordant objects. Then the flashback ends abruptly. Marek Gorsky is, therefore, marked as a Russian-speaking Jew from the start of the series just as much as he is marked as German. His story starts as one of successful acculturation; he seems to live easily in German culture, while he continues to observe Jewish customs and speak other languages (Hebrew and Russian).

As Graf's series progresses, however, Gorsky's allegiance to his Jewish family becomes increasingly intertwined with his work as a German police officer, causing tension between him and Stella yet moving him closer to the truth about Grischa's murder. To be a policeman is, in the eyes of both the Jewish and Russian characters in the series, to be a *Mussar*, an epithet meaning "trash." Gorsky is therefore treated with great mistrust and disrespect by extended family members and acquaintances, and even his mother and sister lament his choice of profession. The series' thematization of ethnic belonging, family loyalty, personal revenge, and codes of honor on both sides of the law allows it to expand the crime genre to include elements of the family drama and the gangster story

Figure 12.2. Gorsky visits his brother's grave. Source: Screenshot, Ascot Elite Home Entertainment.

that, by Graf's own admission, pay homage to Francis Ford Coppola's *Godfather* films from the 1970s as much as they reference gritty U.S. police series like *Hill Street Blues* (Bochco and Kozoll, 1981–1987) and *NYPD Blue* (Bochco and Milch, 1993–2005).[20] Film and media scholars like Kathrin Rothemund therefore classify *Face to Face with the Crime* as "complex crime," a mixed genre that mediates "between traditional television crime fiction and the . . . gangster's world presented on the big screen."[21] Gorsky, too, must mediate between his own desire to avenge Grischa's death and his chance to fight organized crime as a member of Berlin's State Bureau of Investigation (*Landeskriminalamt*, or LKA). He does his best work when these two goals align, as they do in the pursuit of Sokolov, who is both Grischa's murderer and one of the LKA's prime targets.

Through multiple scenes that show Gorsky reaching out to other Jewish characters—visiting his parents on the Sabbath, finding Grischa's ex-lover Lisa, going to Uncle Sascha's shoe-repair shop—in order to connect Grischa's murder to Sokolov, Graf and Basedow lure viewers into thinking that Gorsky can reconcile his police work with his Jewishness. And yet the conversations he has in these scenes indicate an increasing alienation from the Jewish world of his family and the strengthening of his allegiance to the state due to his role as policeman and hence a civil servant. For example, after Grischa's former girlfriend Lisa (Valery Tscheplanowa) gives Gorsky her eyewitness account of Grischa's murder, she talks in a bittersweet tone about how she found peace after his death, stating "I married a goy." The camera jumps briefly to Gorsky, who throws up his hands in a gesture of bemused resignation, and Lisa continues, "You're a cop. I'm a nurse. We both do something useful. That counts for something." Although the

Figure 12.3. The muscle Jew, naked and armed, emerges into the sunlight as the "German man." Source: Screenshot, Ascot Elite Home Entertainment.

conversation between Lisa and Gorsky alternates between Russian and German, Lisa delivers these lines in German. More than any other scene in the series, this one makes a case for Jewish assimilation that goes back to European Enlightenment pleas for the legal emancipation of the Jews—to what Presner describes as "the normalization of [Jewish] participation in civil society" and "the overcoming of Jewish particularity through intermarriage, conversion, and assimilation."[22] Presner presents the eighteenth-century writings of German thinkers like Christian Wilhelm von Dohm as providing the ideological foundation for the muscle Jew and the project of regeneration the figure embodies, for Dohm argued that "the Jews . . . will fulfill the obligation to defend the society which has given them equal rights," and that they will exhibit "the good will, also the soldierly courage and physical fitness" required to defend German society.[23] As a nurse, Lisa works to improve the health of German residents and citizens, while as a cop, Gorsky restores the "social equilibrium" of the state by fighting organized crime.[24] Engaging in this fight means first concealing, then ultimately relinquishing, his Jewishness.

The interpretation of Marek Gorsky as a muscle Jew who saves Germans from Russian invaders is such a compelling one because of the way in which Graf's series represents physical bodies, particularly men's bodies, and also because it reanimates the idea of the German body politic fighting criminal invasion. With very few exceptions, the Russian Mafiosi are depicted as lean and muscular fighters (Stella's husband, Mischa, trains in the boxing ring, while his wolfish antagonist Andrej is pictured jogging), while the Germans tend to range from paunchy (the corrupt policeman Hollmann) to obese (the decadent, corrupt investor Lenz is repeatedly called "Fat Lenz"). Even the sympathetic Lottner is too rotund for his bulletproof vest and gets shot in the exposed ring of flesh in the final showdown with Sokolov. Only Gorsky's sinewy body comes close to those of the Russian crime bosses, which is why the camera focuses on him during a key moment in a racially tinged motivational speech given in episode four by the head of the LKA, Nico Roeber (Arvid Birnbaum). Disheartened by a failed arrest, Roeber prods his team into action by offering them a vision of their own demise as Germans. Employing the rhetoric of degeneration, Roeber says of the Mafia bosses, "In their eyes, it looks like we Germans are a dying breed. . . . We're dumb German money. They're the victors, the proud barbarians. They've inundated our country." As Roeber speaks these lines, the images shown onscreen alternate between midrange shots of Roeber's face in front of a map of Berlin with photographs of wanted criminals like Sokolov and shots of the criminals themselves, some of them reveling—dancing, womanizing, snorting cocaine—in their corrupt lifestyles and some of them living a seemingly respectable life in luxury villas with their wives and children. As Roeber delivers the following lines, however, the camera hones in on Gorsky: "They're superior to us in their will to live and their strength." The darkened background of this shot serves to accentuate Gorsky's defiant gaze and strong jawline, therefore representing him as the one person in the room who could prove Roeber wrong. The muscle Jew saves Germany, but in so doing, he must embody the impenetrable, potentially violent masculinity that is so often coupled with nationalist chauvinism.[25]

With Roeber's monologue, Graf's series gives a voice to contemporary German xenophobic fears by reinvigorating nineteenth- and early twentieth-century anxieties regarding degeneration and invasion. The journalists Katja Nicodemus and Christof Siemes aptly refer to Roeber's tirade as a "blood and soil speech" reminiscent of fascist rhetoric, and they ask Graf whether or not he thinks that the speech's "drastic" nature undermines the more complex narrative of the series.[26] Graf's answer is, on the one hand, naïve: he claims that Roeber's speech does not constitute an "ethnic generalization" about Russians. And yet the series repeatedly indulges in ethnic generalizations and offensive stereotypes, especially in its representations of Eastern Others like the Turks (who are portrayed as lascivious and brutal) and the Vietnamese cigarette smugglers (who are either feminized dandies or destitute street peddlers referred to by the Russians as the "Vietcong"). On the other hand, Graf conveys to his interviewers what he thinks is the main message of the scene: the police are supposed to see through the façade of the Mafia bosses as respectable businessmen and see them instead as an existential threat. His answer—more than the scene itself—reveals the "double bind" inherent to assimilation, in which the host culture demands that foreign Others erase all traces of their difference, and yet the host culture assumes that the foreign others want to destroy the host culture from inside; that these Others are, to quote Geller, "constitutionally incapable of eliminating their difference."[27] *Face to Face with the Crime*, I would argue, wrestles with questions of assimilation, taking great pains to present Gorsky as someone who can—and even should—assimilate successfully into German culture. Perhaps his Jewishness makes this easier; certainly the German state has deliberately tried to make Jewish migration to and integration into German society as smooth as possible, and it has thrown up fewer barriers to Jewish migrants than to any other migrant group to post-Wall Germany.[28] Unlike the Russian criminals, for whom the idea of learning German is a running joke, Gorsky speaks the language. But like many of the Russian men, he is young, strong, and virile (most of the Germans in the series are childless, while the Russian Mafia bosses are repeatedly shown with their many children) and can therefore carry the hope of regeneration for a German nation with an aging population and low birthrate.[29]

The hope that Gorsky will be both a warrior for the German nation and a fertile father becomes manifest, rather ironically, in his love relationship with the Ukrainian Jelena, who consistently refers to him as "a real man" and "a German man." Despite her inside knowledge of Berlin's criminal underworld and the German investors, like Heinrich Lenz (Bernd Stegemann), who keep it running, Jelena holds fast to the idea that "Berlin is paradise" and to her desire to learn German and settle down with Gorsky. She is a model migrant: hard-working, ready and willing to learn the language of the host culture, and eager to start a family. It is also Jelena's insistence upon saving her friend Svetlana (Katharina Nesytowa) from sexual enslavement in Belarus that prompts Gorsky to prove his muscular masculinity beyond German borders. In the penultimate episode of the series, he frees Svetlana from a roadside brothel and fights one of her captors to the death in a harrowing nighttime scene punctuated by flashes of lightning. The motif of the woodland lake at the Eastern edge of Europe returns again—first as a scene of nightmarish violence, and then as a site of rebirth. After Gorsky strangles and drowns their pursuer, Gorsky, Jelena, and Svetlana swim to safety and hide in a fishing shack until the next day, when Gorsky emerges from the shack into the bright sunlight, naked and armed with a pistol. He then drives to town, and as a self-proclaimed German, he wrests Svetlana's passport from the corrupt chief of police. The film scholar Felix Lenz reads Gorsky's "existential nakedness" alongside Graf's use of "the essential elements of fire, water, earth, and air" in the scene at the Belorussian lake as signs of "metamorphoses from guilt to innocence, from old to new life."[30] The struggle to the death in the Belorussian stream becomes Gorsky's baptism; hence his rebirth as the "German man." In this episode and the final one, in which Gorsky once again proves his mettle by apprehending Sokolov, no more mention is made of his Jewishness.

Why do all traces of Gorsky's Jewishness disappear? I think there are several viable explanations, and the first has to do with the world of mainstream German crime television. By so clearly staging Gorsky's assimilation, Graf's work reveals the limitations of the television crime series when it comes to portraying

Germany as a multiethnic society. As Michelle Mattson argues in her groundbreaking essay on the most popular and longest-lasting German television crime series in history, *Tatort* (*Scene of the Crime*), "Acknowledgment and acceptance of ethnic diversity . . . goes only so far. . . . The conventional wisdom of *Tatort*'s producers seems to be that the German public will tolerate social plurality only insofar as the *foreigner* has successfully completed the process of social integration or is actively attempting to do so."[31] Placing German characters' anxieties about their own future alongside Jelena's dream vision of Gorsky as her lover and the German capital as paradise, Graf's series seems, at first glance, to follow the model that Mattson describes. But *Face to Face with the Crime* is not *Tatort*, despite the fact that it aired on the same public television channel (ARD) in the popular Friday evening time slot usually reserved for *Tatort* reruns.[32] In its depiction of complex familial and ethnic dynamics, and with its multiple, interlocking plotlines, *Face to Face with the Crime* is more than a police series, and it delivers something other than a plea for German integration. Indeed it offers at best a nebulous sense—and at worst an empty view—of what it means to be German in 2010. Gorsky's sister, Stella, gives the most striking example of the use of "German" as an empty category. When Gorsky is forced to take part in a police raid of the Odessa restaurant and then has the uncomfortable task of scrutinizing the papers and belongings of his sister and her husband, Mischa, Stella breaks into tears and issues Gorsky a string of accusations: he does not adhere to Jewish rituals nor does he have any Jewish friends; he may speak Russian but he is not Russian; he is "somehow just German." Stella's stinging indictment of Gorsky is also an indictment of assimilationist politics as a process that alienates the migrant from his first language, his religion, and his family. By depicting Gorsky as a muscle Jew who becomes a model German, I would argue that Graf's series can be seen as an example of just how much post-Wall Germany has relied on Jewish stories in order to develop its own sense of itself as a nation.[33] What the series also does, however, is tell stories that push back against assimilationist and German-centric narratives.

Face to Face with the Crime ultimately leaves viewers with open questions, one of which is the same question that Lottner poses in his final lines: after being shot by Sokolov, Lottner lies in an ambulance with Gorsky by his side. As the ambulance races back to Berlin, the audience sees an aerial, nighttime shot of Berlin and hears Lottner's voiceover saying, "I read that in one hundred years there will be only ten million Germans. Can you imagine what it will look like here?" Instead of indulging the anti-Russian sentiment that might hide behind his partner's question, Gorsky looks quizzically at Lottner and says, "We'll see." The vagueness of his answer captures the ambivalence of the series and hints at a future notion of Germanness that will "decouple German ethnicity from national belonging."[34] After all, its most German characters are those who are often cast as outsiders, the Jew (Gorsky), the Ukrainian (Jelena), and the East

German (Lottner). Gorsky's own final words of the series, uttered to an impatient Jelena who wants desperately to end up with the hero in her underwater vision, are "There is a time for everything." The exhaustion in his face in this final scene, paired with the inscrutable gaze with which he stares into the camera in the closing shot, lead viewers to wonder if the burden of the muscle Jew and new German hero isn't just too much to bear.[35] At the same time his sentence, underscored as it is by the more hopeful, nondiegetic music that usually plays when Gorsky and Jelena lock eyes, implies that there is a future for them in the German capital and that it will be one that includes multiple stories of Eastern European migration, some of which are Jewish.

Old Odessa in Berlin: Honor among Thieves

To conclude this essay as the series does, with Gorsky as the ambivalent hero gazing into an equally ambivalent German future, would be to forget that there is at least one other Jewish hero in Graf's series: Uncle Sascha. It is Uncle Sascha, not Gorsky, who has the power within the world of organized crime to save Jelena from Andrej and issue a stern admonishment to her pimp, Kolja. It is Uncle Sascha who, flanked by two other silent Mafia bosses, sits in judgment over Andrej in the final episode and decides whether he should live or die. Sascha's final scene takes place in the back room of a sleek, high-end restaurant and reveals to the viewer once and for all what the series hinted at from the start—that Uncle Sascha, a former street bandit from Odessa, commands the highest respect by working to preserve honor and counter unbridled greed within the world of the Russian Mafia. Sascha is a ubiquitous character in the series, appearing first at the Gorsky family's table and joining them in mourning Grischa, while also telling patriotic anecdotes about the Soviet victory over the Nazis. In subsequent episodes he is shown at tables in both Mischa and Stella's Restaurant Odessa and the Italian restaurant frequented by Andrej (a clear nod to the Italian Mafia), and when he takes Jelena in, viewers see his elegant yet austere apartment. But the space associated most closely with Sascha is his humble shoe-repair shop that is covered, from floor to ceiling, with the shoes of those who came to Germany from the former Soviet Union and who have either died, like Grischa, or abandoned their shoes, like Gorsky. The abandoned shoes are a striking reminder of the painful history of the Jewish Diaspora, but the figure of Sascha eschews any hint of victimization.

In a key scene in episode three, Stella seeks marital advice from Sascha and visits him in his repair shop. As she enters the room, she runs her fingertips over some of the shoes and boots that hang from the ceiling and inhales, remarking in Yiddish on the good smell of the leather. The camera remains in motion throughout the scene, zooming in to show close-ups of Sascha's tattoos, some of which mark him as a former bandit and others that mark his Soviet background—but

Figure 12.4. Ryszard Ronczewski as Uncle Sascha and Sascha Alexander Gersak as Kolja in *Im Angesicht des Verbrechens* (*Face to Face with the Crime*). Source: Screenshot, Ascot Elite Home Entertainment.

none of which evokes the suffering of the Shoah. German viewers who might be conditioned to expect concentration camp tattoos on Jewish figures find signs of other Eastern European Jewish identities instead. As Sascha talks proudly about being a Jew from Odessa, the camera zooms in to the old photographs behind him on the wall: a mix of framed images showing bearded Jewish elders in traditional dress next to headshots of a younger Sascha and an unidentified man wearing a driving cap and leather vest, all of which hang next to a German advertisement for a riding expo during the Christian holiday of Pentecost. Just as pronounced as the mixture of visual images is Graf's use of a cacophony of languages and sounds; Stella and Sascha speak in Yiddish, Russian, and for most of the scene, in accented German, while the upbeat diegetic folk music that plays in the shop mixes with the more somber tones of the series' score. The dialogue, too, is a jumble of reminiscences and laments. Sascha contrasts those who live by the law with those who display an insatiable hunger for money, and Stella poses a question that seems, at first, to be a non sequitur: "Am I living in a den of thieves?" While this question is a meant to be a veiled reference to her marriage to Mischa, the fact that it is posed in Sascha's repair shop allows it to refer to the world of honorable thieves that he represents. When taken in the context of Sascha's clear association with the city of Odessa, the shop becomes—much like the restaurant that Stella and Mischa run—a space for Old Odessa to live on in today's Berlin. As Jarrod Tanny shows in his vibrant study of the Ukrainian city, "Old Odessa was alone in having the Jewish gangster crowned king." It was the early twentieth-century fiction of Isaac Babel that sealed the image of Odessa as a "city of swashbuckling Jewish swindlers and sinners, who all at once embodied the physical strength, revelry, and wit" for which the city was known, a "myth that survived the twentieth century and continues to flourish today."[36] In his extended interview with Johannes Sievert, Graf makes explicit reference to Babel's work and the Jewish gangsters that populate them, and he states that he was intrigued to learn about networks of real Jewish gangsters in Odessa that existed from the early twentieth century, through the Second World War and the Soviet era. This type of Jewish story, one that persists despite the Shoah, he claims, "is what makes it so special and particularly important for Germany—tricky and ambivalent. But also exciting and funny, provocative. And I like the idea of telling stories about Russian-Jewish gangsters, here and now in Germany."[37] The list of adjectives Graf uses to describe his own project—ambivalent, tricky, exciting, funny, provocative—are ones that could also describe the rebuilding of Jewish life in postunification Germany, particularly within the cultural realm. These adjectives articulate the possibility that twenty-first-century German culture will embrace a cacophony of Jewish stories embracing humor and alternative codes of honor as well as other national, ethnic, and familial affinities. It also suggests that this will allow them to clash or mix with the narratives of mourning and remembrance that have been so central to the narrative about Jews and Germans since 1990. In so doing, German culture might just reflect the vibrancy of Jewish culture in today's Berlin and learn to revel in the sound of German with an accent.

NOTES

1. *Im Angesicht des Verbrechens* (*Face to Face with the Crime*), DVD, directed by Dominik Graf (2010; Regensburg, Germany: MFA+ Film Distribution, 2012). All translations from the German are based on the English subtitles provided in the DVD, with slight alterations of my own. The miniseries is composed of ten fifty-minute episodes, and Jelena's opening line is always included in the recap before each new episode.

2. Interview with Dominik Graf in *Dominik Graf, Im Angesicht des Verbrechens, Fernseharbeit am Beispiel einer Serie*, ed. Johannes F. Sievert (Berlin: Alexander Verlag, 2010), 47. Unless indicated otherwise, all translations from the German are mine.

3. As Jeffrey M. Peck documents in his 2006 book *Being Jewish in the New Germany* (New Brunswick, N.J.: Rutgers University Press), "85% of the Jewish population in Germany is from the former Soviet Union," with the majority of migrants hailing from Russia, Ukraine, and the Baltic States (41). Recent ethnological work estimates that twenty-five thousand Jews live in Berlin. That said, exact numbers for the Jewish population in Berlin are hard to find due to the fact that many Jews from the former Soviet Union do not define Jewishness in a strictly religious sense and therefore do not subscribe to the traditional matrilineal definition (halacha) of Jewishness. The Central Council of Jews in Germany claims that in 2016 the Jewish community of Berlin had fewer than ten thousand members, but recent studies argue that fewer than 50 percent of the approximately two hundred thousand Jews who live in Germany officially belong to the Jewish community. See Alina Gromova, "A City of Mind: Berlin in the Perception of Young Russian-Speaking Jewish Migrants," in *Contemporary Jewish Reality in Germany and Its Reflection in Film*, ed. Claudia Simone Dorchain and Felice Naomi Wonnenberg (Berlin: de Gruyter, 2012), 73; "Gemeinden," Zentralrat

der Juden in Deutschland, accessed 8 March 2018, https://www.zentralratderjuden.de/vor-ort/gemeinden/; and Karen Körber, ed., *Russisch-jüdische Gegenwart in Deutschland: Interdisziplinäre Perspektiven auf eine Diaspora im Wandel* (Göttingen: Vandenhoek & Ruprecht, 2015), 2.

4. Graf in Sievert, *Dominik Graf*, 48–49; Basedow in Sievert, *Dominik Graf*, 222–223. See also Katja Nicodemus and Christof Siemes, "Bei den Russen ist da dieser Stolz," Interview with Dominik Graf, *Die Zeit*, April 15, 2010. Graf and Basedow began working together in the 1990s on single episodes of popular German crimes series such as *Der Fahnder* (The detective) and *Polizeiruf 110* (Police emergency 110), and Graf filmed Basedow's feature-length milieu study of a small-time pimp in Berlin in *Hotte im Paradies* (Hotte in paradise; 2002) and his sociocritical profile of Leipzig, *Eine Stadt wird erpresst* (A city gets blackmailed; 2006). For Graf's filmography and documentation of his work with Basedow, see Chris Wahl, Marco Abel, Jesko Jockenhövel, and Michael Wedel, eds., *Im Angesicht des Fernsehens: Der Filmemacher Dominik Graf* (Munich: edition text + kritik, 2012), 316–332. I deliberately refer to Marek Gorsky as "Gorsky" throughout this essay, in keeping with the crime genre convention of referring to police by their last names. I often use his full name when discussing his place in familial dynamics.

5. In her comprehensive survey of crime fiction in German, Katharina Hall deliberately points to "the lacuna of Jewish-German crime fiction," meaning that neither crime fiction authors nor their main characters are Jews. Katharina Hall, ed., *Crime Fiction in German: Der Krimi* (Cardiff: University of Wales Press, 2016), 22, 26. This lacuna exists in the visual medium as well.

6. Britta Hartmann, "'Berlin ist das Paradies:' Inszenierung der Stadt" in Dominik Grafs *Im Angesicht des Verbrechens*; Thomas Arslans, "Im Schatten," in *Die Lust am Genre. Verbrechergeschichten aus Deutschland*, ed. Rainer Rother and Julia Pattis (Berlin: Bertz + Fischer, 2011), 169–186, here 180 (emphasis added); and Peter Körte, "Schichten und Geschichten einer Stadt," in *Dominik Graf*, 308–313.

7. Brad Prager, "Gegenspieler und innere Dämonen: Dominik Grafs *Im Angesicht des Verbrechens*," in *Im Angesicht des Fernsehens*, ed. Wahl et al., 215–237, here 221.

8. Todd Samuel Presner, *Muscular Judaism: The Jewish Body and the Politics of Regeneration* (London: Routledge, 2007), 59.

9. Moshe Zimmermann, "Muscle Jews versus Nervous Jews," in *Emancipation through Muscles: Jews and Sports in Europe*, ed. Michael Brenner and Gideon Reuveni (Lincoln: University of Nebraska Press, 2006), 13–26, here 13 and 24. On the Jewish male body as feminized, see Sander Gilman, "The Construction of the Male Jew," in *Freud, Race, and Gender* (Princeton, N.J.: Princeton University Press, 1993), 49–92.

10. Presner, *Muscular Judaism*, 4, 14. See also xxiii, xxiv, 19, 34, and 190. As Daniel Boyarin argues, the masculinization of the Jewish man was part of his "Westernization," his abandonment of a gentler form of manhood (the *mentsh*) in exchange for the ideal of the muscle Jew, "a figure almost identical to his 'Aryan' confrers." See Daniel Boyarin, *Unheroic Conduct: The Rise of Heterosexuality and the Invention of the Jewish Man* (Berkeley: University of California Press, 1997), 37.

11. Jarrod Tanny, *City of Rogues and Schnorrers: Russia's Jews and the Myth of Old Odessa* (Bloomington: Indiana University Press, 2011).

12. Graf, in Marco Abel, "'I Build a Jigsaw Puzzle of a Dream-Germany': An Interview with German Filmmaker Dominik Graf," *Senses of Cinema* 55 (July–September 2010), http://sensesofcinema.com/2010/feature-articles/%E2%80%9C%E2%80%98i-build-a-jigsaw-puzzle-of-a-dream-germany%E2%80%99-an-interview-with-german-filmmaker-dominik-graf%E2%80%9D-2/. On the myth of Berlin as Babylon, particularly the clichéd representation of Berlin as the "Whore of Babylon," see Jill Suzanne Smith, *Berlin Coquette: Prostitution and the New German Woman, 1890–1933* (Ithaca, N.Y.: Cornell University Press, 2013), 3, 192. On Old Odessa as Babylon, see Tanny, *City of Rogues and Schnorrers*, 6.

13. Max Nordau, "Muskeljudentum," *Juedische Turnzeitung* (June 1903) and republished in Nordau, *Zionistische Schriften* (Cologne: Juedischer Verlag, 1909), 379–381. This article also appears as "Jewry of Muscle," trans. J. Hessing in *The Jew in the Modern World: A Documentary History*, ed. Paul Mendes-Flohr and Jehuda Reinharz, 3rd ed. (New York: Oxford University Press, 2011), 616–617.

14. Nordau, "Jewry of Muscle," 616; John M. Efron, "The Jewish Body Degenerate?," in *Medicine and the German Jews: A History* (New Haven, Conn.: Yale University Press, 2001), 143, 149. On the concept of "degeneration" and its widespread usage in nineteenth and twentieth-century Europe, see Daniel Pick, *Faces of Degeneration: A European Disorder, c.1848–c. 1918* (Cambridge: Cambridge University Press, 1989).

15. Efron, *Medicine and the German Jews*, 149. See also Presner, *Muscular Judaism*, 201.

16. Presner, 26.

17. Jay Geller, "The Conventional Lies and Paradoxes of Jewish Assimilation: Max Nordau's Pre-Zionist Answer to the Jewish Question," *Jewish Social Studies* 1, no. 3 (Spring 1995): 129–160, here 144.

18. Paul Lerner, Benjamin Maria Baader, and Sharon Gillerman, "German Jews, Gender, and History," in *Jewish Masculinities: German Jews, Gender, and History* (Bloomington: Indiana University Press, 2012), 14.

19. On comic figures in postunification Jewish film, see Jill Suzanne Smith, "Reviving German-Jewish Comedy: Dani Levy's Family Farce *Go for Zucker!*" *Journal of Modern Jewish Studies* 13, no. 2 (July 2014): 231–248. On Jewish men as romantic interests in contemporary German visual culture, see Lea Wohl von Haselberg, "Between *Self* and *Other*: Representations of Mixed Relationships in Contemporary German Film and Television," in *Contemporary Jewish Reality*, 85–98. For discussions of the muscle Jew as central to the representation of Israeli masculinity in visual art and film, see Presner, *Muscular Judaism*, xv–xxiv, and Felice Naomi Wonnenberg, "Sissy and the Muscle-Jew Go to the Movies: The Image of the Jewish Man in Film after 1945 and Its Reception in Germany" in, *Contemporary Jewish Reality*, 205–230.

20. Graf in Sievert, *Dominik Graf*, 38 (on *The Godfather*), 45 (on *Hill Street Blues* and *NYPD Blue*); see also Graf's interview with Abel, "Jigsaw Puzzle," and Christian Buß, "Berliner Mafia-Saga im TV. Von Bullen und anderen Schweinen," *Spiegel* online, 27 April 2010, accessed January 2018, http://www.spiegel.de/kultur/tv/berliner-mafia-saga-im-tv-von-bullen-und-anderen-schweinen-a-691483.html.

21. Kathrin Rothemund, "Facing Complex Crime: Investigating Contemporary German Crime Fiction on Television," *Northern Lights: Film and Media Studies Yearbook* 9 (2001): 127–142, here 139. See also Abel, "Jigsaw Puzzle."

22. Presner, *Muscular Judaism*, 28.

23. Christian Wilhelm von Dohm, *Ueber die buergerliche Verbesserung der Juden* (Berlin, 1781). Translated by Helen Lederer and reprinted in excerpts as *Concerning the Amelioration of the Civil Status of the Jews* in *The Jew in the Modern World*, 27–34, here 33–34.

24. Rothemund, "Facing Complex Crime," 131.

25. There is still no better work on militant masculinity as defined through impenetrable, muscular bodies than that of Klaus Theweleit, *Male Fantasies*, trans. Stephen Conway, 2 vols. (Minneapolis: University of Minnesota Press, 1985–1989). See also Boyarin, *Unheroic Conduct*, 42, on the association of "violent physical activity" with Christian European masculinity and/or *goyim naches*, forms of behavior traditionally derided by Jews.

26. Nicodemus and Siemes, "Bei den Russen ist da dieser Stolz," Interview with Dominik Graf. All subsequent quotes by Graf in this paragraph come from this interview.

27. Geller, "The Conventional Lies and Paradoxes of Jewish Assimilation," 139–140.

28. As Körber shows, Jewish migrants who entered Germany from the former Soviet Union as "contingent refugees" fleeing economic and political turmoil as well as anti-Semitic violence starting in 1990 and running until 2005 enjoyed a privileged status compared to

other migrant groups. They could apply for German citizenship after eight years, and their entire family was able to accompany them to Germany. See Körber's essay "Zäsur, Wandel oder Neubeginn? Russischsprachige Juden in Deutschland zwischen Recht, Repräsentation und Realität," in *Russisch-jüdische Gegenwart in Deutschland*, 19.

29. Various Russian characters mockingly deliver the following line in heavily accented German in the course of the series: "Speak German, learn German. We're only guests in this country." With this line, Graf and Basedow mock the rhetoric of integration but also criticize those who do not abide by it. On Germany's declining population, see the 2015 study by the *Statistisches Bundesamt* (Federal Statistical Office): *Germany's Population by 2060*, accessed March 2018, https://www.destatis.de/EN/Publications/Specialized/Population/GermanyPopulation2060_5124206159004.pdf?__blob=publicationFile.

30. Felix Lenz, "Urelemente und Milieu. Die *Coming-of-Age*-Filme von Dominik Graf," in *Im Angesicht des Fernsehens*, 159.

31. Michelle Mattson, "*Tatort*: The Generation of Public Identity in a German Crime Series," *New German Critique* 78, Special Issue on German Media Studies (Autumn, 1999): 161–181, here 171.

32. The *Tatort* viewers did not respond especially favorably to Graf's series. After its exuberant reception at the Berlin Film Festival in February 2010, the series was aired first in April 2010 on Arte, a German-French channel known for its focus on independent films and educational programming, and then on ARD in October 2010. Viewership for the Arte broadcasts was quite strong (300,000) by that channel's standards, but the 2.1 million viewers who watched on ARD constituted disappointing numbers for the public channel. The negative comments made by the ARD viewers prompted the channel to end the series one week earlier than planned. See Chris Wahl, "Dominik Grafs Karriere als Filmemacher zwischen Kino und Fernsehen," in *Im Angesicht des Fernsehens*, 32–59, here 55–56.

33. On Germany's post-Wall aimlessness and its reliance on German-Jewish memory politics to develop a unified national identity, see Dmitrij Belkin, "Wir können Avantgarde sein: Die Zukunft des Patchwork-Judentums," in *Russisch-jüdische Gegenwart in Deutschland*, 153–161, here 154. See also Graf, who refers to Germany as a country that is "still wavering between being a Banana Republic and being the bureaucratic state par excellence," in Sievert, *Dominik Graf*, 58.

34. Lerner, Baader, and Gillerman, "German Jews, Gender, and History," 15.

35. I am not as sanguine in my interpretation of the series' ending as Prager is, who reads the ending as "optimistic" and is confident that Gorsky and Jelena will end up together. See Prager, "Gegenspieler und innere Dämonen," 237. Basedow gives the audience reason to doubt a happy end with Lottner's description of Gorsky in the first episode as "a tough nut to crack" and "not the happy ending type."

36. Tanny, *City of Rogues and Schnorrers*, 18, 3.

37. Graf in Sievert, *Dominik Graf*, 57.

CHAPTER 13

"YOU ARE MY LIBERTY"

ON THE NEGOTIATION OF HOLOCAUST AND OTHER MEMORIES FOR ISRAELIS IN BERLIN

Irit Dekel

On the river Spree, there we sat and drank when we remembered Zion.

—Avital Yomdin, *Spitz*

The young Israelis in Berlin give the impression of making their way around the city's hip districts unencumbered by history.

—Kathrin Schrader, *The Pulse of Germany*

Fascination with the Israeli Jewish migration to Germany—and specifically to Berlin—in the German and Israeli media is itself a phenomenon, and a transnational one. Media coverage peaked in 2015, on the occasion of fifty years of bilateral relations between the two countries. The Israeli media, as well as the German, has celebrated the migrants' Jewish roots and viewed them predominantly as the descendants of Holocaust victims. In both media cultures, they have been presented as part of Berlin's thriving "young creative" scene and as secular, educated Jews attracted to the inexpensive and cosmopolitan city, creating a vibrant Israeli community there. This migration occupied the national press for many months, disproportionally so in terms of its absolute size and as a percentage of global migration in these years.

In the German press, a Google search for pieces written in German reveals that between 1 January 2012 and 3 January 2018 there were about 7,450 articles on the topic of "Israelis in Berlin, migration" (and about 9,740 when the search term is "Israelis in Germany, migration"). Beginning in summer 2015, the German media's interest in this migration was constrained somewhat by increasing discussion of the refugees coming to Germany, as Ofri Ilany suggests.[1] Thereafter, articles about Israelis in Berlin or Germany shifted their focus to discussions of anti-Semitic attacks involving Jews and Israeli citizens. The Israeli press was similarly preoccupied with the phenomenon. About 5,770 articles were published in the Israeli press in Hebrew on the topic in the same timeframe. Articles about the quality of life in Germany by Israelis living there as well as think pieces about "Germans" have appeared in the Israeli media often, suggesting that this migration became a source of reference and for comparison to life in Israel. The Israeli press predominantly presented this migration as economically motivated, linking it to the "milky protest"[2] ensuing from the demonstrations of 2011 against growing social inequalities in Israel. This chapter explores how three senses, or understandings, of "liberation" function within the discourse in both Israel and Germany surrounding Israelis in Berlin.

Israeli Jews discuss economic motivations to move as often as they will present the move as liberation from the grip of the nationalistic climate in Israel. Precisely for that reason, they are also free from the Holocaust memory taught in Israel as the motive to reside in Israel—the only place where Jews are safe, experiencing their minority status as a source of freedom and comfort. They think anew their Jewish identity with respect to observing religious and ritual practices, rethinking their forms of attachment to and distance from the culture in which they are a majority. The German press, meanwhile, presents and celebrates the phenomenon as liberating from its own historical guilt over the Holocaust: that Jews chose to live and thrive in Germany is proof of Germany's transformation into an open society. Curiously, there is also a focus on how Jews enrich Berlin nightlife, a topic to which we will return.[3] As for the local Jewish community in Berlin, a certain resentment toward the migrants and their choices can be detected as represented, for example, in the *Jüdische Allgemeine* article entitled "Cheap in Berlin."[4]

Commentators on this Israeli migration to Berlin, together with the migrants themselves, use and react to the symbolic index of Holocaust memory performance available to them.[5] By "symbolic index" I am referring to the indexical association that concerns the causal or proximal relation between signified and signifier: Jews and the Holocaust. If Jews, generally, are signified by their visibility as reminders of the Holocaust and successful Holocaust memory, then the indexical relations to Jews would summon Holocaust memory and the memory of anti-Semitism or the possible danger to Jews posed by anti-Semitism.[6] A few of the artists discussed in this piece refuse these indexical relations and claim, as Max Czollek does, "Now I do not anymore play the Jew for you." This refusal can come from Jews, like Czollek, who grew up in Germany or from Jews who grew up in Israel, as in the case of Noam Brusilovsky in his 2016 audioplay "How to Recognize a Jew: An Investigation." In this respect, we must note the growing number of voices in Germany and Israel who discuss the danger of a putatively resurgent anti-Semitism that could now be directed at the Israeli Jews, following the rise of the far-right AfD (Alternative für Deutschland, Alternative for Germany) in September 2017, with a parallel fear of Muslim citizens and migrants. This mistrust of four million Muslim residents is intensified and considered justified by the rush to protect Jews and Israelis as possible victims.

I suggest that the trope of liberation is composed of three modes of interpretation, which often appear in combination:

1. Emancipation: Individuals and groups emancipate themselves from the national gaze, from economic hardship, and from lifelong narratives that bound them to modes of life they recognize as limiting.[7] Both the Israeli and German media predominantly highlight the reason for migration to Berlin as economical: Berlin is an affordable European capital, as Daniel Mosseri emphasized.[8] At the same time, the Israeli Hebrew magazine *Spitz* as well as some media coverage in Germany affirmed the claim that in Berlin, for Jewish Israelis, "one can be oneself" or be liberated from the kind of societal pressure one might have experienced "at home." This feeling of emancipation might then be extended to the possibility of experiencing other groups through, for example, having romantic relations with non-Jews and developing friendships or affinities with Palestinians as well as Muslims who, for some Israeli migrants, might be viewed as minorities with similar needs and desires, such as daily products.[9]
2. Undoing Zionism: This is sometimes framed as "returning Jews to Europe," in which the iconic relations between Tel Aviv and Berlin and the reference to "Tel Aviv on the Spree" frame the yearning for a renewed Jewish Diaspora, now *after* Israel in a spatiotemporal frame. In both the German and Israeli press, Israeli and German cultural elites present Berlin as the better, more affordable Tel Aviv, while Tel Aviv is framed as coming to Berlin and giving it an edgy, liberating "kick." Additionally, in this interpretational frame Berlin and Central Europe, where Hebrew literature developed and thrived before the Holocaust, are now where Mizrachi and Ashkenazi Jews, with others, live and perform Holocaust memory—in and through the nation but also outside its grip. The German press, for instance, viewed many of the Jewish migrants as originating from Germany and hence "returning" in an ironic inversion of the Jewish right of return to the State of Israel.
3. Lamentation and Loss: Liberation discourse is romantic, often ironic, and rests on a third pillar of lamentation. Both German and Israeli press articles focus on the historical irony of Israeli Jews migrating to Germany, disrupting the metaphors of *Aliya* (ascending), *Yerida* (descending), and *Exodus* (exiting). The Israeli press and Israeli authors residing in Germany discuss the reasons that made them choose to leave Israel and reside in Berlin, thinking—or not—of return. The German press often

speaks about the passion to live in Berlin and of how the city, Berlin, proves itself free with the coming of Israelis.

Before we discuss each mode of liberation, I would like to present the case and how it has been studied.

Representations of Israelis in Berlin, within these three frames of liberation and reactions to them, are central to the modes of self-fashioning and understanding of migrant communities.[10] I use a discourse analysis methodology that defines press releases and newspaper articles as genres used in the formation and negotiation of public opinion and self-presentation by different actors.[11] I describe what Forchtner and Schneickert[12] call the *discursive means* surrounding the phenomenon as "dramatic" on two accounts: first, Israeli Jews leave Israel or, in the language often used, they "descend" from Israel. The second dramatic element is that these Israeli Jews have decided not merely not to live in Israel but also to live in Berlin (or Germany)—quite remarkable in light of the Holocaust as well as the (real or perceived) dangers to Jews in Germany today. The focus on discursive means helps grasp the emphasis of the migrants' class, gender and sexual orientation claims, ethnic background, and generational makeup: they are relatively young, the majority Ashkenazi, have academic educations, and secular. But there are also many observant, non-Ashkenazi migrants as well as Palestinian citizens of Israel who are less visible in the press in both Israel and Germany. The migrants are perceived as culturally fitting within a social field that historically was their families' habitat, and as such it is easier both for them and for the German press to explain their choice to live in Berlin and in Germany.

As a diasporic phenomenon, "Israelis in Berlin" is composed of Jews and non-Jews in Berlin, Paris, and other European cities and includes intellectuals, artists, and activists in Israel. They choose their position in response to the discourse about themselves. In the theater discussions and performances during the Disintegration Festival in Berlin's Maxim Gorki Theater held in 2016 and 2017, authors specifically reflected on the choice to react to the reading of their Jewish identity in Jewish means, or *ceasing* to do so, and the responses that such a refusal entail on the part of the German public. We can best understand this through the analysis offered by Forchtner and Schneickert (2016),[13] following Bourdieu.[14] Thus understood, if the Ashkenazi habitus fits the requirements of the German social field, the more likely they are to use strategies that are presupposed and successful *without* being intentional, and the more likely that the "field" will accept them as locals.

This is indeed how the German press views Israeli migrants. This light and neutralized mobility also accounts for the German discussion of the phenomenon being less morally charged, since the migrants are presented as both Israeli and European or as almost nonmigrants but instead as home-comers moving with the lightness of fish in water, as one epigraph to the following article suggests: "The young Israelis in Berlin give the impression of making their way around the city's hip districts unencumbered by history." The second part suggests a freedom from the past, a freedom not available to others such as the so-called biological German or earlier generations of Jews who learned, even in the hip areas, to embody Holocaust memory. This easiness is also not reported on by or for other migrants, for whom nothing is or should be unquestioned or easy.

In the Hebrew press, meanwhile, many analyses struggle with the Zionist narrative, which envisions meaningful Jewish existence in Israel only, while the German press wonders about the meaning of Jews choosing Berlin as their "home." Interestingly, both discourses produce a surprising juxtaposition of the Holocaust and the easygoing "party" lifestyle of Berlin, with Israelis contributing to its party scene. In both contexts the Holocaust, as a cultural event and symbol, has no strongly determined and immediate "positional meaning" as studied by Victor Turner and Tamar Katriel.[15] Rather, its meaning relates to another symbol and event: the party. To write about the Holocaust alongside that of a party is to mark their oppositional meaning for both the German and Hebrew press, thereby making the Holocaust central to understanding the phenomenon of Israeli migration to Berlin.

Who Are the Migrants and How Are They Studied?

The Israelis in Berlin constitute about 2 percent of Israeli emigres. According to Dani Kranz, about 10 percent of the 8,371,600 Israeli citizens live abroad, and of those, 90 percent live in the United States.[16] Hence our analysis concerns the media fascination with approximately 20,000 Jewish migrants. The migrants comprise a diverse group in terms of religion, ethnicity, and politics, although studies show that they tend to be educated, secular, and liberal. This includes a majority of Jews whose families originated from European countries (a number of whom possess European passports),[17] Jews from the former Soviet Union who lived in Israel prior to migrating to Germany,[18] Palestinian citizens of Israel, Mizrachi or Arab Jews, and Ethiopian Jews. This fact points to the diversity of those who choose to live outside Israel, also with respect to their intended duration of stay, class, and level of education.[19]

The number of migrants is reported to be between about four thousand Israelis who are officially registered with the Israeli embassy as residing in Berlin and thirty thousand, the highest estimate given in the press.[20] This attempt to count migrants, however, risks falling into deploying numbers either for or against the interests of the State of Israel. More important, the desire to count subjects conforms to the German narrative of Israelis as exemplifying a certain freedom from the burden of the Holocaust and Holocaust memory. This narrative relies on statements such as that Israelis are free or that, as a repeated trope in the German press has it, they say they feel "*Sababa*."[21]

As for the generational aspects of this group, studies show that most of their grandparents were from Central Europe, albeit not necessarily from Germany.[22] It is also clear that it does not make any difference in how the Israeli grandchildren in Germany deal with Holocaust memory, as Israeli socialization bestows the status of possible victims equally on people with Ashkenazi or Mizrachi origins. However, as we will see, being an Israeli Jew in Berlin enables a recognition of the state of strangeness that those migrants share with Palestinians, Turks, and others of Middle Eastern origins living in Berlin and longing (or not) for the same home.

I suggest that we ought to understand this group and the German and Israeli fascination with it not only within a dialectic of Middle Eastern and European memories of the Holocaust but also within a dialectic of the Berlin and West Bank walls. Both walls are present in iconic representations of this migrant group and are where the Israeli Jews act and are understood as both European and "Arab" in their longing for and production of food, music, and literature. As Cohen and Kranz put it, "While . . . Israeli collective memory of the Shoah, shape the initial experiences of present-day Israeli migrants to Berlin, once they arrive in the city, their experiences are much more defined by current Israeli social and geopolitical issues."[23] I would like to expand this claim by adding that the Israeli migrants are also decisively affected by local politics and are in touch with other migrants in language courses, visa applications, and in everyday encounters with their strangeness from "locals." Even after language and social conventions are acquired and deployed, Israelis, myself included, report that they are often asked by Germans about their personal safety and experience of anti-Semitism; their life in Germany is still imagined inseparably from the Holocaust.

From 2010 through 2019, I have been an Israeli living in Berlin. In following a discourse of which I was part—first to Berlin, later for a year spent in the United States, and now again while living in Berlin—I "played ethnographer in my own backyard," as Tamar Katriel puts it.[24] I was thus able to ponder taken-for-granted tropes in articles about the phenomenon in Hebrew and in German. I have participated in a historical moment in which many authors and migrants recognize aspects of the discourse on belonging and ethnicity, a time during which it has also changed. I have been invited to reflect on my own experience in Berlin, mostly in the German academy and public but also for European audiences. Often, the invitation is to speak from the position of a Jew who, since possibly in danger, may substitute for the dying survivors.

Holocaust Memory and Historical Contingency

In discussing the question "Why are Israelis migrating to Berlin?" we have addressed a combination of economic reasons (embracing changes in the Israeli economy and possibilities in the German economy, among other factors) and culture. As I argue in my book on action at the Holocaust Memorial in Berlin, both of these factors are at work in the performance of memory in Germany since the 1990s.[25] The role Jews play in this work is also relevant.[26] The concept of historical contingency takes into account the dynamic of those factors together with engaging in politics and society in the present. Following Moishe Postone's reading of Marx's historically specific forms, I suggest that overcoming the constraints Israelis list as reasons to migrate to Berlin entails overcoming structural and cultural constraints on action that are historically determined.[27] The Israeli migration to Berlin, in this sense, belongs to the realm of politics—a position that many of its critical members take and to which we will return later.

From the German side, overcoming historical contingency must stand the trial of the rigid roles that Jews play in the German public as possible victims and descendants of victims. These roles lead to the trope of personal as well as cultural emancipation in the German media and may account for the visibility and interest in many Jewish-Palestinian projects that thrive in Berlin and react, contingently, to the Christian moral demand of reconciliation. For instance, the Berlin daily *Tagesspiegel* reports on a Jewish-Palestinian owned restaurant, *Kanaan*, as follows: "Jalil Dabit und Oz Ben David solved the Middle East conflict in their Berlin kitchen. They serve hummus and international understanding (*Völkerverständigung*)." We will return to hummus later. For now, it is important to understand what Jeffrey Olick and Daniel Levy describe as "the trope of reconciliation" that is a cultural aspect of Holocaust memory among "German Jews," Germans, Israeli Jews, and Palestinians.[28]

The German press is eager to show projects in which peace between Jews and Palestinians is possible in Germany as part of discussing Israelis in Germany. The need for Israeli culture in Berlin is another focus, as seen in a press release of the Bundestag on 16 October 2015 announcing the Israel-Germany (ID) Festival supported by the German Ministry of Culture, which was started as a cooperation between Israeli and German artists. The press release read, "Israeli-German Festival Berlin shows the reconciling and forward-looking power of culture."[29] The historical contingency of the emancipation symbol does not make freedom an ontological category; rather, for both Israeli and German popular discourses, Israelis in Berlin present a rare opportunity to see beyond a stifled discussion about Jewish migration, conflict in the Middle East, and reconciliation between Germans and Jews.

The importance of this political dimension does not reduce but even enhances the intimacy of "home," its memory, and its absence for many Israelis in Berlin, as Noam Brusilovsky and Ofer Waldman reflect on in their award-winning audioplay *We Love Israel*.[30] For instance, in one of the many social media groups of Israelis in Berlin, the questions "Why did you come to Berlin?" and "What do you like here / miss from Israel?" are often discussed. Such questions are integral to the experience of migration more generally as a form of longing that may also be innovative and inventive with regard to the objects of longing, as Özlem Savas shows in the case of Turkish tastes among migrants in Vienna. The reasons to migrate to Germany listed on social media include the following: public transportation, affordable rent, and in particular from women, "that men don't ask me to smile" or "that people do not ask me when I will marry."[31] Importantly, gender inequality as a reason to migrate can be viewed in the context of the large LGBTQIA+ community in Berlin, as Preser as well as Amit analyze.[32] Preser interviewed members of the Israeli lesbian diaspora in Berlin and found out that their migration to a society with other sexual imaginaries enabled diversity of desire and choice in subjects, which for these women was not possible or imaginable in Israel. The migrants' rigid social position as outsiders in renting an apartment, finding a job, and through everyday reactions to their accents, grammatical errors, habits, or how to raise their children becomes a point of associating with other migrant communities. Preser calls this association "becoming a Jew" or seeing oneself as a racialized migrant in a process that Bodemann and Yurdakul termed "learning diaspora."[33]

Cohen and Kranz claim that Israeli Jews have a similar fascination and shared interests with Palestinians that they also feel toward Germans.[34] The German press reflected on what this migration means for Holocaust memory and moved between seeing the migrants themselves as unburdened to seeing the Germans in Germany unburdened as an outcome, since Jews chose to live in Germany. What is more, the many gay Jews are seen to enrich the nightlife of a city whose nightlife was already pretty cool. As Hannah Lühmann ironically writes, "The [reflexive] German . . . has deep in his heart the feeling: at last, again Jews, and then also gays. Somehow we've done really well."[35]

Amit, in her study of queer migration outside of Israel to New York, London, and Berlin, illuminates the choice to live outside the time and territorial space of Israel as a rejection of a heteronormative national and collectivist culture but then again marks the "us and them" division, which signifies the boundary work that still considers Israel as the spatiotemporal and cultural referential point of existence.[36] Thus becoming a Jew or refusing to establish a family according to Israeli norms can be liberating and enable new relations to oneself and others. The phenomenon is also symbolically anchored in two cities: Berlin and Tel Aviv. Some commentaries claim that they became one and the same, or that Berlin is an improved Tel Aviv: it is liberal, Ashkenazi, and cool. Many Israelis reside in the Kreuzberg neighborhood in Berlin. It is important to note that conversely, when people call an area in Kreuzberg "little Istanbul," it is not thought of as an improved Istanbul but more of a cultural ghetto. Among Israelis in Berlin, references to ghettos are present in relation to the fear that as migrants they will not muster the German language and culture. Thus learning to be a minority among other, predominantly Muslim minorities is paramount to understanding this migration.

I defined this migration as transnational, which is necessary in order to see how its members in their actions often transgress national borders. Transnationality can be a position benefitting the most highly educated professional migrants as well as a phenomenon characteristic of the underprivileged migrants whose maintenance of ties across borders underlines their marginality and economic instability.[37] The migrants come for a limited period of time and often move between different European cities and Israel. According to Thomas Nail, "Most people fall somewhere on the migratory spectrum between 'inconvenience' and 'incapacitation.'"[38] Indeed, as we will see in the media reports, the more the migrant is defined by her minority position(s) in Israeli society (Palestinian, Mizrachi, gay, disabled), the closer she is to the "incapacitated" pole. Israeli and Palestinian artists in Berlin critically respond to the pedagogical impulse to bring Jews, Syrians, and Palestinians together in Europe as well as in Israel/Palestine so as to affect the conflict in the Middle East and bring about reconciliation. This is also seen in a play entitled *The Situation*, 2016 winner of the Play of the Year prize from Theater Heute, written for the Maxim Gorki Theater by Yael Ronen, one of four in-house directors.

Gad Yair interviewed Israeli Jews about their choice to live in Berlin and was interested in the narrative of liberty and freedom they use as they are thinking about their own identities and belonging. In a newspaper interview about his findings, he explains, "In Berlin you can be yourself. Everyone is a desert island." He continues that most of these young migrants will return to Israel since they are "too different" from "the Germans" and that "nobody wants to raise a German child and this will ultimately happen if you stay there."[39] The drama of leaving and the choice to live in Berlin is thus further intensified by a choice to have a family in the city, or country, and the prospect of one's own child becoming "German." This dichotomy recognizes the sense of liberation but fails to see the diasporic project, as it identifies two distinct entities and fetishizes them as national. It is a point that Nail recognizes in his study of the figure of the migrant from the perspective of stasis—that is, of the migrants perceived as derivative figures with respect to place-bound social membership, or as a failed citizens.[40]

Nail maintains that "migratory figures function as mobile social positions and not fixed identities."[41] He suggests studying them through their movement, critically understood. Following a similar view, Yael Almog offers a reading of the Israeli migration to Berlin in her analysis of the collection *We Don't Forget We Go Dancing*, which was published as a cooperation of the Ministries of Foreign Affairs in both countries in German and Hebrew.[42] In collective migrant stories, she found the trope of young, partying Israelis meeting reconciliation-seeking Germans and concluded that the encounters between Germans and Israelis are driven by a compulsive repetition of the Holocaust narrative. In a more recent piece, Almog shows that the recent migration of Israelis to Germany marks the trajectory of normalizing Germany as a land to which descendants of former

Holocaust victims can now move. She also suggests that this migration of young people reflects a crisis of and within Israeli culture.[43]

In the summaries and critiques of authors such as Preser, Amit, Yair, and Almog, we can see contrasting versions of the three narrative modes of liberty in German and Israeli pieces about Israelis in Berlin. Let us now examine these intertwined tropes in closer detail.

Emancipation

The German press often presents the decision of Israelis to live in Berlin not only as an expression of their emancipation from social and economic pressure but also as an indication of German emancipation from the experience of Jews as murdered. Robert Pausch, writing in *Zeit*, put Israeli migration in nationalized terms, under the headlines of "Israelis in Berlin" and "The State Turns One into a Jew." He wrote, "Today, 70 years after the end of Hitler-Fascism, the German media and politicians proudly observe . . . Young Israelis present Berlin as their yearning place. There is currently talk of a 'new exodus' from the Promised Land to the German capital."[44] This quote frames the attraction of Israelis to Berlin in terms of a "story of mutual infatuation," considering the overtones of desire or even obsession that permeate the trope of Israelis crowning the royal Berlin nightlife. The experience is cast as mutually liberating—the city of the final solution now a free and tolerant city Jews long to see, finding Germans longing for Jews.

Ruth Wodak claims that "texts are often sites of struggle in that they show traces of differing discourses and ideologies contending and struggling for dominance."[45] Here, the questioning voice is on the German public to imagine the exodus of Jews from Israel, the biblical Promised Land, to Germany's capital, which is taken as a metonym for "Hitler-Fascism" (not "National Socialism"). In this and the next section, we will see how these traces emerge and are organized around the relation to the Zionist ethos: through features of the immediate context such as speakers, hearers, settings, expectations, and intentions. According to Katriel, "The strong accent on the community" and "primacy of the collective voice has been a central strand in the Israeli nation-building ethos," but this has been gradually shifting to a more individual(ist) perspective.[46] In the Israeli press, especially *Ha'aretz*, the discussion of the phenomenon turned personal and intimate as, for example, when an author addressed his childhood friend in Berlin.[47]

Ofri Ilany writes both in his own blog *Eretz Haemori* and in *Ha'aretz*, and he reflects on this irony of migrants who are not treated as social surplus but as members of an elite who take action and leave the elite statuses they enjoyed in Tel Aviv. He writes in *Eretz Haemori*, "What are we looking for, there? Usually people go abroad to find there the difference, not sameness. But this is perhaps the point: for Tel Aviv, Berlin is not really abroad. It is more like diaspora (Gola), or an un-geographical place that connects people with similarities. It is very easy to get to Berlin so we live our lives between travels. But we don't leave at once. We swing for years between the one leg that is there and the one here."[48] "There" is Berlin, "here" Tel Aviv, and vice versa. The protagonists, in first-person plural, find individuals just like them in this diaspora state, written and experienced in Berlin and Tel Aviv and in Paris, Amsterdam, and other European cities.

Personal emancipation was reflected on in the German press as well. For instance, in *Tagesspiegel*, a headline read, "Israelis in Berlin: Berlin Lets You Be Many Persons in One." The article explained, "With culture and party the capital presents itself in Tel Aviv. [. . .] for many Israelis, the city has become a place of longing."[49] This *topos* of longing is entangled as much in lamentation as it is in emancipation. *Spitz* had a special Passover issue titled, "Berlin as a Freedom Lab," in which Dana Rothschild wrote about a liberated Jewish existence in West Berlin: "Fasanenstrasse reverberates for me another existential form of Jewish life, liberated and free. Liberated from Israeliness, which covers a large chunk of its natives' identity and makes shallow parts of the Berlin-Jewish identity, free also of the uprootedness that accompanies migration. Every migration."[50] In this quote, the migrant writes in the first person singular about the hardship of migration together with the possibility of creating a new Hebrew culture in Berlin that is nevertheless connected to the first modern Hebrew culture insofar it is not looking toward Zionism but past it. Such new cultural possibilities can also be found in the visual arts. For example, photographer Benyamin Reich, an Israeli Jew who grew up in the ultraorthodox Bnei Barak and whose work is presented in the Jewish Museum in Berlin and celebrated as "local," claimed that it was in Berlin that he learned to see more colors in art and Judaism.[51]

Palestinian migrants who left Israel/Palestine discuss their feelings of emancipation as well, although they reflect a deeper existential crisis in their life in Israel. In interviews to the Israeli press as well as to *Spitz* about their choice to migrate to Berlin, Palestinians say that in Berlin they can live freely, because they are not afraid to speak Arabic in public and they can live without having to face daily the social judgment of their identity.[52] Dani Kranz, who studied the phenomenon of Israelis in Berlin and is often asked to explain it to the German press, said, "Many Israelis affected by the Middle East conflict say in Berlin: now I can finally breathe freely, again."[53] This sense of freedom from personal and societal threats—along with the longing for the possibility of "normalized" Jewish German as well as Jewish Palestinian and Arab relationships—connects with the broader post-1989 German narrative of normalcy as described by Konrad Jarausch.[54] In the words of an article from *Die Welt*, "The city, where the final solution was decided on, is free, tolerant and relaxed today."[55]

Undoing Zionism and Returning Jews to Europe

In October 2014, the project Olim Leberlin (Ascending to Berlin), which was initiated by Naor Narkis, called on Chancellor Merkel to provide twenty-five thousand working visas to Israelis wishing to come to Berlin. But soon thereafter Narkis announced that he was returning to Israel, for "I know where my home is," and he shut down the project's Facebook page. This act quickly prompted interest from the media about the broader phenomenon of Israelis migrating to Berlin. Channel 10 in Israel dedicated a series called *The New Yordim* (*The Newly Descending Ones*) composed of reports by young Israelis who confessed that Berlin is where they can realize their middle-class aspirations. While different, these two examples are similar in that they do not question the nation as a center of identity and meaning. However, many Israelis—Ashkenazi as well as Mizrachi—do reflect on the possibility of questioning and departing from such narratives. "It is funny, the Zionists met in Basel, we too," said poet Adi Keissar in the first *Ars Poetica* meeting in the Maxim Gorki Theater.[56]

Keissar and other Mizrachi poets from Berlin and Israel share the space of Hebrew poetry in its original as well as in translation into English and German, and German poetry in translation, opening up the possibility of converging paths of making and remaking Hebrew culture in Berlin alongside the remaking of German culture. The ironic element of an Israeli group of Mizrachi poets celebrating the diversity of this enterprise in Berlin, alluding to the first Zionist congress in Basel in 1897 as the place and time of its birth, underscored the project's aim to open up possibilities yet unknown.

Jews have contingent relations to Holocaust memory in Germany and so do other migrant groups. We have already discussed how migrants impact Germany's culture of remembrance, and numerous educational programs now target Muslims (migrants or not) in trying to challenge anti-Semitic sentiments that are believed to be held by Muslims. Esra Ozyurek shows that the Muslim migrants are seen as most threatening to the integrity of the German narrative of mastering memory.[57] Victoria Bishop Kendzia shows that Muslim pupils' experiences are not welcome in the Jewish Museum in Berlin, where majority-German educators see them as suspicious, unable to join the German cultural memory, and unable to participate in it as equal citizens.[58] What Rothberg and Yildiz termed "memory citizenship," or the assessment of a particular group's ability to participate in German culture through the performance of Holocaust memory work, has been discussed in the German media to such an extent that Muslim Germans now find it necessary to respond to it.[59] Naika Foruntan claims that the Holocaust should cease belonging purely to German history;[60] hence, other groups, with their various memories, should be allowed to participate in remembering it. Adelson discusses such participation in the case of German-Turkish literature.[61]

Illouz and Böhm connect the discourse in Germany on collective guilt to that of Israel's guilt, or its lack thereof, over the destruction of Palestinian life in Palestine in and after 1948. They claim that ironically, "it is only the theatrical collective staging of a victim role—a reflection of the German theatrical collective staging of guilt—that has enabled the Israelis to reject the experience of guilt and responsibility."[62] Similarly, claims Ulrike Schleicher, "today, the Holocaust seems to connect more often than it divides."[63] Illouz and Böhm suggest that Jews and other observers and participants in the new Jewish migration to Berlin ought no longer to make themselves complacent with the negative symbiosis between Israelis and Germans and thereby "replace the collective victimhood and collective guilt with a real responsibility for our past and our future."[64]

The dialogical space among and between these various positions in the "Israelis in Berlin" phenomenon transcends Zionism, since it calls for a universalistic, humanist, and diasporic project. As Galit Saada-Ophir shows, the boundary work that such activists perform creates a broader space of negotiation—not simply rejection—for critical choices or chances inside or outside of Israel.[65] The rich correspondence between Tel Aviv and Berlin as havens and ideas that individuals imagine and play cannot be captured by Zionism and its putative opposite(s).

Poet Mati Shemoelof describes the possibilities of such transnationalism as follows: "The Germans tend to talk about the Israelis in Berlin out of the perception that the Jew stands behind the Israeli. But what happens when the Germans discover that there are more complex identities than those in their imagination? What happens when they hear about an Israeli-Palestinian who sees himself both as an Israeli and as a Palestinian? How do they respond to the thousands of Palestinians who emigrate from Israel to their city? And how is their memory and guilt organized towards the Nakba?"[66] Germans meeting both Jews and Palestinian migrants in Berlin discuss their positions vis-à-vis Israel and the occupation, a discussion that affects their narratives about the Holocaust as well as their responsibility toward both Jews and Palestinians. Having said that, Shemoelof stresses that Palestinians often go unseen in the German exploration of Israelis in Berlin: "Of all places in Berlin, Arab Jews have the freedom to get to know their sisters and brothers from the Arab world." Palestinians as well as Arab Jews can newly experience their state of strangeness within the migratory space they enact.[67]

Anya Topolsky claims that the agency Jews and Muslims enjoy in Europe is somewhat reduced by the state, which uses theological-political mechanisms of managing minorities.[68] The State of Israel manages this minority through the label of *Yordim*, while the German state manages it in one of two ways: by perceiving Israelis (1) as "good migrants" who can "integrate" and become true Germans or (2) as possible brokers, with Palestinians on German soil, of reconciliation in the Middle East. Those asymmetrical power relations are balanced by the presence of

Israeli Jewish intellectuals in the German media and by Israeli groups refusing to accept the definition of minorities imposed on them.

For instance, an Israeli Jewish migrant shared a post from a Facebook group: "I have a really strange question. It really bothers me that the drawing with the Star of David on the Berlin wall is scribbled over. Who can I write in this regard, you think? The municipality or who's responsible?" The many amused reactions came with little delay: "Tell him to come and clean it off himself"; "Maybe he is looking for a place to crash when he comes to check out the berlin wall"; "I am really shocked by your reactions. What did he ask you to do?"; and "Tell him you don't know who is in charge, but that he can go ask in the [Hebrew-language] group 'our Berlin.'" The question and replies reveal a rich field of intimate national signification in which the Israeli citizen living in Berlin is expected to serve as a mediator on things related to doing Holocaust memory right or reproaching "the Germans" for doing it wrong (often mixing up and condensing different historical periods) and the ability of the newcomers to intervene in a way one would in Israel.

As stated earlier, migrants do intervene in the discourse about integration. For instance, Tal Hever-Chybowski, editor of the Hebrew-language annual magazine *Mikan Ve'eylakh* (From here onward) asks in his piece "Integration?" which was written for the ID Festival in 2017, about the subject-object position ambiguity in the term *integration*. This ambiguity, he claims, reveals the obvious hegemony of the majority over the minority: "Integration is a universalist-humanistic pretense, whose function is to conceal the fundamental intolerance of hegemonic power systems toward manifestations of the particular."[69] This cultural artifact underscores the dialogical nature of the German-Israeli fascination with the migration of Israelis. Another example is the consideration of Tomer Gardi's novel *Broken German* for the Bachmann literature prize, which Noam Brusilovsky adopted as a podcast.

We have thus far seen the intercultural and intergenerational exchange by groups that respond both to Holocaust memory as it is performed in Israel and Germany and to the condition of migrant groups in Berlin in recent history, which is extensively debated. I will show how this particular migration and its representation in Israeli media opens up a space for negotiation of national and intersectional identities, and less so in Germany, where the possibility of seeing and sharing time and space with Jews is fraught with seeing them as possible victims. In the latter, Jewish Israelis, Ashkenazi and Mizrachi, remember the Holocaust with other minorities and negotiate within a rigid memory regime, which denies them—together with other Jews and members of other minorities—a subject position other than their presupposed position in the fixed framework.[70] Those modes of remembrance are taken from Israeli contemporary memory culture.[71] They are then reimagined and interpreted in the Hebrew Diaspora in cosmopolitan capitals of Europe.

Lamentation and Loss

The third form of liberation in the discourse on Israelis in Berlin is of lamentation and loss. The political-moral move to not stay within the confines of the Zionist culture of Jews in Israel is at first experienced as emancipatory but then is lamented as a loss. For example, issue 10 of *Spitz* (Passover 2014) was called *You Are My Liberty: Berlin as a Freedom Lab*.[72] Writers were asked to reflect on the topic of liberty, as we saw in the example of Dana Rothschild on the topic of feeling free in Western Berlin, where Hebrew writers lived and worked in the early twentieth century. In *Spitz* as well as in the German and Israeli press generally, the city was viewed as enabling freedom as well as being itself "free." "Berlin as a freedom lab" also discursively marks the project as plural and contingent, adding to the transgression of national narratives. The attempt to be free in the lab, with other "researchers" in a controlled environment, marks both a break with the past and the possibility of failure.

Uri Avnery, journalist, author, and peace activist, called on young Israelis living in Berlin to return to Israel, stating that their excellence will be better recognized in Israel and that they are needed to fight and change the course of the country's nationalistic right-wing ascendancy. In this public dialogue, Avnery sees the migrants not as a mobile social surplus, as Thomas Nail characterizes them, but rather laments their loss as agents crucial to rejuvenating the Israeli nation.[73] Na'aman Hirschfeld, a doctoral student studying in Berlin, struck a similar tone of lament: "Leaving is a political act against the rhetoric of 'here' as the only possible place for self-realization and affecting politics."[74]

Tal Hever-Chybowski responded in the blog *Ha'oketz* as follows: "And today, whoever does not want to live by the sword in the bible land and on the edge of Moab, can live a life no less political in Moabit, the neighborhood in Berlin where new refugees arriving in the city register." Here the lamentation is not about the choice to leave Israel but the choice of Avnery not to see possible paths of political resistance against right-wing sentiments in Berlin. Indeed, Hever-Chybowski alludes to the biblical Moab, an area and people paramount to thinking about relations with non-Israelites in the Old Testament: instead of focusing on the decision to live on the brinks of war in Israel, a political choice in and of itself, Hever-Chybowski turns his attention to Berlin's Moabit neighborhood, itself named after biblical Moab, as a new place of refuge.[75]

In yet another example, we can see the importance of biblical metaphors and images: the reception of the cover image for the first issue of *Spitz*. As journalist Kathrin Schrader described the image, "Beside the door is a newspaper rack [with] the first issue of Berlin's Hebrew-language magazine *Spitz*. . . . The cover shows the globe of Berlin's Television Tower floating beside a little white cloud in a blue sky, a picture that might have been taken from a children's book."[76]

Figure 13.1. Avital Yomdin's illustration for the first cover of *Spitz* magazine, July 2012.

The author does not describe the women sitting with a bottle of beer, probably because she did not read the accompanying text.

Embedded in the illustration of the river Spree and the iconic Oberbaum Bridge that links Friedrichshain and Kreuzberg, a symbol of Berlin's post-Wall unity, is a play on Psalm 137: "On the river Spree [not *Babylon*], we sat, and drank [not *cried*], as we remembered Zion." Here the irony of having a choice of where to sit or reside, and what to do, drink, or where to party, brings the *memory of Zion*—not Zion—to the Spree. The magazine title was "Not Alone in Berlin," a reference to Hans Fallada's very popular novel in Israel, *Alone in Berlin*, which tells the story of violence between individuals and Germans under National Socialism. Returning to the image, one also sees that the figure is a single woman who is smiling as she holds a bottle of beer. The political positioning of the woman sitting, as it were, on top of where the Wall stood, over the Spree, with the train behind her and the sculpture connecting times and places is ignored in German journalists' gaze at the self-presentation of the "Israeli." In opposition to this self-presentation, Tal Alon, editor of *Spitz*, claimed, "We are not a Jewish magazine. We are concentrated on the contemporary life in Berlin." Nevertheless, she and her work are often described precisely as what she says she and *Spitz* are not: "Tal Alon is the editor of the first Hebrew magazine published in Berlin after the Holocaust," an article from *Berliner Morgenpost* reads.[77] Here we see that the Berlin newspaper insists on connecting the Hebrew language to the Holocaust. The rhetorical device[78] of lamentation is juxtaposed with the celebration of the lightness with which the new migrants move in the city, their young ages, and the putatively naïve choices they make.

The use of Psalm 137 on the cover of *Spitz* assumes prior knowledge of both the text and the context of lamenting leaving Israel and the Holocaust. As Almog writes,[79] this choice is intoxicating for both Germans and Jews. This is evident in another German-Jewish cooperation, the ID Festival. It was celebrated in the German press: "The makers of the ID festivals bring back a culture that the generation of its grandparents brought from here to Israel," marking a cycle of people and cultures enabled by the Holocaust.[80]

Uri Avnery, in his previously discussed call for migrants to return to Israel, refers to this verse from Psalms, arguing that if everyone who can resist the crisis in Israeli democracy will surrender and "move to the cafes on Unter den Linden or Champs Elysees, there he will sit and cry as he remembers Zion." Interestingly, the reference to the famous avenues in Paris and Berlin mistakes where Israelis in those cities actually live, work, and play, exposing Avnery's assumptions about the economic success, tourist destinations, or limelight those individuals seek. The lamentation over the failure of the Zionist project is performed also in reaction to the flourishing Hebrew literature in Berlin and Europe—either from a position of rage and dismissal or from a matriarchal position relating to the angry "chicks," as in Fania Oz-Salzberger's otherwise positive reading of *Mikan*

Ve'eylakh, whose title implies that you can *both* take from Israeli literature *and* celebrate diasporic Hebrew.[81]

The intimate relations between Hebrew and German culture since the 1980s, based on the rich legacy of Hebraism and bilingual writing, have been explored by Amir Eshel and Naama Rokem. To quote them, "Increasingly, the German–Israeli encounter is triangulated with the Israeli–Palestinian dialogue, in works of literature—such as short stories by Savyon Liebrecht and Uri Zeig—or of popular culture—such as Ethan Fox's film *Walk on Water*."[82] The intimate embodied relations are seen in the Israeli culinary scene, which Ofer Waldman describes in the Middle Eastern exile neighborhood of Neukölln. Waldman is aware of the colonial sentiments described by Daphna Hirsch, where hummus is signified as an Arab dish whose Arab identity "functions as a resource employed by actors who are embedded in various political, social, and economic projects."[83] However, unlike Jews consuming hummus in Palestinian neighborhoods in Israel/Palestine, the shared space of consuming hummus in Berlin seems to reflect the longing for a not-yet-existing mutual future, a shared Jewish-Arab space populated by a third group—the Germans. Waldman writes about "trusted strangeness" and describes how one street, the *Sonnenallee*, turned from a place of longing for the collapsed GDR to a boulevard of longing for the Middle East by Arabs and Israeli Jews together, a longing he poignantly termed "*Nah-ostalgie*," or "Near *East*" nostalgia.[84]

The ground that characterizes and motivates the relationship between sign and object can be indexical (i.e., with causal or proximal linkages)—namely, that of the same people consuming the same dish remembering a historical (Berlin) and a present (West Bank) wall. Here the consumption of hummus also signifies Israelis as ethnic, foreign, and newly local together with Palestinians, who are often second-generation local, with the German gaze to which all this is not only appealing and delicious but with which political claims are made. As Ofer Waldman notes, however, it is often the Palestinian who exclaims "Here we are not enemies" or "Everyone is welcome in my business." At the same time, it is often the Israelis who are asked whether they are worried that those Muslims will attack them. A sign, "Make hummus not walls," is printed on the walls of an Israeli-owned hummus restaurant in the center of Berlin, and a photo of graffiti by Moodi Abdalla that makes the same call on the separation wall in Bethlehem is on the restaurant's website.[85]

The Jewish community in Berlin, itself a diverse group, was also skeptical and to an extent lamented this migration. Asked by *Jüdische Allgemeine*, "How many of them are there really?" Ilan Kiesling responded, "Most Israelis who moved from Israel to Berlin are more secular and seldom visit a synagogue . . . additionally many Israelis, apart from cultural events and celebrations, perceive the community as a purely religious institution, and this changes, when a child needs kindergarten or school."[86] The (legally established) German-Jewish Community's lamentation is that the Israelis are not the Jews they were hoping for, though eventually they might become those Jews after living in Germany for some time.

The lamentation on the German Christian side is often celebratory, showing surprise at how Israelis *and* Palestinians love Berlin, as a study by the Konrad Adenauer Foundation revealed.[87] This study also showed that 19 percent of Israelis have relatives in Germany and continued, "To these relatives clearly belong the over 20,000 members of the Israel community in Berlin or 'Spree-Aviv,' as they call it. Neukölln or Kreuzberg, where also many Muslims live, are sought after spots." In this quote, the majority sees perhaps a danger to the (Jewish) minority who is not aware of it, so comfortable as they are as newcomers on the Spree. In another example, the celebration of Jews choosing to leave Israel for Berlin is looked at as a temporary moment to party: "The fact that Israelis are partying in Europe's cheapest metropolis is not new, but the political context in which the story is told by the Israelis leaving their Jewish homeland and moving to Germany has changed."[88]

Dani Kranz was asked about Jewishness and replied that the Israeli migrants have very little to do with the Jewish community, since they see themselves first as Israelis and second as Jews, while only a few search for contact with the Jewish community: "The German-Jewish and the Israeli-Jewish identities are completely separated."[89] From my conversations with Israeli Jews who sought such contact, a complex picture arises: they failed to garner interest from the community or to raise funds for a Hebrew library, a youth movement, or a Jewish nonreligious school. The picture is different in Frankfurt, Hamburg, and Munich, where the Israelis and the Jewish community do converge.

Concluding Remarks

"I wanted to develop modes of writing in a language by which the power relations will be other than what I have in Hebrew," said author Tomer Gardi, playing with the possibility that by writing in German he became an "author without authority"—a choice possible to explore in Berlin.[90] This was indeed the impression of the jury for the Bachmann prize as well as that of an audience in the presentation of the sound installation *Broken German* in the Maxim Gorki Theater in February 2018. They asked themselves whether the text is actually written in Hebrew, whether this is the price Germans and the German language had to pay for the "broken German" in Israel due to the Holocaust, or even for accepting refugees to their land—reflecting the interpretational frame of "undoing Zionism." Gardi, interviewed by Gadi Goldberg in *Spitz*, reflected, "When they say 'The Israeli Tomer Gardi' it bothers me. Because I think precisely about the way in which they do not manage to think of literature separately from the nation. This is a problem that the literary worlds of both Germany and Israel share. It is the reading resists the act of writing."[91]

The power relations in the struggle over the definition of "otherness" in the city one chooses to live in were explored in this piece through the symbolic use of liberty and emancipation in the discussion of Israelis in Berlin. In this chapter, I have understood this migration as part of a transnational diaspora that partakes in redefining ethnic belonging while recognizing the fragility and temporal contingency of that very project of redefinition in terms of a lab or even a party. I believe that the breadth of this diasporic project enables its members to negotiate mobility and social boundaries from a position that may change and transgress rigid categories for them as well for other groups.

NOTES

Epigraphs: Avital Yomdin, *Spitz*, no. 1, cover, 1 July 2012; Kathrin Schrader, *The Pulse of Germany*, 6 November 2012, a project supported by the German Ministry of Foreign Affairs.

1. *Ha'aretz*, 13 October 2017.

2. Hadas Cohen and Dani Kranz, "Israeli Jews in the New Berlin from Shoah Memories to Middle Eastern Encounters," in *Cultural Topographies of the New Berlin*, ed. Karin Bauer and Jennifer Ruth Hosek (New York: Berghahn Books, 2017), 322–346.

3. An exploration of the aesthetic of the Jews of the night, the transvestites' images, and other curiosities should merit a separate study.

4. Ayala Goldman, "Chocolate Pudding as a Reason for Migration: Israeli Calls on Facebook for Migration to Europe," *Cheap in Berlin*, 8 October 2014.

5. Irit Dekel, *Mediation at the Holocaust Memorial in Berlin* (Basingstoke, U.K.: Palgrave Macmillan, 2013).

6. Irit Dekel, "Subjects of Memory? Holocaust Memory in Two German Historical Museums," *Dapim: Studies on the Holocaust* 30, no. 3 (2016): 296–314.

7. Hilla Amit, "The Revival of Diasporic Hebrew in Contemporary Berlin," in *Cultural Topographies of the New Berlin*, 253–271.

8. Daniel Mosseri, "Berlin and Tel Aviv: Story of an Infatuation, How Berlin became the New Mecca for Young Israelis" (diss., Freie Universität Berlin, Internationales Journalisten Kolleg, 2015).

9. Ruth Preser, "Lost and Found in Berlin: Identity, Ontology, and the Emergence of Queer Zion," *Gender, Place & Culture* 24, no. 3 (2016): 413–425.

10. Nelly Elias and Daphna Lemish, "Between Three Worlds: Host, Homeland, and Global Media in the Lives of Russian Immigrant Families in Israel and Germany," *Journal of Family Issues* 32, no. 9 (2011): 1245–1274.

11. Ruth Wodak, "Pragmatics and Critical Discourse Analysis: A Cross-disciplinary Inquiry," *Pragmatics & Cognition* 15, no. 1 (2007): 203–225.

12. Bernhard Forchtner and Christiaan Schneickert, "Collective Learning in Social Fields: Bourdieu, Habermas and Critical Discourse Studies," *Discourse & Society* 27, no. 3 (2016): 293–307.

13. Forchtener and Schneickert, "Collective Learning," 296.

14. Pierre Bourdieu, *Distinctions: A Social Critique of the Judgment of Taste* (London: Routledge, 1990).

15. Victor Turner, *The Ritual Process: Structure and anti-Structure* (New Brunswick, N.J.: Transaction, 1977); Tamar Katriel, *Communal Webs: Communication and Culture in Contemporary Israel* (Albany: State University of New York Press, 1991).

16. Dani Kranz, *Israelis in Berlin: Wie viele sind es und was zieht sie nach Berlin?* (Gütersloh: Bertelsmann Stiftung, 2015), 11.

17. Dani Kranz, "Forget Israel—the Future Is in Berlin! Local Jews, Russian Immigrants and Israeli Jews in Berlin and across Germany," *Shofar* 34, no. 4 (2016): 5–28; JDC International Centre for Community Development and Machon Kehilot, *The Israeli Diaspora in Europe: A Survey about Israelis Living in Europe*, 2017.

18. Larissa Remennick, "Generation 1.5 of Russian Speaking Immigrants in Israel and in Germany: An Overview of Recent Research and A German Pilot Study," in *Integration, Identity and Language Maintenance in Young Immigrants, Russian Germans and German Russians*, ed. Ludmila Isurin and Claudia Maria Riehl (Amsterdam: John Benjamins, 2017), 69–98.

19. Mosseri, "Berlin and Tel Aviv."

20. See, for instance, a piece in the October 2014 issue of the *Juedische Allgemeine*, http://www.juedische-allgemeine.de/article/view/id/20597. Estimates vary widely and certainty is difficult because it is so easy for "an Israeli" to live in Berlin without officially being registered as an Israeli, as living in Berlin, or either.

21. See, for instance, Tagesschau24, "Zion an der Spree: Was Israelis in Berlin Machen," television news broadcast, 13 September 2015.

22. Cohen and Kranz, "Israeli Jews." Fania Oz-Salzberger, "Kinderlach, You Can Do Both: On the Brilliant, Raging Raise of Hebrew, Non-Israeli Literature in Europe," *Hashiloach* 1 (2016): 163–169.

23. Cohen and Kranz, 323.

24. Katriel, *Communal Webs*, 1.

25. Dekel, *Mediation*.

26. Y. Michal Bodemann, *Gedächtnissthater. Die Jüdische Gemeinschaft und Ihre deutsche Erfahrung* (Hamburg: 1996); Irit Dekel, "Jews and Other Others at the Holocaust Memorial in Berlin," *Anthropological Journal of European Culture* 23, no. 2 (2014): 71–84.

27. Moishe Postone, "History and Helplessness: Mass Mobilization and Contemporary Forms of Anticapitalism," *Public Culture* 18, no. 1 (2006): 93–110.

28. Jeffrey K. Olick and Daniel Levy, "Collective Memory and Cultural Constraint: Holocaust Myth and Rationality in German Politics." *American Sociological Review* 62, no. 6 (1997): 921–926.

29. Press release of the government on the occasion of the Israel-Germany festival, accessed 21 February 2018, https://www.bundesregierung.de/Content/DE/Pressemitteilungen/BPA/2015/10/2015-10-16-bkm-israelisch-deutsches-festival-berlin.html.

30. Noam Brusilovsky and Ofer Waldman, *We Love Israel*, 2018, SWR in cooperation with Deutschland Radio.

31. Özlem Savas, "Taste Diaspora: The Aesthetic and Material Practice of Belonging," *Journal of Material Culture* 19, no. 2 (2014): 185–208.

32. Preser, "Lost and Found"; Hila Amit, "Exit Points: The National Temporal Axix and Queer Migration from Israel," *Theory and Criticism* 45 (2015): 91–113; Hila Amit, *A Queer Way Out: the Politics of Queer Emigration from Israel* (New York: State University of New York Press, 2018).

33. Y. Michal Bodemann and Gokce Yurdakul, "Learning Diaspora: German Turks and the Jewish Narrative," in *The New German Jewry and the European Context*, ed. Y. Michal Bodemann (Basingstoke, U.K.: Palgrave Macmillan, 2008), 73–95.

34. Cohen and Kranz, "Israeli Jews."

35. Hannah Lühmann, "Oi, Berlin, Junge, Muss es Wirklich Sein?," *Welt Kultur*, 4 May 2014.

36. Amit, "Revival."

37. Karolina S. Follis, *Building Fortress Europe: The Polish-Ukrainian Frontier* (Philadelphia: University of Pennsylvania Press, 2013).

38. Thomas Nail, *The Figure of the Migrant* (Stanford, Calif.: Stanford University Press, 2015), 2.

39. Gad Yair, *Love Is Not Praktisch: The Israeli Look at Germany* (Tel Aviv: Hakibbutz Hameuchad, 2015).

40. Nail, *Figure of the Migrant.*

41. Nail, 3.

42. Yael Almog, "Migration and Its Discontents: Israelis in Berlin and Homeland Politics." *Transit* 10, no. 1 (2015): 1–7.

43. Yael Almog, "Europe Will Be Stunned: Visualization of a Jewish Return," in *The German Hebrew Dialogue: Studies of Encounter and Exchange*, ed. Amir Eshel and Rachel Seelig (Berlin: De Gruyter, 2018), 197–209.

44. Cited in Mosseri, "Berlin and Tel Aviv."

45. Ruth Wodak, "What CDA Is about—A Summary of its History, Important Concepts and its Developments," in *Methods of Critical Discourse Analysis*, ed. Ruth Wodak and Michael Meyer (London: SAGE, 2001), 1–13.

46. Katriel, *Communal Webs*, 4.

47. Asaf Ronel, "Na'aman, Come Back from Berlin to Jaffa," *Ha'aretz*, 4 August 2016.

48. Ofri Ilany, "Zurückbleiben Bitte," blog post on *Eretz Haemori*, 16 September 2010, https://haemori.wordpress.com/2010/09/16/zuruckbleiben-bitte/.

49. Lissy Kaufmann, "Berlin lässt dich viele Personen in einer sein," *Der Tagesspiegel* online, 7 October 2013.

50. Dana Rothschild, "Shelter/Sanctuary-City," *Spitz* 10 (April 2014): 9 [Hebrew].

51. He made this statement in November 2017 while discussing the film, which bears the same title as a film by Daniel Laufer. The film is a coproduction of DAGESH KunstLAB ELES und Asylum Arts with support from the German Ministry of Education and Research.

52. Nir Yahav, "In Israel, You Cannot Escape' Your Arabness. Here You Can Rest," *Walla*, 15 January 2015 [Hebrew], https://news.walla.co.il/item/2820101.

53. Elke Vogel, "'Endlich wieder frei atmen'—Junge Israelis in Berlin," *Rhein-Neckar Zeitung*, 29 July 2015 https://www.rnz.de/wissen/gesellschaft_artikel,-Gesellschaft-Endlich-wieder-frei-atmen-Junge-Israelis-in-Berlin-_arid,115739.html.

54. Konrad Jarausch, "Normalisierung oder ReNationalisierung? Zur Umdeutung der deutschen Vergangenheit," *Geschichte und Gesellschaft* 21, no. 4 (1995): 571–584.

55. Freia Peters, "Berlin, a German Longing for Jews," *Die Welt*, 23 April 2012.

56. Gorki, "Radical Jewish Cultural Days," 4 November 2017, https://gorki.de/de/ars-poetica.

57. Esra Ozyurek, "Export-Import Theory and the Racialization of Anti-Semitism: Turkish and Arab-Only Prevention Programs in Germany," *Comparative Studies in Society and History* 58, no. 1 (2016): 40–65.

58. Victoria Bishop Kendzia, *Visitors to the House of Memory Identity and Political Education at the Jewish Museum Berlin* (New York: Berghahn, 2017).

59. Michael Rothberg and Yasemin Yildiz, "Memory Citizenship: Migrant Archives of Holocaust Remembrance in Contemporary Germany," *Parallax* 17, no. 4 (2011): 32–48.

60. Malte Lehming, "Wie Migranten das Holocaust-Gedenken verändern," *Tagesspiegel*, 13 January 2018.

61. Leslie A. Adelson, "Touching Tales of Turks, Germans, and Jews: Cultural Alterity, Historical Narrative, and Literary Riddles for the 1990s," *New German Critique* 80 (2000): 93–124.

62. Eva Illouz and Omri Böhm, "Kollektive Schuld, Kollektive Opfer," in *Israel und Deutschland, Kultur Austausch* a special edition of *Kulturaustausch*, ed. Micha Brumlik (Instituts für Auslandsbeziehungen, 2015): 16–18.

63. "Meine oder Deine Geschichte," *Deutsche Welle*, 7 November 2013, https://p.dw.com/p/1ABgz.

64. "Meine oder Deine Geschichte," 18.

65. Galit Saada-Ophir, "Mizrachi Subaltern Counterpoints: Sderot's Alternative Bands," *Anthropological Quarterly* 80, no. 3 (2007): 711–736.

66. "Nobody Talks about Palestinians in Berlin," *Ha'aretz*, 15 June 2015 [Hebrew], https://www.haaretz.co.il/literature/study/.premium-1.2659531.

67. "Nobody Talks about Palestinians in Berlin."

68. Anya Topolski, "Good Jew, Bad Jew . . . Good Muslim, Bad Muslim: 'Managing' Europe's Others," *Ethnic and Racial Studies* (2017): 1–18.

69. Tal Hever-Chybowski, "A Parable on Integration," *Protocols*, no. 2 (2018).

70. Dekel, "Subjects of Memory."

71. Jackie Feldman, "Between Yad Vashem and Mt. Herzl: Changing Inscriptions of Sacrifice on Jerusalem's 'Mountain of Memory,'" *Anthropological Quarterly* 80, no. 4 (2007): 1147–1174; Tamar Katriel and Yifat Gutman, "The Wall Must Fall: Memory Activism, Documentary Filmmaking, and the Second *Intifada*," in *Cultural Memories of Nonviolent Struggles*, ed. Anna Reading and Tamar Katriel (Basinstoke, U.K.: Palgrave, 2015), 205–225.

72. At Heruti is a reference to a famous song by Georges Moustaki, "You Are My Liberty."

73. "Youth of Berlin, Return to the Land," *Ha'Aretz*, 28 July 2016 [Hebrew], https://www.haaretz.co.il/opinions/.premium-1.3021448.

74. "No Thanks, I Stay in Berlin," *Ha'Aretz*, 31 July 2016 [Hebrew], https://www.haaretz.co.il/opinions/.premium-1.3024138.

75. This is a point that Dani Kranz illuminates in her analysis of the *allos* ("Other") discourse on Israel migration to Berlin and the refugees' "welcome culture" since 2015.

76. Kathrin Schrader, "Tel Aviv an der Spree," *So tikt Deutschland*, 6 November 2012, https://www.deutschland.de/de/topic/leben/gesellschaft-integration/tel-aviv-an-der-spree.

77. Marion Bernhardt. "Berlin heißt בדלק," *Berliner Morgenpost*, 27 July 2014, https://www.morgenpost.de/printarchiv/biz/article130596669/Berlin-heisst.html.

78. As these are analyzed by Wodak in "Pragmatics."

79. Almog, "Migration and Its Discontents."

80. Esther Slevgot, "Kunst braucht Platz," *TAZ*, 12 October 2017, https://www.taz.de/Archiv-Suche/!5452253&s=ID%2BFestival&SuchRahmen=Print/.

81. Fania Oz-Salzberger, "Kinderlach, You Can Do Both," *Ha'shiloach*, 19 January 2017, https://hashiloach.org.il/קינדערלאך-אפשר-גם-וגם/.

82. Amir Eshel and Naama Rokem, "German and Hebrew: Histories of a Conversation," *Prooftexts* 33, no. 1 (2013): 1–8.

83. Daphna Hirsch, "'Hummus Is Best When It Is Fresh and Made by Arabs': The Gourmetization of Hummus in Israel and the Return of the Repressed Arab," *American Ethnologist* 38, no. 4 (2011): 617–630.

84. Ofer Waldman, "Berlin als arabisch-israelischer Begegnungsort," Deutschlandradio Kultur, 24 December 2017, https://www.deutschlandfunkkultur.de/auf-neutralem-boden-berlin-als-arabisch-israelischer.942.de.html?dram:article_id=406702.

85. This is graffiti by Moodi Abdalla on the separation wall in Bethlehem.

86. Alice Lanke, "Wie viele sind es wirklich?," *Jüdische Allgemeine*, 30 October 2014, https://www.juedische-allgemeine.de/article/view/id/20597.

87. "Israelis and Palestinians Both Love Germany," *TheLocal.de*, 12 January 2015, https://www.thelocal.de/20150112/israelis-and-palestinians-a-positive-view-of-germany.

88. James Kirchick, "Was soll die israelische Begeisterung für Berlin?," *Frankfurter Allgemeine Zeitung*, 29 July 2015, http://www.faz.net/aktuell/feuilleton/debatten/zieht-es-wirklich-so-viele-israelis-nach-berlin-13723985.html.

89. Elke Vogel, *op. Cit.* (see note 54).

90. Gadi Goldberg, "Tomer Gardi's Book Was Written in Broken German and Challenges the Most Basic Assumptions by and about Migrants," *Spitz-Magazin*, August 2016, http://spitzmag.de/culture/8765.

91. Goldberg.

EPILOGUE

Jay Howard Geller and Michael Meng

In the early 1960s, Israeli journalist and writer Amos Elon journeyed across divided Germany to investigate the country's transformation after Nazism. Through a series of nuanced observations about West and East Germany, he explored whether Germans had fundamentally changed. Had the country learned from the errors of its past? As he witnessed untold former Nazis in positions of political, judicial, and economic power; as he noted that most Germans wished an end to war-crimes trials; and as he failed to engage his interlocutors in a critical examination of the past, he ultimately concluded that Germany had in fact not changed. In his first book, entitled *Journey through a Haunted Land: The New Germany*, he argued that Germany had failed to transform itself into a tolerant, self-critical nation-state committed to humanitarianism.[1] Though West Germany had adopted democracy, xenophobia and illiberalism still persisted. All in all, Elon left Germany with a view of a country that was largely in denial about its past and unwilling to change from it.

While Elon spoke with many Germans about the Holocaust and elicited their attitudes toward the Jews during his time in Germany, it seems that he only minimally engaged with the Jewish community in West Germany. He commented offhandedly that "the Jewish population of West Germany is a negligible minority (0.04 percent against 0.9 percent before the war)" and that "the few Jews who returned to Germany after the war were most old or sickly, pensioners or small businessmen."[2] He failed to interrogate their motives for remaining in Germany or to examine the quality of their lives in Germany. And with the exception of organized Jewry in Communist East Germany—a minuscule population—he failed to investigate the changes to German-Jewish life and its prospects for the future.[3] He did interview a few Jews with unusually prominent positions in West German society, including the literary critic Marcel Reich-Ranicki and the Hessian state attorney general Fritz Bauer. Yet those discussions focused more on

German confrontations with the past rather than on the Jewish experience in the present.

If Elon had looked closely at Jewish life in West Germany, he would have encountered many of the issues examined by this volume. He would have seen how the community structured itself and worked behind the scenes to achieve its aims—namely, support for communal institutions and reparations. He might have noticed that members of the community sought to build on the prewar German heritage through the postwar establishment of archives and institutes for the study of German-Jewish history. And he would not have missed the internal tensions within the Jewish community, particularly between German Jews and Eastern European Jews.

Elon, who lived until 2009, returned to Germany on many occasions; however, he never wrote a direct sequel to *Journey Through a Haunted Land*. If he had, he would have had to chronicle the fundamental transformation in West Germany only a few years after his book appeared. Under the leadership of Social Democratic chancellor Willy Brandt, accompanied by an upsurge of youth activism, West German society finally began a public reckoning with its past. Additionally, as noted in essays in this volume, the Jewish community in Germany, while still small in size, began to assert itself publicly.

By 2002, as Elon published his final book, *The Pity of It All: A History of the Jews in Germany, 1743–1933*, the community had grown significantly through the immigration of Russian Jews and achieved real visibility in German society. Many of the challenges faced by the Jewish community in Germany in the first decades of the twenty-first century differed significantly from those of thirty years prior. The integration of the Russian Jews, their relationship to the existing community, religious and cultural pluralism in a diversified society, and the position and influence of Israeli Jews in "German" Jewry became topics of consideration alongside previous issues, such as age structure and anti-Semitism.

Moreover, Germany itself has changed significantly, including its attitude toward Jews and, more broadly, toward the ethnocultural nationalism of its past. Today, Germany stands out in contemporary Europe for its public, official opposition to anti-Semitism; for its commitment to the transnational project of the European Union; and for its embrace of the universalistic principles of the liberal constitutional state. While ethnocultural nationalism poses a threat with the recent electoral success of the right-wing political party Alternative for Germany, it appears more likely than not that Germany will remain a supporter of transnationalism and democracy in continental Europe. Indeed, Germany's transformation after Nazism has prompted several prominent German historians to narrate postwar German history as a tale of successful rehabilitation.[4]

However, the postwar narrative of German rehabilitation often reduces the complex history of Jews in divided Germany to explaining the progressive transformation of Germany into a liberal democracy. Put somewhat differently, such a narrative assimilates the experiences of Jews into a national story. Looking toward new approaches to considering Jewish life in Germany, how might one research and write about Jewish experiences in Germany after 1945 in a manner that does *not* assimilate those experiences into a German national story? This question applies as much to "German" scholars as it does to "Jewish" scholars.

This volume suggests some alternative ways of narrating these historical experiences. One way is local history. Local history permits, through meticulous archival research, an up-close look at the intricate, everyday lives of Jews, as this volume's chapters on Hamburg, Frankfurt, and Berlin show in detail. Another way is through the history of individuals, some of whom, such as Barbara Honigmann and Ernst Bloch, call into question narrow national identities or undermine them altogether. More broadly, the history of individuals eludes generalization by offering an in-depth look into the lives and thoughts of a single person. Still another approach is institutional history. As the first set of chapters in this volume demonstrate, institutional history can capture the movement of actors, ideas, and projects across national borders. International and transnational history also offer fruitful means of interrogating the Jewish presence in Germany since 1945, particularly as the community in the Bonn Republic was largely composed of Jews from Eastern Europe and the community in the Berlin Republic is overwhelming "Russian," with a sizeable contingent of Israelis. A final approach is interdisciplinary history. If all the essays in this volume can be characterized as historical insofar as they address a distinct period of time in the past, they are not all written by historians, which is a beneficial feature of the volume because historians tend to be more wedded to the conventional, generalizing pattern of linear narration than are, perhaps, their colleagues in other disciplines.[5]

We wish to conclude by proposing some alternative ways of narrating postwar German-Jewish history that this volume does not explore but that serve as possible avenues for future scholars to pursue. The possibility of transcending the nationalistic claim that each individual belongs to a particular group or *ethnos* was advanced, in different ways, by the religious and philosophical traditions that have shaped European history since the ancient period. Although the philosophical attempt to transcend nationalism through reason by thinkers such as Jürgen Habermas has received extensive scholarly treatment,[6] less attention has been paid to religious expressions of universalism in the post-1945 period, most notably as advanced by Judaism, Christianity, and Islam. Explorations of these religious traditions, especially as they relate to each other, could be a fruitful way of considering alternatives to national narratives in the postwar era. Moreover, multinational and comparative approaches to the study of German-Jewish history can help break the confines of traditional national history. The challenges of reconstructing Jewish life after the Holocaust were of course not limited to the case of Germany. Jews in Germany's neighboring countries—France, Austria, Poland, Czechoslovakia, Hungary, and Italy—faced similar challenges. By examining these cases from comparative or transnational perspectives, future scholars can reconstruct more deftly the richness and plurality of Jewish experiences in Germany and Europe.

NOTES

1. Amos Elon, *Journey through a Haunted Land: The New Germany*, trans. Michael Roloff (New York: Holt, Rinehart, and Winston, 1967).

2. Elon, 43, 236.

3. Elon, 130.

4. See, for example, Konrad Jarausch, *After Hitler: Recivilizing Germans, 1945–1995* (New York: Oxford University Press, 2008); Ulrich Herbert, ed., *Wandlungsprozesse in Westdeutschland: Belastung, Integration, Liberalisierung 1945–1980* (Göttingen: Wallstein, 2002); Heinrich August Winkler, *Germany: The Long Road West*, vol. 2, trans. Alexander Sager (New York: Oxford University Press, 2007).

5. For an innovative reflection on the conventionality of historical narration, see Yair Mintzker, *The Many Deaths of Jew Süss: The Notorious Trial and Execution of an Eighteenth-Century Court Jew* (Princeton, N.J.: Princeton University Press, 2017).

6. Jürgen Habermas has devoted his career to defending the possibility of overcoming narrow, particular interests through the exchange of reasons in the public sphere.

NOTES ON CONTRIBUTORS

JOSEPH CRONIN has published on Jewish identity in Germany since the 1980s. His PhD, undertaken at the Leo Baeck Institute London, focused on how Russian-Jewish immigrants were received into Germany's Jewish communities between 1990 and 2005. He has held a research fellowship at the German Historical Institute London and teaches at Queen Mary University of London.

IRIT DEKEL is a cultural sociologist. She was a research associate at the Jena Center for Reconciliation Studies at the Friedrich Schiller University Jena before joining the Department of Germanic Studies and Jewish Studies Program at Indiana University, where she currently works. Dekel is the author of *Mediation at the Holocaust Memorial in Berlin* (Palgrave Macmillan, 2013); "Subjects of Memory? On Performing Holocaust Memory in Two German Historical Museums," *Dapim: Studies on the Holocaust* 30, no. 3 (2016); and, with Vered Vinitzky-Seroussi, "A Living Place: On the Sociology of Atmosphere in Home Museums," *European Journal of Cultural and Political Sociology* 4, no. 3 (2017).

TOBIAS FREIMÜLLER is vice director of the Fritz Bauer Institute at Goethe University in Frankfurt am Main. His recent publications include "Alexander Mitscherlich oder wie ein Grenzgänger zum Makler der psychosomatischen Medizin wurde" in *Auf der Suche nach einer anderen Medizin. Psychosomatik im 20. Jahrhundert*, edited by Alexa Geisthövel and Bettina Hitzer (Berlin: Suhrkamp, 2019) and "Bürgertum, Rasse und Eugenik" in *Wie bürgerlich war der Nationalsozialismus?* edited by Norbert Frei (Göttingen: Wallstein, 2018).

KATJA GARLOFF is a professor of German and humanities at Reed College in Portland, Oregon. She is the author of *Words from Abroad: Trauma and Displacement in Postwar German Jewish Writers* (Wayne State University Press, 2005) and *Mixed Feelings: Tropes of Love in German Jewish Culture* (Cornell University Press, 2016) as well as the coeditor of *German Jewish Literature after 1990*

(Camden House, 2018). She is currently completing a new book on the reemergence of Jewish literature in contemporary Germany and Austria.

CATHY S. GELBIN is a professor of film and German studies at the University of Manchester. She has worked on Holocaust representations and modern German-Jewish culture with particular interest in issues of gender, sexuality, and race. She is coeditor of the *Leo Baeck Institute Year Book* (Oxford Journals) and serves on the Board of Directors and Trustees of the Leo Baeck Institute London. Recent publications include *Cosmopolitanisms and the Jews* (2017) and *Jews on the Move: Modern Cosmopolitanist Thought and Its Others* (coeditor, 2018), both with Sander L. Gilman.

JAY HOWARD GELLER is the Samuel Rosenthal Professor of Judaic Studies and a professor of history at Case Western Reserve University. He is the author of *Jews in Post-Holocaust Germany, 1945–1953* (Cambridge University Press, 2005) and *The Scholems: A Story of the German-Jewish Bourgeoisie from Emancipation to Destruction* (Cornell University Press, 2019) He is the coeditor of *Three-Way Street: Jews, Germans, and the Transnational* (University of Michigan Press, 2016).

CONSTANTIN GOSCHLER is a professor of modern history and dean of the faculty of history at the Ruhr-University Bochum. He is the coauthor of "1968–1989: Alignments" (with Anthony Kauders) in *A History of Jews in Germany after 1945: Politics, Culture, and Society*, edited by Michael Brenner (Indiana University Press, 2018). He also edited *Compensation in Practice: The Foundation* "Remembrance, Responsibility and Future" *and the Legacy of Forced Labour during the Third Reich* (Berghahn, 2017) as well as *Robbery and Restitution: The Conflict over Jewish Property in Europe* (Berghahn, 2007), which he coedited with Martin Dean and Philipp Ther.

JASON LUSTIG is a lecturer and Israel Institute Teaching Fellow at the Schusterman Center for Jewish Studies at the University of Texas in Austin. He has previously been a Harry Starr Fellow in Judaica at Harvard University's Center for Jewish Studies and a Gerald Westheimer Early Career Fellow at the Leo Baeck Institute. His research focuses on the development of Jewish archives in Germany, the United States, and Israel/Palestine in the twentieth century, and he is currently preparing his book *A Time to Gather: Archives and the Control of Jewish Culture*.

MICHAEL MENG is an associate professor of history at Clemson University. He is the author of *Shattered Spaces: Encountering Jewish Ruins in Postwar Germany and Poland* (Harvard University Press, 2011) and coeditor of *Jewish Space in Contemporary Poland* (Indiana University Press, 2015) and *Modern Germany in Transatlantic Perspective* (Berghahn, 2017).

MIRIAM RÜRUP is a professor of history and director of the Institute for the History of the German Jews in Hamburg. Previously, she worked as a research fellow at the German Historical Institute in Washington, D.C., among other positions in Göttingen, Berlin, Jerusalem, and Leipzig. Her publications include articles on statelessness; a coedited volume of essays, *Space and Spatiality in Modern German-Jewish History* (Berghahn, 2017); and *Ehrensache: Jüdische Studentenverbindungen an deutschen Universitäten 1886–1937* (Wallstein Verlag, 2007).

ANDREA A. SINN is an O'Briant Developing Professor and an assistant professor of history at Elon University. Previously, she served as a DAAD professor at the University of California, Berkeley. Among others, her recent publications include *Jüdische Politik und Presse in der frühen Bundesrepublik* (Göttingen: Vandenhoeck & Ruprecht, 2014) and *Die Erfahrung des Exils: Vertreibung, Emigration und Neuanfang—Ein Münchner Lesebuch*, with Andreas Heusler (Berlin: Walter de Gruyter, 2015).

JILL SUZANNE SMITH is the John S. Osterweis Associate Professor of German at Bowdoin College in Maine. She is the author of the book *Berlin Coquette: Prostitution and the New German Woman, 1890–1933* (Cornell University Press, 2013). Her research focuses on gender and sexuality, Jewish studies, and the city of Berlin from the Wilhelmine era to the present. Smith has published articles and essays in the *German Quarterly*, the *Journal of Modern Jewish Studies*, and in the recent volume *German Women's Writing in the Twenty-First Century*. She is currently working on a book-length study of representations of Weimar Berlin in contemporary German literature and visual culture.

ALEXANDER WALTHER is a PhD candidate at Friedrich Schiller University Jena. His dissertation project investigates the multifaceted forms of commemoration practices of the Shoah within the GDR's antifascist culture of remembrance. In previous work, he has analyzed the memoirs of former Yugoslavian refugees of the 1990s war. Since 2015 he has worked as a research associate at the Europäisches Kolleg Jena. He has published on Holocaust memory in the GDR and Poland as well as on memories of former Yugoslavian refugees.

INDEX

Page numbers in *italics* refer to figures.